Haunted English

Haunted English

The Celtic Fringe, the British Empire,
and De-Anglicization

LAURA O'CONNOR

The Johns Hopkins University Press
Baltimore

© 2006 The Johns Hopkins University Press
All rights reserved. Published 2006
Printed in the United States of America on acid-free paper
2 4 6 8 9 7 5 3 1

The Johns Hopkins University Press
2715 North Charles Street
Baltimore, Maryland 21218-4363
www.press.jhu.edu

Library of Congress Cataloging-in-Publication Data
O'Connor, Laura, 1959–
Haunted English : the Celtic fringe, the British Empire, and
de-anglicization / Laura O'Connor.
p. cm.
Includes bibliographical references and index.
ISBN 0-8018-8433-0 (hardcover : acid-free paper)
1. English poetry—Celtic authors—History and criticism.
2. English poetry—Celtic influences. 3. Yeats, W. B. (William
Butler), 1865–1939—Criticism and interpretation. 4. MacDiarmid,
Hugh, 1892– —Criticism and interpretation. 5. Moore,
Marianne, 1887–1972—Criticism and interpretation. 6. English
language—Political aspects. 7. Politics and literature.
8. Postcolonialism in literature. I. Title.
PR8491.027 2006
821'.912098916—dc22   2006001443

A catalog record for this book is available from the British Library.

For my mother,
Vera Hannon O'Connor,
And in memory of my father,
Donal O'Connor

Contents

Acknowledgments

The seed of this work goes back a long time, at least as far back as my first day at school when I answered "anseo" (present) to my de-Anglicized name, Laura Ní Chonchubhair. Although the book ultimately derives from my background and education in Ireland, it was conceived and shaped by graduate work at Columbia University and research and teaching at the University of California, Irvine.

Haunted English began as part of my doctoral research at Columbia University. It was my great good fortune to have had the late Professor Edward Said as my supervisor, and I shall always be indebted to him for his example, encouragement, and inspiration. His groundbreaking comparativist studies of postcoloniality undergird my analysis of linguistic imperialism (as an integral part, yet distinct phenomenon, of cultural imperialism) and of the countervailing de-Anglicization movement at the turn of the twentieth century. His commitment to close literary analysis and abiding interest in questions of style also informs the main part of the book, which examines how the colonial history of English inflects the literary vernaculars of Anglo-Celtic modernists W. B. Yeats, Hugh Mac-Diarmid, and Marianne Moore. I also wish to thank, my second advisor, Professor Ann Douglas, whose intuitive sympathy for my subject helped me to clarify my ideas at an early stage of the project.

I have benefited greatly from the stimulating and supportive intellectual community at the University of California, Irvine. This book was slow to reach completion, and would have taken longer yet were it not for the timely intervention of my friends and colleagues, Vicki A. Silver and Jayne E. Lewis. Their loving friendship, solidarity, and practical help enabled me to regain equilibrium at a critical juncture. I am also indebted to my colleagues Brook Thomas, Margot Norris, J. Hillis Miller, Ngũgĩ wa Thiong'o, Gabriele Schwab, Linda Georgiana, Jim McMichael, Jim Steintrager, and Ann Van Sant, and to my students, especially Erika Nanes, Ann Mikkelson, Aisling Aboud, and Laura Knighten. I would like to thank the following friends and mentors, whose encouragement and support has helped me more than I can say: Lisa Botshon, Terence Brown, Borgie Brunner, Ross Chambers, Antoinette D'Alton, John Doyle, Joe Dunne, Tom Dunne, Luke Gibbons, Michael Griffith, Allen Grossman, Brendan Kennelly, Nicola Mason, Mary J. Murphy, Jennifer O'Connell, Marianne O'Connor, Mary O'Connor, Donna Perreault, Jean Roche, Sally Shiels, Sophie Smyth, Ann Tobin, Renee Tursi, and Shelly Zavala.

I have been particularly fortunate in the institutional support I have received while at work on this project. Fellowships from the American Council of Learned Societies and the University of California President supported the sabbatical leave that allowed me to write much of the book. I also wish to thank Columbia University, the Josephine De Kárman Foundation, and the Charlotte W. Newcombe Foundation for the fellowships I received as a graduate student.

I am very grateful to my editor, Michael Lonegro of the Johns Hopkins University Press, for his assiduous care and helpfulness in guiding *Haunted English* to publication. Versions of two portions of chapters three and four have been published in *Postmodern Culture* 15, no. 2 (2005), and in *Critics and Poets on Marianne Moore: A Right Good Salvo of Barks*, eds. Linda Leavell, Cristanne Miller, Robin Schultze (Bucknell University Press, 2005). An article on Frank O'Connor and W. B. Yeats's translations "from the Irish," which appeared in *Yeats Annual*, no. 15 (2002), expands on one section of chapter two.

I am forever grateful to my husband, James, whose understanding of what I aspired to do with this project and steadfast confidence in my ability to accomplish it was a constant source of encouragement. For welcome reminders that play is as necessary as work, I thank my daughter, Marina. *Haunted English* is dedicated to the memory of my father and to my mother, whose generosity of spirit, resilience, and abundant good humor I admire all the more as I get older.

Introduction

In *My Fair Lady* (1956), the Lerner and Loewe musical based on George Bernard Shaw's "shameless potboiler," *Pygmalion* (1914), Henry Higgins sings a catchy lyric bemoaning how East End flower seller Eliza Doolittle mangles the English language into a cacophonous "Aooooooooooow!":

Look at her—a pris'ner of the gutters;
Condemned by ev'ry syllable she utters.
By right she should be taken out and hung
For the cold-blooded murder of the English tongue!

.   .   .   .

Oh why can't the English learn to set
A good example to people whose English is painful to your ears?
The Scotch and the Irish leave you close to tears.
There are even places where English completely disappears.
In America, they haven't used it for years![1]

Shaw conceived the Galatea plot and cast his beloved, Mrs. Patrick Campbell, in the "East End doña" role in 1897, at a time when his compatriot William Butler Yeats was in the throes of protest, with Maud Gonne, against the celebration of "the famine queen" Victoria's 1897 jubilee.[2] He was also organizing a centennial of the 1798 rebellion by the United Irishmen, but he paused to hatch a sequel for Gonne's West-of-Ireland doña role in *The Countess Cathleen, Cathleen Ni Houlihan*. In *Cathleen Ni Houlihan* (1902) the eponymous personification of Ireland lures a young man from his wedding to join the French in the 1798 revolutionary war against the English oppressor: "They that have red cheeks will have pale cheeks for my sake," she prophesies ominously, "and for all that, they will think they are well paid. [*She goes out; her voice is heard outside singing*]":

They shall be remembered for ever,

They shall be alive for ever,

They shall be speaking for ever,

The people shall hear them for ever.[3]

The Irish are condemned to remain anonymous vagrants in their native land, irredeemably alienated from the ruling symbolic order, *Cathleen Ni Houlihan*'s lyrics suggest darkly, unless they heed her clandestine call to rout the English "strangers" and revitalize the Gaelic sovereignty she personifies.

These murderous assaults on the reigning English symbolic order, from the heart of the metropole and the colony, are represented by both playwrights as the metamorphosis of a female pauper into an erotic icon "with the walk [and the talk] of a queen." Eliza's Anglicizing makeover appeals to a fantasy that one can "conquer . . . the greatest possession we have," the English language, by expunging every audible and legible trace of one's humble origins (86). Her confidence that she'll have a "loverly" life once she masters the *winner*-language is a mirror image of Cathleen Ni Houlihan's conviction that the *killer*-language has alienated the Irish from their birthright. In the Anglicized young man who hears her, her songs trigger a dim memory of a once-sovereign, ancestral Gaelic culture, and thus the play gratifies a wish that Anglicization would fail to sever all ties with a largely supplanted ethnic culture.

Haunted English explores the ways these ties indeed remained unsevered and how the ghostly voices that Cathleen Ni Houlihan prophesies will be "speaking for ever" managed to do so within spoken English and written English literature. Their uncanny persistence in the language ultimately equipped them for re-animation in the hands of three "Celtic" modernists—W. B. Yeats, Hugh Mac-Diarmid, and Marianne Craig Moore. The term *Celtic* emerged in the eighteenth century to codify an ancient and increasingly imperiled European cultural tradition.[4] In the British Isles it was invoked to sanction the polarization of Britons into two racialized groups, the best (Anglo-Saxons) and the rest (Celts). The pan-ethnic term posits a sameness among the Irish, Scottish, Welsh, Cornish, and Manx which singles out their difference from the "Anglo-Saxon" English: they have an ethnic link to Britain's "other" languages, whether or not they speak them, and conversely, irrespective of their mastery of English, they remain in some sense "other-than-English" speakers of English. Unlike the self-descriptive particularism of "Irish" (Yeats), "Scottish" (MacDiarmid), and "Scotch-Irish" (Moore), "Celtic" is a philological abstraction imposed from the outside by scholars and adopted by cultural commentators as a composite term for other-than-

English Britons. To declare that "I am a Celt" is to allude to a personal ethnicity encompassed by the pan-ethnic tag, to differentiate oneself as "not-Anglo," and to embrace otherness in a characteristically "je est un autre" modernist gesture.

The Celtic identification of Yeats, MacDiarmid, and Moore marks them as other-than-English writers in English and betokens a double linguistic alienation. English is their first language and one that affords them an international audience. It is also the colonial tongue that almost destroyed the Gaelic culture underpinning their Celtic ethnicities. These poets' knowledge of Gaelic was at best vestigial, and thus they were dependent upon English translations and the colonialist discourse of Celticism for access to their ancestral culture. Moreover, the dominant English tongue is a killer *and* a winner language for Anglo-Celts because the Anglicization that alienated them from their ancestral ethnic tongue also enabled many of them to enjoy the fruits of empire.

Cultural critics writing in English have analyzed many dimensions of the racialist discourse of Anglo-Saxon and Celt, but they have largely overlooked the constitutive role of a specific variety of racism, linguicism, in Anglo/Celtic cross-cultural relations.[5] Linguicism, the discrimination against others on the basis of language and speaking style, has been, by contrast, a dominant preoccupation of Gaelic-, Welsh-, and Scots-language advocates. I use Robert Phillopson's term *linguicism* more loosely than he does by way of emphasizing the interlocked concepts of English as a "killer language" (an instrument of Gaelic lingui*cide*) and English as a medium of linguistic ra*cism* and ethnicized class antagonism, which produces and maintains the social differentiation that elevates members of the Anglo elite over their audibly different inferiors.[6] Linguicism is as old as ethnocentrism (the Greek *barbaros,* an onomatopoetic imitation of incomprehensible speech, *barbarbar,* shuns those outside the *civis*) and the competitive pursuit of social status: "The rich man speaks and everyone stops talking; and then they praise his discourse to the skies. The poor man speaks and people say, 'who is this,' and if he stumbles, they trip him up yet more" (Ecclesiasticus 13.23). It has also been an integral part of imperialist ideology and practice, as Edmund Spenser observes in his blueprint for the military subjugation and Englishing of Ireland, *A View of the Present State of Ireland* (1596): "It hath bene ever the vse of the conqueror to dispise the language of the conquered, and to force him by all means to learne his" (87).[7]

The history of Anglicization in the British Isles is figured as the providential advance of "the English Pale" and concomitant recession of the Gaeltacht (Gaelic-speaking areas) and Welsh Wales into a notional "Celtic Fringe." In late-medieval Ireland "the Pale" referred to the ramparts separating the English-speaking colonial garrison from the native population, or, from a Gaelic perspective, the boundary dividing the *Galltacht* from the *Gaeltacht* (the non-Gaelic-speaking "strangers" from the Gaelic-speaking community). In Spenser's *View* the Pale is the frontline of a perilous linguistic struggle to Anglicize the natives before they could Gaelicize the colonial settlers. The Anglicization of the British Isles is usually envisioned in spatial terms, as a series of images from a linguistic atlas charting the steady encroachment of English and the reciprocal retreat of Welsh and Gaelic to the western and northwestern peripheries. This mental map evoking the progressive contraction of the Celtic Fringe supplies an enduring iconography for linguicide, or *glottophagie* (linguistic cannibalism)—Louis-Jean Calvet's provocative metaphor for the process in which subordinate languages are "eaten up" by dominant, imperial, or "killer" languages.[8] The cartographical image of the English Pale devouring the Celtic Fringe needs to be supplemented, however, with a vertical image of the ascendancy of English. By the eighteenth century the Pale had come to represent the social pyramid that legitimates speakers of "proper English" and discriminates against speakers of "accented" or vernacular Englishes and Celtic languages as "beyond the Pale." Anglicization drastically altered the demographics of English and Celtic speech-communities, and it did so by creating a society that fostered and perpetuated the political and cultural supremacy of an Anglo elite. The axes of geographical and socioeconomic marginalization are both expressed in the colloquialism "beyond the Pale," a phrase that puts the Gaeltacht at the greatest distance from the metropole and which disdainfully recoils from those whose speaking styles place them lower down in the social pecking order.

The *Celtic Fringe* refers territorially to the western and northwestern pockets of Welsh Wales and the Gaeltacht and symbolically to the zone where Britons' English-only self-image begins to fray and merge into otherness, an archaic fragmentary past, and a subliminal sense of loss.[9] The Pale is a limit; the Fringe is consistently associated with liminality: twilit zones, misty horizons, chimerical visions, and vanishing lore. The constitutive nebulousness and malleability of the Fringe draws attention to its phantasmatic nature, to how it consists of that which haunts and unsettles the borders that circumscribe stable identities. The Fringe refers not to the Gaeltacht as such but, rather, to a Romantic image of the Gaeltacht as it has been "translated" by the Anglophone world since the phenomenal success of James Macpherson's *Ossian* (1760–65).[10]

Although the term *Celtic* would seem to flaunt the linguistic basis of ethnic difference among Britons, historically it has served to suppress it by representing Gaelic and Welsh cultures as geographically and historically remote. English culture is here and now; Gaelic and Welsh cultures, by contrast, are transposed into a Celtic Fringe that recedes into the distant mists of a faraway place and a once-upon-a-time mythic space. The effect of the peripheralization is to deny the contemporaneity of adjacent Gaelic- and Welsh-speaking cultures by imagining them as a storehouse of an ancient cultural tradition, which can be salvaged, through translation into English, as a "Celtic" heritage for all Britons.

Matthew Arnold's influential work *On the Study of Celtic Literature* (1867) argues that the disinterested study of Celtic literature could help to transform Anglo/Celtic antipathy into a creative interracial symbiosis: what the poetic, spiritual, ineffectual, and primitive Celt lacks, the prosaic, materialistic, worldly, and progressive Anglo-Saxon can supply, and vice versa. Ernest Renan's influential argument in *Poésie des Races Celtiques* (1854) that Celts' excessive "poetic life" renders them unfit for politics has been widely contested by critics. Yet the anomalous use of literary genres as a racial category to divide Britons into "prosaic" Anglo-Saxons and "poetic" Celts goes unexamined, as does the notion that at the pinnacle of empire English is a utilitarian medium in need of a poetic Celtic infusion. An elegiac nostalgia for a Celtic culture of yore which simultaneously tunes out living Gaelic and Welsh cultures is a means of envisioning British culture as if it were exclusively English-speaking while yet acknowledging, at least on a subliminal level, some of the cultural losses entailed by linguistic imperialism. I interpret Arnoldian Celticism as an oblique and evasive discourse about the impact of Anglicization on Celtic and English language-communities, at once a denial of the multilingual diversity of contemporary British culture and an anxious compensation for the English-only monolith imagined in its stead. The way in which warm-and-fuzzy Celticism obfuscates how speakers of Gaelic, Welsh, Scots, and "accented" English are marginalized by the Anglophone mainstream is suggested by the conjoined semantic overtones of "decorative embellishment" and "social outcast" in *fringe*.

In this book I use the metaphor of the "Pale/Fringe" to track how the linguicism that went hand in glove with the Anglicization of the British Isles became a constitutive and pervasive feature of British cultural life. The Pale/Fringe refers to the linguistic contact zone in which the contours of cultural identity (British, Celtic, Anglo-Saxon, English, Gaelic, Irish, Scottish, Welsh, Highlander, Lowlander, Scotch-Irish) and popular images of those ethnic groups and their vernaculars are established, contested, renegotiated, and changed. The Pale is the frontier of linguistic imperialism, and the Pale/Fringe draws attention to how the Pale is necessarily defined by what lies *"outwith"* it, to borrow the suggestive Scots synonym for *beyond*, the outermost limit that bounds and coexists *with* it. Mary

Louise Pratt borrows *contact zone* from linguistics as a more fitting term than *colonial frontier* to refer to "the space of colonial encounters, the space in which peoples geographically and historically separated come into contact with each other and establish ongoing relations, usually involving conditions of coercion, radical inequality, and intractable conflict."[11] The fact that the Celtic Fringe component of the Pale/Fringe dyad is largely an Anglophone construct exemplifies Pratt's point that cross-cultural interactions among colonizer and colonized are determined by "radically asymmetrical relationships of power."

It is no accident that *Cathleen Ni Houlihan* and *Pygmalion* were first conceived by Irish playwrights in the 1890s because the plays stage a shift in language attitudes which was given definition and force by the salvo that launched the Gaelic Revival in Ireland, Douglas Hyde's lecture "The Necessity for De-Anglicizing Ireland" (1892). Hyde felt obliged to coin a neologism, *de-Anglicize*, for "the want of a better" word in English to convey the desired cultural transformation. He acknowledges that *de-Anglicization* has a harsh, virulent, and rebellious edge, but in his view the toxic effects of Anglicization merit an alienating terminological rejoinder.[12] By dramatizing the transformational impact of Anglicization on social identity and on the vernaculars that were brought into contact as a result of it, the plays likewise call into question what heretofore had been treated as a natural and inexorable phenomenon. The representation of Anglicization as a questionable ideology roundly contests the Victorian dogma that the providential spread of English is inextricable from the onward march of progress. The discordancy and instrumentalist connotations of *de-Anglicization* carry the considerable rhetorical advantage of setting Anglicization apart as something harmful that needs rectification and of implying at the same time that Anglicization can be, and ought to be, reversed.

Hyde's "de-Anglicizing" lecture contends that to overcome the cultural cringe that inclines the nation to defer to the superiority of English and to demean Ireland's Gaelic heritage, a concerted effort must be made to restore the widespread use of spoken Irish and to create a modern literature in the language. De-Anglicizing ideology promulgated the idea that the re-Gaelicization of Ireland would restore the damaged colony to prelapsarian harmony. It is steeped in Victorian Celtophilia and Romantic nationalism, laced with a Jacobite millennialist hope that the turn of the century would bring about a reversal of fortunes for empire and colony. As the "de-Anglicizing" concept caught on, a growing realization among ordinary people that they were in ideological thrall to the English of their everyday lives made language the object of political and philosophical inquiry. People without advanced formal education began to ponder how minds are formed by language (i.e., by language as such as well as by the specific contours of English, Irish, and Irish-English).

The dramatization of Anglicization in *Pygmalion* as an art of verbal passing which can be learned by any aspiring self-made aristocrat and in *Cathleen Ni Houlihan* as a tyranny to be overthrown portray obverse valuations of the winner / killer language. They also stage almost diametrically opposed takes on how identity is constituted by language, as a script to be performed and as an inalienable core subjectivity. De-Anglicizing rhetoric propagated idealized notions of lost organic unity, but because de-Anglicizing praxis made linguistic mediation an object of critical observation, it also promoted deep linguistic skepticism by disseminating popular versions of the Wittgensteinian insight that "the limits of my language mean the limits of my world."[13] Hyde's de-Anglicizing salvo inaugurated a rupture with Victorian antiquarianism and a renewal of Herderian Romanticism, and the movement launched by the "rebellious" and "virulent" word also set in motion what were to become two major political and philosophical developments in twentieth-century literature: the emergence of language and literature as a medium of decolonization; and the emphasis on the primacy of "language as such" in European cultural modernism.[14]

The first chapter of this book explores the history of Pale / Fringe linguicism and the complexity of Hyde and Yeats's efforts to redress its psychocultural legacy by de-Anglicizing Ireland's linguistic milieu and literature. The internal context of the British Isles provides fertile ground for examining the role of language in colonization and decolonization. The close proximity of English to Gaelic and Scots (and Welsh, though Welsh Wales only features in passing in this study),[15] and the long history of their interaction, generated substantial direct and oblique discourse about the impact of Anglicization on British multilingual culture. Drawing on this discourse, the first part of the book explores the cultural logic of English-only Anglicization and the countervailing turn-of-the-twentieth-century de-Anglicization movement.[16]

The main part of *Haunted English* explores how the literary vernaculars of W. B. Yeats, Marianne Moore, and Hugh MacDiarmid are shaped by their respective efforts to work through and remake their conscious and unconscious memories of Pale / Fringe linguicism. Such "memories" haunt the poets' minds, the medium of their art, and the social fabric and cultural unconscious of their societies. By working through a kind of inscribed melancholia and by unlocking a spectral linguistic resource still present within English, each of these writers gives birth to his or her own signature style. Chapter 2 tracks the influence of collaborative translation and the changing symbolic status of the (national) Irish and (colonial) English languages on Yeats's literary vernacular as he conflates his own life and the "matter of Ireland" into the overtly self-constituting "Collected Yeats." Chapter 3 examines how Hugh MacDiarmid creates a literary Creole, Synthetic Scots, to dismantle the normative grip of the English Pale in Scotland by inter-rogating the ambivalence that keeps the stereotyping of Scotticisms and Scottish national "character" in place. Chapter 4 explores how self-avowed "purely Celtic" American poet Marianne Moore uses her hallmark quotational method to cri-tique the Victorian stereotype of the feminine Celt and the gender politics of the English Pale in Ireland. Their styles are wrought out of struggles to work with and against the symbolic domination of the English-only Pale, and thus their poetry illuminates—and is illuminated by—the dynamics of Pale/Fringe interaction.

Haunted English

CHAPTER ONE

Beyond the Pale

To Anglicize is "to make English in form and character," and *Anglicization* is grounded in a metaphorics of translation. The formation of Irish, Scottish, English, and British cultural identities shows the intimate reciprocity between the Englishing of people and the Englishing of texts. Or one might say, instead, the "forging" of cultural identities because the space of translation between Pale and Fringe was often a site of violent struggle over originals and counterfeits. Tracking the role of linguicism in the advance of the English Pale begins with Spenser's *View*, a blueprint for gaining absolute control over cultural memory by "translatinge" the Irish natives into subordinate Anglicized serfs before they could translate the settler caste into Gaelicized degenerates.[1] Spenser's plan for "newe framing [Ireland] as yt were in the forge" seeks to obliterate Gaelic language and culture in order to ready Ireland for "carrying across" and "planting" the English standard (121). English-only Anglicization propagates a superficial sameness that upholds the power and privilege of the colonizer by the institution and maintenance of "the Pale," the boundary separating the colonial caste from those who are destined to remain, in Homi Bhabha's memorable phrase for the Anglo-Indian, "almost the same but not quite" as the English themselves.[2] Over time the territorial Pale of early modern Ireland came to define the limits of the speakable for the Anglicized British bourgeois subject.

It is highly significant, as Susan Bassnett observes, both to the ascendancy of the idea that the "New World" colonies are inferior copies, or "translations," of the Great European Original and to its recent contestation that the early colonial period coincided with the explosion of print technology and the ensuing commonsense notion that the author is the exclusive "owner" of an "original" text.[3] English supremacy in print capitalism enhanced the cultural prestige of the language and helped to fix an image of an implicitly English "literate speaker" which set the standard for self-improving Scots and others who endeavored to pass as fully Anglicized Britons. Translation is a means of bridging linguistic barriers and promoting international understanding, but it is also, as Maria Tymoczko claims, "paradoxically the means by which difference is perceived, preserved, projected, and proscribed."[4] English-only Anglicization and one-way translations from Gaelic to English, vernacular to standard, and the spoken to the written word extend the domain of the English Pale by extinguishing cultural alterity. The linguicism underpinning the movement to global English accordingly aroused deep ambivalence among those who Anglicized their speech. As a result, the arduous effort by Enlightenment Scots to translate themselves into fully Anglicized Britons contributed in turn to a compensatory salvage of cultural alterity in the form of a Highland romance which became the ground of a new Scottish national heritage. The Celtic Fringe was largely fabricated out of literary translations—preeminently James Macpherson's alleged forgery, *Ossian* (1760–65)— and ethnographies. The ideology of "the Celtic Fringe" proscribes Gaelic culture even as it enshrines Celtic genius, providing a prism for perceiving cultural identity through an alterity that is projected beyond the Pale. In their different ways Spenser's *View* and Macpherson's *Ossian* demonstrate how our images of vernaculars and their speakers are profoundly influenced by our received texts about them.

ENGLISHING THE OVERSEAS COLONY

"English-only" ideology has a long history in Ireland.[5] The Statutes of Kilkenny (1366), which prohibited English settlers from using Irish language and customs among themselves, were enforced by a king's justiciar, who was none other than the accomplished Gaelic poet Gearóid Iarla (and the inspiration for "Earl Gerald" in Marianne Moore's "Spenser's Ireland"). The figure of the Gael- icized Anglo-Norman earl raises the specter of settler "degeneracy" in Spenser's *View*, as one of the precursor colonists who are "so farr grow[n] out of frame . . . in so shorte space [as to] quite forgett theire Countrie and theire own names" (84). Poyning's Law (1494), which instituted a parliament loyal to the English Crown, significantly stopped short of proscribing what was then a general use of Gaelic and instead required settlers in the Dublin area to surround the diminishing colonial enclave with a six-foot double ditch (OF *pal*, stake), the Pale of idiomatic memory. Its double ramparts nicely signal the Pale's dual function of exclusion and restraint, constructed simultaneously to keep the dispossessed and barbarous Gaels out of the confiscated territories and inner sanctum of colonial society and to quarantine English settlers from the toxic Gaelic influence that might induce them "to growe out of frame." All other stratagems for maintaining and retrenching the segregated two-tier society of the overseas colony "wilbe but lost labour by patchinge vpp one hole to make manye," Spenser contends, "for the Irishe doe stronglie hate and abhorr all reformacion, and subiection to the englishe, by reason that havinge bene once subdued by them, they were thrust owt of all theire possessions" (121).

In the colonial war for dominance, language is recognized as a formidable weapon by both sides. As the medium of cultural identity, common memory, and the social customs that form the thick experience of everyday life, language represents the collective wills of warring settlers and natives. The language that prevails over the long haul determines the ultimate victor of the colonial enterprise for Spenser, who treats language both as a component of culture and as the basis of it.[6] At the turn of the seventeenth century Gaelic was spoken everywhere in Ireland except the Dublin Pale and a few small settlements, and so its culture posed an omnipresent threat, at once readily absorbed by the English colonists— "Lord how quicklie doth that Countrie alter mens natures" (196)—and stubbornly indigenous, rendering the Irish recalcitrant. In order to make the cordon sanitaire that perpetuates the English colony in Ireland permanent, the Crown must seize absolute control over cultural memory by a radical Englishing of Ireland.

Spenser's *View* is a blueprint for securing the symbolic domination of the English Pale in Ireland, staged as a dialogue between an Irish colonist, Irenius, and an English interlocutor of moderate opinions, Eudoxus.[7] It combines an ethnography of Ireland with an exhaustively detailed blueprint for the country's permanent military occupation. Spenser uses *translate* to describe transplanting or resettling natives elsewhere, with the proviso that "in noe place under any [English] landlorde there shall be manie of them planted together, but dispersed wyde from theire acquaintances, and scattred far abroade [so they cannot] conspyre what they will" (160–61). Moreover, Gaels should be induced to "forgette [their] Irishe nation" in order to secure expropriated territories because if they remember the antecedent Gaelic society, they will reject the usurping English master text (201). Eradicating Gaelic also protects against that "most dangerous Lethargie," which inclines English settlers and their progeny to assimilate into the native way of life. Here Spenser sounds what became a persistent motif in colonialist discourse: the asymmetry between the amnesiac English colonist, who "conquered and peopled half the world in a fit of absence of mind," and the re-membering natives, whose retentive memories nurture an abiding resentment.[8] Spenser adjures settlers to avoid intermingling with natives in the early phase of conquest because "with the streame the greater [number] will carry awaye the lesse." Once Gaelic culture is eradicated, the "blank slate" of Ireland may be safely inscribed with the great English "original." At some unspecified time in the remote future, a cautious "translatinge" of the Irish into the Pale of English civility may even "bringe them to bee one people," but only on the colonizer's terms (197).

A *View* engages a propaganda war over Ireland's image. Irenius advances "the vse of the conqueror to dispise the language of the conquered" by defaming several Gaelic customs as barbarous "Scotes or Scythian" survivals (87, 50). In so doing, he widens the Pale between settlers and natives, distancing the feminized barbarous Gaels from the zone of (implicitly masculine) English civility. Because Scythian practices perpetuate a "tribal" memory, binding the Irish to one another and to a past "more auncyent than most that I know in this end of the world" (49), Irenius recommends that "all the Oes and mackes [Gaelic patronymics] be utter-lye forbidden and extinguished" and replaced with English names so as to "much enfeeble" the social cohesion and ancestral awareness they foster (201). In a similar vein keens (*caoineadh*, ritual laments) and war cries (*sluaigh-ghairm*, com-pounds yoking the Gaelic *abú* [forever] to the clan name or motto) must be outlawed because they cement kinship and solidarity among the Irish. English common law must replace Gaelic Brehon law, but Gaels will be denied equal civil rights because they would manipulate English laws to advance Irish interests: "Therefore since wee cannot now applye lawes fytte to the people, as in the first instytucion of common wealthes yt ought to bee, wee will applye the people and fytte them to the lawes, as yt most conveniently maye be" (183). In short, an Englished Ireland will perpetuate the privileges of the Anglo-Irish settler caste, produce a comprador class of much resented "middlemen," and reduce everyone else to amnesiac serfdom.[9]

A *View* genders the colonial cordon sanitaire against the barbarity of the Scyth-ian horde: it is the fear of Irishwomen's almost cannibalistic powers of seduction and assimilation which drives Irenius' imperative to Anglicize "them" before they Gaelicize "us." For Spenser the imperviousness to state control of kinship ties and their underlying maternal authority is exemplified by the female preroga-tive of keening the dead, which Irenius cites as proof that the Irish-Scythian *anthropophagi* drink "not theire Enemies but frindes bloode": "at the execution of a notable tratour at Lymbricke called Murrogh Obrien, I sawe an old woman which was his foster mother tooke vpp his heade whilst he was quartered and sucked vpp all the blood running there out sayinge that the earth was not worthie to drincke yt, and therewith also steeped her face and brest and tare her haire cryinge and shriking out most tyrriblie" (81). As she closes the circle of kinship by consuming the blood of the slain traitor she suckled, she keens an ominous theme: the three most dangerous "infeccions"—intermarriage, fosterage, and the Gaelic language—may yet outlast and prove mightier than English swords.

Intermarriage with Irishwomen can "but bringe forth an evill race, seinge that comonlye the child taketh most of his nature of the mother . . . for by them they are first framed and fashioned, so as they receave any thinge from them, they will hardlie ever after forgoe" (89). Settlers' adoption of the Gaelic custom of fosterage means that their infants imbibe the disposition, mind, and language of the Irish "with their sucke": "insomuch as though he afterwards bee taught Englishe, yet the smacke of the first will alwayes abyde with him . . . for the mind followeth much the temperature of the bodye: and also the wordes are the Image of the mynde, so as they proceding from the mynde, the mynde must bee needes effected with the wordes: So that the speach beinge Irish, the harte must needes bee Irishe, for out of the aboundance of the heart the tonge speaketh" (88).

Indigenous culture is a reminder of an alternative and antecedent social order to that of the colonizer and, as such, a seedbed of resistance to colonial rule. This seedbed is nurtured in a prelinguistic cultural unconscious that Spenser elaborates by applying a Platonic concept of anamnesis (remembrance of what one has never consciously known) to the matriarchal basis of acculturation. Irish "sucke" potentially nurtures a visceral antipathy in natives toward the alien symbolic order, while (according to Spenser's asymmetrical logic) its toxic influence on the progeny of English settlers may foster the "most dangerous *Lethargie*" that causes them to "growe [so farr] out of frame." The barbarous Scythian calumny is animated less by snobbish disdain toward Gaelic than by the precarious position of the settler who seeks to occupy the host country without ever being either ejected from or assimilated into its bosom. Anxiety about whether the parasitic English settlement can feed off the Irish colony without being ultimately assimilated into it drives the "eat-or-be-eaten" logic of linguicide (*glottophagie*).

The difficulty involved in destroying Gaelic language and culture while yet (in the aggregate) sparing the Gaelic people is resolved by Irenius in an extraordinary proposal that literalizes the question of who eats whom. From his experience with Lord Grey, lord deputy of Ireland, in the clearance and plantation of Munster (the source of his estate at Kilcolman), Spenser expounds a final solution of the Irish problem: after mobilizing a huge English army of occupation, serving the Irish with a twenty-day evacuation notice, and laying waste their land, those Irish "rebels" who refused to comply would not nobly "fall by the sworde" but, instead, would be ignobly compelled by starvation into "consuming them selves and devouring one other" (135). During the clearance and plantation of Munster, "ere one yeare and a half, they were brought to such wretchedness, as that any stonie harte would have rewed the same . . . they looked Anatomies of death, they spake like ghosts cryinge out of theire graues, they did eat of the dead Carrions . . . in shorte space there were none almost left and a most populous and plentyful countrye suddenlie left voyde of man or beast, yet sure in all that warr there perished not many by the sworde, but all by extremitye of famyne, which they themselves had wrought" (135). Spenser's modest proposal displaces colonial rapacity onto cannibalistic natives, with English colonists—their unbloodied swords for all intents and purposes sheathed—standing by as blameless witnesses of Irish depravity. The appalling spectacle provides an allegory for Irenius' point that culture cannot be expunged by external force alone but must be renounced by its adherents to the point that the collapse of kinship bonds in a state of extremity might delude the victims into supposing that "they themselves had wrought" their own devastation. If such self-annihilation may be said to anticipate the ways in which famine and "the Clearances" came to signify a traumatic severance of both Irish and Scots from their Gaelic past, it also permits an English fantasy of moral and cultural quarantine, uncontaminated by blame and so not unlike the disavowal of linguicide at the heart of Anglicization.

Cannibalism provides a resonant metaphor for the Pale/Fringe contact zone because it entails a double movement of polarization and interaction. Maggie Kilgour writes that "cannibalism involves both the establishing of absolute difference, the opposites of eater and eaten, and the dissolution of that difference, through the act of incorporation which identifies them, and makes the two one."[10] The English Pale cannot "eat up" the Gaeltacht without itself being translated by what it ingests because when cultures are brought into contact, even under conditions of radical inequality, both act as "host" to the other. Spenser's representation of Gaelic linguicide perversely undermines the project of consigning the language to oblivion by depicting the starving, dispossessed Gaels who "spake like ghosts crying out of theire graves." The chorus of de-differentiated Gaelic orality, impaled in English print, survives as an untranslatable, yet eminently quotable, indictment of the policy document in which it is interred.

SELF-ANGLICIZING MAKEOVERS AND THE
ALIENATION OF GAELIC AND SCOTS FROM LITERACY

The historical fact that Irish and Scots Gaelic had once enjoyed literate parity with English was of the first importance to de-Anglicizing modernists, who cite it as evidence that the vernaculars were not intrinsically less literary or cultured than English but were reduced by barbarous means to abject status. While Irenius is not slow to defame Gaels, he nonetheless acknowledges that Gaelic, the oldest written vernacular in Europe after Greek and Latin, can lay claim to an august literary tradition and, moreover, that "the Saxons of England are said to haue theire lettres and learned men from the Irishe" (53).[11] Irenius testifies to the existence of a sophisticated Gaelic literary culture, for he had requested the bards' "prayses and disprayses of men . . . be translated vnto me, that I might vnderstand them, and surelie they savored of sweete witt and good invencion" (94–98). Yet Gaelic literary culture must be excised precisely for its eloquence, since the bards immortalize those who oppose the colonizer: "whomever [they] fynde to bee most lycentious of lyfe, most bold and lawlesse in his doinges, most dangerous and desperate in all partes of disobedyence, and rebellious disposition, him they sett vpp and glorify in theire rymes . . . tendinge for the most part to the hurte of the Englishe . . . this evill Custome therefore needeth reformacion" (94–98). Reformation as Spenser conceives it came swiftly. The hereditary caste of bards, who maintained the standard vernacular now known as classical Irish and created a literature based on conservation and emulation, was ruined by the loss of patronage which ensued from "the flight of the earls" (Irish clan chiefs) to the Continent after the Battle of Kinsale in 1601. The Statutes of Iona (1609) formally prohibited Scottish clan chiefs from patronizing their bards, and the collapse of the bardic schools led inexorably to the fragmentation of classical Irish into regional spoken vernaculars. The alienation of spoken Gaelic from literate expression was key in marginalizing the Gaeltacht from the public sphere, as Victor Durkacz argues.[12] Gaelic high culture never fully made the transition from chirographic or manuscript to print culture, and the active proscription of Gaelic literacy reduced the language and its speakers to a disenfranchised state of orality. The comprehensive influence of the Reformation on vernacular literacy in Europe scarcely registered in Ireland, which remained predominantly Catholic, and the English defeat of the Jacobites at the Boyne and Aughrim in 1691 was followed by a series of penal laws restricting Catholic access to civil rights and education.

In Scotland "the political end of extirpating the Gaelic language prevailed over the religious aim of evangelising through Bible literacy in the mother tongue."[13]

In a similar vein Scots, which had thrived as a literary language on a par with English until the early sixteenth century, steadily lost ground with the post-Reformation circulation of the Englished Geneva Bible and English Psalter (1560), and later the King James translation (1611), all of which immeasurably enhanced the prestige of English as the superior vernacular in the British Isles. "Scots" (initially known as "Inglis" and later as "Scottis," in contradistinction to "Southron" English) developed out of a Northumbrian dialect into a literary vernacular in the fourteenth century and became the official language of the kingdom of Scotland for two centuries.[14] The broad consensus among Enlightenment Scots to "leave behind" the vernacular in favor of English transformed the linguistic profile of Scottish civil society. From a sociolinguistic perspective the Scottis-Sudron bidialectalism of the fifteenth century polarized into *diglossia:* that is, the coexistence of a "High" (English) vernacular with a wide range of functions; and a "Low" (Scots) vernacular with a restricted usage.[15] The sociolinguistic shift toward diglossia is inextricable from the psycholinguistic or attitudinal shift that enabled it because the High/Low valuations put on English and Scots would have no force unless people accepted their validity. Whereas the Pale in early modern Ireland was established by the colonizers' interests in controlling the circulation of common memory in order to win the them-or-us war of linguicide, the contours of the modern British Pale are determined by how the competitive struggle to speak English "without an accent" makes language a key component of social stratification and discrimination (linguicism).

The striving "to talk more genteel," as Eliza Doolittle puts it in *My Fair Lady,* is crucially dependent upon a pervasive belief that to sound genteel is to sound English and to sound literate, which of course lends those who sound English the distinct advantage of coming across as elegant "literate speakers" who seem more authoritative and more educated than their hapless counterparts who sound Scottish or Irish. The "beyond the Pale" phrase calls attention to the intimate reciprocity between the dispositions that are ingrained into our bodily demeanors and the circulation of social prestige "out there" in the public sphere, a symbiosis between the formation of bourgeois subjectivity and the flow of cultural capital which Pierre Bourdieu has theorized in a French context. The consensual adoption of English as the standard British vernacular changed the tacit rules of what Bourdieu calls the "linguistic marketplace" so that those who could perform the accredited English speaking style were given a respectful forum to say their piece, while those who could not were cut short with the "who is this" put-down noted by Ecclesiasticus.[16] Cognizant of the social reality of this linguicism, Anglophone Scots schooled themselves to measure up to the prestigious English standard by shunning the vernacular.[17] Their self-improving endeavors widened the High/ Low divide by enhancing the prestige of English at the cost of devaluing Scots, and this in turn intensified the pressure to jettison the vernacular in favor of the standard, and so on in a self-perpetuating loop. This loop, which delineates "the Pale" of modern British society, is propelled forward by the structural disparity between the relatively rare competence in the legitimate vernacular and the much more uniform recognition of it,[18] which allows those who have mastered the high-prestige variety of English to command deference from those who recognize it as "the best" speaking style but are not quite able "to talk proper" themselves. Self-Anglicizing aspirants became hypersensitive to "How do I sound?" and "How well received is my speaking style compared to that of my peers?" since the purpose of reconditioning every nano-reflex of their speaking style was to succeed at verbal passing in a higher echelon of the Pale or at least to avoid falling behind in a rapidly Anglicizing society. The Pale operates as a form of auditory censorship, inhibiting speakers with anticipatory anxiety about not sounding right and surrounding them with an echo chamber that magnifies audible "lapses" into Scotticisms.

The competitive pursuit of "insider" status exacerbated the frequently noted obsession with accent in British society. Popular stereotypes of the English depict them as obsessed with how accent betrays how much class one has.[19] Stereotypes of the Scottish and Irish portray them as bedeviled by their irrepressible "brogues," a Gaelic loanword whose popular currency probably owes something to the way it allows users to mimic the very inflections that are under censure by relishing the enunciation of rolled *r*, broad vowel, and hard *g* sounds.[20] In a situation where the degree to which one can neutralize one's braid Scots brogue becomes a measure of how much class one has, accent is a highly charged signifier of ethnicity, class, and of the cross-wired conflation of class and ethnicity which regulates the social differentiation delineated by the Pale.

The legitimacy of English as the standard language for Britain and its empire was further reinforced by English supremacy in mass print capitalism. As Tom MacArthur points out, the word *standard* has connotations of war, measurement, and schooling which are pertinent to the cultural sway of "Standard English."[21] The earliest *OED* citation refers to the flag (OF *estandart*) around which English soldiers rallied against the Scots at the 1138 Battle of the Standard, a usage that anticipates how Standard English would serve as an expanding guarantor of English imperial identity as well as the demarcation of its political-economic reach (102–3). The "king's standard" came to regulate world trade, not to mention schooling, in which the "standards" of student proficiency were constantly monitored by school inspectors such as Matthew Arnold. Language standardization has a scriptist bias insofar as it assumes that the relative permanence and transmissibility of written speech makes it superior to a more context-bound, and so ephemeral, orality.[22] Scriptism intersects with Anglocentrism in Samuel Johnson's magisterial effort to fix the English standard in *A Dictionary of the English Language* (1755). His dictum that "the best general rule" of pronunciation is established by "the most elegant speakers who deviate least from the written words," sets up a Pale between speakers of "proper" English, whose purportedly unaccented speech is assumed to correspond exactly with ordinary spelling, and speakers of other class and regional sociolects, whose speech is indicted by contrast as "low," "provincial," and "sub-standard."[23]

The "commonsense" opinion that print-standardized English is preferable to other varieties of spoken English is evident in the argument, and the rhetoric, of George Campbell's *Philosophy of Rhetoric* (1776):

> Thus, though in every province they ridicule the idiom of every other province, they all vail to the English idiom, and scruple not to acknowledge its superiority over their own. For example, in some parts of Wales (if we may credit Shakespeare) the common people say *goot* for good: in the South of Scotland they say *gude*, and in the North *gueed*. Whenever one of these pronunciations prevails, you will never hear from a native either one of the other two; but the word *good* is to be heard everywhere from natives as well as strangers. The provincials may not understand one another, but they all understand one who speaks properly.[24]

In his observations Campbell follows Johnson's Anglocentric image of the "literate speaker" by assuming a homology between the orthography and phonology of "good (i.e., English-) English," as against the disparity between the written and spoken word evinced by the pronunciation of less *goot/gude/gueed* English speakers. The spelling variants are no longer seen to represent the particularity of English and Scots, as they would have done in the heyday of middle Scots, but are codified instead as deviant "Scotticisms" that fall short of proper and standard usage. The belief that there is only one correct way to spell and pronounce words, and it is the English way, exponentially increased the normative authority of English as a universal language of logic, clarity, and formal grace. Nonetheless, while the scripting of Scots as a *hamely* dialect indirectly associated a vernacular speaking style with the stigma of illiteracy, it also garnered connotations of character, lack of affectation, homespun sagacity, and spontaneity in comparison with "standardized" English. Campbell evidently approves of Britons' consensual embrace of the "language of Shakespeare," but his citation of Shakespeare's landmark use of nonstandard orthography in the "what ish my nation" passage of *Henry IV* is revealing. It betrays how a "four-nations" concept of British identity simmers beneath the surface of consensual Anglicization, animated in no small part by subliminal memories of the linguicism visited upon Celts.

Popular perceptions of standard English tend to oscillate between the laudatory and derogatory poles of the language of Shakespeare and the stilted English of those who are trying too hard to be good. Campbell's observations about the spread of "good English" were written at a time when the field of rhetoric and belles-lettres was changing emphasis in ways that would influence the future institution of English literary studies. Ian Duncan argues that the shift away from "the traditional goals of inculcating civic virtue towards an emphasis on the stylistic formation of polite discourse and the cultivation of sensibility . . . involves the programmatic realignment of the national culture upon a conception of literacy, set against (yet in crucial ways dependent upon) a primitive orality."[25] Macpherson's *Ossian* served as a catalyst for this realignment, and it is indicative that the great interpreter of those texts—Hugh Blair, the professor of Rhetoric and Belles Lettres at Edinburgh—was instrumental in creating the discipline of English Studies, as was Matthew Arnold. In the nineteenth and twentieth centuries English Studies served to propagate Anglicized "literate speakers" throughout empire and to promote an image of (English-) English as intrinsically superior to other languages and varieties of English. It also invested literature as such with enormous symbolic consequence, motivating other-than-English writers in English to leave their literary imprint on the language of Shakespeare and Spenser.

THE FENIAN REVENANT:
THE RETURN OF THE GAELTACHT AS THE CELTIC FRINGE

How did Gaelic live on in the aftermath of such intensive efforts at coerced and consensual Anglicization? Four centuries after Spenser rang Gaelic's death knell, it remains a living language—the daily vernacular of some 140,000 people and a second language for 1.5 million more.[26] The fact requires emphasis because Gaelic has been enshrouded in a rhetoric of moribundity and obsolescence which denies the contemporary vitality of the language.[27] Celtic antiquarianism and philology emerged during the eighteenth and nineteenth centuries, when Gaelic and Welsh were expected to disappear as living languages. The proactive project of saving the doomed vernaculars through translation, ethnography, and the salvage of antiquities, which was crucial to the formation of the Celtic Fringe, over-laid the Gaeltacht with the belated aura of the archive.

The movement from suppression of Gaelic culture to nostalgic recuperation is presaged by Spenser, who concludes *A View* with Eudoxus plaintively reminding Irenius of an unfulfilled promise to "declare vnto vs these your obseruations which yee haue gathered of the Antiquities of Ireland" (219). The projected sequel to *A View* speaks volumes about the politics of antiquarianism over the next three hundred years because it ironically makes Irenius—the architect, as it were, of Gaelic linguicide—custodian and curator of the Gaeltacht's cultural remains. The desire to salvage Gaelic culture, apparently so at odds with Irenius' determina-tion to eradicate it, attests to the ambivalence aroused by linguicide. In *A View* this ambivalence is expressed through the largely silent figure of Eudoxus, who is fascinated by the "manye sweete remembrances of antyquities" which Irenius glosses over in his disquisition on customs "offensyve and repugnante to good gouernment." Instead of being won over by Irenius' ruthless prescriptions, Eu-doxus is enraptured by what remains unsaid about Gaelic culture: "I was all that while as yt were entranced and carried soe farr from my self, as that I am now right sorye, that yee ended so soone" (78).

The debate over antiquities inaugurates Gaelic's illustrious afterlife as a "dead" language, that is, a language like Latin that is preserved in written form and thus recoverable from the mass grave of the world's "disappeared" indigenous lan-guages. With the catastrophic loss of the bards' patronage system, the intricate syllabic structures and feudal topoi of classical Irish verse gave way to the popular meters of the *amhrán* (ScG *òran*, song) and a vibrancy of personal utterance which refreshes even as it recalls the impoverished conditions out of which it came. Eighteenth-century *òrain* track Jacobite Gaels' opposition to the 1707 Union of Parliaments and the 1714 Hanoverian succession, their support for a Jacobite restoration in "the fifteen" and "the forty-five," and the desolation following their brutal defeat at Culloden in 1746. Jacobite *amhrán/òrain* were orally transmitted as songs, and they circulated in manuscript among the literati, who managed to maintain a written literary tradition against the odds.

The polarizing effects of the diglossic split between the dead letters of Gaelic antiquity, on the one hand, and a despised spoken vernacular, on the other, is evident in the title of the first book of original Gaelic poems to appear in print, Alasdair Mac Mhaighstir Alasdair's *Ais-eirigh na Sean chanoin Albannaich; No, An Nuadh Òranaiche Gaidhealach* (The Resurrection of the Ancient Scottish Tongue; Or, New Gaelic Lyrics [1751]). The antiquity redivivus/New Poems split in the title is riven by Mac Mhaighstir Alasdair's dilemma: the normalcy of *new poems* makes an optimistic pitch at the dim prospect of this being the first of many such publications, while *Ancient Scottish tongue* suggests the molder of the archives. *Ais-eirigh* presents itself as a "revenant" text, a work that speaks out of an immemorial past to potential audiences in the future because the likelihood of finding a positive reception in the Anglocentric culture of the time was so slim. Conscious of the unilateralism attending Gàidhealtachd/Galltachd relations, Mac Mhaighstir Alasdair appeals in an English preface to the Gaelic anthology for more such new poems in Gaelic, as well as translations of contemporary and traditional Gaelic verse, and decries "the great ill-will of the Lowlander" in a dedicatory paean to Gaelic:[28]

> Is ge h-iomadh cànain
> O linn Bhabeil fhuair
> An sliochd sin Adhaimh,
> Is i Ghàihlig a thug buaidh
>
> .   .   .   .
>
> Mhair i fòs,
> Is cha téid a glòir air chall
> Dh'aindheoin gò
> Is mìoruin mhòir nan Gall.
> Is i labhair Alba
> Is gallbhodaich fèin.

In translation the poem reads:

> Although many languages
> came from the age of Babel
> with Adam's race
> It was Gaelic that won the victory
>
> .   .   .   .
>
> She still survives,
> and her glory will not be lost
> in spite of the deceit
> and great ill will of the Lowlander.
> She is the speech of Scotland,
> and of Lowland churls themselves.[29]

Mac Mhaighstir Alasdair's pride in Gaelic as a national language of Scotland and as a bridge to a primordial past treats its antiquity as an expression of lived continuity with the bardic tradition itself.[30] To ensure that the "glory [of Gaelic would] not be lost," the classical past was ever more frequently invoked to refute the defamation of Gaelic as primitive and somehow inadequate to the sophisticated demands of contemporary taste and usage.[31] The focus on Gaelic antiquity, however, inexorably fed the Anglophone image of the Gaeltacht as anachronistic. From the eighteenth century onward, Pale/Fringe relations were characterized by what anthropologist Johannes Fabian calls the "denial of coevalness"—that is, the metropolitan tendency to represent the observed culture as somehow inhabiting a time other than and previous to the eternal present of print shared by ethnographer and reader alike.[32]

A decade after Mac Mhaighstir Alasdair's *Ais eirigh*, James Macpherson published *Fragments of Ancient Poetry* (1760), putatively translated shards of a Gaelic epic attributed to a blind third-century bard named Ossian. Not surprisingly, given the dearth of fragments, Macpherson initially resisted the blandishments of the Edinburgh literati to retrieve more, protesting that "no translation of his would do justice to the spirit and fire of the original" and expressing skepticism about a favorable reception for Fenian legend.[33] After doing his "fieldwork" in the Highlands, Macpherson, a native Gaelic speaker who had received a belletristic education at Aberdeen University, composed his "new" material into *Fingal* (1761) and *Temora* (1763), in consultation with Professor Hugh Blair, who appended a critical dissertation to the 1765 edition of the *Poems of Ossian*.

Blair's scholarly appendix and Mac Mhaighstir Alasdair's English preface share the assumption that a Gaelic text requires more than an interlingual translation to attract English readers: it needs a rhetorical frame to persuade a previously indifferent or even hostile audience of its worth. There was no "normal" cross-cultural interchange between Gàidhealtachd and Galltachd, and the one-way Gaelic-English translations were extremely selective, excluding "New Poems" by Jacobite Gaels in favor of the safe, because seemingly antiquarian, *Ossian*. The Celtic Fringe was fabricated out of literary translation and ethnographies in a context in which the English "target" culture had enormous power to fashion the Gaelic "source" culture to its own ends. The Pale is normative; the Fringe is exotic and elusive, a place that needs to be explained to others and which presents itself, tantalizingly, as something that resists pinning down. The distancing lens of ethnography and romance made it seem that Gaelic culture, and the Celtic Fringe, could only be approached with a hermeneutic guide to frame and interpret the view. Two kinds of cultural intermediaries played an important role in the formation of the Celtic Fringe: ethnographers such as Renan and Arnold, and predominantly metropolitan scholars such as Blair; and the revenant, an indigenous Gaelic literary device for bridging gaps between epochs and worlds.

Ossian draws on the *fiannaíocht,* a cycle of Irish and Scottish Gaelic lays about a band of warriors (the *fianna*) led by Fionn MacCumhaill / Fingal, which had been preserved—in what seemed a miraculous anachronism to the Enlightenment mind—for over a millennium in the Gaelic oral tradition, even as the narrative itself entails the anachronism of the revenant Ossian relating the heroic culture of vanished pagan Gaels. Manuscript evidence of Scots Gaelic *fian* lore, traditionally ascribed to Fionn / Fingal's son, Oisín / Ossian, extends back to the twelfth century and the Irish collection *Acallam na Senorach (The Colloquy of the Ancients)*, whose contents can be traced still farther to the seventh.[34] It is because Macpherson made use of an ancient oral tradition that *Ossian* cannot be summarily dismissed as a literary hoax, though it is far from the "literal" translating of an exhumed Gaelic past to which Macpherson obstinately laid claim.[35] Rather, *Ossian* can be regarded as a "cultural translation" that combines the antiquarian, linguistic, anthropological, and literary tasks of unearthing and translating source texts, conceiving a cultural context for them, and imaginatively reframing them in a print epic genre designed to suit contemporary metropolitan tastes.[36]

The revenant is a vehicle through which the past can be made to "appear" in the present. The figure of the revenant, one who returns after death or long absence, is an apt trope for the potential of translation to traverse linguistic, cultural, and temporal barriers. The ambiguous ontological status of the revenant, and the uncertainty hovering over "death or long absence," resonates with the diametrically opposed images of Gaelic culture which evolved out of the denial by Anglophones of the coevalness of the Gaeltacht. When the monastic compilers of the twelfth-century *Colloquy of the Ancients* set about recording ancient Irish history from the *filí* (poets, with archaic connotations of seer), the revenant device enabled them to represent Oisín and Cailte's return from the otherworld as an occasion for Saint Patrick to catechize them about the remote pagan past they inhabited. The dialogical device makes coevalness the sine qua non of cross-cultural exchange and juxtaposes contemporary Christianity with ancient paganism to create a sense of the past in accordance with perceived present needs. Macpherson does not develop the ironic potential of such a colloquy but, instead, creates a rapport between revenant and reader, achieving coevalness not so much of cultural exchange but of sensibility.

Macpherson's Ossian is the romantic embodiment of bardic memory, an autochthonous voice that emanates from a desolate, windswept rock, a locus of durability and imminent submersion. The roll of his rhythmic prose, as the pitch shifts from exclamatory to reflective, mournful to exhortative, has a mesmeric effect, deepening the melancholy of its prolonged *ubi sunt:* "Roll on, ye dark-brown years, for ye bring no joy on your course. Let the tomb open to Ossian, for his strength has failed. The sons of song are gone to rest: my voice remains, like a blast, that roars, lonely, on a sea-surrounded rock, after the winds are laid" (170). His reminiscences augment his melancholy pleasure, "the joy of grief belongs to Ossian, amidst his dark-brown years" (283), and in the apostrophe to the sun that concludes "Carthon" it achieves a sublime detachment from a transient life (a favorite of Thomas Jefferson, who received "daily and exalted pleasure" from *Ossian*) (133–34).[37]

Ossian created a sensation in the British Isles and internationally. The benchmark in translation scandals was translated into twenty-six languages, to become a foundational text for European Romanticism. Unfazed by the storm of controversy surrounding Macpherson's Gaelic source texts, a rapturous British public took the Gaelic Homer to its heart, making *Ossian* the touchstone for a hyperbolic version of Scottish culture and the Gàidhealtachd. In the past many Lowlanders had dissociated themselves from the Highlanders, who derisively labeled them "Sassenach" (English), but now they invoked the Highland ridge to claim a symbolic difference from their erstwhile allies.

The Scottish theme park of bagpipes, tartans, clans, bards, and sublimely empty (because depopulated) landscape was fabricated in English yet authenticated by reference to a Gaelic antiquity and Jacobite fealty to a nobly lost cause. If the pastoral romance did little to improve the material conditions of Gaeltacht life, it made the Celtic Fringe "the privileged home of subjectivity as such . . . an ideal country, until even those who seek to uphold its interests against the core find that they are doing so in the glowing and reverent language which ratifies its oppression."[38]

Anticipating the journey westward of future Celtophiles, in 1770 Johann Herder confesses that his idea of Eden is "an ancient Celtic hut on a rugged mountain, amidst cold and storm and mist": "should I ever reach the coasts of Britain, I will only hurry through, see some theatre and Garrick, and say Hello to Hume, and then it will be up to Wales and Scotland, and to the Western Isles, on one of which Macpherson sits, Ossian's youngest son."[39] Herder's fantasy—which accompanies a full critical engagement with the text—conflates the author of *Ossian* with the revenant figure and inserts himself into the Highland romance as the privileged outsider (like Saint Patrick) to whom *fian* lore is passed on. Meeting Macpherson in London or Edinburgh, where he was most likely to be found, presumably would not satisfy Herder, who hopes to find in the bracing weather and acoustic texture of the Western Isles something akin to the receptive mood evoked by *Ossian*.

The Celtic Fringe connotes receptivity: a lyrical and storytelling ambiance in which one is "carried away" by reverie and reminiscence. It is a place of evocative moods, especially melancholy, nostalgic, sublime, and elegiac moods, and a setting where the imagination can take flight and the mind is free to wander where it will. It is also an ethnographic topos inviting exegesis and cultural translation, an exotic discursive object to be "carried across" to the normative mainstream. The Celtic Fringe became a kind of lint screen for cultural anxieties and psychocultural projections, an "empty" panorama that attracted and absorbed all kinds of psychic and cultural baggage. Over time it has served as a vehicle for defining the other across the gamut of polar oppositions: progressive/primitive, masculine/feminine, pragmatic/visionary, prosaic/poetic, and so on. Hence, *the Celt* and *the Celtic Fringe* serve as proxies for debate about modernity, gender, secularism, the changing status of literary genres, and other issues as well as a repository of discourse about the impact of Anglicization on English and Celtic languages. The role of the Fringe as a transferential lint screen dramatizes how in encounters with alterity—other people, the texts we read, other cultures—we "carry across" and "transfer" more than we know and more than we can know.

The formation of the Celtic Fringe is illuminated by Gabriele Schwab's theory of literary transference, which tries to factor the effects of intercultural transference on cross-cultural translations into our understandings of the anthropological encounter and of literary reception. Her theory is useful because it provides a tool for thinking about the translation of literary alterity *into* the individual and collective psyche, in addition to thinking about transference in the colloquial, pejorative sense of offloading one's psychic baggage *onto* others. Following Christopher Bollas's concept of "a receptively derived unconscious, as partner to a repressed unconscious," which he defines as a prelinguistic "grammar of being" which later inhabits language as an "unthought known," Schwab argues that "it is this very grammar that expresses itself in the form of moods, and that literature engages and modifies by providing a form susceptible to unconscious resonance."[40] She draws attention to the common experience of forgetting the content but remembering the mood awakened by a literary work, or the experience while reading of being transported far away to an undifferentiated wordless world that nonetheless remains deeply internal, to describe the subliminal "unthought known" at the core of aesthetic experience.

Schwab conceives of literary texts as "evocative objects" that can facilitate the working through of unconscious projections by providing narrative forms for psychic elaboration and acoustic and imagistic effects that reverberate in the unconscious.[41] She argues that formal aspects of poetic language such as rhythm, rhyme, and image are the primary evocative agents of literary transference because they conduct the moods, or "voice-feelings" (*stimmung*), which resonate with as yet inarticulate unconscious ideas to form the psychic genera that coalesce into one's "grammar of being." The sympathy occasioned by an evocative literary scene, word, or rhythmic cadence is a mix of estrangement and familiarity, a start of recognition that this evocative object somehow matches our inchoate sense of the order of things, as if it were till then an unconsciously missed element of our expressive repertoire. The Ossianic bard whom "as yt were entrance[s] and carrie[s] soe farr from [one]self" is introjected as a revenant within, a link between "timeless" reverie and the stuff of everyday life.

Literature makes possible a transference between the psychic and the social, Schwab contends, because rather than enforce an epistemological divide between the cultural, political, and psychological dimensions of human being, it "transcodes" and integrates these spheres, permitting an exchange between them by giving narrative form to formless preoccupations and anxieties.[42] Such transcoding is observable in the Jacobite *aisling*, in which the erotic functions as an allegory for the cultural and the political, and vice versa. Similarly, the bardic device of the revenant creates the literary illusion of coevalness between "the unthought known" and cultural consciousness and the return, however partially and obliquely, of the Gaelic world to the realm of English-only. Transcoding is the subliminal task of the Jacobite *aisling*, the dream vision genre in which the three poets Yeats, MacDiarmid, and Moore compose and which was circulated primarily through oral channels in the eighteenth and nineteenth centuries.

Cathleen Ni Houlihan translates a translated eighteenth-century Jacobite *aisling* song, Liam Dall Ó'hIfearnáin's "Caitilín Ní hUallacháin," into theater. In Jacobite *aislingí* the muse-like *spéirbhean* (skywoman; Gaelic sovereignty goddess) returns to incite or prophesy the routing of the usurper. The Jacobite *aisling* is not based on ancient Fenian legend as such, but—like Ossian—the *spéirbhean* represents the vigilant (un)dead who return to rue the passing of a Golden Age and to contest the legitimacy of the ruling status quo. If the figure of Macpherson's Ossian is a reassuring revenant, a sage if melancholy keeper of tradition who represents continuity and stability in the face of cultural upheaval, the Jacobite *spéirbhean* is distinctly the disturber of an illusory because oppressive peace, one whose fleeting visit arouses disquieting passions that may rupture the status quo. The reception of *Ossian* is intimately bound up with solitary reading for pleasure, whereas the reception of the *aisling* is enmeshed in the convivial context of an imagined Jacobite subcommunity. The transference between the social and the psychic is crucially mediated by the technologies of literary transmission.

Ernest Renan observes that "the essential element of the Celt's poetic life is the *adventure*—that is to say, the pursuit of the unknown, an endless quest after an object ever flying from desire" (9). "No other [race] has conceived with more delicacy the ideal of woman, or been more fully dominated by it; [i]t is a sort of intoxication, a madness, a vertigo," Renan declares, and nor is he acquainted with any literature in which "woman appears . . . as a kind of vague vision, an intermediary between man and the supernatural world" (8). And yet the Renanean *adventure* conforms almost exactly to the plot of the *aisling*. The ravishing *spéirbhean* disturbs a male intermediary, inspiring him with hope and passionate desire. She delivers her "as once, so again" typological message, placing the onus on him to keep faith with her. She vanishes, since this embodiment of former harmony can appear only fleetingly during this hostile time. She can return but can never stay because the time is out of joint and she out of place in a forsaken world. Yet her message lingers, bracketing present political conditions as an anomalous chapter in a glorious national destiny that remains to be fulfilled. The *aisling* became a vehicle for disseminating what Roy Foster calls "the story of Ireland," an accepted version of Irish national memory which "is linked to the expectation that something alien to the present will or must occur."[43] The *aisling* sublimates memory into desire so effectively, however, that "the story of Ireland" conveyed by the genre might equally be dubbed an accepted version of Irish national aspiration.

Renan writes that Celtic "poetic life" (by which he means something close to a cultural unconscious) is animated by "that indomitable hope, that tenacity in the affirmation of the future, that belief that the salvation of the kingdom will come from a woman" (24): "Thence arises the profound sense of the future and of the eternal destinies of his race, which has ever borne up the Cymri and kept him young still beside his conquerors who have grown old. Thence that dogma of the resurrection of the heroes, which appears to have been one of those that Christianity found most difficult in rooting out. Thence *Celtic Messianism*, that belief in a future avenger . . . Nearly all great appeals to the supernatural are due to peoples hoping against hope" (10). He portrays the Celts' anachronistic "fidelity" to abandoned traditions as less a matter of nostalgia for the past than of an unquenchable desire for a better future, which is projected as the typological fulfillment of Celtic "destiny." In Renan's view it is the "intoxication" with supernal beauty and the "invincible need of illusion" which alienates the Celtic people from the "cheerful but commonplace" lives of their neighbors and renders them viscerally incapable of adapting to the compromises of realpolitik. In *Poetry and Jacobite Politics* Murray Pittock contrasts the Jacobite treatment of "history as recurrence and return," which has recourse to the typological understanding of "the marginalized and defeated," with the Whig tradition of progressive, incremental history (2–3). The two historical modes are entirely at cross-purposes. Several times Renan comes close to admitting the latent revolutionary potential of Celtic messianism, but on each occasion his commonsense progressivism gets the better of him, with the result that he touts the typological cast of their political unconscious as proof of Celts' lack of political savvy.

When Hugh MacDiarmid sought Gaelic inspiration for *To Circumjack Cencrastus* (1930), an epic that attempts to encompass the Gaelic heritage of Scotland, he rejected his compatriots' militant Jacobite verse in favor of the erotic messianism of the Irish *aisling*. A prototype of the genre, "Gile na Gile" (c. 1715) by Aogán Ó'Rathaille (c. 1675–1729), was a key intertext for him.[44] Ó'Rathaille was the first poet to adapt the ancient Gaelic sovereignty myth (in which a tutelary land goddess mates with the rightful king) to a Jacobite context. In Ó'Rathaille's hands the conceit does not describe the inauguration of Gaelic sovereignty but, rather, its subversion, in which the goddess is mated not with the king but with an alien churl. Ó'Rathaille's verse frequently conflates the Stuart deposition with that suffered by the patrons of his matrilineal ancestors, the MacCárthaigh Mór family. He cannot remember this family because it was despoiled of rule long before his birth, but the golden age of its patronage typifies for Ó'Rathaille what it would mean for Gaels to come into their own again. "Gile na Gile" appeals for the future restoration of a past that the poet himself never knew, except by way of intuiting a primal fall behind the present calamity. In so doing, he illustrates the tendency, noted by Mary Louise Pratt, to predicate a homogeneous, feminized "linguistic utopia" at the core of an imagined speech community.[45]

As Breandán Ó'Buachalla observes, Ó'Rathaille's attribution of calamity to the overthrown sovereignty of clan and kingdom is simultaneously mythological and political, for the two spheres are intertwined, not conflicted, in the typological Gaelic tradition.[46] MacDiarmid's source, Daniel Corkery's influential study *The Hidden Ireland* (1924)—a revisionist history that treats eighteenth-century Gaelic poets as precursors to twentieth-century Irish nationalists—reprints a translation of "Gile na Gile" made by poet-translator James Clarence Mangan in the 1840s under the shadow of the famine and the Young Ireland movement. Mangan's translation, "The Brightness of the Bright," testifies to the enduring erotic appeal of the *aisling* and helps bring into clearer focus the habitus of Gaelic language and lyric from a translator's perspective.

The Gaelic "Gile na Gile" is approached through a series of receding frames because the encounter with the *spéirbhean* is represented as a vision outside the realm of ordinary experience. It portrays the scene of poetic inspiration and the scene of the mésalliance which, by destroying the Gaelic social order, has made poetic production impossible. Ó'Rathaille's proud allegiance to the bardic profession made the mating-conceit uniting the sovereignty myth and the poet-muse symbiosis completely appropriate to him: it is the expression of a once-idyllic order—political, social and poetic—which has now fallen into utter disarray. The lonely, roving, poet-speaker encounters a resplendent radiant beauty (*gile na gile*, the brightness of the bright) who, equally forlorn, brings news of the rightful king's return, the routers who expelled him, "and somewhat else she told me which I dare not sing" ("'s fios eile ná cuirfead im laoidhthibh le fíor-uamhan"). He is captivated by her—made prisoner by the prisoner ("im chime ag an gcime") —but startles her by "call[ing] on Holy Mary" in fear. She vanishes, fleeing to "bruín Luachra" (the *sidhe*/fairy dwelling at Luachair).

The luminous *gile na gile* has a subtle phantasmatic tie to the landscape (the sweep of her hair draws dew from the grass) which emphasizes the evanescence of boundaries and yet involves a spiraling, entangling, and even carceral quality. She is that Renanean "object ever flying from desire," a figure that Ó'Rathaille represents as a kind of ineffable logos or source of harmony in the Gaeltacht—a feminized beauty and purity of life that has been ravaged by the colonizer. "O'er mountain, moor, and marsh" ("tré imeallaibh curraigh, tré mhongaibh, tré shlímruaidhtigh"), the speaker pursues her "till I reached the magic palace reared of old by Druid art" ("go hionad na n-ionad do cumadh le draoidheacht dhruadha"). There he is greeted with derision by goblins and maidens who force him to witness the fateful mésalliance: "And I felt as though I never could dream of Pleasure after/When I saw the maid so fallen whose charms deserved a crown" ("i ngeimhealaibh geimheal mé cuirid gan puinn suaimhnis,/'s mo bhruinneal ar bruinnibh ag bruinnire bruin-stuacach"). (In Kinsella and O'Tuama's more literal translation, these lines read: "They bound me in bonds, denying the slightest comfort,/and a lumbering brute took hold of my girl by the breasts.") Aghast, the speaker reminds her of her Stuart suitor, "But answer made she none; she wept with bitter weeping" ("Ar chloistin mo ghothu dhi goileann go fíor-uaibhreach").

In an act of characteristic license Mangan's translation inserts the speaker himself (as against the prince) into the mating-scene by having him berate the *spéirbhean* for wedding a churl, "When a bridegroom such as I was longing to enfold her/To a bosom that her beauty had enkindled into flames." The voyeurism of the spectacle is thus compounded, evoking the pathos of both the speaker's and the *spéirbhean*'s devastated pride: two lonely and proud (*fíor-uaigneach*, *fíor-uaibhreach*) captives tortured by the consciousness of how the world ought to be and once was. Escorted from the otherworldly dwelling, the speaker despairingly concludes that no remedy is near until "our lions" (the Stuarts) come over the sea. The speaker mediates between the otherwordly logos and his community, acting both as a participant who fully identifies with the *spéirbhean*'s traumatic bondage and degradation, and as a detached observer who then returns as a revenant to report on the catastrophe engendering cosmic disorder.

The concentrated reflexivity of Ó'Rathaille's verse owes much to the anaphoric use of genitive metaphors for *gile na gile* which, as Mangan's opening stanza illustrates, defy satisfactory translation:

> The Brightest of the Bright met me on my path so lonely;
> The Crystal of all Crystals was her flashing dark-blue eye;
> Melodious more than music was her spoken language only;
> And glorious were her cheeks of a brilliant crimson dye.
>
> Gile na gile do chonnarc ar slighe i n-uaigneas,
> Criostal an chriostail a guirmroisc rinn-uaine,
> Binneas an bhinnis a friotal nár chríon-ghruamdha,
> Deirge is finne do fionnadh n-a gríos-ghruadhnaibh.[47]   (1–4)

Frank O'Connor, an accomplished translator of Ó'Rathaille who nonetheless felt stumped by "Gile na Gile," comments that "in Irish the poem is pure music, each line beginning with assonantal rhymes on the short vowel *i* (like *mistress* and *bitter*), which gives it the secretive, whispering quality of dresses rustling or of light feet scurrying in the distance" (104). The assonantal music is based on an interlacing of vowel sounds that Dinneen and O'Donoghue scan as a "five-stressed homogeneous UA-poem." It is homogeneous because the verses of each quatrain conform to an "(i—i—u—ee—UA)"; significantly, the final UA stress bearer is *uaigneas,* "lonely."[48]

Because Gaelic is an inflected language whose elements can be rearranged for emphasis and euphony, such intricate assonantal and internal-rhyming textures can be achieved without semantic compromise. A noun-centered language, Gaelic often couples nouns for adjectival purposes—for example, *amadán fir,* a fool of a man—and Ó'Rathaille's genitive metaphors are attributive intensifiers with a more fluid semantic reference than is apparent from their tautological English equivalents. "Gile na Gile" is translated as "brightness of brightness" by O'Connor and Dinneen/O'Donoghue and as "brightness most bright" by Kinsella/O'Tuama, and they render "binneas an bhinnis," respectively, as "sweetness of sweetness," "melody of melody," and "sweetness most sweet." Their translations preserve the salient reduplication, but because the genitive case lenites the initial consonant and modifies the final syllable of the second noun, lending "binneas an bhinnis" the whispering tonality of "biniss on vinish," they cannot recreate its aural texture. In the Gaelic original, the hushed inflections accentuate the magical aura evoked by the reduplicative anaphora, drawing the reader into the mysterious liminal world of *gile na gile*.

Gile na gile is unnamable. The lyric is composed out of the quest to approximate her name and to convey the collapse of social cohesion and naming and kinship systems. The assonantal filigree of "Gile na Gile" displays many of the translational cruces created by the incompatibility between Gaelic and English syntax and prosodic worlds. Yet the *aisling* proved eminently transmissible *as a genre*, especially in the form of popular Jacobite songs. Over time the need to fit English words to Gaelic melodies, words that could negotiate the linguistic habitus shaping the music, led to a host of inventive improvisations that then became part of the vernacular idiom. For example, when Mangan translates another Jacobite *aisling* song, "Caitilin Ni Uallachain," he lingers over the trisyllabic *Cait-il-in* to accommodate O'hIfearnáin's music and adds the possessive pronoun *our* ("*our* Caitilin Ni Uallachain"), two changes that accentuate the lilt of the Gaelic *amhrán* and the difference between "our" wavelength and theirs.

The appearance of Gaelic shibboleths such as "Caitilín Ní Uallacháin," *Róisín Dubh*, and *Shan Van Vocht* or well-known Jacobite melodies signal that a seemingly innocuous love song is a clandestine political allegory. The starts of recognition and sympathy aroused by these songs are intimately enmeshed in the fabric of a Jacobite subcommunity that is defined by opposition to the mainstream, not to mention possession of the cipher that decodes the lyric. The convivial sense of solidarity created by the Jacobite argot reinforces the feeling that "*our* Caitilin Ni hUallachain" sets "us" apart from the dominant "them" and potentially reminds listeners of a collective aspiration to overturn an untimely regime that comes between them and their proper destiny.

The codedness of these familiar names paradoxically gives them an estranging quality, and the *aislingí* often make the fading cachet of a revered name part of their theme. In an anticipation of Hyde's ideology of "de-Anglicization," a prefatory headnote to the translation insists on the propriety of preserving the *Ní* (daughter of) in English, and the Yeats/Gregory play *Cathleen Ni Houlihan* (1902) obeys this injunction.[49] The play borrows little more than the name from Mangan's translation of O'hIfearnáin's *aisling* and instead develops a version of the sovereignty myth in which an old hag (*cailleach*) is rejuvenated by her avenging prince. Vestigial renown attends the eponymous heroine, the Old Woman, disclosing how the world she represents has dwindled to a smattering of subliminal clues and faint echoes of old songs. Her deferred naming of herself as "Cathleen, the daughter of Houlihan" triggers the young man's memory of the *aisling* genre. The memory prompts him to join forces with those who understand what these "songs on the wind" mean and at the same time, in an interesting conjunction with *gile na gile's* association with the fairy mounds, makes him appear "touched" and "far away" to his family.[50] In effect, he enacts the double transcoding of the *aisling:* he deciphers the allegory connecting him with the Jacobite-Fenian sub-community even as he undergoes the radical psychic transformation that betroths him to the cause. His touched state somehow precipitates the *cailleach's* meta-morphosis at the play's end into a girl "with the walk of a queen." Her "transla-tion" adumbrates a de-Anglicizing reversion of her name to its Gaelic etymon—*uallach,* "proud."

With Maud Gonne bringing her immense sexual charisma to the title role, *Cathleen Ni Houlihan* enthralled Abbey audiences. By many accounts 1916 in-surrectionists rehearsed their destiny in "the story of Ireland" by attending the play as "a sort of sacrament."[51] Much as *Ossian* invites readers to insert them-selves into colloquy with the revenant, the poet-speaker of the *aisling* models the participant-observer activity of literary reception. Three of the insurrection-ists composed *aislingí* in Irish and English and brought a much deeper knowl-edge of the tradition to the play than Yeats had. "Did that play of mine send out / Certain men the English shot?" asks the poet-speaker in "Man and the Echo" (1938), and, in doing so, inscribes the play as a typological event in the story of Ireland.

One might equally hold Hyde's 1892 de-Anglicizing manifesto responsible. Six of the seven signatories to the 1916 proclamation were Gaelic League activists. When a Republican caucus led by Patrick Pearse thwarted Hyde's efforts to keep the league apolitical by changing its constitution in 1915, Hyde resigned from the presidency in protest.[52] This was no conventional infiltration of a centrist organi-zation by a radical cabal because it evolved out of the revolutionaries' sustained and intense immersion in learning, teaching and translating Irish, composing poetry in Irish and English, rendering folklore into literature, and cultivating a de-Anglicized "tone of thought." The 1916 Rising showed, contrary to Renan, that dreamy messianism and literary activism can alter the political landscape. It had a galvanic impact on all three poets in my study: it provided the occasion for signifi-cant poems by Yeats and Moore and boosted MacDiarmid's efforts to revive Scots.

In the 1890s this all lay in the future. Jacobite and Fenian lyrics and lore are a catalogue of dashed hopes, but the refrain of renewal and new beginnings continues regardless. The shift at the turn of the twentieth century toward "revival"—*athbheochan na Gaeilge*, the *revivification* of Irish, and the literary renaissance—was embedded in a Jacobite rhetoric of renewal, the *fin*-again wake of a Fenian revenant.

THE GHOST IN THE MACHINE OF VICTORIAN CELTICISM

In 1865 Matthew Arnold—poet, critic, and inspector of schools—delivered a series of lectures "On the Study of Celtic Literature" in his capacity as professor of poetry at Oxford. It was a surprising choice of topic because in 1865 public interest was low and his knowledge of the subject for once superficial. Deeply influenced by Ernest Renan, on whose *Sur la poésie des races celtiques* (1854) the lectures heavily rely, Arnold felt that Britain should emulate French success at "attaching" the Celt.[53] A visit to Brittany in 1859 had reminded him of his maternal Cornish ancestry, and in 1864 he spent a blissful holiday walking the Welsh hills, chanting Thomas Gray's 1754 poem "The Bard" "some hundred times" to his brother.[54] The experience of familial affinity with the Celtic was a novel one because his formidable father had taught him "to think of Celt as separated by an impassable gulf from Teuton" in such a way as to make "this estrangement immense, incurable, and fatal" (14–16).[55] Interposing himself between the hostile English and Celtic parties, Arnold argues that encouraging the disinterested study of Celtic literature would foster cultural and political reconciliation: "Let us consider that of the shrunken and diminished remains of this great primitive race, all, with one insignificant exception, belongs to the English empire . . . They are a part of ourselves, we are deeply interested in knowing them, they are deeply interested in being known by us . . . let it be one of our angelic revenges on the Philistines, who among their other sins are the guilty authors of Fenianism, to found at Oxford a chair of Celtic, and to send, through the ministration of science, a message of peace to Ireland" (*SCL* 149, 152).[56]

To "know the Celt" one journeys westward or northwestward to the periphery, where the *residuum* of things Celtic may still be found. Joep Leerssen defines this pilgrimage, which opens Renan's and Arnold's essays, as the "foundational scenario" of Celticist discourse, noting that travel to the Fringe is routinely represented as "a flight from contemporaneity" into "a preterite temporal zone that hovers ambiguously between a straightforward past tense or else a narrative mood, a 'once upon a time.' "[57] Renan's *Sur la poésie des races celtiques* accordingly begins:

> Everyone who travels through the Armorican peninsula experiences a change of the
> most abrupt description, as soon as he leaves behind the district closely bordering

upon the continent, in which the cheerful but commonplace face of Normandy and Maine is continually in evidence, and passes into the true Brittany, that which merits its name by language and race. A cold wind arises full of a vague sadness, and carries the soul to other thoughts; the tree-tops are bare and twisted; the heath with its monotony of tint stretches away into the distance; at every step the granite protrudes from a soil too scanty to cover it; a sea that is almost always sombre girdles the horizon with eternal moaning. The same contrast is manifest in the people: to Norman vulgarity, to a plump and prosperous population, happy to live, full of its own interests, egotistical as are all those who make a habit of enjoyment, succeeds a timid and reserved race living altogether within itself, heavy in appearance but capable of profound feeling, and of an adorable delicacy in its religious instincts. A like change is apparent, I am told, in passing from England into Wales, from the Lowlands of Scotland, English by language and manners, into the Gaelic Highlands; and too, though with a perceptible difference, when one buries oneself in the districts of Ireland where the race has remained pure from all admixture of alien blood. It seems like entering on the subterranean strata of another world, and one experiences in some measure the impression given us by Dante, when he leads us from one circle of his Inferno to another.[58]

Renan was raised in a bilingual French-Breton home, but there is little in the essay to indicate that he is returning to his birthplace. Rather, he presents himself as a cosmopolitan making an archetypal passage through intervening stages into an unknown realm. In the fashion of Dante's epic, Breton Brittany is construed in relation to the pilgrim's approach, for he never altogether arrives at the periphery, which recedes northwest into a great beyond and downward into the protruding granite substrate. Brittany emerges as both terra incognita and the bedrock of France, a geopolitical conundrum that introduces one of the anomalies of Celticism, its domestic exoticism. For Celticism doubles as a discourse of alterity, in which the aberrant Celts define the French or English norm, and as a discourse about Gaulish-French and composite British origins.

It is indicative that Renan likens the abrupt sense of dislocation on crossing the nonexistent border between Normandy and Breton Brittany to a movement counterclockwise into an underworld. Passing beyond the pale, or notional boundary, between the metropolitan and the exotic, Renan enters an antipodal zone that requires from the traveler a radical reorientation of bearings, so great are the polarizing forces that set Brittany apart from Normandy. Stranger still than this sense of planetary incompatibility is Renan's extraordinary repression of the one clear and inescapable difference between the two places: that he is now surrounded by Breton speakers of the mother tongue that he rarely hears else-where. When Renan went away to school in Paris, the homesick fifteen-year-old wrote in French to his mother of the pleasure he had conversing with an *abbé* from Tréguier "dans le langage de notre bon pays" (in the language of our good country). Late in life, summering in Brittany, he reports that as soon as he speaks Breton, the locals unhesitatingly accept him as one of their own.[59] Yet in the Brittany of *La Poésie* the wind sighs, the sea moans eternally, and the human landscape is as mute as granite. There is scarcely a trace of conviviality or contem-porary Breton culture to be found in Renan's sixty-page opus, which leaves the reader with a decided if mistaken impression that Breton culture had ceased centuries earlier, after it had contributed to another Victorian preoccupation: the chivalric sentiment that shaped medieval romance.

The opening of Arnold's essay likewise treats Celtic culture as a panoramic fossil of the past and almost entirely suppresses the contemporary world of Welsh Wales. Poised at the threshold of Llandudno, he is dissatisfied with the view eastward to Liverpool—"the horizon wants mystery, the sea wants beauty, the coast wants verdure"—and we can anticipate that the view westward will disclose the desired utopia: "Wales, where the past still lives, where every place has its tradition, every name its poetry," the enraptured Arnold declares, citing Welsh place lore as proof that the prosperous Anglo-Saxons have by contrast forgotten their own history (*SCL* 1–2):

> As I walked up and down, looking at the waves as they washed this Sigeian land which has never had its Homer, and listening with curiosity to the strange, unfami-liar speech of its old possessors' obscure descendants,—bathing people, vegetable-sellers, and donkey-boys,—who were all about me, suddenly I heard, through the stream of unknown Welsh, words, not English, indeed, but still familiar. They came from a French nursery maid, with some children. Profoundly ignorant of her rela-tionship, this Gaulish Celt moved among her British cousins, speaking her polite neo-Latin tongue, and full of compassionate contempt probably, for the Welsh bar-barians and their jargon. What a revolution was here! How had the star of this daughter of Gomer waxed, while the star of these Cymry, his sons, had waned! What a difference of fortune in the two, since the days when, speaking the same language, they left their common dwelling-place in the heart of Asia . . . the poor Welsh-man still says, in the genuine tongue of his ancestors, *gwyn, goch, craig, maes, llan, arglywdd;* but his land is a province, and his history petty, and his Saxon subduers scout his speech as an obstacle to civilisation; and the echo of all its kindred in other lands is growing fainter and more feeble; gone in Cornwall, going in Brittany and

the Scotch Highlands, going, too, in Ireland;—and there, above all, the badge of the beaten race, the property of the vanquished. (*SCL* 3–5)

In the ordinary way of things it seems likely that the accomplished multilinguist would be "listening with curiosity" to Welsh speech so as to assess the difficulty of learning a language that would give him access to the literature his lectures extol. Instead, Arnold filters the indigenous language on British soil through the ears of a French nanny. Lacking the scholar's knowledge of its Indo-European pedigree, he imagines that she would listen with "compassionate contempt, probably, for the Welsh barbarians and their jargon." Arnold transforms "this daughter of Gomer" into a regal embodiment of historical hindsight by hailing her with an allusion to Edmund Burke's 1790 *Reflections on the Revolution in France:* "What a revolution was here!" The revenant-muse transports her beholder on a journey through time, and the bustle of Welsh Wales is converted into a tableau of the diverging fortunes of the Indo-European family, as the ruins of successive civilizations pass before the compassionate gaze of Mother Asia.

In my view the unconscious silencing of Breton, Welsh, and Gaelic cultures enacted here by Renan and Arnold is the most striking feature of the "foundational scenario" of Victorian Celticism, though this selective deafness goes unremarked by critics. Renan does not hear Breton when he is wearing his cosmopolitan hat, and Arnold soon disengages himself from Welsh Wales by transposing it to ancient Gaul and central Asia. They both tune out the thick texture of Breton and Welsh culture and sublimate it into something else, an abstract notion of "the Celt" which transforms Brittany and Wales into a spectacle of ruin. Such "switching-off" denies Breton, Welsh, and Gaelic speakers the minimal social recognition of acknowledging their existence. The disregard is accompanied by lavish idealizations of the Celt and wistful yearnings after exotic Celtic traits. Arnold's projections onto the unwitting nanny enact this double move of screening out Celtic languages and apotheosizing Celtic culture onto a pedestal. The benign "timeless" aura masks and disavows contempt toward the "backward" culture while nonetheless reinforcing the image of Welsh Wales as "behind the times."

It is important that Arnold's and Renan's "tuning out" is an unconscious reflex, but the double move of deprecating and exalting in Arnold's reverie perfectly accords with his cultural prescriptions. Although initially he separates himself from the fond contempt that he projects upon the French nanny and the "Saxon subduers who scout [Welsh] speech as an obstacle to civilization," he soon forgoes this momentary tolerance and admits to sharing Saxon opinion "as to the practical inconvenience" of Welsh:

The fusion of all the inhabitants of these islands into one homogeneous, English-speaking whole, the breaking down of barriers between us, the swallowing up of separate provincial nationalities . . . is a necessity of what is called modern civilization, and modern civilization is a real, legitimate force . . . The sooner the Welsh language disappears as an instrument of the practical, political, social life of Wales, the better; the better for England, the better for Wales itself. Traders and tourists do excellent service by pushing the English wedge farther and farther into the heart of the principality; Ministers of Education, by hammering it harder and harder into elementary schools. (*SCL* 10–11)

The ideology of English-only is conflated with the "real, legitimate force [of] modern civilization," which drives a wedge between the Welsh and their perversely undead language, the better to hasten its extinction. Tolerating Welsh and Gaelic cannot be countenanced because the vampire-like vernaculars imperil the lifeblood of the British Isles in some unexplained way. This unexpected outburst is succeeded by what appears to be another reversal of ideas, in which Arnold protests that he "would not for the world have the lineaments of the Celtic genius lost" since, unlike most Saxons, he has "no passion for finding nothing but myself everywhere" (*SCL* 12). The apparent contradiction is shortly resolved by Arnold's solution: scholars and translators in the academy can distill the "genius" from Celtic literary remains and feed the doctored spirit back into the mainstream as a spiritual antidote to English philistinism. Lay the ghost of British multilingualism, and raise the sublimity of English literature to new heights.

Arnold approvingly cites French physiologist W. F. Edwards to the effect that historians' bias and the obscurity of early British history "allowed the contempt of the conqueror and the shame of the conquered to become fixed feelings," arousing the expectation that his disinterested criticism will avoid this regrettable dichotomy (*SCL* 79). Our interest in knowing the Celt, he remarks, "is enhanced if we find him to have actually a part in us," and then elaborates Edwards's observation to contend that "Celtic elements . . . [are] insensibly mixed up . . . in the English race" (*SCL* 74–75). Although Arnold repeatedly struggles to resist the siren call of Saxon contempt, his efforts are in vain, both because he supports Celtic linguicide in the name of modern civilization and because his linguicism involves a profound anxiety about Anglo-Saxon susceptibility to the "loser" proclivities of the Celt. The epigraph from *Ossian* which headlines the published essays—"they went forth to the war, but they always fell"—shows how he conceives Celtic languages not simply as minority languages but as "the property of the vanquished." When he tolls the decline of Celtic cultures, "gone in Cornwall, going in Brittany and the Scotch Highlands," his largesse abruptly founders on recollecting Ireland, and contempt overtakes the respectful elegiac tone: "going, too, in Ireland, and there, above all, the badge of the beaten race, the property of the vanquished" (5).

As he advocates the pleasures of Celtic literature, Arnold recalls the "start of sympathy" he felt on reading Whitley Stokes's observation that "though the names *Triton, Amphitrite,* and those of corresponding Indian and Zend divinities, point to the meaning *sea,* it is only the Irish *tráith* [sic] which supplies the vocable" (70). In the published lectures *tríath* (sea, noble) is misspelled as *tráith* (seashore, ebbing or reflux of tides).[60] The mistranscribed *tráith,* which has to have been an inadvertent error, reverberates uncannily with Arnold's reveries about the waning of empires. The near-antithetical word overlays a vocable with Fenian connotations of nascent nobility with Celticist associations of inexorable decline. Had Arnold's cultural predisposition been different, *tríath/tráith* might well have coalesced into a poem for the poet of "Dover Beach." Instead, the disinterested "start of sympathy" is snuffed out by transference from his own, and his society's, "poetic life."

How "delightfully that [*tráith*] brings Ireland into the Indo-European concert!" Arnold rhapsodizes, "what possibilities of affinity and influence are here hinted at; what lines of inquiry suggest themselves" (70). Yet as he confronts the inadmissible knowledge that Celtic elements are indeed insensibly mixed with English, his urbane composure collapses into sputtering uncertainty:

> By the forms of its language a nation expresses its very self. Our [English] language is the loosest, the most analytic, of all European languages. And we, then, what are we? what is England? I will not answer, A vast obscure Cymric basis with a vast visible Teutonic superstructure; but I will say that that answer sometimes suggests itself, at any rate,—sometimes knocks at our mind's door for admission; and we begin to cast about and see whether it is to be let in.
>
> But the forms of its language are not our only key to a people; what it says in its language, its literature, is the great key, and we must get back to literature. (*CLT* 70–71)

The luminous materiality of *tríath,* a vocable for "noble form arising out of the formless sea," momentarily transfigures Gaelic into a living, palpable language in a manner that threatens to topple the superstructure of the English Pale. Arnold regains his Saxon poise by retreating from the vitality of Gaelic to the transcendent realm of Literature. The paradigmatic swerve permits him to deny the coevalness of Celtic and English languages in the modern moment and to perpetuate the linguicism that sanctions the recuperation of Celtic literary genius at the cost of obliterating its living forms.

The swerve away to literary criticism provides fertile ground for analyzing the traits that distinguish Celts from their English and French observers. In true circular fashion the profile that emerges uncovers a rationale in Celtic "character" for Pale/Fringe diglossia. *Francisation* is a providential civilizing force of good for Renan, as Anglicization is for Arnold, and the two critics are in agreement on most fronts.[61] The issue on which they differ, Renan's characterization of Celts as "an essentially feminine race" (8), reveals how their concepts of the Celtic are decisively if unreflectively colored by their ethnic loyalties to opposite sides of the Pale/Fringe divide. Renan's ideological commitment to *Francisation* vies with his emotional investment in preserving Breton Brittany. He temporizes by portraying Bretons as "a domestic race . . . alien to all ideas of aggression and conquest, little desirous of making its thought prevail outside itself," who have graciously withdrawn to remote fastnesses, whence they "make an invincible resistance to [their] enemies" (5–6).

The race "has worn itself out . . . in defense of desperate causes . . . in taking dream for realities, and in pursuing splendid visions," and this dogged pursuit of unattainable ideals, in concert with a "charming shamefastness [*charmante pudeur*]" in public, means that the Celts have "no aptitude for political life" (7–8). Without disturbing his imperialist assumptions, Renan assuages his Breton pride with a racial profile of "shamefast" Bretons, who neither importune France with their grievances nor internalize the inferiority of a subject race: "Feeling themselves to be strong inwardly and weak outwardly, [Celts] protest, they exult," he writes, egging them on: "thus . . . little people dowered with imagination revenge themselves upon their conquerors" (10). Renan then concludes *La Poésie* on a messianic note, "hoping against all hope" that by hardening themselves to criticism, the Celtic race might yet undergo a national resurgence, as Germany had done a century before (60).

Renan's profile of "the timidity and delicacy of the Celtic nature, its preference for a retired life, its embarrassment at having to deal with the great world," boggles Arnold's mind, and he protests that "however well it may do for the Cymri (Bretons and Welsh), [it] will never do for the Gael" (83, 84). "How little [*charmante pudeur*] accords with the popular conception of an Irishman who wants to borrow money!" he counters, dismissing the risible notion by opining that "if the Celtic nature is to be characterized by a single term, 'sentimental' is the best term to take" (*SCL* 83–84). "Sentimentalism, *always ready to react against the despotism of fact*," Arnold famously begins his anatomy of the Celt's "habitual want of success."[62]

From the vantage of the Anglo insider their Celtic neighbours are a shameless bunch, ingratiating themselves as if they were equals, endlessly venting their grievances, and habitually overreacting. Yet at the zenith of empire, Arnold declares, "this is the moment when Englishism pure and simple, which with all its fine qualities managed always to make itself singularly unattractive, is losing that imperturbable faith in its untransformed self which at any rate made it imposing" (xvii–xviii). The cause and the treatment of this malaise consists in the composite as against integral nature of the English, and hence Arnold replaces Renan's gender dichotomy with a tripartite racial compound. The "Germanic part *triumphs* in us," he observes, "but not so wholly as to exclude *hauntings* of Celtism . . . and our want of sureness of taste, our eccentricity [come] from our not being all of a piece . . . we have Germanism enough to make us Philistines, and Normanism enough to make us imperious, and Celtism enough to make us self-conscious and awkward" (*SCL* 112; my emph.). Like Renan, he identifies social gaucherie as a Celtic trait. He feels that if the English are to shore up a faltering national identity, they must cultivate a balance of Celtic spirituality, Teutonic science, and Norman diplomacy.

The Victorian Englishman at the hub of empire hallucinates a vision of the eccentric Englishman, sinking into obscure irrelevance from a surfeit of awkward self-consciousness: "if we are doomed to perish (Heaven avert the omen!), we shall perish by our Celtism, by our self-will and want of patience with ideas, our inability to see the way the world is going; and yet those very Celts, by our affinity with whom we are perishing, will be hating and upbraiding us all the time" (*SCL* 146). Arnold's debate with Renan over the character of the Celtic Fringe reveals that the feelings of contempt and shame which overtly keep Pale/Fringe diglossia in place are nonetheless more fluid and ambivalent than at first appears, with contempt bleeding into shame, and vice versa. Renan's *charmante pudeur* converts the shame of conquest into what the Scottish-Gaelic poet Sorley Maclean calls "the hauteur of humiliation" (*ardàn tamàilte*), while Arnold's uneasy suspicion that "Englishism" does not quite cohere in the eyes of the world confounds the conquering Anglo with diffuse shame and casts a pall over the prospects of empire. Their "disinterested" ethnographies are decisively influenced by transference from their own, and their respective societies', "poetic life."

MYTHS IN DISGUISE: THE FOLKLORIC FRINGE

The titles of Yeats's first book of poetry and collection of folklore—*The Wanderings of Oisin and Other Poems* (1889) and *The Celtic Twilight* (1893)—advertise the extent to which the author set about deliberately filling the niche created by

Arnoldian Celticism. Writing for the Boston *Pilot* under the pseudonym "the Celt in London," he shuttled between Dublin, Sligo, and London, earning his living as an anthologist, reviewer, and commentator on Irish affairs and the Celtic Fringe.[63] When in London, he haunted the British Museum, devoting himself to the study of Celticist scholarship and popular Irish literature in translation and establishing in the process a canon of Irish writings in English out of which he himself would emerge as a representative talent. The Celt-in-London sobriquet connotes, on the one hand, a native informant and antiquarian of Celtic relics and, on the other, a Fenian subversive, paving the way for a cultural revolution. Yeats was both and neither of these things. His marginal positioning of himself at the center of empire illuminates, however, the peculiar predicament confronting the Irish writer in Victorian England. Most nineteenth-century Irish prose writing in English, Joep Leerssen argues, represents Irish quaintness to (implicitly English) readers through "'the cracked looking-glass of a servant.'"[64] Alternatively, Irish writers could take the London stage by storm and outshine English writers at their own game, as George Bernard Shaw and Oscar Wilde did, and, in the course of so doing, mockingly invert some English standards.

Between them Yeats and Douglas Hyde moved the center of Irish literary production to the Celtic Fringe, conceived by Hyde as the Gaeltacht and by Yeats as "the folk mind," "peasant imagination," or the Celtic "element" he re-signifies as "primitive melancholy." Geoffrey Hartman has felicitously remarked that "we can only know ourselves through the detour of a text."[65] Transmuted into Hyde's fervent Gaelic revivalism and into the bardic persona Yeats fashions for himself, the Celtic Fringe becomes a textual detour through which the nation might "know [it]self." Yeats and Hyde were agreed that renewed contact with the Gaelic past was vital for restoring national self-esteem and fostering critical and creative autonomy. Whereas for Hyde restoring Irish language and traditions was essential for regenerating the "[broken] continuity of Irish life,"[66] for Yeats it lay in the matrix of a national literary tradition provided by "the matter of Ireland."

Yeats and Hyde were leading members of the Dublin-based National Literary Society, a group who saw themselves as heirs to the cultural nationalists of the 1840s Young Ireland movement. In his inaugural presidential address to the National Literary Society, "The Necessity for de-Anglicizing Ireland," in November 1892, Hyde excoriates the nation's tendency to slavishly imitate discarded English fashions in the erroneous assumption that the most innovative and prestigious speech, literature, and culture come from the English metropole after an inevitable "lag." In such essays as "Hopes and Fears for Irish literature" (August 1892) and "Nationality and Literature" (May 1893), Yeats argues that if they are to cultivate a truly national literature (as opposed to the nationalistic literature of the Young Ireland movement), Irish writers must begin at the beginning with Irish mythological cycles and legends and reimagine how to create a distinctively Irish literature. Over the next decade the National Literary Society regrouped around two coeval "revival" movements: the Gaelic Revival, spearheaded by the Gaelic League, which was cofounded in 1893 by Hyde and Eoin MacNéill; and the Irish Literary Revival, which centered around the Abbey Theater and was led by Yeats, Lady Gregory, and John Millington Synge. A good number of cultural nationalists participated in both groups, which collaborated on several projects, and the two movements shared a common goal of undoing the internalization of colonialist contempt toward native culture flagged by the cunning *de-* prefix in *de-Anglicization.* I treat the Irish Literary Renaissance as a de-Anglicizing movement insofar as it, too, strove to work through and dismantle the cultural cringe caused by the impact on the national psyche of the Pale / Fringe linguicism. Irish Literary Revivalists undertook to write a de-Anglicized literature in English which would not be "English" but, rather, "Irish" and "national." Many Gaelic Revivalist writers felt that an authentic Irish national literature must perforce be written in Gaelic, however, and not in the colonial tongue. I mark this crucial divergence between their de-Anglicizing ideologies by characterizing them respectively as movements "to re-Anglicize with a difference" and "to re-Gaelicize." The two movements were each defined in relation to one another, and Yeats's fifty-year career intersects at many junctures with the formative influence of de-Anglicizing ideology on the transformation of the colony into a nation-state. Yeats is an exemplary figure in this book not only for this reason, and because he set the stage for the Celtic modernists who followed in his wake, but also because the "first principle" of "A General Introduction for My Work" (1937), based on Giambattista Vico's philosophical precept that "we can only know what we have made," provides the concept of autopoiesis (self-making) which directs the critical approach of *Haunted English.*[67]

The radical revisions of Arnoldian Celticism at the turn of the twentieth century owe much to the transformational impact of "folklore" on the imagination and politics of Hyde and Yeats. The term *folklore* was coined in 1846 to replace *popular antiquities,* and it encompasses living popular traditions and the purportedly vanishing legends and folkways that are preserved in print as antiquities by the literati. Hyde's and Yeats's formation as intellectuals straddled the divide between "institutional" folklore (the print-circulated lore and legend of Celticist antiquarians and philologists which overlays the Fringe with an exotic and anachronistic aura) and "organic" folklore (the popular orature, beliefs, and customs that are produced and disseminated beyond the Pale).[68] Their intimacy with a folkloric purview honed their instincts for imaginatively reconstructing the oral tradition "from the inside," while their position as connoisseurs "from the outside" helped them to view folklore itself, and the clash of Pale/Fringe values it brought into focus, from a critical distance. Moreover, they were both convinced, albeit for disparate reasons, that ignorance of folk tradition contributed to their Celticist and Young Ireland precursors' fundamentally misguided constructions of Irish national culture and Celtic genius. For them folklore includes but extends beyond the Irish oral tradition to constitute an artistic manifestation of the cultural unconscious Herder calls "volksseele" and Giambattista Vico (and Antonio Gramsci) term "common sense": "the judgment without reflection, shared by an entire class, people, nation, or the entire human race."[69]

Organic folklore is associated with rootedness, immediacy, and conviviality, while mediated folklore is predicated upon distance. Institutional folklore is based on the social distance between the leisured classes, who select and interpret the lore and their informants, the common "folk"; the temporal distance between the archivists' modernity and the vanishing antiquities of popular tradition; and the generic distance between the written media in which the lore is preserved and the oral media in which it is first produced and disseminated. The discipline of folklore emerged when it seemed that folk customs and orature were disappearing, as Diarmuid O'Giolláin observes, and this aura of belatedness means that folklore is associated with the demise of tradition even as it also connotes, in a different register, living popular tradition (8). The emergence of print-mediated folklore as folk customs and orature were declining coincided in Ireland with the contraction of the Gaeltacht. Moreover, the distance between the up-to-date ethnographer and peasant source demarcates the Pale dividing the Anglo-Irish Ascendancy from those of Gaelic ancestry in Ireland. The Anglo-Irish who had been largely responsible as a class for supplanting Gaelic culture were a major cohort among the literati who collected, interpreted, and "saved" Gaelic and Irish-English lore, as Yeats acknowledges, provocatively, in "A General Introduction," when he characterizes antiquarian Celticism as "a gift of the Protestant aristocracy" (511). The aura of neo-feudal largesse surrounding that "gift" was psychologically crucial to Yeats, who elected to approach peasant lore by way of a colonial enclave, Coole Park. Yeats made High/Low class politics an intrinsic part of the ethnographic encounter as he collaborated with Lady Gregory in what he liked to portray as a long-standing creative symbiosis between the Anglo-Irish gentry and the Irish peasantry. Hyde and Synge, by contrast, strove to elide the class barriers that separated them from their peasant informants, but all of the Revivalists participated perforce in the romanticization of peasant culture. Their writings are rife with Arnoldian "turns" to Celtic/peasant genius in order to find there what Anglo culture most lacks, and thus their interpretations are refracted through the Pale's image of the Fringe.

Hyde argues that comparative philology endorses the universality of Fringe lore because the recurrence "of a body of tales such as we might any of us invent to amuse children with" in Hyderabad and Siberia proves that Irish folktales are "myths in disguise" (*LLL* 94). From a comparatist vantage the lore discounted as the primitive flotsam of a despised Gaelic vernacular made Ireland an estimable player in what Arnold calls "the Indo-European concert." The nation's state of disenfranchised orality combined with the antiquity of the Gaelic tradition to make Irish legend and orature unusually rich and certainly more highly prized by scholars than English orature. Hence, the "matter of Ireland" easily held its own in the arena of world literature, offering a firmer foundation for Irish literary and cultural development than pale imitations of English literary trends.

Signs of folklore's crucial agency in the de-Anglicizing shift appear in two tales of abduction by the *sidhe* (fairies, shape-shifters): Hyde's "Teig O'Kane and the Corpse" and Yeats's "The Stolen Child," both published in Yeats's edition of *Fairy and Folk Tales of the Irish Peasantry* (1888). Hyde's tale, which Yeats regarded as the gem of the collection, features an irresponsible youth, Teig, whose father threatens to disinherit him unless he marries the young woman he has made pregnant. That evening Teig finds himself besieged by a host of the *sidhe* who place him under *geis*, or taboo, compelling him to carry a corpse on his back and lay it to rest by dawn. This is easier said than done, and the corpse drives Teig around all the graveyards in the vicinity (an interesting mix of consecrated, unconsecrated, and forgotten burial grounds, including what may be a mass grave from the Famine), directing whither they go by pointing a bony finger. After a harrowing nocturnal odyssey, the harassed Teig finally discovers the corpse's resting place just before daybreak, and the chastened rake returns to wed the girl.

One of the tale's manifold delights is its topography, as the audience reconstructs Teig's nocturnal odyssey around the better-known burial grounds of Leitrim, trying to place precisely where the unmarked graveyards are located. The *sidhe* chorus of "The Stolen Child" similarly locates liminal zones in familiar places around Sligo: "*Where* dips the rocky headland/Of Sleuth Wood in the lake, / *There*" (my emph.). The source for Hyde's story was a Gaelic ballad, structured as a dialogue between Teig and the corpse, which he had heard just once and could only corroborate by a fragmented version in manuscript. He nonetheless succeeded in converting this uncanny ballad into a prose fable, which was published in English in Yeats's anthology and in Irish in his own collection, *Leabhair Sgeulaigheachta* (Book of Storytelling), in 1889.[70] Yeats's poem "The Stolen Child" works in the opposite direction, adapting fairy legend into song lyric, which faithfully re-creates through the contrapuntal refrain an eerie effect similar to the dialogue between living and dead in Hyde's Gaelic original:

> *For here he comes, the human child,*
> *To the waters and the wild*
> *With a faery, hand in hand,*
> *From a world more full of weeping than he can understand.*

Dinnsheanchus (place lore), a prominent feature of Irish folklore, translates the local landscape into a mythical terrain. Lovers' trysting places throughout the country are accordingly graced by the presence of the legendary Diarmuid and Grainne, and Saint Gobnait's adventures unfold in Ballyvourney and Ventry.

Dinnsheanchus and *síscealta* (fairy legend) potentially endow the most insignificant thorn-bush with an epic genealogy and cosmology, inspiring hopes like those of historian Standish O'Grady, that "a day will come when Slieve-na-mon will be more famous than Olympus" (GI 152). If their Anglo-Irish backgrounds put Yeats and Hyde at a distance from popular orature, the situatedness, intimacy, and untrammeled expression of the lore fostered in them a greater sense of belonging to the people and their respective Sligo and Roscommon neighborhoods than they may otherwise have enjoyed. Moreover, the genius of folklore appealed to the pronounced strengths of their very different temperaments. Yeats responds to the visionary and melancholic purview of legend, while Hyde's gregarious nature is stimulated by the vernacular and performative dimensions of orature, the way a teller melds local knowledge, "the matter of Ireland," and the here-and-now occasion of storytelling into an artistic performance.

Hyde (like Yeats) was attracted to an oral tradition devalued by the mainstream, and his boyhood autodidacticism shaped his life's work. He persuaded Seamus Hart, the local keeper of the bogs whom he revered as a father figure, to teach him Irish. His journals include awkward transliterations of the Gaelic language into English orthography, including a song he recorded at thirteen by Anthony Raftery—"Condae Mhuigh Eo": "In syth joc na fail Breedah/Baen yil au sheena/Ohil-mae in muchanee."[71] Yet Hyde had no idea that the song was by Raftery because the unlettered Galway poet did not "appear" in mainstream culture until Hyde and Lady Gregory brought him to public attention over fifteen years later. Still more telling of Anglocentric disregard, his early stab at transliterating the song reproduces the deplorable conditions of Gaelic print culture at the time. Gaelic has a distinctive orthography, alphabet, and type font, but by 1822 there was no Gaelic type founder in Ireland, and catechetical prose was transliterated into English orthography and then printed in roman characters.[72] (Gaelic itself was not printed in roman font until the 1930s, and this practice only became official policy in the 1950s.) As a boy, it seemed natural for Hyde to write down Gaelic songs in the only form available to him, but as a man, he thought it was a scandal that the nation had ever acquiesced in these printed travesties of "Gaelic" literature. Healing the alienation of spoken Irish from the printed word, and renewing the fertile reciprocity between orature and literature which had once obtained in Ireland, became a critical component of de-Anglicizing praxis for him.

Yeats's poetics and poetry is anchored in the "secret fanaticism" that led him as a youth to gather stories of apparitions and, significantly, to break free from his agnostic father's overwhelming charisma (*Au* 79). "I did not believe . . . with my intellect, but I believed with my emotions, and the belief of the country people made that easy," he recalls, and he returns the courtesy by never discrediting peasant or occult belief, though he was often baited to do so (78). "Nobody ever laid new milk on their doorstep" for the "mortals beautifully masquerading" as fairies in English literature, he writes in the 1888 preface, and the fact that *sidhe* lore is embedded in everyday peasant observances made it an essential element of the nation's "poetic life" for him.[73] The "*human* child" replies to the difficulty of writing about the *sidhe* (one of the few Gaelic loanwords in Yeats's lexicon) in the English language, which inexorably diminishes them into "mortals beautifully masquerading" as fairies. In his play on the *sidhe* abduction theme, *The Land of Heart's Desire* (1894), he tries to break the impasse of translation by adding a program note that "the characters are supposed to speak in Gaelic"—in effect, recommending the audience to imagine his English dialogue as Irish.[74] Yet unlike many of his peers, Yeats made only a faint-hearted effort to learn Irish himself.[75] Instead, he tackled the epistemological divide by making the study of magic "next to my poetry the most important pursuit of my life," declaring that he has "always considered myself a voice of what I believe to be a greater renaissance—the revolt of the soul against the intellect—now beginning in the world."[76]

For Yeats folk belief and orature are "myths in disguise," but in a very different sense from Hyde's conventional one. He sees myth as a product of an encounter between the artist and "the imperishable moods" (1895)—the gyring dialectic between human consciousness and the dead "dreaming back" their memories into the instincts of the living elaborated in *Per Amica Silentia Lunae* (1917) and schematized in *A Vision* (1925, 1937). Furthermore, as well as their ultimately irreconcilable differences over the relative status of Gaelic and English in Irish national cultural life, Hyde and Yeats perceive language from their very different vantages as cultural activist and poet. For Yeats the matter of Ireland and the English language are the stuff of his art and the medium with which he hopes to hone a style that is both inimitably his own and unmistakably Irish. For Hyde the genius of the matter of Ireland emerges in and through vernacular use. It is there to be used by the people who produced it, and not to be salted away as an archival treasure. If the nation could relearn how to use the national vernacular—Irish language, folk traditions, and orature—they might recover the sense of people-hood and critical-aesthetic discrimination which he believes they have lost.

DE-ANGLICIZING IRISH NATIONAL "SENTIMENT"

Hyde strongly dissents from the Arnoldian premise, in *The Study of Celtic Literature,* that "the sooner the Welsh [and Gaelic] languages disappear as an instrument of the practical, political, social life of Wales," Ireland, and Scotland, and are "swallowed up . . . into one homogeneous, English-speaking whole . . . the better for England, the better for Wales [and Ireland and Scotland]" (10). He sees the swallowing up of Celtic cultures by the homogenizing English Pale as a catastrophic cultural loss in itself and as a profoundly damaging assault on the morale and creative agency of Celtic communities. He challenges his audience to unravel the conundrum of their "most anomalous position." "It has always been very curious to me how Irish sentiment sticks in this half-way house," he re-marks, "how it continues to apparently hate the English and at the same time continues to imitate them; how it continues to clamour for recognition as a distinct nationality, and at the same time throws away with both hands what would make it so"—namely, the Irish language (*LLL* 154). Over the past sixty years, Hyde contends, the nation has been "possessed with a mania for changing" Gaelic names to English. He "de-Anglicizes" the Anglicized names through an etymological salvage that reminds his audience of the residual kinship bonds preserved in Gaelic clan names and the wealth of local lore obscured by the crass transliteration of place names.[77] He links the mania for self-deculturation with the seventeenth-century colonialist drive to destroy Irish common memory by citing Spenser's recommendation in *A View* that clan names and Gaelic place names be outlawed because with "the O's and Macs . . . utterly forbidden and extinguished," social cohesion and solidarity among Gaels would be "much en-feeble[d]," and with storied Gaelic place names Anglicized, the colonizer could usurp natives' cognitive ownership of the land (*LLL* 162).

Hyde's sixty-year time frame dates this Anglomania back to Daniel O'Connell's heyday, when the Irish Penal Laws ended with Catholic Emancipation (1829) and an Anglophone educational system was established for the nation (1832). He is conspicuously silent about how the trauma of the Irish Famine (1845–49) and the pandemic of emigration which ensued may have strengthened the belief that the language was unsustainable.[78] The prevailing outlook on the language shift, in Victorian Britain and Ireland alike, was that the social advancement expected from educational opportunity and emigration would soon render Gaelic obsolescent. Hyde rejects what he wryly calls the "Philistine idea" that minority language communities are "a barrier to progress" because his philological background makes him aware of many counter-examples. "All the world knows that bi-linguists are superior to men who know only one language," he observes elsewhere, "yet in Ireland everyone pretends to believe the contrary."[79]

Hyde believes that a significant factor in the precipitous shift from bi- to monolingualism is that the native intelligentsia and political leaders (notably O'Connell) have at best tacitly discouraged the speaking of Irish. A transcript of the "De-Anglicizing" lecture, given in 1905 to a capacity crowd at Carnegie Hall, contains an anecdote exposing what Hyde regarded as the moral bankruptcy of such "leadership." He recounts how, in County Sligo, a pleasant chat he had in Gaelic with a little girl was interrupted by her brother saying (Hyde mimics her brother's voice), " 'Now Mary, isn't that a credit for ye?' and not a word could I get out of Mary from that time on [audience laughter]. You laugh, gentlemen, and, God forgive me, I laughed too; but when I went home and thought it over, I swear to you that I cried, because I saw that it was the tragedy of a nation in a nutshell [audience applause]" (186).[80] That Hyde, who had initiated the conversation out of profound respect for the language, should then so readily collude with the boy's ridicule of his sister, captures the intractable shame felt by the Irish toward their national tongue. Neither Hyde at the time of the incident nor his audience on its retelling quite understand *why* they spontaneously laugh at the girl's expense; the deprecatory laughter discharges embarrassment about the stigma on Irish once tragically imposed and now cultivated by its own people. Tellingly, the two most frequent epithets for Irish in post-Famine Ireland were *drochmheas* (contempt) and *náire* (shame) (*LLL* 20). The nation is unconsciously behaving in an unconscionable manner toward its national heritage, and a "melancholy" aspect of the current stampede to English "is that not one single word of warning or remonstrance has been raised, as far as I am aware, against this colossal cringing" (164).

Given that they "hasten to adopt, pell-mell, and indiscriminately, everything that is English simply because it *is* English" and rush to abandon their national culture (153), Hyde asks why "the Irish millions" across the globe applaud the "sentiments" of this song:

> They say the British empire owes much to Irish hands,
> That Irish valour fixed her flag o'er many conquered lands;
> And ask if Erin takes no pride in these her gallant sons,
> Her Wolseleys and her Lawrences, her Wolfes and Wellingtons.
>
> Ah! these were of the Empire—we yield them to her fame,
> And ne'er in Erin's orisons are heard their alien name;
> But those for whom her hearts beats high and benedictions swell,
> They died upon the scaffold and they pined within the cell.   (155)

In Hyde's view the fact that popular song glorifies nationalist martyrs, and not the heroes of British imperialism, should give the Irish pause. He speculates that the "dull ever-abiding animosity" that makes Ireland "grieve when [England] prospers and joy when she is hurt" and "very composite" mix of nationalist and anti-imperialist sentiment are a distorted expression of aggrieved national pride (154–55). Behind the reflex antagonism lies "the half unconscious feeling . . . that the Ireland of to-day is the descendent of the Ireland of the seventh century," an awareness that what was "then the school of Europe and the torch of learning . . . is now—almost extirpated and absorbed elsewhere—making its last stand for independence on this island of Ireland and do what they may the race of to-day cannot wholly divest itself from the mantle of its own past" (155–56). "As long as [the nation] is actuated by motives so contradictory" as anti-national *and* anti-imperial sentiment, he contends, Ireland cannot come into its own.

To tip the balance in favor of "cultivat[ing the Irish-language culture] they have rejected, and build[ing] up an Irish nation on Irish lines" and to prove his contention that "there is no earthly chance of [the Irish] becoming good members of the Empire," Hyde makes a populist appeal to Anglophobic and anti-imperial sentiment (154). In an extended reference to Spenser's *View* and to Victorian tirades about the inassimilable Irish, he transvalues the racial stereotypes of the stolid, worldly Saxon and the atavistic, rebellious Celt to proffer a loaded dilemma:

> Let us suppose that a century of good government and able husbandry of national resources were to make Ireland fat, wealthy, and populous, but with every spark of national feeling stamped out; every thought and idea that was Irish extinguished; every external that at present differentiates us from the English lost or dropped; all our Irish names of places and people turned into English names; the Irish language completely extinct; Irish intonation changed by English schoolmasters into some-

thing English; our history no longer remembered or taught; the names of our rebels, martyrs, and battlefields blotted out; the fact that we were not of Saxon origin dropped out of sight and memory, and let me now put the question—How many Irishmen are there who would purchase prosperity at such a price?[81]

Hyde's largely rhetorical question drew "shouts of None, and great applause" at Carnegie Hall, as did his claim that "nine Englishmen out of ten would jump to accept it, and I equally believe that nine Irishmen out of ten would indignantly refuse it" (183). The chauvinistic appeal assumes that the threat of Gaelic's irreversible loss will rouse the nation to reclaim the national tongue as a cherished birthright, but this assumption cannot fully account either for his own inflammatory rhetoric or for its sensational impact upon an audience. It would seem more in keeping with Hyde's revivalism to picture a future Ireland as a proud, self-determining, and Gaelic-speaking state that assumes its rightful place in the community of nations. Yet it is the very prospect of replacing the Ireland of famine, poverty, and forced emigration with a "fat, prosperous, and populous" quasi-English state which excites Irish outrage at Carnegie Hall. How did Hyde make the English-only mania that until now had seemed unexceptionable, and even desirable, come to seem symptomatic of a collective malaise with dire cultural consequences to his audiences?

Hyde's millenarian rhetoric places Ireland at a historic crossroads, where the "unparalleled frivolity" with which Gaelic is being cast aside becomes a crime against posterity. Hyde's "View of the Future State of Ireland" conjures a world in which future generations of children could recite the prayer then displayed in Irish classrooms without irony:

I thank the goodness and the grace,
That on my birth has smiled,
And made me in these Christian days,
A happy English child.

The imaginary child of the future with no inkling of the past is a vapid creature, living testimony that "England 'has definitely conquered us, she has even imposed upon us her language, that is to say, the form of our thoughts during every instant of our existence' " (159–60). Needless to say, this image of future oblivion and obliviousness works powerfully upon a people who passionately commemorate the nation's rebels and martyrs.

A residual identification with Gaelic culture and the colonial struggle are not the only reasons Hyde's audience is appalled by "this awful idea of complete

Anglicisation" (155). The notion that anyone with Irish ethnicity might ever be treated by the English as one of their own provokes the deepest skepticism. As his Anglicized audience who have "ceas[ed] to be Irish without becoming English" know all too well, Anglicization is predicated upon maintaining an impassable Pale between those who are English and those who are caught in the endlessly deferred state of becoming English (153). Consequently, the Irish suffer from what Anne Anlin Cheng describes, in a different context, as "racial melancholia": the "deep-seated, intangible, psychical complications for people living within a ruling episteme that privileges that which they can never be."[82] "Irish sentiment" is stuck in "a half-way house" because the Anglicized Irish are unable to get over the unavowed, intertwined losses that Anglicization has produced: a thwarted and hotly denied ambition to adopt the Englishness that is interminably withheld; and a repressed identification with the Gaelic culture that is reviled as worthless and yet revered.

Hyde understands that a primary effect of Anglicization is affect, the "very composite" and "half unconscious feelings" of contempt, antagonism, pride, disillusion, and grievance which animate national "sentiment." In making the case that the nation is all unawares in the throes of an identity crisis and beset by cultural cringe, his analysis coincides with the Freudian reading of melancholy as ego impoverishment "on a grand scale." In "Mourning and Melancholia" (1917) Freud distinguishes mourning, the arduous work of acceptance which gradually frees the mourner from libidinal attachment to a lost loved one or ideal, and melancholia, the devastating self-abasement that ensues when the mourner refuses the freedom of grief and projects the now intensified ambivalence of its previous attachment onto the self. Thus, one aspect of the ego is objectified as notionally beloved or ideal, a displacement that allows the now riven subject at once to sustain the libidinal attachment and lament it all at once. "In grief the world becomes poor and empty; in melancholia it is the ego itself," Freud writes, and the ambivalence of melancholia "casts a pathological shade on the grief, forcing it to express itself in the form of self-reproaches, to the effect that the mourner himself is to blame for the loss of the loved one, i.e. desired it" (246, 251). At the same time, Freud sees self-reproach, which is usually moral in nature and cultivated almost artistically as lamentation, as providing the melancholic with a neurotic pleasure and peculiar assurance that the sufferer is loath to relinquish.

It is arguable that whereas the Jacobite *aisling* laments the Gaelic present in pursuing the beloved revenant of past and future glory, Anglomania is the pathological repression of that grief, which returns in the form of disdain and vilification of Gaelic culture. The revenant-*spéirbhean* of "Gile na Gile" plays something like the role of an objectified Irish self, forever mourning the nation's catastrophe as it in turn is lamented by the Anglicized speaker in Mangan's translation, who desires, reproaches, and laments her in the pathological manner of melancholia. Melancholia is understood by Freud to originate in a profound wound to self-esteem given by an influential other, which leads to psychological regression and ultimately to the narcissistic and therefore ambivalent identification of the ego as its own lost love object. As a result, "The ego wishes to incorporate this object into itself, and the method by which it would do so, in this oral or cannibalistic stage [of narcissistic regression], is by devouring it" (249–51). Such self-devouring evokes the living death of Spenser's cannibalized Irish, who by the conqueror's right of despoliation are made falsely to conceive themselves as the cause of their own suffering.

The "pathological shade" cast by its colonial history on Irish grief becomes the melancholia of Anglicization, the otherwise nameless psychocultural malaise that Hyde acutely addresses with his "de-Anglicizing" polemic. The sense of ambivalence, of not quite belonging inside the English Pale of Ireland and Britain—which de jure included Celts and the lower classes in "one homogeneous English-speaking whole" while de facto excluding them in ways both overt and subtle—induces a state of mind not unlike melancholia. Those "beyond the Pale" risk being branded as one of *them* if their speech does not measure up to standard, but acceptance as one of *us* implies that they have repressed part of themselves, objectifying their Irishness in order to spurn it and so opening themselves up to perpetual self-reproach. The melancholia of the Anglicized Celt expresses this ambivalence as grief, distorted by contempt, for a subjugated Gaelic culture and an implacable grievance against the colonizer for destroying the ancestral tongue and upholding a symbolic order that privileges that which they can never be, English. The high-Victorian diagnosis for Celtic disaffection is that Celts need to "let go" of "the past" and their "doomed" vernaculars and "move on." In Hyde's view, by contrast, the best way for the nation to move forward is not by "forgetting" the past but by recovering their Gaelic heritage and recovering from the Anglocentric false consciousness and debilitating shame and contempt that alienate them from it.

The "despotism" of the Pale was brought home to Hyde when he wept at his collusive shaming of the little girl in Sligo. Her mortification and his own unthinking obeisance to the ideology of English-only moves him to harness the system of social contempt which silences Irish speakers and, instead, direct its disdain against anyone who slights the use of Gaelic: "We must arouse some spark of patriotic inspiration among the peasantry who still use the language, and put an end to the shameful state of feeling—a thousand-tongued reproach to our leaders and statesmen—which makes young men and women blush and hang their heads when overheard speaking in their own language" (160). The desired turnaround in linguistic attitudes would rupture the self-perpetuating loop of the English Pale in Ireland. Hyde's solution recognizes the intimate reciprocity between "the colossal cringing" of a linguistic marketplace that automatically defers to English and derogates Irish and the cringe of individual speakers and interlocutors. De-Anglicization necessitates reconditioning on two interdependent fronts because the nation's linguistic habitus is simultaneously deeply internal (inner cringe is necessarily subjective) and inescapably social (because speaking styles are finely attuned to the flow of social prestige "out there" in the public sphere).

Irish sentiment, which means something close to race memory for Hyde, is deployed by him in two separate yet related ways: a "live" anti-imperial, pro-Irish, reflex solidarity that can be ignited in a flash, on the one hand, and a "dim" habitus and Irish-oriented aesthetic-critical feel for things, a "tone of thought" which must be unearthed, revived, and cultivated, on the other. When he considers why a crew of fifteen workmen he knew ceased to speak Irish after an English farmer laughed at them, he treats sentiment as an ingrained habitus in Bourdieu's sense of an embodied instinctive knowingness about how to comport oneself in public and as the automatic, unthinking assumptions that constitute the "common sense" of a group. Hyde seeks to demonstrate that "we" (the manifesto proceeds as a collective consciousness-raising exercise) have lost our embodied instinctive knowingness for who we are, where we are coming from, and what kind of future we want to create. Nevertheless, and paradoxically, we can depend upon ourselves to close ranks and fight back against the invisible blight that has set national sentiment at cross-purposes with itself. The extended roll call of Anglicized Gaelic names and the appealing portrait of Gaelic conviviality and custom convey the message that the Irish belong to the Gaelic tradition and it potentially belongs to them, if only they would repossess it.

As the de-Anglicizing message caught on over the next decade, those who attempted "to snuff out [Gaelic] by their tacit discouragement" hazarded being reproached as anti-national and as betraying unbecoming cultural cringe (160). Hyde felt strongly that the Irish must inculcate "a tone of thought" which would make it as "disgraceful for an educated Irishman to be ignorant of his own language . . . as for an educated Jew to be quite ignorant of Hebrew" (161). But de-Anglicization remained a daunting task for that very reason, since it required people learning Gaelic voluntarily to create an audience for an as-yet-unwritten

modern Gaelic literature. In order to create resilient pockets of vernacularity amid
the global lingua franca, in which Irish Anglophones would habitually use Irish
in preference to English, "we must teach ourselves to be less sensitive, we must
teach ourselves not to be ashamed of ourselves . . . [and] create a strong feeling
against West Britonism, for it—if we give it the least chance, or show it the
smallest quarter—will overwhelm us like a flood" (169).

Hyde's slur of "West Britonism" refers to the self-segregation of Irish resi-
dents who dissociate themselves from "the natives" and who are disdained in
return because they deny their origins and delude themselves into thinking they
are accepted on "the mainland" as true insiders of the Pale. "West Briton!" is a
popular blazon (a speech genre of interethnic mudslinging and stereotyping
which I explore in chap. 3, on Hugh MacDiarmid), and Hyde's use of it taps into,
and places a new spin on, a historical memory of linguicism.[83] (It also gave a new
lease of life to nativist prejudice and spawned a new form of linguicism, Gaelic-
only linguicism.) The West Briton bogey objectifies the enemy within, receiving
the brunt of that Irish ambivalence which proceeded to polarize the nation into
two tribes: on the one hand, "every Irish-feeling Irishman" and, on the other, the
deracinated, on-the-make "West Briton," who serves as scapegoat for the national
malaise of Anglicization (160).[84]

Among other symptoms of the malaise Hyde equates "this continued West
Britonising of ourselves" with cultural homogeneity (165): his antipathy to
"penny-dreadfuls" and "shilling-shockers" owes less to their English provenance
than to the potentially deleterious effect of a consumerist popular culture and its
mass media on the local orature and folk traditions of the Gaeltacht (LLL 169). He
follows Spenser's and Renan's gendering of the Pale/Fringe divide by painting a
rosy portrait of "our dear mother Erin" to whose "kindly Irish breast" Dane,
Norman, and even the descendants of Cromwellians were drawn and who, "assimilative as she is . . . issued forth in a generation or two fully Irished, and more
Hibernian than the Hibernians themselves" (156). The utopian image of a hospi-
table, Irish-speaking gemeinschaft depicts the Fringe as a redemptive counter-
cultural enclave in a mercantile world and also—though unconsciously in Hyde's
allegory—as a primal, and to that extent regressive, retreat.[85]

In folk memory the "more Irish than the Irish" accolade pays tribute to those
settlers who joined forces with the colonized against the colonizer. Hyde's canny
use of it here embraces both the Anglo-Irish settler caste who may wish to claim
an Irish affiliation by speaking the national vernacular as well as the "native" Irish
who choose to display the traditional "assimilative" hospitality of "mother Erin"
by renouncing any class, sectarian, or nativist resentments they may feel. The

persistence of the "more Irish than the Irish" leitmotif in Ireland's folklore is also, I believe, a tacit comment upon a telltale lack of reciprocity: the Irish cannot become "more English than the English," and it is here, in the unbridgeable gulf between "Anglicized" and "English," that the historical memory of Pale/Fringe linguicism becomes acute. All discursive communities are simultaneously inclusionary and exclusionary, and Hyde's deployment of the "West Briton" and "more Irish than the Irish" blazons mark "where we differ [from excluded others] and where we belong [with included others]."[86] The emphasis on the political significance of voluntary speech acts made it possible for "Catholic and Protestant, Unionist and Nationalist, landlord and tenant" to mark where they belong by speaking Irish. In Hyde's hands the contours of Irish nationality were drawn in cultural and performative terms, rather than ancestral ones. Much in the manner of its precursor, the Arnoldian "Philistine" (but unlike its Scottish equivalent, Hugh MacDiarmid's "canny Scot"), the phantasmatic West Briton elides competing class interests and aspirations among the Irish of landlords and tenants, shopkeepers and peasants.[87] Notwithstanding its purportedly classless ideology, the de-Anglicizing movement transformed the cross-wiring of ethnic and class cues that determine social prestige in the Pale by organizing the lower and middle classes to value what is most Irish over what is most bourgeois, metropolitan, and English.

One complex manifestation of the reconfigured Pale/Fringe hierarchy was the emergence of the West-of-Ireland peasant as an alternative source of cultural authority. As the phantasmatic "true" national (the antithesis of the West Briton), the Irish peasant was invoked to authorize a host of de-Anglicizing initiatives, from the wearing of homespun tweed (recommended by Hyde) to the issuing of tirades against anything foreign, newfangled, or abstract as un-Irish (168).[88] Hyde's more moderate and practical suggestions also employ Gaelic culture as a means to create national community: house-to-house canvassing in the Gaeltacht; re-Gaelicizing the country's nomenclature; reviving Gaelic music, storytelling *ceilidhe* (night visits), and traditional sports. This new solidarity would then provide popular incentive to preserve the vernacular within a predominantly Anglophone society. While gradual at first, the growth of the Gaelic League—the organization founded by Hyde and Eoin MacNéill in 1893 to promote the language revival—underwent a boom after the outbreak of the Boer War, with membership doubling annually until 1904, when there were almost six hundred branches with a total of fifty thousand members.[89]

Hyde was radicalized by the inherent contradictions in the Arnoldian project of preserving the "genius" of Celtic literature while suppressing everyday use of

Celtic languages. Whereas Arnold's brand of Celticism simply widened Pale/
Fringe diglossia, Hyde sought to dismantle its entrenched linguicism by invoking
the international prestige of Celticist scholarship on behalf of the spoken languages: "the Irish language *is* worth knowing, or why would the greatest philologists in Germany, France, and Italy be emulously studying it, and it *does* possess a
literature, or why would a German savant have made the calculation that the
books written in Irish between the eleventh and seventeenth centuries, and still
extant, would fill a thousand octavo volumes" (*LLL* 160). Hyde himself moved
easily between two coteries who shared his conviction about the aesthetic merit of
the lore: the peasantry who composed and exchanged the songs and tales among
themselves; and the (international) scholars who transcribed, collated, and interpreted them. The high value these two groups set on Gaelic orature contrasted
painfully with the hostile reception of Gaelic and folk traditions by the general
Irish public, whose collective urge to stamp out the use of Gaelic is best illustrated
by the notorious "tally-stick."[90] Children were obliged to wear these sticks around
their necks, which were scored whenever they lapsed into Gaelic so that the
penalty or rather its severity might be properly assessed. As a result, Hyde found
himself marveling at the artistic accomplishment of a storyteller (*seanchaoi*) or
singer—the nuanced delivery of a traditional tale or song, skill at improvising a
fitting and sufficient context for a given audience, or a singer's handling of a
series of grace notes—only to observe that the *seanchaoi*'s children set little store
by his art, while his grandchildren could not understand it. Hyde believes that
criticism flourishes where orature is strong because observation by an exacting
audience may strengthen the oral performer's mettle and hone the "edge" of the
vernacular repertoire.

The normative authority of Pale/Fringe diglossia was dramatically reduced
once the Irish became aware of the double-think in their cultural values, and this
changed the relative status of the dominant English and minor Gaelic languages
in the national imaginary. Competence in English was no longer seen as a benign
or neutral asset because it represented the systematic inculcation of colonialist
attitudes. The dominance of English acquired a decidedly oppressive aura, and
Hyde's excoriation of the tendency to imitate the most tawdry aspects of English
consumerist culture gave a nationalist valence to the rejection of the "mass-
produced," "standard," and "uniform." The status of Gaelic shifted from a despised peasant patois to an inestimable source of national identity, linking a
venerable past to a de-Anglicized future. The Gaelic League's slogan, "Beatha
teanga í a labhairt" (A language lives when it is spoken), captures the revivalists'
turn from antiquarian Celticist preservation to the promotion of spoken Irish as

an expression of ethnic and national pride. The emphasis on spoken Irish created a linguistic marketplace in which to speak Irish was to keep it alive and, by the same token, to neglect to speak it was to hasten its demise.[91] Language and the ambivalent feelings of contempt and shame which perpetuate Pale/Fringe diglossia were placed at the forefront of the cultural-nationalist endeavor. The resolve to recover from the cultural impasse besetting the nation's people through language and literary activism served both to alleviate and to intensify public ambivalence about their fraught linguistic heritage. For the zealous de-Anglicizing subject, the desired shift from self-contempt to national pride was often shadowed by self-reproach.

Hyde had a canny and uncanny genius for working a crowd. By making his audiences squirm at their colossal cringing, he roused an indignant surge of passionate nationalist resolve to pursue the revenance of a Gaelic-oriented habitus. As he declares, "When the picture of complete Anglicisation is drawn for them in all its nakedness Irish sentimentality becomes suddenly a power and refuses to surrender its birthright" (155). If the polarizing force of nationalist sentiment could mobilize public resistance to the craven emulation of English culture, the same revolutionary zeal, Hyde recognized, could also derail the slow and gradual restoration of the national language and literature. In order to secure the delicate, laborious work of cultural regeneration, he sought to carve out a sphere of almost Arnoldian disinterestedness which "leave[s] alone all questions of practical consequences and applications, questions which will never fail to have due prominence given to them."[92] It became a key tenet of de-Anglicizing ideology that the state of Gaelic language and culture is a more salient index of robust nationality than "any mere temporary wrangle" over partisan politics and that cultural emancipation is the sine qua non of political autonomy.

The intimate reciprocity and often uneasy symbiosis between political and cultural nationalism is epitomized by the way the revivalist rhetoric of "revivification" appropriates the phoenix imagery of Fenianism, the *risorgimento* ideology of the Young Ireland movement, and the *puella-senilis* topos of the Jacobite *aisling*. In a departure from his usual avoidance of issues that might provoke divisiveness or despondency,[93] Hyde at one point obliquely alludes to the secret underground organization the Fenians, which emerged in the wake of the Young Ireland movement. He remarks parenthetically that the house-to-house canvassing of Gaelic speakers is analogous to the recruitment strategy ("though with a very different purpose") of the Fenian organizer James Stephens, "when he found [Ireland] like a corpse on the dissecting table" (161). Hyde's simile gestures at the presence in his audience of Sir Charles Gavan Duffy, erstwhile prime minister of the Australian state of Victoria and the Young Irelander who supplied the conceit when he declared in August 1855 in the *Nation* that there seemed "to be no more hope for the Irish cause than for the corpse on the dissecting table."[94] The return of this nationalist elder earlier that year had cast a pall over the National Literary Society's first major initiative: the publication of an "Irish Library" series for distribution in reading rooms around the nation. Yeats's plan to publish imaginative literature by upcoming writers was nixed by Duffy's use of the scheme to reissue hackneyed patriotic classics. Hyde's attempt to bottle up the genie of militant Fenianism founders as the metaphor that refuses to die makes yet another return, to raise the twin specters of the de-Anglicizing movement: the risk of dashing raised expectations by producing no greater evidence of de-Anglicization than a Gaelicized rehash of hackneyed staples; and the likely takeover of the movement by Fenian separatists.

The creation of a significant Gaelic literature would prove to the Irish themselves and to the world that the nation had managed, despite centuries of colonial depredation, to retain its cultural autonomy and tradition. The Gaelic literary tradition offers more than potential cultural parity with other nations, however, because Hyde envisions Irish language, literature, and orature as themselves primary media through which "Irish sentiment" may be reawakened, reoriented, transformed, and empowered. In short, language and literary activism is potentially a catalyst of de-Anglicization. Hyde contends that the Irish peasantry were "all to some extent cultured men" because they had maintained residual contact with high Gaelic culture until early in the nineteenth century, unlike the Anglophone elite who had discarded it: "Irish poor scholars and schoolmasters used to gain the greatest favor and applause by reading out manuscripts in the people's houses at night, some of which manuscripts had an antiquity of a couple of hundred years or more behind them, and which, when they got illegible from age, were always recopied" (158). He gives as an example of the vanishing cultured peasantry a Galway peasant who is dismissed as "a mere brute" because he is an unlettered Gaelic monoglot but who has "a marvelous fund" of Gaelic orature, including a hitherto undocumented 400-line Ossianic lay. Meanwhile, the peasant's mastery of the Gaeltacht's legend and lore is being supplanted in the next generation by a rudimentary national curriculum in English, an advance of the Pale's putatively civilizing influence which Hyde denounces with the bitter declaration that "I would as soon have a lump of ashes choked down my throat as the *Third Reading Book* of the National Schools" (186–87). The juxtaposed predicaments of the unlettered Gaelic rhapsode and his literate Anglicized son define the challenges confronting the Gaelic League as it strove to reverse the twofold alienation of the Irish language and the Irish people from literacy. Although the Galway man's orature connects him with ancient Gaelic tradition, Hyde warns that this undocumented repository of high Gaelic culture will "die" with his generation, even as the force-fed "ashes" of the *Third Reading Book* gains literacy for his son at the cost of alienating him from his first language.

Hyde allows Young Ireland literature to be "a most brilliant effort" but contends that because it was "written in the English language and largely founded upon English models [it] cannot be said to have been enduring . . . a new bark, stuck on with English gum . . . failed to incorporate itself with the ancient stem; English gum is no substitute and never can be a substitute for Irish sap" (158, 184). Young Ireland literature, he complains, is demonstrably deficient in "Irish sap" because "it failed to properly leaven our peasantry, who might, perhaps, have been reached on other lines," by rekindling memories of the Gaelic tradition which used to win applause for vagrant poets and scholars (158). A litmus test of Irish sap for Hyde would be if a new work aroused "starts of sympathy" ("leaven") in the Galway rhapsode and he memorized it as an integral part of "the ancient stem." He maintains that the rhapsode's monoglottism is in one sense "all his luck" because it enables him to know the Gaelic tradition from the inside, uncontaminated by colonialist bias, in salutary contrast to his Anglicized compatriots (186). Revivalists envisioned the peasantry as a passive yet discerning audience whose members have the good sense not to be duped by the superficial and the second-rate and yet are dependent upon cultural intervention (they must be "reached" by a literati who speak to their subliminal "cultured" past).

By 1905 Hyde is sufficiently emboldened by the accomplishments of the Gaelic League to express the hope to his Carnegie Hall audience "that we can go a step farther than [the Young Irelanders] went and allow the natural bark, the Gaelic bark, thin though it may be at first," to be grafted. His caution is hardly surprising, given the formidable challenges facing the league. Revivalists had to fashion a literary vernacular out of diversified regional dialects; foster public literacy by suiting the diverse reading needs of Gaelophones and Anglophones learning Gaelic; develop new literary genres, including the novel and drama; and operate within a diglossic context in which *bearlachas* (Anglicisms) and "English gum" percolate through Gaelic. Significantly, however, Hyde's trepidation also acknowledges that writing in Irish does not in itself guarantee a rising of Irish sap. Literary reception works in mysterious ways, and it is only after a work has manifestly quickened dormant Irish sentiment that it can claim the de-Anglicizing power he predicts for an authentically Gaelic literary corpus.

Hyde's lecture is equivocal about the de-Anglicizing efficacy of Irish literature in English, for he treats Anglo-Irish literature as something other than "English" literature when he concludes his list of de-Anglicizing strategies with the remark that "perhaps the principal point of all I have taken for granted . . . [namely,] the necessity for encouraging the use of Anglo-Irish literature instead of English books" (169). Anglo-Irish literature and translated Gaelic texts came to serve as a transitional, stopgap measure in official de-Anglicizing ideology, with Yeats conceding the "most national" laurels to Gaelic while yet determined to establish the Abbey as a national theater and to press his own claim to national representativeness.

Yeats immediately grasped the ramifications of Hyde's populist appeal for his own work and accordingly felt compelled to reply to the "De-Anglicizing" lecture in a letter to the *United Ireland* (1892), which had published it just the week before. Although he had decried Ireland's predicament of being caught between "the upper and nether millstones" of "de-nationalizing" American and English influence in the journal earlier that year (*UP1* 223), he invokes U.S. literary achievement as an exemplary precursor for creating a literature that "shall be none the less Irish in spirit from being English in language" and as quickly cuts "America, with no past to speak of, a mere 'parvenue' among nations" back down to size.[95] Cultural nationalists should not base "our hopes of nationhood" on the Irish language alone, Yeats contends, though he approves the effort to reverse the decay of Gaelic, "preserv[ing] it always among us as a learned language to be a fountain of nationality in our midst." Thus, he repeats the classic Arnoldian move of suppressing the legitimacy of living Celtic languages by swerving away from "the Gaelic tongue of yesteryear" with the claim, espoused by the Young Irelanders as well as Arnold, that the spirit of a nation finds expression through its literature: "When we remember the majesty of Cuchullin and the beauty of sorrowing Deirdre, we should not forget that it is that majesty and that beauty which are immortal, and not the perishing tongue that first told of them."

Yet Yeats also embraces the desideratum of de-Anglicization with a volley of rhetorical questions whose wistful tone suggests that Yeats himself is beset by the melancholia of Anglicization: "Is there, then, no hope for the de-Anglicising of our people? Can we not build up a national tradition, a national literature, which shall be none the less Irish in spirit from being English in language? Can we not keep the continuity of the nation's life, not by trying to do what Dr. Hyde has practically pronounced impossible, but by translation or retelling in English, which shall have an indefinable Irish quality of rhythm and style, all that is best of the ancient literature?" The letter fudges the ultimately irreconcilable difference between Hyde's "re-Gaelicizing" and Yeats's "re-Anglicizing" agendas, but it also zeroes in on the centrality of retelling, reimagining, and reinterpreting Irish legend and folklore to de-Anglicizing praxis. It is no more possible to "de-translate" a translated text (let alone an Anglicized society) back into an unaltered original state than it is to translate the English standard onto a blank slate, but one can retranslate with a view to altering the "tone of thought" of the re-Gaelicized and/or re-Anglicized culture. Yeats's attempts to re-Anglicize with a difference shares Hyde's goal of undoing the nation's cultural cringe, but he also wants to redeem English literature from the post-Enlightenment repudiation of magic, to make English a medium of Irish literature, and to reinscribe the Pale that elevates the Anglo-Irish into a position of leadership.

PRIMITIVE MELANCHOLY: THE AUTOPOIESIS OF STYLE

In a verse epigraph to the 1909 *Collected Works* Yeats claims that he remakes himself in the acting of revising and reconstituting his oeuvre:

> The friends that have it I do wrong
> When ever I remake a song
> Should know what issue is at stake:
> It is myself that I remake.[96]

It is a constant theme of his poetics that the poet is first and foremost a maker, or *poietes,* whose "self" is forged in the recursive process of transfiguring the language and culture out of which he or she was formed. In "A General Introduction for My Work" (1937), which Yeats saw as "an essay on the nature of poetry" as well as a retrospect of his career (Callan ed. 13), he declares that Vico's axiomatic observation in *The New Science* (1725)—that "we can only know what we have made [*verum ipsum factum*]"—is the "first principle" of his poetics. Yet Yeats did not read Vico until 1924: "When the automatic script [that became *A Vision*] began, neither my wife nor I knew, or knew that we knew, that any man had tried to explain history philosophically."[97] Later, after corroborating his theory by reading Vico and related works such as Oswald Spengler's *Decline of the West* (trans. 1926) and Arnold Toynbee's *Study of History* (1934), he realized that "half the revolutionary thoughts of Europe are a perversion of Vico's philosophy" (*V* 261).

The remark that neither he nor his wife "knew, *or knew that we knew,*" Vico's philosophy is a classic expression of Vichean autodidacticism, which Edward Said describes as the primary task of the public intellectual: "The starting-point of critical elaboration is the consciousness of what one really is, and is 'knowing thyself' as a product of the historical process to date, which has deposited in you an infinity of traces, without leaving an inventory, [and] therefore it is imperative at the outset to compile such an inventory."[98] The goal of converting a dim memory of remote ancestral grandeur into an authentic national culture began for many with reimagining how "the matter of Ireland" might have evolved if there had been neither Pale nor Fringe, making Vichean autodidacticism an unacknowledged cornerstone of de-Anglicizing praxis. The Yeats of 1892–93 intuits a fruitful synergy between the cultural-nationalist task of elaborating a de-Anglicized "self" by working through and coming to terms with the manifold traces of Pale/Fringe linguicism on the psyche and the work confronting him as a poet as he tries to synthesize his rival cultural traditions into a poetry in English with an unmistakably Irish style. The Yeats of 1937 is concerned, rather, with distinguishing between the kinds of self-making practiced by the poet *as a poet* and as an autodidact/intellectual. "A General Introduction" is a product of the self-inventorying of the intellectual; the "Collected Yeats" (lifework and literary remains) is composed out of the poet's conscious and *unconscious* inventorying of the language and "Subject Matter" that formed him as a subject into the literary artifact referred to by readers when they declare that they love (or hate) "Yeats."

"A General Introduction" opens with Yeats's Vichean first principle:

> A poet writes always of his personal life, in his finest work out of its tragedy, what-
> ever it be, remorse, lost love, or mere loneliness . . . [yet] even when the poet seems
> most himself . . . he is never the bundle of accident and incoherence that sits down to
> breakfast; he has been reborn as an idea, something intended, complete. A novelist
> might describe his accidence, his incoherence, he must not; he is more type than
> man, more passion than type . . . He is part of his own phantasmagoria and we adore
> him because nature has grown intelligible, and by so doing a part of our creative
> power . . . The world knows nothing because it has made nothing, we know every-
> thing because we have made everything. (509–10)

The proper name Yeats designates the man who breakfasts and writes, the veri-fiable lived life that furnishes his subject matter, and the figure—that which we call "Yeatsian"—which emerges across the oeuvre as a result. The latter entity bears an ontological resemblance to the English precursors mentioned later in the essay: "I owe my soul to Shakespeare, to Spenser, and to Blake . . . and to the English language in which I think, speak, and write[;] everything I love has come to me through English" (519). The slide from Shakespeare and others to the English language shows how Yeats conceives the phantasmagoric poet as an entirely linguistic entity, the amalgam of idiom, meter, rhythm, and imagery which is rendered typical ("Shakespearean" or "Blakean") by time and the literary canon to become "part of our creative power." When Yeats declares that he owes his soul to Shakespeare, he refers not only to myriad ways in which his literary vernacular derives from a Shakespearean type of literature but also to a less tangible yet no less real sense of indebtedness for how passionate contact with Shakespeare has helped him to come into his own. Thus, the phantasmagoric poet-in-the-oeuvre is "more type than man, more passion than type."

Yeats's peroration about the immortality of Cuchulain and Deirdre may have seemed so much "blather" to Hyde,[99] but folkloric "myths-in-disguise" have a supernatural provenance for Yeats. His Arnoldian swerve away from the Gaelic language to "Literature" differs from Arnold's because Yeats conceives of literature differently:

> Literature differs from explanatory and scientific writing in being wrought about a mood, or a community of moods, as the body is wrought about the soul. Everything that can be seen, touched, measured, explained, understood, argued over, is to the imaginative artist nothing more than a means, for he belongs to the invisible life, and delivers its ever new and ever ancient revelation. We hear much of his need for the restraints of reason, but the only restraint he can obey is the mysterious instinct that has made him an artist, and that teaches him to discover immortal moods in mortal desires, an undecaying hope in our trivial ambition, a divine love in sexual passion. (*EI* 195)

"Mood" conveys the idea of a core and cohering impalpable agency—"the invisible life"—which exceeds the limits of the perceptual, the empirical, and the ratiocinative but is no less actual in its manifestations than them, since its best and most complete revelation lies in art and literature and, most especially, in style.

Yeats's doctrine of the moods is entwined with folk belief in a *ceo sidhe* (fairy mist) which separates this world from a parallel otherworld. The belief "that the natural and supernatural are knit together" and "the dead . . . [have] but retreated, as it were, into the hidden character of their neighborhood," which "A General Introduction" describes as the faith he was born into, has lived in, and shall die in (518), made Yeats's folkloric Fringe into something more than an ambiance of poetry and romance. Arnold may fault "the abstract, severe character of the Druidical religion, its dealing with the eye of the mind rather than the eye of the body," and the Celtic "sentiment [that] cannot satisfy itself, cannot even find a resting-place for itself, in colour and form [but] presses on to the impalpable, the ideal" (*SCL* 101–2), but for Yeats there is a higher wisdom in such "sentiment" than the post-Enlightenment mind can conceive.

Knowing less "than we know now of folk-song and folk-belief," Yeats writes in

"The Celtic Element in Literature" (1897), Arnold fails to understand that "literature dwindles to a mere chronicle of circumstance, or passionless fantasies, and
passionless meditations, unless it is constantly flooded with the passions and
beliefs of ancient times" (*EI* 185). In 1924, emboldened by the experience of
collaborating with his wife, George, on the automatic script that he arranged into
A Vision (1917–25), Yeats adds a revealing footnote to this passage, "I should have
added as an alternative that the supernatural may at any moment create new
myths, but I was timid" (185). It is precisely because contemporary literature has
lost contact with "the impassioned meditation," the reverie of the "ancient religion of the world," that this immense mythopoetic heritage is conceived in banal
or reductive, as against visionary, ways (175–76).

The "touch" of the *sidhe* is an early paradigm for the moods, and in 1901 Yeats
conceptualizes the "mysterious instinct" as a daimon, declaring that "myths are
the activities of the Daimons" (*EI* 107). *Per Amica Silentia Lunae* (1917) and later *A
Vision* (1925, 1937) elaborate his theory of daimonic autopoiesis (self-making).
Yeats argues that one realizes one's destiny by progressively honing one's unique
style and personality through "the perpetual warfare" between man and daimon,
the supernatural intermediary from *Anima Mundi* "who would ever set us to the
hardest work among those not impossible" (*Myth* 336).[100] "Myth is not, as Vico
perhaps thought, a rudimentary form superseded by reflection," he contends
elsewhere, but "the spring of all action" through which one can pass to "unity
with the source of [one's] being."[101] Yeats's credo that "the supernatural can at any
moment create new myths" maintains that we know much of what we know
because it is being dreamed in the supernatural realm of *Anima Mundi*.

Arnold contends that English poetry got much of its turn for style and melancholy and nearly all of its natural magic from a Celtic source, adding dismissively
that Celtic poetry "seems to make up to itself for being unable to master the world
and give an adequate interpretation of it, by throwing all its force into style, by
bending language at any rate to its will, and expressing the ideas it has with
unsurpassable intensity, elevation and effect." He goes on describe "that peculiar
kneading, heightening, and re-casting" of language evident in writers such as
Pindar, Virgil, Dante, Shakespeare, and Milton, who represent a tradition in the
sense of transmitting a poetic language and intelligence from one to the other,
giving it a new translation at each step of the way (113, 121). Style, melancholy, and
magic are part of the same continuum in the Yeatsian model of daimonic autopoiesis, and thus he wishes to preserve this congenial image of the Fringe while
distancing himself from the accompanying ethnic put-downs. Thus, he opens the
"Celtic" essay by citing Renan and Arnold extensively, thereby treating Celticism

as a discursive construct, and proceeds to "re-state a little Renan's and Arnold's argument" by claiming that it is founded upon an epistemological error (*EI* 174).

He makes Arnold's contempt for the Celt's "passionate, turbulent, indomitable reaction against the despotism of fact" and Renan's regret that his race "has worn itself out in mistaking dream for realities" into paradoxical tributes to a lost cultural habitus that he conversely believes will not only refine Irish literature but revivify an English literature that is no longer impassioned by "the ancient religion of the world" (*EI* 176). With a similar irony he turns what his Victorian precursors treat as a supremely self-defeating trait into its most profoundly creative and thus effectual power, the visionary insight into the ineluctable transience of things which accompanies "primitive melancholy" (183): "from this 'mistaking dreams,' which are perhaps essences, for 'realities,' which are perhaps accidents, from this 'passionate turbulent reaction against the despotism of fact' comes, it may be, that melancholy [that] did not mourn merely because their beloved was married to another, or because learning was bitter in the mouth, for such mourning believes that life might be happy were it different, and is therefore the less mourning, but because they had been born and must die with their great thirst unslaked" (182). Yeats represents human loss or disappointment as trivial and incidental when the mourner assumes that the desire denied and its ensuing sorrow are the work of particular chance or contingency and not the implacable refusal of an austere destiny. For truly transformational melancholy has its source in the tragic conflict between heroic aspiration and supernal fate, and hence Yeats calls it "primitive melancholy"—to distinguish the *mythos*, the "dream," the "essence" of loss, from its merely accidental occurrence.

The "Celtic element" that Yeats re-signifies as primitive melancholy is not a perverse racial peculiarity but an archaic universal trait similar to Vichean "poetic wisdom," the "wholly corporeal imagination" and capacity to think in poetic characters and fables found in Homer: "All folk literature, and all literature that keeps the folk tradition, delights in unbounded and immortal things" and keeps faith with primitives "who lived in a world where anything might flow and change, and become any other thing, and among great gods whose passions . . . had not our thoughts of weight and measure . . . and were nearer to ancient chaos, every man's desire" (*EI* 178–79). The mode of apprehension Yeats attributes to primordial man, peasants, and visionary poets has the sublimity of "the beyond" and the "vast obscure substratum" that exceeds and subtends any symbolic order. Such visionary apprehension is characterized by "idealism in love and hatred" and the ambivalence of primordial thought which makes the lovingness and lovelessness of the Irishman mean "but the same thing" (181), according to much the same logic as Freud's antithetical words or MacDiarmid's antisyzygies. With primitive melancholy, as with much else for Yeats, there are no negations, only contraries.

Yeats projects primitivist stereotypes onto the Fringe, but he also fashions an occult model of literary transference out of what Renan describes—to cite Yeats citing Renan—as the "vivid feeling for [Nature's] magic, commingled with the melancholy a man knows when he is face to face with her, and thinks he hears her communing with him about his origin and his destiny" (*EI* 173). In *Per Amica* he recalls that when reading poetry on certain glorious occasions, he has been carried away to "the place where the Daimon is, but I do not think he is with me until I begin to make a new personality, selecting among those images, seeking always to satisfy a hunger grown out of conceit with daily diet; and yet as I write the words 'I select,' I am full of uncertainty, not knowing when I am the finger, when the clay" (*Myth* 365–66). The manner in which the reader is moved by "contact" with the text is "magic" in the specific sense that his 1901 essay on the subject describes: the mind's imaginative reverie allows it to traverse the permeable boundaries between individual and collective memory.

Encounters with great literature can restructure the psyche, Yeats argues in an essay on Synge, in which he also observes that the never-ending argument about the rights and wrongs of Irish history may cause the "zealous Irishman" to fabricate "a traditional casuistry for a country . . . that comes between him and English literature, substituting arguments and hesitations for the excitement at the first reading of the great [English] poets which should be a sort of violent imaginative puberty."[102] Antipathy to the Pale may inhibit the Arnoldian "starts of sympathy" which the best literature can inspire and thus deny Irish readers the creative agon of rival sympathies which precedes aesthetic or cultural individuation. The inhibiting effects of the melancholia of Anglicization may be remedied through contact with the primitive melancholy that literally impassions the production, reception, and cyclical development of the arts in his purview. His theory of literary transference parallels, influences, counters, and compensates for Hyde's argument that renewed contact with Gaelic language and literature may revivify the "Irish sap" that courses through Gaelic language, literature, and orature and informs the true basis of the nation's "tone of thought."

A reaction against eighteenth-century rationalism and nineteenth-century materialism, manifest in fin-de-siècle symbolism, Yeats claims, has readied the arts to "utter themselves through legend." Celtic legend "has again and again brought 'the vivifying spirit' of 'excess' into the arts of Europe," he continues, supporting the claim by citing Renan's thesis that the *Mabinogion* and Breton romance "changed the literature of Europe . . . and the very roots of man's emotions by their influence on the spirit of chivalry." The focus on the ways in which "the fountain of [translated] Gaelic legends . . . is a new intoxication for the imagination of the world" highlights the transformational potential of translating literary myths in disguise into the poetic life of the world and the nation and sidesteps the issue of the potential cost to Irish national sentiment incurred by receiving those legends in English translation (*EI* 186–87). Yet the elided Gaelic culture keeps resurfacing. Memories of Pale/Fringe antagonism, for instance, color Yeats's literary examples of the "passion" of folk literature: "a love-poem in [Hyde's] *Love Songs of Connacht* that is like a death-cry"; an *aisling* that anticipates vast bloodshed on behalf of Róisín Dubh; and an Elizabethan Gaelic poet's curse. Because "Irish legends move among known woods and seas" and are part of the nation's imaginative topography, these myths-in-disguise could transform Irish national sentiment and enlarge the imagination of the world by "giv[ing] the opening century its most memorable symbols" (187).

Yeats made his own life and the matter of Ireland the conjoined subject of his poetry by creating the fable of a national bard who is part of his own distinctively Irish phantasmagoria. He "found [his] theme" when "the old Fenian leader, John O'Leary," introduced him to the poetry of the Young Irelanders, which, though it did not appeal aesthetically, "had one quality I admired and admire: they were not separated individual men; they spoke or tried to speak out of a people to a people; behind them stretched the generations" (GI 510). "I wanted, if my ignorance permitted, to get back to Homer," he continues, sounding very much like Vico, "and the Young Ireland poets when not writing mere politics had the same want, but they did not know that the common and its befitting language is the research of a lifetime and when found may lack popular recognition" (511).[103] Getting back to "Homer" and "the common" not only entails reconnecting with the substratum of legend—"tales which are made by no one man, but by the nation itself through a slow process of modification and adaptation" (*UP1* 273–74)—but also means making common cause with the people whose collective past is preserved in that legend.

Finding "a befitting language" for the common is no easy task for a poet who does not know the national language and whose love for English is beset by antagonism toward the colonial persecutor:

The "Irishry" have preserved their ancient "deposit" through wars, which during the sixteenth and seventeenth centuries, became wars of extermination; no people, Lecky said at the opening of his *Ireland in the Eighteenth Century,* have undergone greater persecution, nor did that persecution altogether cease up to our own day. No people hate as we do in whom that past is always alive, there are moments when hatred poisons my life and I accuse myself of effeminacy because I have not given it adequate expression. It is not enough to have put it into the mouth of a rambling peasant poet:

> You ask what I have found and far and wide I go,
> Nothing but Cromwell's house and Cromwell's murderous crew,
> The lovers and the dancers are beaten into the clay,
> And the tall men and the swordsmen and the horsemen where are they?
> And there is an old beggar wandering in his pride,
> His fathers served their father before Christ was crucified.
> *O what of that, O what of that,*
> *What is there left to say?*

Then I remind myself that though mine is the first English marriage I know of in the direct line, all my family names are English, and that I owe my soul to Shakespeare, to Spenser and to Blake, perhaps to William Morris, and to the English language in which I think, speak, and write, that everything I love has come to me through English; my hatred tortures me with love, my love with hate. I am like the Tibetan monk who dreams at his initiation that he is eaten by a wild beast and learns on waking that he himself is eater and eaten. This is Irish hatred and solitude, the hatred of human life that made Swift write *Gulliver* and the epitaph upon his tomb, that can still make us wag between extremes and doubt our sanity.[104]

Yeats loves the English language and literary tradition unreservedly, and to renounce it seems tantamount to relinquishing his soul. Nonetheless, his unqualified commitment to English is assailed by an abiding sense of grievance about the "wars of extermination" waged by the English against the Irishry. Lecky's description of the colonial "wars of extermination" draws on Spenser's recollection of Lord Grey's Munster campaign in the cannibal scenario, and Yeats also cites the cannibalism passage in the introduction to his edition of *Poems of Spenser* (1906). Thus, the contradictions of "owing [his] soul" to an English poet who was a militant advocate of Irish ethnocide is directly confronted here. The accented diction, *Irishry* and *deposit,* is carefully calculated, inserted into the typescript to replace "the Irish people preserve this civilization or memory of civilization through wars" (Callan ed. 105). *Irishry,* a neologism Yeats borrows from Arnold Toynbee (coined on the model of *Jewry*), emphasizes Ireland's history of colonial persecution and its special status as a resilient enclave of antiquity and romance in Europe. The Irishry's "deposit" represents both a cultural heritage, a tradition that has survived against the odds, and an ethnic animus, a corrosive memory of the persecution visited upon Gaelic civilization. Moreover, when coupled with *Irishry, deposit* assumes a phylogenetic valence in which the sedimented deposit of history becomes a bond of kinship uniting those who share a common culture and perhaps a collective sense of grievance as well.

Like Toynbee and Lecky, the Anglo-Irish Yeats feels personally removed from *their* Gaelic civilization, but unlike his authorities, he owns that the shade of grief cast over Ireland by the history of linguicism is *ours*—"no people hate as *we* do"— and *mine:* "hatred poisons *my* life and *I* accuse *myself* of effeminacy because *I* have not given it adequate expression." He then quotes the opening stanza of "The Curse of Cromwell," arguably the most indebted of all his poems to the translated Gaelic canon. Yet he does so to berate himself for not expressing in his own person the hatred that consumes him (as a "not-Gaelic" poet) instead of projecting it onto a feminized rambling *file* persona. He proceeds to reinforce this not-Gaelic identity by reminding himself of his English marriage and surname, and his incalculable debt to the English literary tradition, as if he sought to conquer the paroxysm of Irish outrage and self-loathing through identification with the language of conquest. He recovers a tentative equanimity by recalling Jonathan Swift, an Anglo-Irish precursor who shares Yeats's sense of solidarity with the persecuted Irishry as well as his utter commitment to the culture of their English oppressor. The acute antagonism he ascribes to the condition of Irishry, at once an abused minority and an ancient heroic tradition, momentarily becomes a specifically Anglo-Irish trait as Swift is made to epitomize "Irish hatred and solitude."

The retreat into lofty Anglo-Irish solitude cannot silence the clamoring voices that "again and again" "ask [him] why [he does] not write in Gaelic" (GI 519). He broaches this sensitive topic obliquely, by recalling a formal dinner in London during which the talk had turned to English civil libertarianism. The thought "that England might seem to those confused Indians the protector of liberty" moved Yeats to vehement indignation. Instead of giving a polite after-dinner speech, he "denounced the oppression of the people of India . . . told how they had been forced to learn everything, even their own Sanskrit, through the vehicle of English . . . [and] begged the Indian writers present to remember that no man can think or write with music and vigour except in his mother tongue" (519–20). In a letter he wrote recounting the "social disaster" to Maud Gonne at the time, December 1933, Yeats confesses that the impression he received that every woman present "was a Britannia and was suckling a little Polish Jew" provoked his incit-

ing the Indians to "boycott the English language[;] compel your masters to talk
Pigeon Bengali, Pigeon Hindi, Pidgeon Marratti [*sic*]; [t]hrust upon them the
indignity they have thrust upon you."[105] Evidently, only the Polish Jews were
receptive to this suggestion ("much as they hate Germany for baiting Jews they
hate it more for putting down the Polish language"), and Yeats admits in a striking analogy that "I have been ashamed of myself ever since, just as if I were a cat
and had eaten a canary."

In 1937, having recollected the incident as he composed "A General Introduction," Yeats confides to Ethel Mannin that the process of "analy[zing] my feelings
and relating one feeling to another and so on—dissolves terror": "Two days ago
while trying to analyse my periodical outbursts of political hatred—I remembered
how I had deliberately exasperated a friendly audience. I found it was from fear of
a theme they were thinking of; now [that] I think I have got rid of this fear by
finding its root in my general conception of life I shall keep my temper better. If
one is afraid of looking into the face one hits the face . . ." (he signs off the letter
following the ellipses). The context strongly implies that the unnamed theme
preoccupying him and his notional accusers is that he is not a national poet
because he writes in the colonizers' tongue. Afraid that his audience regards him
as a collaborator (i.e., a "West Briton") his rant against collusion with the English
Pale hits the face he cannot bear to look upon because he fears it is his own. The
equivocation between treating the impromptu outburst as histrionic (to Gonne)
and as a visceral expression of his core identity—"yet when I think of that scene I
am unrepentant and angry" (GI 520)—is also noteworthy. The implicit comparison Yeats draws between the Anglo-Indians' quandary and his own is un-
sound, but it is revealing that he has recourse to a very different colonial experience, India's, in order to define his relationship to Irish; to align himself with the
de-Anglicizing cause; to acknowledge the limitations of being forced to learn the
ancient wisdom of one's national culture through English translation; and to find
a metaphor for his cultural predicament.

The eater-and-eaten simile resonates with the eat-or-be-eaten logic of *glotto-*
phagie (linguistic cannibalism) and the melancholia of Anglicization which sty-
mies the nation.[106] Poets are compelled, as users of language, to translate the
linguistic and cultural heritage that formed them into "something intended, complete," but for the Anglo-Celtic poet the task is complicated by the duality of that
heritage. The specific manner in which the Irishry's deposit gnaws away at his
attachment to English is unique to Yeats, and the metaphor of self-devouring
illustrates the inescapable individuality of the ways culture gets translated into
singular self-experience. Yet the motive and method of Yeatsian autopoiesis en-

capsulated by the eater-and-eaten simile has wider application. The poet-initiate dreams that he is being eaten by a wild beast—which may be allegorized as "the English Pale" (the killer-language in the food chain), the "Irishry's deposit" (eating him up from within), or a Pale/Fringe hydra—only to discover on waking that the act of incorporation dissolves the absolute difference between eater and eaten, the English Pale and the Irishry's deposit, by making the two one. The divided linguistic heritage that preys on Yeats is also his quarry, the subject that consumes him and is consumed by him as he converts this endless antagonism into a haunted English and a style entirely his own. The competing allegiances that threaten to tear him asunder also fuel his work, and thus the poetry is produced because of the constitutive ambivalence as well as despite it.

"Style is mostly unconscious," Yeats remarks, as he resumes the discussion that abruptly ended with the apologia, "Gaelic is my national language, but it is not my mother tongue" (GI 521, 520). "I know what I have tried to do, little what I have done," he adds, and then describes how he tried to cross the "meditative, rich, deliberate" cadences of English prosody with vehement Irish speech patterns to create a "contrapuntal" verse structure "that combines the past and present": "What moves me and my hearer is a vivid speech that has no laws except that it must not exorcise the ghostly voice. I am awake and asleep, at my moment of revelation, self-possessed in self-surrender; there is no rhyme, no echo of the beaten drum, the dancing foot, that would overset my balance" (GI 521, 524). The counterpoint between measured containment and vehement repudiation is maintained by refusing to exorcise either the stately ghost of the English Pale or the keening spirit of the Irishry's deposit. The contending ghostly voices each host the other, both eater and eaten. The thoroughness and intensity of the remaking is crucial: a minor poet can convey "a Celtic note," but few can make the poetic life of their cultures intelligible through their signature style.

In Yeats's artistic theosophy style propels the development of poetry and the arts. In an early lecture, in May 1893, on "Nationality and Literature" to the National Literary Society, Yeats defines their collective task as "trying to grow" a vibrant national culture. He argues that the cultivation of style, "the only thing in literature which is immortal" (quoting Sainte-Beuve), ought to begin with studying the foundation of Irish literature and that of "the old nations" which is "sunk in the legend lore of the people and in the National history."[107] In the mode of Vico's *Principles of the New Science Concerning the Common Nature of the Nations* the lecture does not focus on Irish or English national literary traditions as such but, rather, examines the "general course of literary development, set apart from mere historical accident and circumstances" (*UP1* 268). Yeats argues that the trajectory of literary development "takes place by a constant sub-division of moods and emotions, corresponding to the sub-division of cells in the tree," as it moves successively through epic, dramatic, and lyric phases in a recurrent, spiraling pattern from rugged and simple unity to subtle and complex multiplicity (268). In no small measure this model reinvents Vico's argument that the purposiveness or mindfulness behind cultural production, through which humanity collectively re-creates itself, unwaveringly makes the same circuit—the *storia ideale eterna*—from "poetic wisdom" to the "barbarism of reflection."

The Vichean/Yeatsian first principle of creative recursion—the concept of "the world of nations or civil society" as a self-regenerating cosmos—is a philosophical precursor to contemporary concepts of "autopoiesis," the self-referential organization of society and such institutions as the legal system, the family, and cybernetics.[108] The extended analogy that Yeats makes between literary development and the process of cell differentiation essentially parallels Niklas Luhmann's claim that style is "the genetic material" that propels the autopoiesis of art.[109] "No man can do the same thing twice if he has to put much mind into it, as every painter knows," Yeats observes in the course of reflecting on Vico, for as soon as a school of painting becomes popular, prompting millionaires to outbid one another and reproductions to appear in every shop window, "painters wear out their nerves establishing something else, and this something else must be the other side of the penny—for Heraclitus was in the right[;] [o]pposites are everywhere face to face, dying each other's life, living each other's death" (*Ex* 430). The autopoiesis of art necessitates that artists stay a step ahead of orthodoxy, Luhmann argues, a factor that helps to explain "why art often produces anticipatory signals in social evolution which can be read retrospectively as prognoses" (203). The gist of Yeats's and Luhmann's theories of poiesis is that the style of an oeuvre preserves many traces of how social reality was refracted through the mind of its maker.

Haunted English contends that there is a relationship—though by no means a straightforward one—between the *glottophagie* that occurs within the Pale/Fringe contact zone and that which takes place within the poet and gets expressed as style (e.g., "Yeatsian"). By making the poets' styles the object of imaginative reconstruction (Vico's fantasia) and analysis, one may gain insight into Pale/Fringe relations, and an understanding of the genealogy of the de-Anglicizing motives of literary modernism in turn enriches our interpretations of their poetry. A key tenet of Yeats's poetics is that poetry imparts a different order of knowing than the conceptual knowledge of science or philosophy.[110] Poetry can stimulate the "starts of sympathy" or "violent imaginative puberty" which modify the unthought known at the core of aesthetic apprehension, "and by so doing [become] a part of our creative power" (GI 509). Readers will not hear the haunted English of Yeats, MacDiarmid, and Moore in quite the same way and will make it "part of [their] creative power" differently, and hence the many residues of Pale/Fringe interaction found in their work are amenable to diverse interpretation.

There is "an indefinably Irish quality" to Yeats's English which is at once inadvertent and assiduously cultivated, and it bears a myriad of traces of the Pale/Fringe contact zone out of which and within which it was fashioned. He animates the received forms of the English literary tradition with the antagonisms generated by the dominance of the English Pale to create a "vivid speech that has no laws except it must not exorcise the ghostly voice" (GI 524). All three Anglo-Celtic poets in this book testify to their ambivalence toward the colonial tongue and stake their identities as poets on their verse imparting "an indefinable quality" that would somehow convey a resonance of what animates their solidarity with those beyond the Pale. Anglo-Celtic poets speak out of the dominant English tradition and from somewhere else to give voice to a tradition that has been marginalized from the mainstream. By wrestling with the shadow of Pale/Fringe linguicism on the psyche, the needling atavistic deposit that eats them up in accountable and unaccountable ways, they translate their conscious and unconscious memories of the colonial history of English into a haunted English and style of their own.

CHAPTER TWO

"Eater and Eaten"

The Haunted English of W. B. Yeats

Yeats's eccentric definition of literary genius—"Homer, Aeschylus, Sophocles, Shakespeare, and even Dante, Goethe, and Keats, were little more than folklorists with musical tongues"—discloses the formative role of folklore on his development as a poet.[1] The process of immersing himself in folklore and filtering "the folk mind" through his own knowing and unknowing mind was key to Yeats's autopoiesis, the Vichean process of making "a poet . . . who is part of his own phantasmagoria" intelligible and therefore accessible to "our creative power." Yeats's "knowing" encompasses critical arrogance (distilling "the Celtic element" for bestowal upon "the people") and humble assent to the unknowingness of "mind," which is at once the site of memory, imagination, intellect, passion, and belief.

The "haunted English" of Yeats's oeuvre is thoroughly inflected by the Gaelic provenance of Irish folklore. Folklore matters to Yeats because it is memorable. The fact that the lore has sufficient imaginative truth to inspire the community to preserve and transmit it over generations is of much greater consequence to him than the countervailing fact that the oral tradition manifestly distorts the past. By making the "folk mind," "folk belief," and "peasant imagination" an object of research along with folklore and idiom, and by continually relating his findings to the workings of his own mind and imagination, Yeats engaged in extensive psychical research that was coterminous with the emergence of psychoanalysis, modernist anthropology, and other intellectual endeavors to uncover the "deep structures" of the psyche and of culture.

The complex formation of memory is illustrated by how Yeats frames his earliest memory in *Reveries over Childhood and Youth:* "I remember sitting upon somebody's knee, looking out of an Irish window" (*Au* 5). The adult autobiographer's evident consternation at the banality and affectlessness of his "first" memory flags it as a Freudian childhood "screen memory," a place marker with opaque clues for reconstructing the unconscious repression of a displaced anterior memory. Freud's theory of "the return of the repressed" in "Screen Memories" (1899) and *The Interpretation of Dreams* (1900) reconfigured memory as a process of selective forgetting shaped by the determining influence of the unconscious on psychical life.

Yeats's first memory is evidently reworked by subsequent reverie on the event, making it a multilayered palimpsest of his evolving identity. The necessarily personal remaking of folkloric common memory in the poet's mind is subject to similar modification and distortion. The modification process is epitomized by Yeats's insistence on the Irishness of his first window on the world because the "Irish" window frame would have gone unremarked if he had resided permanently in Ireland. The emphasis highlights his precarious exilic and Anglo-Irish identity and corroborates sociologist Maurice Halbwachs's thesis that individual memory endures only within sustaining "social frameworks" (*cadres sociaux*).[2] Yeats attributes his boyhood sense of isolation and dislocation to having felt excluded from the identity-sustaining frameworks of Irish and English collective memory: "I was divided from all those boys [at Godolphin School in Hammersmith] because our mental images were different. I read their boys' books and they excited me, but if I read of some English victory, I did not believe that I read of my own people. They thought of Cressy and Agincourt and the Union Jack and were all very patriotic, and I, without those memories of Limerick and the Yellow Ford that would have strengthened an Irish Catholic, thought of mountain and lake, of my grandfather and of ships" (*Au* 35). Image and inflection ground his English schoolmates' and the majority of Irish peoples' unhesitating identification with their respective historical romances and their instinctive sense of belonging to their neighborhoods: "no matter how charming the place . . . I knew that those other boys [in London] saw something I did not see. I was a stranger there. There was something in their way of saying the names of places that made me feel this" (49). Yeats's belief that "writers of a spiritual literature must make the land about them a Holy Land" is indebted to the boyhood experience of being out-of-place and the consequent enhanced appreciation for how the folklore, especially the place lore (*dinnsheanchus*) and fairy legend (*síscéalta*) he heard on "somebody's knee" in Ireland, created by contrast a dense and intimate network of *lieux de mémoire*.[3]

The "Holy Land" precept is proposed in "The Tribes of Danu," the first published work to issue from the Yeats-Gregory collaborative collection of folklore. Yeats dedicated himself to lifelong occult and philosophical research to corroborate Irish folk belief in the otherworld of the *sidhe,* whose incursions into quotidian reality are evidence that "revelation [comes] from that age-long memoried self, that shapes the elaborate shell of the mollusc and the child in the womb, that teaches the birds to make their nest; and that genius is a crisis that joins that buried self for certain moments to our daily trivial mind" (*Au* 272). Folklore offered a popular, if residual, vernacular for his philosophy "that all things are made of the conflict between two states of consciousness, beings or persons which die each other's life, live each other's death."[4] Along with a secular view of memory as dependent upon social group corroboration, Yeats subscribes to a magico-religious model of "instinctive" memory which profoundly shapes the undertaking to portray his homeland as a Holy Land.

Yeats's "window" on Ireland is colored by the folk belief of Irish orature and the cosmopolitan tastes of Literary Decadence, antinomial influences he attributes to his parents. He writes in *Autobiographies* that his mother, who "spen[t] hours listening to stories or telling stories," kept alive his longing ("some old race instinct like that of a savage") and love for Sligo, "and it was always assumed between her and us that Sligo was more beautiful than other places" (31). Sligo is seen through the eyes of an exile and those of "a painter's son [whose natural conviction] to believe that there may be a landscape that is symbolical of some spiritual condition awakens a hunger such as cats feel for valerian" (74). Sligo (and the west of Ireland) is "home"; it is also a veritable storyland and a blank canvas primed for a literary phantasmagoria that has yet to be imagined into existence. His "Celtic fringe" is located in the innermost reaches of personal identity and in "an outside" that corresponds with, yet extends "beyond," the western regions of Ireland.

Yeats strove to redraw the boundaries of the cultural imaginary by creating memorable images in his verse. The contours of the "early," "middle," and "late" chapters of the Yeatsian oeuvre receive a certain definition from the prominence of *sidhe* imagery in the early poetry and "Big House" imagery in the later work. Focusing on three poems that are readily identifiable as characteristic of his early, mature, and late styles—"The Song of Wandering Aengus" (1897), "The Tower" (1925), and "The Curse of Cromwell" (1937)—I examine the positioning of the phantasmagoric "Yeats" in a legendary Irish setting as a working through of the poet's complex relationship to Ireland's Gaelic past.[5] The speaker of the poetic sequence "The Tower" (named as "I, the poet, William Yeats" in the adjacent "To

Be Carved on a Stone at Thoor Ballylee") is a figure of towering achievement dictating his will to posterity. The speakers of the two song lyrics, "Aengus" and "Cromwell," are by contrast anonymous, rambling, *filí* (poets) like the two interlocutors summoned by the Yeats persona in the central section of "The Tower," Raftery and Hanrahan. "The Song of Wandering Aengus" and "The Tower" thematize their own composition as produced out of contact with their settings and feature ghostly interlocutors who highlight the reciprocity between poet and place. "Because a fire was in my head," Aengus goes out before dawn to a hazel wood to fish and embarks upon a highly eroticized quest to lay hold of his elusive catch. Troubled by "Decrepit age," the Yeats persona paces the twilit battlements of the tower, "send[ing] imagination forth" to retrieve "images and memories" from the neighborhood. Not coincidentally, these poems feature reveries that are spun out of, and woven into, the speaker's moods and locale.

Looking back on the composition of his early verse, Yeats recalls how "the matter of Ireland" so saturated his imagination, dreams, and thought that "images from Irish folklore" came to him "in moments of vision, in a state very unlike dreaming, [and] took upon themselves what seemed an independent life and became a part of a mystic language, which seemed always as if it would bring me some strange revelation." Yeats combined these images and legendary figures (including Aengus) with Rosicrucian symbols to devise elaborate ceremonies for the Celtic Mystical Order that he hoped to found with Gonne and others at Castle Island on Lough Key.[6] He writes to William Sharp/Fiona Macleod in May 1897 that he had "made out a sacred hazel tree [arranged as a cabbalistic tree of life] which will help in vision—a tree with symbolic fruit."[7] The hazel (a sacred tree of the druids with divinatory properties) exfoliates into "true symbol" as a result of prolonged meditation, elaborate ritual, and by becoming the object of Symbolist *dérèglement.* When Aengus "[goes] out to the hazel wood," he enters a Baudelairean "forêt de symboles" ("Correspondances"), and when he "cut[s] and peel[s] a hazel wand," he signals magical access to the otherworld.

In the light of the "Celtic Element" essay's peroration that "Irish legends move among known woods and seas," however, it is of vital importance that Aengus goes out to *the* hazel wood on the shores of Lough Gill, Sligo. *Autobiographies* recalls how adolescent nocturnal rambles around Lough Gill to quell "bodily desire" supplanted a boyhood interest in natural science, though "moments of observation [continued] . . . how the little moths came out at sunset, and how after that there were only a few big moths till dawn brought little moths again," persuading him that he "had a passion for the dawn [which] . . . though mainly histrionic . . . had moments of sincerity" (67, 74). The seven woods at Coole, which "are so much more knitted to my thought [than the Sligo woods of his deep affection] that when I am dead they will have, I am persuaded, my longest visit," are also part of the setting because it was there "that the first few simple thoughts that now, grown complex through their contact with other thoughts, explain the world, came to me from beyond my own mind."[8]

The temporal setting of *The Wind among the Reeds* (1899) is *Samhain*, the Celtic New Year, legendarily a hiatus during which identities disintegrate and merge and libidinal energies momentarily sunder the veneer of civilization. The "battle of all things with shadowy decay" which characterizes the interregnum (including *sidhe* battles for the harvest, at a man's death, and that "between the manifest world and the ancestral darkness at the end of all things") is related by Yeats, in the extensive notes appended to the volume, to the fabulous beginnings of the Irish nation, the primordial battle between the divine *Tuatha Dé Danann* (tribes of Danu) and the demonic *Fómhoire* (*VP* 810). The struggle to the death of antithetical forces is transformed into a phantasmagoria of ceaseless flux by shape-changing personae and the orgiastic rumblings of imminent apocalypse. Stampeding horses, "Caoilte tossing his burning hair," and the "high lonely mysteries" of a forgotten "white beauty" sighing "[f]or hours when all must fade like dew" crescendo into anguished eroticism: "O beast of the wilderness, bird of the air, / Must I endure your amorous cries?" (140, 156, 177).

Yeats strove with great difficulty to depersonalize the personae of these poems —he writes in the notes to the 1899 volume that "Michael Robartes," "Aedh," and "Hanrahan" are less "actual personages" than elemental "principles of the mind"—and later replaced their names in titles with generics, "The Poet," "The Lover," and "He" (*VP* 803). The revision process shows the influence of the typifying discourse of folklore (which changes individual histories into universal rites of passage such as elopements and initiations through ordeal) on the 1937 concept of the poet as "more type than man, more passion than type." The anonymity of folkloric types offers to Yeats the "escape from personality" sought by T. S. Eliot and other modernists and an opportunity to distill overwrought personal emotion (to paraphrase Eliot) into "significant [passion]."[9] The effect on the revised personae is that they assume the disembodiment of the *sidhe*, and, voided of historical accident and mortal constraint, they tend to merge with their settings.

Although "The Song of Wandering Aengus" bears the allusive burden and psychological drama of some of the more tortured and tortuous poems in *The Wind among the Reeds*, it is disarmingly accessible:

I went out to the hazel wood,
Because a fire was in my head,
And cut and peeled a hazel wand,
And hooked a berry to a thread;
And when white moths were on the wing,
And moth-like stars were flickering out,
I dropped the berry in a stream
And caught a little silver trout.

When I had laid it on the floor
I went to blow the fire aflame,
But something rustled on the floor,
And some one called me by my name:
It had become a glimmering girl
With apple blossom in her hair
Who called me by my name and ran
And faded through the brightening air.

Though I am old with wandering
Through hollow lands and hilly lands,
I will find out where she has gone,
And kiss her lips and take her hands;
And walk among long dappled grass,
And pluck till time and times are done
The silver apples of the moon,
The golden apples of the sun.

Yeats's attempt to realize the "folklorists with musical tongues" precept can be seen in how he conveys "symbolical" material through a limpid storytelling style and balladic mnemonics. The speaker's storytelling has the unhurried pace and attention to detail of his careful "hook[ing] a berry to a thread." Every couplet narrates an element of the tale, assigning equal weight to each aspect. The simple idiom and paratactic structure of the verse—"I went . . ./Because . . ./And cut . . ./And hooked . . ./And when . . ./I dropped . . ./And caught . . ."—follows a chronological denouement, and doesn't falter on logical, spatial, or temporal implausibilities. The Ovidian metamorphoses of the event and setting are reported in the definitive terms of completed action—"It had become a glimmering girl"—and fact segues into fable without any explanation or register of incongruity. Because "Aengus" leaves much unsaid and does not act as a hermeneutic guide by subordinating and rearranging elements of the tale, readers are left to attach their own meanings to the narrative. Aengus has little of the charisma of the storyteller, and, less a man of passionate nature than one who has been overcome by passion, his quest is described in the somewhat passive terms of what happened to him. Although he functions as a rather flat "type," he nevertheless pursues the fire he purportedly wishes to escape, as the sly innuendo "I went to blow the fire aflame" implies.

The allusions in each stanza to fire—the "fire in my head," the cooking fire, and the anticipated apocalyptic conflagration of solar and lunar apples—form a symbolic economy that unites subjective, objective, and transcendental reality. The fruition of the apple blossom–bedecked girl into a harvest of lunar and solar apples is likewise part of this dense economy in which everything is interconnected though the connections remain obscure.[10] The elusive beloved is everywhere: she is the fire in his head, the bounty of the natural environment, and the destiny awaiting him. Helen Vendler argues that the poem's magical ethos is augmented by verbal patterns that re-create the reduplicative nature of spell-casting by accenting the magical over the semantic connections between words: *wand*ering Aengus cuts a *wand;* his *head* finds a *thread.*[11] The lexical associative links are in turn strengthened by contiguous images—the "moth-like" stars—and by the aura of cosmic fusion created by subliminal awareness that the beloved's metamorphoses complete a Heraclitean cycle. Cast out of water, she becomes an earthy girl, fades into air, and then transfigures into a muse leading Aengus to incandescence. The shadowy sense of cyclic completion overtakes the anti-closural, centrifugal orientation of ongoing metamorphosis with the arresting image of solar and lunar apples in the final couplet. The hyper-closural conceit is accompanied by a shift from the preterite tense of a chronological ballad to the apocalyptic present of an anticipated *Samhain* harvest when the symbolic fruit shall be plucked "till time and times are done." The closural device of the emblematic apples neatly concludes the series of pictorial tableaux, while the alchemical ground of the metaphor imposes cosmic design on its surreal magic.

The tale of how Aengus' shape-shifter "calls [him] by name" and vaporizes into landscape unfolds, like fantasy and reverie, along a metonymic axis. The recourse to metaphor at the conclusion circumscribes the wayward movement of fantasy by imposing symbolic meaning on the anticipated consummation of the quest. The shape-shifting tale mimics the structure of fantasy: the *sidhe*-haunted hazel wood provides "a stage-setting for desire" in which Aengus is present "in a desubjectivized form, in the very syntax of the sequence in question."[12] Like fantasy, the tale of metamorphosis enacts the "proliferation of identifications that puts the very locatability of identity into question,"[13] whereas metaphor, by contrast, reduces the singularity of phenomena by postulating resemblance. The ensuing tension between the centripetal force of the solar and lunar apples and the centrifugal energy of the glimmering girl operates on several levels, most apparently in the contrast between unconstrained, free-spirited eroticism and the sublation of desire into artifact. The counter-pull between centrifugal and eschatological drives in "Aengus" raises a question that troubled Yeats, whether the urge to wander "away" is a death-wish or, to restate Renan's words with a positive valence, an essential part of "poetic life" and the "invincible [human] need of illusion" (*Poésie* 9). The poet is repeatedly forced to choose between incompatible options, Yeats maintains in "The Choice," "Words," and "Sailing to Byzantium": to be caught in the "sensual music" of the heart or to be gathered "into the artifice of eternity," either one embraced at the cost of forgetting the other (*VP* 407–8). It is the constant theme that Yeats draws from folk belief, which posits an otherworld coexisting with this one, a realm in which any given "here" is also always an elsewhere and where to be "touched" by the otherworld is to become out of touch with this one.

Like the Celtic element itself, the *sidhe* have an unstable local and universal aspect: they inhabit the purely aesthetic realm of "immortal moods" ("that mysterious instinct [that makes one] an artist"), and they are neighborhood ancestral spirits, "dreaming back" their memory into the instinctual lives of the locality. The verse itself doesn't address Aengus by name (the name only features in the title), lending the glimmering girl's call the generality of a rite of passage or a poet's inspiration by a divine muse. At the same time, a call-by-name from the *sidhe* of *the* hazel wood at Lough Gill marks the persona as a recognized member of that community.

The issue of names goes further, however, because the poem itself, first published as "A Mad Song" while Yeats was at Coole and featured as Hanrahan's composition in "Hanrahan's Vision" (*Secret Rose*, 111–13), was retitled "The Song of Wandering Aengus" for publication in 1899. The name change, which reverses the overall trend of replacing proper names with the anonymity of *He*, indirectly alludes to the Gaelic *aisling*. In a different context (the notes to *The Shadowy Waters*) Yeats remarks that "poor translations of the various Aengus [and Edain] stories . . . had so completely become part of my own thought" that "in 1897 . . . I saw one night with my bodily eyes, as it seemed, two beautiful persons, who would, I believe, have answered to their names" (*VP* 817). Aengus is "both Dionysus and Hermes," Yeats writes, "the old Irish god of love and poetry and ecstasy."[14] The eighth-century *Aislinge Óenguso* (the dream vision of Aengus), redacted as "The Dream of Angus Og" in Gregory's *Cuchulain of Muirthemne*

(1902), narrates how Aengus fell into a wasting love-sickness because the beautiful woman who visited him in a dream vision eluded him. After much searching, he discovers that his beloved changes into a bird every alternate *Samhain,* and he wins her after they mate in the form of swans.[15] By ascribing the (untitled) lyric to Hanrahan, the poet-protagonist of *Stories of Hanrahan,* based on *aisling*-poet Eoghan Rua Ó'Súilleabháin (c. 1748–84), the eighth-century *aisling* is implicitly linked to the Jacobite *aisling* of the eighteenth century.

By renaming the persona "Aengus," Yeats embeds the lyric in Fenian mythology, including that of Diarmuid and Gráinne, in which Aengus plays a tutelary role. By eliding his debt to "poor" translations (the notes cite a Greek folksong and merrow tales alone as sources), he makes the lyric's provenance seem exclusively oral. The move deflects awareness from a key de-Anglicizing tenet, namely that the oral tradition has residual links to the high-literary Gaelic culture of the remote precolonial past, when monastic Ireland was "the school of Europe and the torch of learning." Two forms of translation are involved in the composition of his Aengus: the Gaelic-English translations read and obscured by Yeats; and the attempt to extend poetry in English toward the Celtic Element, which he redefines as the "primitive melancholy" of those who have not unlearned "the impassioned meditation which brings men beyond the edge of trance" to an animistic "world where anything might flow and change and become any other thing" (*EI* 178, 175, 179). By emphasizing the latter and not acknowledging the former, Yeats's "Aengus" shifts attention away from Gaelic to "the imperishable moods" around which (according to him) literature is wrought.

Between 1892 and 1905 Yeats revised *Stories of Red Hanrahan* several times, first to rework the stories of the "touched" poet into a quasi-Grail quest (1897), and later, with Gregory's help, to bring the stories "closer to the life of the people" by colloquializing his idiom (1905).[16] The protagonist, named "O'Sullivan the Red" in 1892 and renamed "Hanrahan" in 1897, is based on the *spailpín* (journeyman) Munster poet Eoghan Rua Ó'Súilleabháin (c. 1748–84). *Stories* includes a tale based on a Gaelic song, "Casadh an tSúgáin" (The Twisting of the Rope), which tells how a woman sidesteps the obligatory deference to poets by tricking the rakish Hanrahan (who is charming her daughter) into inadvertently crossing back over her threshold by enlisting him to twist a rope. "Lady Gregory and I wanted a Gaelic drama, and I made a scenario for a one-act play founded upon an episode in my *Stories of Red Hanrahan,*" Yeats writes in *Autobiographies,* "I had some hope that my invention, if Hyde would but accept it, might pass into legend as though he were an historical character" (439). Hyde certainly knew the folk motif of enticing an unwanted poet-suitor out of the house by rope twisting,[17] and yet Yeats claims it as his "invention," taking credit for the success of the first play in Irish, *Casadh an tSúgáin,* in which Hyde played the title role of Hanrahan.

Yeats refashions folk hero and poet Ó'Súilleabháin into Hanrahan and then makes Hanrahan "seem traditional" by asking Hyde to translate the persona into a Gaelic drama "as though he were an historical character." Hanrahan passes into legend as part of the Yeatsian phantasmagoria, rendering the poet as well as his persona legendary. The division of cultural labor here, with Lady Gregory and Yeats as patrons, Yeats as inventor, and Hyde as purveyor of the Yeats-patented invention into circulation among the Irishry, is revealing. The presumption of patronage casts a protective aura of cultural control around "Lady Gregory and I," a positioning that allows Yeats to maintain access to, and yet personal distance from, the alien Gaelic culture through an intermediary, Hyde, who, despite his Anglo-Irish background, is placed outside their elite circle because of his Gaelic affiliation.[18] Here Yeats views translation into Gaelic as a kind of accelerated weathering, akin to distressing new furniture or stone-washing denim, which lends a well-seasoned traditional timbre to the translated text. Yeats's collaborative scheme for *Diarmid and Grania,* which shared a double-bill premiere with *Casadh an tSúgáin*—that it would be written in French by George Moore, translated into English by Lady Gregory, into Irish by Tadhg O'Donoghue, back into English by Lady Gregory, and would have style put on it by Yeats—also subscribes to this notion of translation.[19]

The character of modern Gaelic literature was decisively shaped by the move to develop the literary standard out of the contemporary spoken vernacular, *caint na ndaoine* (the speech of the people), rather than basing it on the classical Irish of the seventeenth century, as some Revivalists advocated.[20] The *caint-na-ndaoine* touchstone is paralleled by the Abbey writers' attempt to develop a literary vernacular in English which would be distinctively Irish without being "stage-Irish." Revivalist writers in Irish and Irish-English alike honed their literary vernaculars in the Pale/Fringe "contact zone" between Gaelic and English, orature and literature, classical and demotic, and the spoken and written word. Crafting a literary idiom out of "the speech of the people" was both a means of working through the stigma of "dialect" and of attempting to rekindle the vestigial literary sensibility of the peasantry which Hyde calls "Irish sap."

From the turn of the century, chiefly at Coole and on the Abbey stage, Yeats "continually test[ed] both my verse and my prose by translating it into dialect," adding, "I remember nothing with pleasure [of the early Abbey years] except my excitement during those first months when dialect was being reshaped as literature."[21] Hyde, Gregory, and Synge worked their respective variations on standard

English by emphasizing idiomatic usages that are overtly inflected by Gaelic speech patterns and by favoring the implicit reciprocity of vernacular exchange over an impersonal, explicit style. In short, they wrote an English that often reads like a word-for-word translation from *caint na ndaoine,* and considerable internal textual evidence suggests that they often mentally translated their English into Gaelic and back again to achieve the desired effect.[22] Gregory's redaction of the Cuchulain mythological cycle, *Cuchulain of Muirthemne* (1902), composed in part to challenge the 1900 Commission on Secondary Education's ruling against making Irish a school subject on the grounds that "there was no imagination or idealism in the whole range of Irish literature" (7), was a crucial literary translation for Yeats. In his laudatory preface to "the best book that has come out of Ireland in my time," Yeats admits that he "was sometimes made wretched [that he] knew of no language to write about Ireland in but raw modern English" (11–12). Cofounder of the Gaelic League Eoin MacNéill likewise expressed warm, if rueful, admiration in a letter to Gregory: "A few more books like it, and the Gaelic League will want to suppress you on a double indictment, to wit, depriving the Irish language of her sole right to express the innermost Irish mind, and secondly, investing the Anglo-Irish language with a literary dignity it has never hitherto possessed."[23]

Yeats felt that Gregory had found a courtly idiom, made venerable by archaism and yet tempered by the spontaneity of storytelling and speech patterns, by retelling the legends in "an old vivid speech with a partly Tudor vocabulary, a syntax partly moulded by men who still thought in Gaelic" (GI 513). The Tudor and Gaelic residues in Gregory's English belie the historical antagonism between Tudor and Gael to suggest a harmonious blend of "Anglo" and "Irish" as well as fulfilling the golden rule of Yeatsian poetics, to "seem traditional" (GI 522). To Yeats's ear the Irish-English of *Cuchulain of Muirthemne* combines the poetry of the coteries (which developed gradually within the written tradition) and the poetry of the people (which developed gradually within the unwritten folk tradition) which he claims are "both alike strange and obscure and unreal to all who have not understanding" in the essay "What Is 'Popular Poetry'?" (1901). *Cuchulain of Muirthemne* was a breakthrough in his quest for "the common and its befitting language," a hybrid of "ancient idealism" and "living speech" out of which he could fashion his own bardic voice.

On August 25, 1900, the evening before he gave the *Casadh an tSúgáin* scenario to Hyde, Yeats publicly discarded "the phrases 'Celtic note' and 'Celtic Renaissance' because both are vague and one is grandiloquent, and because the journalist has laid his ugly hands upon them" in a letter to the editor of the *Leader,*

D. P. Moran, who was a loud proponent (in English) of Irish-Ireland nativist opinion and a castigator of the Celtic revival as "spurious" and "unIrish." Earlier on that "red-letter day," while attending a Gaelic League event (organized by Gregory and Hyde) to place a commemorative headstone at the unmarked grave of unlettered Gaelic poet Anthony Raftery (1784–1835) at Killeenan, he had an insight into the de-Anglicization movement and his own role within it. As he stood on the grave of the Gaelic precursor he would later mythologize as the Irish Homer, Yeats writes in "Literature and the Living Voice," he realized that "the decisive element in the attempt to revive and preserve the Irish language . . . [is to restore] a way of life in which the common man has some share in imaginative art." Pale/Fringe diglossia permeates every facet of Irish national life, and he would make the antagonism between Irish orature and English print culture the donnée of his own work: "Irish poetry and Irish stories were made to be spoken or sung, while English literature, alone of great literatures, because the newest of them all, has all but completely shaped itself in the printing press. In Ireland today *the old world that sang and listened is,* it may be for the last time in Europe, face to face with *the world that reads and writes,* and their antagonism is always present under some name or other in Irish imagination and intellect."[24] Through collaborative de-Anglicizing translations he had found an edgy new note, that of a combative bard in colloquy with "the people," whose "living speech" is overheard by the (print) mainstream. In a 1913 letter to his father he describes the shift to a poetics of "personal utterance" as follows: "Of recent years instead of 'vision,' meaning by vision the intense realization of a state of ecstatic emotion symbolized in a definite imagined region, I have tried for more self-portraiture. I have tried to make my work more convincing with a speech so natural and dramatic that the hearer would feel the presence of a man thinking and feeling."[25] It is the voice of the public poet in colloquy with his nation, celebrating, exhorting, and upbraiding them.

Yeats's home, Thoor Ballylee, is a metonymic mask for the poet and the governing symbol of *The Tower* (1928), *The Winding Stair and Other Poems* (1933), and "The Tower," a centripetal poem in which the process of constructing "Yeats" is conspicuously and self-consciously displayed. In striking contrast to the evanescent, generic *He* of the early poems, the first-person *Yeats* persona "[writes] his will" with flamboyant bodily gesture and charismatic soliloquizing utterance. A monumental assertion of artistic and reproductive virility, the tower is linked in related poems to "the far high tower where Milton's Platonist/Sat late, or Shelley's visionary prince" and to the Anglo-Irish lineage he was then cultivating assiduously: "I declare this tower my symbol; I declare/This winding, gyring, spiring treadmill of a stair is my ancestral stair;/That Goldsmith and the Dean, Berkeley and Burke have travelled there."[26] Although purchased before he decided to marry (notwithstanding the stone inscription: "I, the poet William Yeats/ .../Restored this tower for my wife George"), Thoor Ballylee was soon renovated into "befitting emblems of adversity" for his "bodily heirs."[27] It is a domestic sanctuary and "some high lonely Tow'r" for the epic poet, a defensive shoring up against a leveling modernity and a strategic domicile from which to influence the Irish Free State. The adjacent sequence, "Meditations in Time of Civil War," quizzically asserts that since such sanctuary is wrested from violence, a public confronted with imposing "Ancestral Houses" can "but take our greatness with our violence."

During the 1920s Yeats strove to revitalize the leadership prerogative of the Anglo-Irish Ascendancy by mythologizing the benign influence of the superseded colonial network of "Ancestral Houses." He wishes such a "house/Where all's accustomed, ceremonious" for his daughter because ancestral houses wield the exemplary "powerful character" of Lady Gregory at Coole Park that

> Could keep a swallow to its first intent;
> And half a dozen in formation there,
> That seemed to whirl upon a compass-point,
> Found certainty upon the dreaming air.[28]

Onto the primitive landscape emblazoned with "Here are ghosts" (*Myth* 15), a "Here Yeats lives" legend is inscribed, mapping Thoor Ballylee onto local, national, and international consciousness.

The densely intertextual poem "The Tower" is replete with Yeats's "ancestral voices," as Stan Smith argues, and "poses discourse against discourse" in recursive doublings "to speak of a subject 'who has lost his totality and no longer coincides with himself.'"[29] Chief among these discursive confrontations is the antagonism between "the [Irish] old world that sang and listened . . . and the [English] world that reads and writes" (*Ex* 206). Two key intertexts for understanding how "The Tower" is constituted out of Pale/Fringe diglossia are the Irish pseudohistory by the blind unlettered Gaelic poet Anthony Raftery, "Seanchus na Sgeiche" ("The Dispute with the Bush") and Walt Whitman's "Song of Myself," an epic of the parvenu U.S. literature, which has by contrast "completely shaped itself in the printing press."[30] Neither Raftery nor Whitman "[ever] dramatized anybody but himself" (*Ex* 214), and their "self-portraiture" is made convincing by a speech that attunes the hearer (the reader's mental ear rather than deciphering eye is in question) to the "presence" of a "feeling and thinking" author. "Our own

Raftery will stop the tale to cry, 'This is what I, Raftery, wrote down in the book of the people'; or, 'I, myself, Raftery went to bed without supper that night,' " Yeats writes in *Explorations* (215), and similar self-dramatizing asides in the Whitmanian "barbaric yawp" help to make *Leaves of Grass* a "book of the people." The *aural* signature gives Raftery/Whitman a corporeal *presence* to establish an atmosphere of rapport which in turn reinforces the symbiosis between the people and their bard sought by Yeats. Whitman's incorporation of U.S. national space into the phantasmatic body of "Walt Whitman . . . a Kosmos, of mighty Manhattan the son" (l. 492) is a performative act of cultural independence which is also, and indivisibly, an emphatic gesture that the poet is "not-English." The overt self-constitution of *Leaves of Grass* and the *Collected Yeats* are extravagant gestures of cultural autonomy; no English Victorian felt the need to create such an ostentatiously self-delimiting corpus.

Yeats expropriates Raftery's signature in "The Tower" by renaming him "Homer" and representing him as a summative embodiment of the Irish oral tradition in accordance with Vico's definition of Homer as "an idea or a heroic character of Grecian men insofar as they told their histories in song."[31] Raftery signs off "Seanchus na Sgeiche" (which narrates how the poet curses the bush for inadequate shelter from rain and the bush responds by disclosing the history of Ireland from the flood to defeat by the Williamites and by prophesying Catholic Emancipation) with this closing couplet: "Sin mar chuir Raiftearaí síos ar Éirinn/é féin is an sceach i bpáirt a chéile" (This is how Raftery put down upon Ireland/Himself and the bush, both joined together). In *The Celtic Twilight* (1893) Yeats represents the narrative as a spontaneous overflow from "the cauldron of Fable" and anticipates how Raftery and Mary Hynes (the local Ballylee beauty immortalized in Raftery's songs) shall grow more fabulous under the patented *Yeats* signature:

> a man at Coole says, "When [Raftery] put his finger to one part of his head, everything would come to him as if it was written in a book"; and an old pensioner at Kiltartan says, "He was standing under a bush one time, and he talked to it, and it answered him back in Irish. Some say it was the bush that spoke, but it must have been an enchanted voice in it, and it gave him the knowledge of all the things of the world. The bush withered up afterwards, and it is to be seen on the roadside now between this and Rahasine." There is a poem of his about a bush ["Seanchus na Sgeiche"], which I have never seen, and it may have come out of the cauldron of Fable in this shape . . . It may be that in a few years Fable, who changes mortalities to immortalities in her cauldron, will have changed Mary Hynes and Raftery to perfect symbols of the sorrow of beauty and of the magnificence of dreams. (M 29)

Yeats represents Raftery's witty authorial conceit as unwittingly shaped by "Fable," portraying his precursor as a preliterate Homer, an uncritical conduit of immemorial "Irish sap." Raftery's signing-off extends more credit to his arboreal muse than Yeats does to him. Raftery's enviable colloquy with the Irish-speaking bush may be surpassed for Yeats by how the peasantry reads Raftery's signature in the bush "to be seen on the roadside now between this and Rahasine." The remembering bush, withered by hardship and perhaps by the blight of Raftery's curse and depletion of divulging the past, has taken root in peasant imagination, validating the history itself and the circumstances of its chronicling. In the Irish tradition of *dinnsheanchus* the bush stands, as Yeats wishes Thoor Ballylee to stand, as "a permanent symbol of [the poet's] work plainly visible to the passer-by . . . all my art theories depend on just this—rooting of mythology in the earth."[32]

For Yeats, as for Giambattista Vico, the compatibility between "the peasant's unreflective passion" (the "folk" imagination) and "Homer's" propensity to think in poetic characters is proof of how *memoria* (which means, crucially for Vico, memory *and* imagination), and hence historical consciousness, is based on the image, not the concept.[33] Of the three aspects of memory defined by Vico, "memory when it remembers things, imagination when it alters or imitates them, and invention when it gives them a new turn or puts them into proper relationship," Donald Verene argues that it is the middle term, *fantasia,* the necessarily subjective sense of remembering particulars so that they have a total shape, which holds together a philological remembering that allows us to derive an event from its beginning and a philosophical invention of history involving principles of explanation.[34] The unifying fantasia of Yeats's tower is indebted to how Whitman subsumes U.S. national space into the phantasmatic national bard in "Song of Myself." Yeats, whose recollection of "Walt Whitman in his pocket" at age seventeen faithfully enacts the *fantasia* scripted by *Leaves of Grass,* absorbs the U.S. example of cultural secession without, however, adopting Whitman's egalitarianism. The youthful optimism, robust health, and manifest destiny of Whitman's expansive "I dote on myself, there is that lot of me and all so luscious" (l. 544) contrasts strongly with how the Yeats persona battles against entropy and strives for supremacy. In order to annex folk imagination without surrendering the will to master, the figure-in-the-tower must prevail as a deictic "center that [can] hold."[35]

The figure-in-the-tower is figurally and rhetorically hyperbolic. The extravagant "over-the-top" figure, at once phallus, owner-occupier-speaker, and panoptical garrison, dramatizes the figurative continuum between these valences by morphing back and forth between them. The Yeats persona is the "I" who speaks and the "I" who is spoken, the deictic center of the instance of discourse which is the poem and its presiding image. "Aengus" could perhaps be revised from a first- to a third-person persona, but the hypersubjectivized "I" is the sine qua non of "The Tower," its primary fantasia. The poet enacts his will in the final, philosophical, section of the tripartite sequence:

> It is time that I wrote my will;
> I choose upstanding men
> That climb the streams until
> The fountain leap, and at dawn
> Drop their cast at the side
> Of dripping stone; I declare
> They shall inherit my pride,
> The pride of people that were
> Bound neither to Cause nor to State,
> Neither to slaves that were spat on,
> Nor to the tyrants that spat,
> The people of Burke and of Grattan
> That gave, though free to refuse—
> Pride like that of the morn,
> When the headlong light is loose,
> Or that of the fabulous horn. (121–36)

In the act of making a will, saying (under signature) is doing, as J. L. Austin's theory of illocutionary speech acts reminds us. The assertion of timeliness draws the reader-witness into the fictive covenant scenario, lending the lines the peculiar intimacy of the first (and only) articulation of "last words," which, however, are frozen in the reiterative "timelessness" of lyric apostrophe. "Now shall I make my soul" reinforces the declaration (l. 181), urging acceptance of the text before us as the will and soul of the phantasmagoric Yeats become intelligible (GI 509). The pact is conducted through gesture: one is drawn into the mounting motion of the chosen "upstanding" men whose climb recalls Yeats's reminiscence in the sequence's opening section of boyhood summer days on "Ben Bulben's back" (l. 9). The mounting and ejaculative movements—the "fountain leap," "dripping stone," spitting tyrants, and "fabulous horn"—in the taut trimeter lines suggest that the tumescent tower is on the move, surging upward. Evidently determined to stay on top, the Yeats persona leads the way, and, while he may "stop somewhere waiting for you" (to quote the final line of "Song of Myself" [l. 1346]), such tarrying on high ground exudes an attitude of Ascendancy condescension. He bequeaths a dash of hauteur to his spat-upon countrymen (women do not enter the patrimony exchange) by modeling the arrogation of *I* as a royal *we* through intonation. The "I declare . . . my pride" Yeats persona coincides with the Senator Yeats who declaims in a 1925 speech against divorce that he is a "typical man" of "we, the minority . . . of Burke; Grattan; . . . of those who created most modern Irish literature and the best of [Irish] political intelligence."[36] The tone of this minatory "I," which vaunts a signature blend of persecuted elitism which is inflected by caste aloofness and of "Irishry" protestation, is ultimately inextricable from the figure-in-the-tower.

Yeats's dramatization of himself in the ascendant is indebted to Edmund Burke. Alasdair MacIntyre contends that Yeats learned from Burke how to unify poetic form and philosophical content through the image and that many of his mature poems show how images can disclose their imaginative incoherence and sterility when they are used with integrity.[37] Burke and Raftery both use the organic image of a genealogical tree to impose continuity on discontinuity. If the Homeric Raftery represents the first historian of the nation, Edmund Burke is Yeats's first historian of the state, as the companion sequence, "Blood and the Moon," proclaims: "And haughtier-headed Burke that proved the State a tree,/ That this unconquerable labyrinth of the birds, century after century,/Cast but dead leaves to mathematical equality" (*VP* 481). The Burkean tree is a hierarchical image that subordinates lower classes, lesser races, and women (through the patrilineal "family tree") within a putative organicism. The disjunctive yoking of tower and cottage in the Thoor-Ballylee image draws attention to the violent history subtending the disparity between the grandeur of the Burkean oak on an entailed landed estate and the squalor of Raftery's vagrant bush shelter. The philological central section, which displays in the making the double and inter-dependent process of creating Yeatsian *dinnsheanchus* and the phantasmagoric "Yeats," is enacted from the superior positionality. "I am delighted with all that joins my life to those who had power in Ireland," Yeats confides in *Autobiographies* (22), and the Prospero-like opening of section 2 is similarly unabashed. "I pace upon the battlements and stare," the autopoietic drama begins,

> And send imagination forth
> Under the day's declining beam, and call
> Images and memories
> From ruin or from ancient trees
> For I would ask a question of them all.

The soliloquizing "I" casts his surveillant eye "beyond that ridge" to Mrs. French's aristocratic house, and his reverie then draws inward to the Ballylee townland of Mary Hynes, Raftery, and Hanrahan (who was touched at Slieve Echtge nearby) before returning to Thoor Ballylee's former occupant. One might expect that the Yeats of 1925 would draw a Tower-peasantry-Coole demesne as he does in "Coole and Ballylee, 1931," but instead he portrays a fictive demesne, whose center is Thoor Ballylee and whose circumference is a neighboring "Ancestral House." The anachronistic high/low map juxtaposes the Pale, conjured as the outside limit, against the rambling peasant life inside. Yeats's four ghostly interlocutors are figures of violence in the manifold textual, gestural, and illocutionary senses in which the figure-in-the-tower is one. Yeats's Big House/folk map was formed in the 1890s when he first saw the tower (which then belonged to the Gregorys) and retold stories of Raftery and Hanrahan. It is contoured by the four larger-than-life legends whose independent nonsynchronous eighteenth- and nineteenth-century histories are germane to the 1920s task of renovating the nation-state. As "types," their lineup replicates that of the foursome in "Easter 1916": a termagant and a loutish mercenary flanking two Gaelic-identified poets. The ostentatiously random drift of these legends through the "thinking and feeling" mind of the Yeats persona belies how the quadrumvirate represents the yoking together of Anglo-Irish and Gael; State and Poetry; and Beauty and (delirious) Action in which "The Tower" is engaged.

Monarch of all he surveys yet flaunting his senility, the Yeats persona's seriatim summoning of local shades for questioning falters as he fails to put the question, wanders off on digressive anecdotage, and suffers a conspicuous bout of amnesia. The presiding fiction that the persona's reverie unfolds in "a fit of absence of mind" is undercut by the overdetermined nature of the apparently associative string of anecdote.[38] Ruminating on the legends that his surveying eye/I sweeps up from the neighborhood, the Yeats persona craves reassurance that he is not unheard, unheeded, and unlikely to become the stuff of legend himself.

Yeatsian *dinnsheanchus* unfolds through a Whitmanian metonymic incorporation of local legend. Randall Jarrell's observation that "we see the *ands* and not the *becauses*" of Whitman's metonymic style applies also to the paratactic chronicling in "Seanchus na Sgeiche" and (in a rare departure for Yeats, whose poetry has a strong metaphoric bias) to the apparently rambling, disjointed, and inconclusive denouement of this philological middle section.[39] The "becauses" of Yeats's complex relationship to diglossic Irish culture are to be discerned not only in the *style* of the reverie performed by the Yeats persona but also in how Yeatsian style hybridizes Irish diglossia by posing the self-prescribed Pale of English versification against the rambling, vestigial, Gaelic culture. I would like to amplify this point in some detail by considering, in the light of Yeats's discussion of "Style and Attitude" in "A General Introduction," how the opening section of "The Tower" attunes us to the wavelength in which the Pale/Fringe confrontation becomes audible.

In "A General Introduction" Yeats writes that his stylistic breakthrough came when he realized that he must seek "not as Wordsworth thought, words in common use, but a powerful and passionate syntax, and a complete coincidence between period and stanza" (521–22). The "contrapuntal structure of the verse . . . combines the past and the present," Yeats explains, and then elaborates his prosodic rule by scanning the opening line of *Paradise Lost* as if it were crossed with a four-stressed emphasis of impassioned prose:

Of man's first disobedience and the fruit.   (524)

Yeats does not wish to "break the pentameter" but to shake it up; "Irish preference for a swift current" makes it impatient with the "meditative, rich, [and] deliberate English mind of the Thames valley" (521).[40] Since the Anglo-Irish poetic tradition was largely forged through singing English words to a Gaelic tune, as Robert Welch, Bernard O'Donoghue, and others argue, the effects of translation, and negotiating between the two languages' syntactical and metrical incompatibilities, played a crucial role in the shake-up.[41] Why Yeats, ignorant of Gaelic and tone-deaf, succeeded where others failed at perfecting the interaction of the slow *amhrán* with the iambic line through trisyllabic substitution remains a critical conundrum. The effect of the crossover, as Sean Lucy illustrates, is also to reduce the pentameter to four stresses. The Yeatsian pentameter is counterpointed by the stresses of vehement speech and the additional unaccented syllables of the *amhrán*'s melancholy lilt. By "compel[ing] [him]self to accept those traditional metres that have developed with the language," Yeats acknowledges that he goes against the grain of his fellow modernists, who "wrote admirable free verse." If he did not so compel himself, "[he] would lose himself, become joyless like those mad old women" whom he invokes earlier to exemplify "the passionate, normal speech . . . [that] comes most naturally when we soliloquise, as I do all day long, upon the events of our own lives" (522, 521). "If [he] spoke [his] thoughts aloud they might be as angry and as wild" as those of the "denouncing and remembering" slum women, he confides, and therefore he requires formal constraint, the Pale of stately English prosody, to transmute them into significant passion (521). The agitated Yeatsian measure is made clearer by scanning the slum speech he cites as a Yeatsian pentameter:

How dare you and you without health or a home! (521)

The one-iamb-followed-by-three-anapests structure is determined by the exclamatory force and agrammatical syntax of the vituperative statement, which is almost impossible to enunciate with five stresses. The contempt climaxes with the reiterated, redundant anacoluthon "and you," which follows logically, but not grammatically, from the first clause. The anacoluthic tail wags the exclamatory force of the English "how dare you!" by deferring the caesura to the end of the line and thereby skewing the iambic meter. When the slum speech pentameter is placed in dialogue with Milton's, the social relations governing the utterances become apparent. To hear it as Eve's riposte to a marriage proposal from postlapsarian Adam affords some allegorical pleasure, but the harsh reality cannot be gainsaid that the utterance repudiates what is not on offer. The slum woman's magniloquence is inversely proportionate to her social clout, and hence her only power lies in the magical cursing power of the disempowered.

Yeats counterpoints the magisterial, meditative, cadences of English prosody with vehement Irish talk and lilting Gaelic tunes. By attempting to become the vehicle for transforming disenfranchised, female-identified, Irish repudiation into the dominant, male-identified English traditional forms, Yeats appropriates the suppressed culture and tries to animate the dominant culture with the antagonisms generated by its dominance. His verse equivocates between the unmistakable regularity of traditional prosody and the subjective referentiality and agonism of the impassioned soliloquist. The opening rhymed pentameters of "The Tower," doubly haunted by the patrician stateliness of "a sixty-year-old smiling public man" and the peremptory wildness of slum invective (*VP* 443), buttonholes the implied reader into the role of interlocutor:

> What shall I do with this absurdity—
> O heart, O troubled heart—this caricature,
> Decrepit age that has been tied to me
> As to a dog's tail?
> Never had I more
> Excited, passionate, fantastical
> Imagination, nor an ear and eye
> That more expected the impossible. (1–7)

The Vichean argument in lines 5–7 that the cerebral faculty of Memory/Imagination is grounded in corporeality is made through the Yeatsian pentameter.[42] The sputter of polysyllabic abstractions, "Excited, passionate, fantastical," peaks on the two-stressed *fantastical* (which is accentuated further by the rhyme word *impossible*), gesticulating beyond, while conforming to, the containment of the pentameter. The assertion that his imaginative power exceeds the vigor of boy-hood when "with rod and fly" (alluding to Wordsworth's poem *The Prelude*) he "climbed Ben Bulben's back" is also a declaration of intent (8–9): "Yeats" shall march to a different drum in old age than "Wordsworth who wither[ed] into eighty years, honoured and empty-witted" (*Myth* 342).

"Decrepit age" atomizes the Yeats persona into a bundle of bodily synecdoches —heart, imagination, ear, and eye—whose grotesque fissure into self and cari-cature-of-self is encapsulated by the recoupled "ear and eye." The impression of fissured duality in the recombined Cyclopean image (which is illustrated by the figurative immediacy of the Irish for "ear and eye," *leathchluas agus leathshúil* [half of a pair of ears/eyes]) is reinforced by the call-and-response slapstick of the section, in which the ego's assertions of creative potency are almost instantane-ously "derided by/A sort of battered kettle at the heel" (15–16). The eye/ear drama, in which the will-to-prevail of the surveillant Yeats persona is mocked by the auricular mirror of skewed reception, structures the fantasia of "The Tower." It is a universal quandary that how others receive one's dictated will cannot be controlled, either during life or from beyond the grave, but Yeats's inscription of that will into the high/low cartography he imposes on the Ballylee hinterland roots the dilemma in the diglossic struggle between "the [English] world that reads and writes and the [Irish] world that sings and listens." Political injustice makes reciprocal communication between the master-surveyor (identified with the Yeats persona, the erstwhile owner of the tower, and Mrs. French) and the peasantry (who are all ears) into a grotesque parable of speaker inequality.

The spiriting of Mrs. French into colloquy with the Yeats persona introduces a multilayered version of the parable which requires unpacking like a series of Russian dolls. The first "doll" is the "complete coincidence between period and stanza" achieved by crossing the rambling soliloquy of a spoken Irish-English sentence with a neatly boxed eight-line stanza.[43] The interaction "between period and stanza" can be seen at play when the stanzaic form is turned "Fringe"-side out, so to speak, by relineating it as a prose sentence: "Beyond that ridge lived Mrs. French, and once when every silver candlestick or sconce lit up the dark mahogany and the wine, a serving-man, that could divine that most respected lady's every wish, ran and with the garden shears clipped an insolent farmer's ears and brought them in a little covered dish" (25–32). Despite the absence of *I* in the sentence, the emphatic demonstratives make the speaker an omnipresent refer-ential center. The opening inversion underscores how significance is conferred on "that ridge" by the gazetteer, who makes it his point of departure for storytelling. Yeats's unbound use of the reflexive pronoun *that* (instead of the *wh*— pronouns of standard English), is a feature of the Gaelic-influenced habit of reordering syntax for emphasis and of a colloquial, context-dependent orality that eschews the explicitness of syntactic subordination. "Beyond *that* ridge" where "*that* lady" lives situates the reader in the middle of a story where what happened "once" is subject to infinite reiteration. The ambiguity about whether or not "a serving-man, *that* could divine" is restrictive (are his divinatory powers exceptional or typical of his class?) is characteristic of the interpretive cruxes raised by the oscillation between the logical indeterminacy of Yeats's colloquial usages of Irish-English, on the one hand, and the unmistakable orthodoxy of traditional metrics and forceful assertion, on the other. The tale is counterpointed by the rhythm and tight rhyme scheme (*aabbcddc*) of an eight-line stanza, modeled after Abraham Cowley's "On the Death of Mr. William Hervey" and first used by Yeats in the poem "In Memory of Major Robert Gregory" (1918). The elegiac decorum is enlivened by the folk ballad material and the near-flippant levity of semantically charged end rhymes: "once, sconce; wine, divine; wish (shears, ears), dish." A formal feature of the Cowley stanza—how the rhymed pentameters of lines 5 and 8 envelope the rhymed tetrameters of lines 6 and 7—scores the accelerating delivery of the sentence-long story and introduces thereby the comic strains of a "Three Blind Mice"–like ditty. The difficulty of assigning the ghostly voice of the comic ditty exclusively to the Cowley meter or to the speaker's gusto for sensational anecdote illustrates how the style created out of the diglossic struggle cannot be neatly disassembled into the Pale / Fringe divisions out of which it is forged.

The next layer of parable pertains to hyperbole and to how the social accreditation of figurative "excess" is governed by "the Pale." In a macabre parody of how the colonizer displaces the violence of expropriation onto the violated culture, Mrs. French's tenant farmer's ear is severed because *her* ears are offended by his insolence. Yeats learned of the incident from Sir Jonah Barrington's *Personal Sketches*—Mrs. French was Barrington's grandmother—in which it is cited as testimony "of the mutual attachment between the Irish peasantry and their landlords in former times." The Frenches were tried, and "they were, of course, acquitted" on the grounds that they could not be held accountable for their servant's insufficient grasp of the figurative subtleties of English.[44] The wry *wish/dish* rhyme suggests that it is unexceptional in this feudal economy for the serving man to "divine" the lady's wish as his command. When the "real" event is recirculated as legend, it enters the preexistent genre of servant bulls, a subgenre of Irish bulls which ridicule how servants' misprision of instructions betrays their ignorance of polite society. It is axiomatic of Irish bulls that the meaning of the utterance is controlled by the (Anglicized) auditor, not by the (laughably half-Anglicized and supposedly unwitting) speaker. The joke depends on overriding the straightforward intended meaning through exaggerated emphasis on the solecism's logical inconsistency. With servant bulls, however, this speaker/interpreter hierarchy is inverted, and the comic target becomes the servant's over-literal interpretation of a figurative expression. The ground rules for deciding what constitutes "excessive" figurativeness or literalness are rigged to favor the master and to censure the servant. The play within the anecdote between the historic depredations of colonialism (which makes harvesting peasant ears for supper seem plausible) and the tendentious circulation of bulls to caricature the Irish peasantry as beyond the Pale of normal social intercourse starkly encapsulates how colonial violence is perpetuated through the English language. In all of its figurative splendor English itself became an instrument of colonial oppression when it was harnessed to widen the gap between colonized subjects with the competence to communicate in English and the elite, who have the much rarer competence to compel others to attend carefully to what they mean to say.

There is a further Russian doll layer to consider: how is the Yeats persona's summoning of Mrs. French as his first ghostly interlocutor to be interpreted? The laconic epithet "Mrs. French/Gifted with so fine an ear" (93–94) has an element of self-satire toward the poet-speaker's imperious call to neighborhood ghosts to lend him their ears and collaborate in telepathic *dinnsheanchus*. While the epithet ironizes Yeats's own nostalgia for the "mutual attachment" of noble and peasant and his noblesse oblige attitudes, he nevertheless renounces neither his privileged position nor his relish for a fine anecdote. "All the well-known families [around Sligo] had their grotesque or tragic or romantic legends," Yeats writes in *Autobiographies*, noting how the maternal Pollexfens had greater renown than the Yeatses because they were more feared and disliked, "and I often said to myself how terrible it would be to go away and die where nobody would know my story" (17–18). The Yeatsian "first principle" situates the poet as "part of his own phantasmagoria" because poets make and know their souls in relation to those whose stories overlap with their own. The shades also function as alter egos: "Homer's" service to the Ballylee "Helen" obviously refers to Yeats's mythologization of Gonne, and "An ancient bankrupt master of this house" (line 80) and Hanrahan likewise function as masks. Moreover, Yeats's Swedenborgian ontology means that he conceives the haunted hinterland of his reverie as inhabiting his mind in a very dynamic way. The "sleeper" in the following lines may well refer to the poet who breakfasts at Thoor Ballylee:

And certain men-at-arms there were
Whose images, in the Great Memory stored,
Come with loud cry and panting breast
To break upon a sleeper's rest.   (Ll. 84–87)

The blurring of poet/phantasmagoria boundaries renders the poet-speaker's "rambling" reverie about his "rambling" (i.e., dispossessed by colonialism) Gaelic precursors and the "singing and listening" Gaeltacht very complex.

Yeats's attempt to become legendary emulates the mythic stature achieved by certain Gaelic poets, a fame paradoxically shadowed by anonymity since it involves "the people" singing lyrics without knowing whose words they sing and converting actual personages into folkloric types. Yeats strove to authorize his aristocratic singularity with the signature of "the common" by projecting an imagined peasant audience of people who sing and listen to his verse in the fields, perhaps occasionally attributing them to *that* poet who lived in *that* tower. The would-be legendary Yeats evolved through contact with Raftery (Homer) and Ó'Suilleabháin (Hanrahan). The 1925 poet's recollections about the turn-of-the-century popularizations of Raftery and Hanrahan are charged with consciousness of the influence on Irish history of the Revivalists' collaborative retranslations; the impact of the contact with Raftery and Hanrahan on his growth as a poet; and the psychological travails he invested in the personae. The Nobel laureate, senator, and master of Thoor Ballylee revisits the scenes of formative youthful encounters with his Gaelic precursors through the haunting replay of Raftery's song, "Máire Ní h-Éidhin," and by a disturbing reprise of the quest inaugurated when local sovereignty-goddess Echtge "touched" Hanrahan.

The Gaelic lyric that replays in some distorted and fragmentary fashion in the Yeats persona's mind is silenced in "The Tower." It is evoked, instead, through the *aisling* topos, the recollection of a supernal Beauty who disappears into the landscape and the reiteration of an insurgent desire to repossess that lost beauty. "Some few remembered still" the Ballylee beauty (Máire Ní h-Éidhin/ Mary Hynes), the reversed-chronological sequence of the poet-persona's reverie begins (33). "So great a glory did the song confer" that farmers jostled to glimpse her, and some, "maddened" by the lyric evocation of beauty, were lured to destruction: "Music had driven their wits astray—/And one was drowned in the great bog of Cloone" (ll. 40–41, 47–48). The will-o'-the-wisp melody of "Máire Ní h-Éidhin" emanates from "the great bog of Cloone," an autochthonous "Great Memory" that preserves fugitive traces of the past. Yeats then relates Raftery's lyric powers to epic by representing the unnamed poet and beauty as "Homer" and "Helen"

(Gonne in the Yeatsian phantasmagoria) in a move that consigns Gaelic culture to anonymity and prepares for his own world literary significance with the concluding declaration: "For if I triumph I must make men mad" (l. 56). The spiraling reverie "back to Homer" hearkens prospectively to the "triumph" of "Some few remember[ing]" Yeats's lyrics and Tower signature in years to come (from ll. 56 and 33, the last and first lines of the three-stanza narrative).

The recessive structure places the phantasmagoric Yeats in a summative position as one of the last surviving witnesses of an expiring "Homeric" tradition. The segue to reflection on how "the tragedy began/With Homer" swerves away from the tragedy that befell Gaelic culture to highlight the universality of a Yeatsian Homer who embodies an ancient oral tradition (ll. 51–52). The move back to Homer finesses what compromises Yeats's authority as a figure of continuity, namely the fact that the language and culture of "Máire Ní hEidhin" remains foreign to him. The self-positioning as the last in an Irish Orphic line via Raftery anticipates the revenant persona of "The Curse of Cromwell," a poem that inscribes into the Yeatsian oeuvre what his cotranslator of the 1930s, Frank O'Connor, calls the "characteristic backward look" of Gaelic literature. Gaelic literature is "haunted by the revenant" who returns to "find that Ireland, under the Christians, has gone to Hell," O'Connor remarks: "The Irish are like Orpheus, forever looking back at the Eurydice they are attempting to bring home from the Shades."[45] The attempted return to a Golden Age before the tragedy of Eurydice/ Gile na Gile/Cathleen Ni Houlihan began is "the [Vichean] master key" both to the formation of the "Collected Yeats" through the poet's lifelong research into "the common and its befitting language" and to de-Anglicizing re-translations (GI 511).

The translation of Raftery into Homer and of Ó'Suilleabháin into Hanrahan is at once expropriative and affiliative. "The Tower['s]" tone of "triumph" becomes unrestrained in the Hanrahan colloquy when the poet of the colonizer caste exults in the victimization of his hireling Gaelic precursor. This performance by the Yeats persona is matched by Yeats's at best "casual" disregard for his precursors' intellectual property.[46] Yeats habitually downplays his incalculable debt to translated Gaelic literature and often misconstrues the written Gaelic tradition as orature. He treats the matter of Ireland as "common property" awaiting salvage and renovation by a truly creative writer. Under these circumstances the muting of Gaelic words into a wordless melody that is absorbed into Yeatsian "will" displays how "Celtic melancholy" can function as crocodile tears for a "dying" Gaelic culture in the very act of cannibalizing it so artfully. The pleasurable mull-

ing over picturesque local legend, each one a singular yet representative episode
in the "melodrama of . . . villain and victim" which makes up the plot of the "story
of Ireland," also has, however, an obsessional quality—the insistent iterativity of
the melancholic who is "eaten up" by loss and unable to "get over it" (*Au* 206).
Yeats, who identifies with the villain caste and shares the persecuted Irishry's
sense of loss, is both eater and eaten.

"And I myself created Hanrahan/And drove him drunk or sober through the
dawn" (57–58), the Yeats persona continues, introducing Hanrahan as though he
were a Caliban of his own Prospero-like production. The 1890s revisions of
Stories into a Grail quest draw on Arthurian romance ("once, it seems, the cauldron of an Irish god," according to the "Celtic Element" essay) and Fenian legend
about Diarmuid, who was led up "Ben Bulben's back" to his death, a topographical detail that acquires additional salience in "The Tower." "Hanrahan" served as a
mask for Yeats to work through his unrequited love for Gonne, the nationalist
ambivalences that were intensified by his involvement with her, and the ambition
to "accounted be/True brother of a company/That sang to sweeten Ireland's
wrong" (*VP* 137). The success of Hyde's Hanrahan in *Casadh an tSúgáin* and
Gonne's performance in the Yeats-Gregory dramatization of "Red Hanrahan's
Song about Ireland" contributed to the cultural-nationalist sentiment behind the
1916 Rising. Enmeshed in the matter-of-Ireland, transfused with Revivalist synergy, and saturated with Yeats's "poetic life," Hanrahan's significance lies in the
fact that he is *not* an exclusive Yeatsian creation. Nevertheless, the Yeats persona
undertakes a sole-owner performance of directing Hanrahan through the Grail
ordeal by retelling *Stories* in verse:

> Caught by an old man's juggleries,
> He stumbled, tumbled, fumbled to and fro
> And had but broken knees for hire
> And horrible splendour of desire;
> I thought it all out twenty years ago. (Ll. 60–65)

The circus master seems to exult in the contrast between the *spailpín*'s unbounded
passion and his "broken knees" (the synecdochic reduction is accented by the
Gaelic-influenced *but* locution).[47]

Launched into an outdoing momentum, the enthusiastic retelling of Hanrahan's quest by "Yeats" violates an otherwise absolutely upheld "complete coincidence between period and stanza," so that the narrative frenzy of the enjambed
stanza outstrips the reported delirium of its subject:

Hanrahan rose in frenzy there

And followed up those baying creatures towards—

O towards I have forgotten what—enough!   (Ll. 71–73)

The respite plea "—enough!" breaks off and resumes the narrative on a different
tack, suggesting that the reprise of the quest evokes a surfeit of disturbing memories. Yeats spectacularly trips up the Yeats persona's rambling reverie by transgressing the rigidly observed versification rule and underscores the rupture by
following it with an equally flagrant violation of the laws of fiction. Dismissing the
assembled shades, he turns suppliant toward Hanrahan: "Go therefore; but leave
Hanrahan,/For I need his mighty memories" (103–4). If Hanrahan were indeed
a mere Yeatsian fictional "creation," he would not have any memories beyond
those assigned him by his creator. The metapoetic ruptures twice enact the return
of the repressed, a traumatic "remembering" that so strains the soliloquizing
narrative of "The Tower" that it "stutters" and *reaches the limit* that marks its
outside and makes it confront silence."[48] The persona's mimicry of the loss of
nerve and consequent amnesia that had set the "touched" Hanrahan on his quest
"stutters" that Hanrahan's *aventure* is an ongoing Yeatsian quest.[49] It reveals
how the process of revising Hanrahan to remake the "Collected Yeats" was, and
continues in 1925 to be, a way of working through the poet's personal "poetic
life." The second stutter transmogrifies Hanrahan into the deceased Eoghan Rua
Ó'Súilleabháin (or a similar, perhaps local, poet), who is now engaged in the
dreaming back. In "the Dreaming Back," *A Vision* explains, the spirit relives the
events that most moved it first in order of their intensity and then in order of their
occurrence, finding the names and words of the drama from some incarnate
mind "because all spirits inhabit our unconsciousness or, as Swedenborg said,
are the Dramatis Personae of our dreams" (226–27). As it happens, the Gaelic for
"to go west," *ag dul siar,* has a further connotation of "to go back over" in the sense
of retracing for recall, and thus the Gaelic for reflecting back over one's life, or
"dreaming back," is *ag dul siar ar do shaol.*

In "The Tower" Hanrahan is a Virgilian guide to the Gaelic past and to the
future neighborhood haunt of Yeats's afterlife. The intertwining of Yeats's soul-
searching with Hanrahan's/Ó'Súilleabháin's dreaming back positions Hanrahan
as a Yeatsian daimon. To the Yeats persona of "The Tower," Hanrahan has lived
and loved more passionately than he, belonged to the people more fully than he,
and now, from the posthumous omniscience of his Ballylee Hades, has a more
comprehensive perspective on the living poet's life than he himself has:

Old lecher with a love on every wind,
Bring up out of that deep considering mind
All that you have discovered in the grave,
For it is certain that you have
Reckoned up every unforeknown, unseeing
Plunge, lured by a softening eye,
Or by a touch or a sigh,
Into the labyrinth of another's being;

Does the imagination dwell the most
Upon a woman won or woman lost?
If on the lost, admit you turned aside
From a great labyrinth out of pride,
Cowardice, some silly over-subtle thought
Or anything called conscience once;
And that if memory recur, the sun's
Under eclipse and the day blotted out.   (Ll. 103–20)

The attempted seduction of narrative from Hanrahan, like the earlier driving
of him through a proxy quest, creates a reciprocity between poet and shade which
climaxes when the apostrophized *you* in "admit you turned aside" turns self-
accusatory (not least because Yeats does not credit his Gaelic precursors with
"silly over-subtle thought"). The mulling over the past has the quality of remorse
over specifics, which Deirdre Toomey links to a crisis in 1898 when Yeats backed
away from commitment to Gonne.[50] The memory, which is obscurely related to
Hanrahan's "mighty memories," is approached and "blotted out" before it can
recur, as the stage-managing persona precipitately draws the curtain on section 2.
The "blott[ing] out" enacts the silencing of censorship, performed by way of
repressing a remembrance that refuses to be forgotten and by not writing certain
mighty memories into the record. It also prepares for another "blott[ing] out," the
silencing of death and supersession implicit in writing a will which preoccupies
section 3.

The figure-in-the-tower, a censor and a symbol of conquest, is embedded in the
uncanny womb/tomb terrain of the dispossessed, rambling *file*. In this topography the controlling act of censorship is haunted by the romance of inside knowledge of a "softening eye," "touch," and "sigh" which is outside the ken of him
whose aerial view provides a detailed itinerary to the maze below. By etching
detailed topographies that are haunted by a colonial past onto international cul-

tural consciousness, Yeats and Joyce succeeded in putting Ireland, and Irish aspiration for political and cultural autonomy, "on the map." In a path-breaking essay, "Yeats and Decolonization," Edward Said argues that Yeats exemplifies "the primacy of the geographical element . . . in the imagination of anti-imperialism" because he grasps the central importance of imaginatively "reclaim[ing], re-nam[ing], and reinhabit[ing] the land."[51]

Yeats's decolonizing topography also has neocolonial elements, which can be observed in how Yeats's legendary Holy Land at once preserves and usurps Gaelic *dinnsheanchus.* In his 1941 study of how European Christians constructed the commemorative landscape of "the Holy Land," Maurice Halbwachs traces how the Christian "collective memory" of the life of Jesus was mapped onto the terri-tory of Palestine through a network of pilgrimage sites.[52] He notes how the topographical referents dotted across the authoritative Holy Land act as a brake on the modifications to oral traditions about Jesus which might otherwise have oc-curred. The staying power of a symbology that is rooted in a verifiable geography (and linked to a known history) governs the construction of the "Collected Yeats." It is the lesson of "seem[ing] traditional" which Yeats drew from folklore and from Edmund Burke, and he shares the conservationism of both sources. Halbwachs also contends that because the Christian Holy Land was constellated around a preexistent network of sacred Jewish sites it then partially displaced, it has an unavowed Jewish "deep structure." Yeats's "re-Anglicizing with a difference" has a Gaelic deep structure that is variously obscured, celebrated, and refash-ioned. The yoking-together of cottage and tower annexes peasant culture to his Ascendancy-identified power base. His *sidhe* pastoral merges a folk tradition of weaving an otherworldly realm into the local hinterland with a metropolitan mix of Hermetic Neoplatonism, agrarian nostalgia, and the evasions that *Finnegans Wake* lampoons as the "cultic twalette" (344).

In "Dante . . . Bruno . Vico . . Joyce" Samuel Beckett draws attention to an-other *Wake* neologism, "in twosome twiminds," which is equally applicable to Yeats's *sidhe* pastoral. Unlike the "abstracted-to-death" word *doubt,* which "gives us hardly any sensuous suggestion of hesitancy, of the necessity for choice, of static irresolution," Beckett writes, in *twosome twiminds* has a Vichean "savage economy of hieroglyphics" and hence exemplifies how "Mr. Joyce has desophisti-cated language."[53] The *sidhe* were crucial to Yeats's "de-sophistication" of English because *sidhe* lore provided a de-Anglicizing vernacular for showing that "the mechanical theory has no reality, that the natural and supernatural are knit to-gether" (GI 518), and for coming to terms with the nation's "anomalous condi-tion" of "ceasing to be Irish without becoming English." The protagonist of "The

Man who dreamed at Faeryland" who dreams at Drumahair, Lissadell, Scanavin, Lugnagall is enmeshed in a familiar geography to those who know Sligo. The litany of place names plays a de-Anglicizing tune to those who can detect residual Gaelic etymologies or sonic texture in the Anglicized place names, and the "foreignness" of the names likewise differentiates Sligo from the Lake District or other English places for international readers.[54] The sense of estrangement enhances receptivity to the poem's theme of how worldly composure can be unexpectedly ambushed by traumatic incursions from the otherworld. The folkloric locale is picturesque, but its pictorial quality is one in which any given here oscillates to an "away, come away" singsong to create an uncanny place of reverie.

Yeats approaches the task of making a panoramic, legendary Holy Land out of the western part of Ireland as though he were painting a reverie in words. Taking exception to Arnold's characterization of Celts as "sentimental," Yeats writes in the "Celtic" essay that the popularity of Oisin's anaphoric lament "the clouds are long above me this night" in the Gaeltacht attests to how "all dreams withering in the winds of time lament in his lamentations," and a decade before he wrote "The Tower" he describes how an Arnoldian "criticism of life" thwarted all attempts to portray this quality of "primitive melancholy" adequately:

> Years afterwards when I had finished *The Wanderings of Oisin*, dissatisfied with its yellow and dull green, with all that overcharged colour inherited from the Romantic movement, I deliberately reshaped my style, deliberately sought out an impression as of cold light and tumbling clouds. I cast off traditional metaphors and loosened my rhythm, and recognizing that all the criticism of life known to me was alien and English, became as emotional as possible but with an emotion which I described to myself as cold. (*Au* 74)

The outcome of the stylistic struggle to avoid the sentimentality of Romantic Ossianism and establish thereby some common ground with his Gaelic precursors is evident in the style and subject matter of the closing lines of "The Tower." The couvade image of nesting birds in lines 166–72, a Yeatsian symbol for the transmigration of souls and for how "it is the dream martens that, all unknowing, are master masons to the living martens" (*Myth* 359), effects a tonal shift from hectoring supremacism to a letting go that is serene without being quiescent:

> Now shall I make my soul,
> Compelling it to study
> In a learned school
> Till the wreck of body,

Slow decay of blood,

Testy delirium

Or dull decrepitude,

Or what worse evil come—

The death of friends, or death

Of every brilliant eye

That made a catch in the breath—

Seem but the clouds of the sky

When the horizon fades;

Or a bird's sleepy cry

Among the deepening shades.   (181–95)

The poignant succession of images of bodily decrepitude and loss of companionship (magnificently epitomized by setting apart "every brilliant eye" with catches
of breath) is orchestrated into a kind of mortality countdown by the spare trime-
ters. The austere beauty of the closing quatrain results from an ascetic pursuit
of the exact tonality for "the deepening shades" that draw Yeats toward the daimonic precursors who share an impassioned attachment to the hazel woods,
rocky places, and homesteads of his native land. Beckett's play for television, . . .
but the clouds . . . (1976) *dreams back* these lines in tacit tribute to how their
poise between sensuous hesitancy and intrepid will conveys the "primitive melancholy" around which art was wrought for Yeats. The "contrapuntal structure of
the verse . . . combines the past and present" by integrating into contemporary
consciousness the affects and percepts that may have shaped how Aengus and
others from remote epochs apprehended their world. The pensive reverie of
recollective fantasia leads to an uncanny place of solitude—"I am awake and
asleep, at my moment of revelation, self-possessed in self-surrender"—where the
unexorcised "ghostly voice" of "vivid speech" that "moves me and my hearer" is
made and heard (GI 524).

   In contrast to the moody reveries of Yeatsian *dinnsheanchus,* the conviviality of
song evokes an imagined subcommunity of people who share that ethnic repertoire. "Mad Song" became a means of cultivating tragic gaiety in the final decade
of Yeats's life, and an intensified renewal of interest in folksong and in translations "from the Irish" is evident in the oeuvre from *Words for Music Perhaps* (1932)
onward. During the 1930s Yeats collaborated with Frank O'Connor on "translations from the Irish"; F. R. Higgins on setting his lyrics to music; and Lady
Dorothy Wellesley on ballad collection and publishing ballad broadsheets (she
succeeds the late Lady Gregory as an aristocratic co-folklorist). "The Song of

Wandering Aengus" and "The Curse of Cromwell" (1937), composed forty years apart, feature speakers whose "in twosome twimindedness" reveal much about the translation aesthetics developed to confront the cultural ambivalences of the 1890s and 1930s, two decades of so-called decadence which coincided in Ireland with intensified anxiety about the imperilment of Gaelic culture.

The foundation of the Irish Free State / Saorstát Éireann in 1922 changed the parameters of the language debate, shifting responsibility for reviving Gaelic from grassroots voluntarism to state-sponsored initiatives. Membership of the Gaelic League declined precipitously, from 819 branches in 1922 to 139 branches in 1924.[55] Over the next decades successive Free-State governments carried out a re-Gaelicization program that depended primarily upon making Irish a major (though not exclusive) medium of instruction in elementary schools. "Compulsory Gaelic" in schools meant that the grandchildren of those who had been subjected to "tally-stick" Anglicization were routinely punished for failing to master the grammar of an officially venerated "national" language that the adult population was manifestly neglecting to acquire. As the gap between the rhetoric and achievement of re-Gaelicization in the Free State widened, Irish came to occupy the feminized position of a "mother" tongue, marginalized from the public sphere to the elementary school and to token appearances on state occasions. The twice-iterated, twice-deferred *wish* in Yeats's Senate speech—"I wish to say that I wish to see the country Irish-speaking"—neatly captures a widespread popular desire for an Augustinian "but not yet" conversion to bilingualism.

Yeats's contributions as a senator to the debate display the same obtuseness about the logistical challenges of reviving Gaelic which mar his assessment of Hyde—for example, he opposes bilingual railroad signs by treating the issue as if Gaelic-only signs were in question. His intimate understanding of the ambivalent passions aroused by Gaelic are apparent, however, in the way he weighs the pros and cons of "compulsory Gaelic" in a 1924 essay of that title in the *Irish Statesman*. Their fishing spoiled by a dynamited stream—an allusion to "Easter 1916" and to the postcolonial context of "a bunch of martyrs were the bomb and we are living in the explosion"[56]—two legislators take up the compulsory-Gaelic issue in the bipartisan debate format of Spenser's *View*. "Paul's" view that Gaelic counters "the damnable convenience of the English tongue" with "disturbing intellectual force" is contested by "Peter," who sees prescriptive Gaelicization as neocolonial servitude, "a stronger subconscious desire than England ever knew [in replacing Charles with Cromwell] to enslave and be enslaved" and a danger in a culture in which "there is no public emotion but resentment" and "praise is unreal . . . but our vituperation is animated and even joyous." An adjudicative third party, "Timothy," opines that "whatever imagination we have in Ireland today, we owe to Gaelic literature or to the effect of Gaelic speech upon the English language," and recommends a diversified experimental approach: "after all, imitation is automatic, yet creation moves in a continual uncertainty[;] if we were certain of the future, who would trouble to create it?"[57]

A far more influential contribution to the debate in that year, Daniel Corkery's study *The Hidden Ireland* (1924), is also charged with anxiety about realizing the 1916 insurrectionists' high hopes for re-Gaelicizing Ireland. Corkery's subaltern history—a key source for Hugh MacDiarmid's conversion to "the Gaelic Idea" in the late 1920s—finds in the rambling Gaelic poets of the eighteenth century an ancestral peasant intelligentsia for the emergent ruling class of the ex-colonized. He represents the survival of a Gaelic high culture (epitomized by the *aislingí* of Aogán Ó'Rathaille and Eoghan Rua Ó'Suilleabháin, among others) amid the squalor of the pauperized peasantry's "slatternly" mud cabins as little short of miraculous. The "hidden Ireland" concept is an implicit rebuttal of Yeats's coterminous gilding of Ascendancy munificence and Anglo-Irish eighteenth-century achievement. (Corkery dismissed Yeats as "a poseur" when they met in 1905, and his antipathy to "Anglo-Irish" revivalism permeates *Synge and Anglo-Irish Literature* [1931]).[58] Corkery was Frank O'Connor's "first love,"[59] the teacher who awakened the nine-year-old's enthusiasm for the hitherto despised language of his grandmother. O'Connor's passion was rekindled by reading Pearse's Gaelic poetry and the Cuchulain saga and by joining the Gaelic League in the aftermath of 1916 and continued in 1923 when, as a prisoner in a Republican internment camp, he began the Gaelic translations that brought him AE and Yeats's attention in 1925. Anguish over whether Gaelic would become a fountain of "imagination" or a prescriptive bludgeon in Free-State Ireland colors O'Connor's 1926 review of *The Hidden Ireland*, which he welcomes for its "enthusiasm" and for restoring balance to a historical record that "to us was maddening in its one-sidedness" while warning against the use of it to bolster complacency when Irish-Ireland needs to confront "its own nakedness."[60]

As the national will to revive and use Gaelic became an increasingly hollow orthodoxy, politicians, intellectuals, and official and would-be state censors drew on the considerable symbolic prestige of Gaelic and popular notions of the "hidden Ireland" concept to authenticate their versions of "true" Irishness. Once again, Gaelic-English translation became highly politicized. The O'Connor/Yeats collaboration on Gaelic-English translation crossed caste (i.e., Papist Gael/Protestant Ascendancy), generational, and class lines to engage in a combative revision of the Revivalist aesthetic that Yeats had helped to fashion and which had had a formative influence on O'Connor's life (1903–66) and self-education (he left school at age fourteen). Hyde, Gregory, and other Revivalists had tried to close the gap between the spoken language and the literary archive by undertaking colloquial redactions of antiquarian scholarship which simulated the spoken arts of the storyteller and balladeer. Their collective effort "to restore dignity to Ireland" by reintegrating the "ancient idealism" associated with a precolonial heroic age into demotic speech had stressed the ennobling antiquity of Gaelic culture. The upcoming generation of writers, by contrast, felt stifled by the official and indirect censorship carried out in the name of Mother Ireland's "dignity" and focused, instead, on the satiric and iconoclastic energy of demotic orality and adversarial balladry.[61] The contrastive strategies are crucially determined by the related but different types of cultural ambivalence motivating them: the turn-of-the-century interregnum of "ceasing to be Irish without becoming English" invoked to galvanize the public against irremediable cultural loss; and the anticlimactic experience of "ceasing to be English without becoming Irish" facing citizens of the new Free State.

The O'Connor/Yeats collaboration—together they re-created the verse that O'Connor had translated from Irish—apparently renewed some of the synergistic energy of early Revivalist collaborations. O'Connor recalls how "even in extreme old age when he was looking most wretched and discontented, quite suddenly that blaze of excitement would sweep over the face like sunlight over a moor, and from behind the mask, a boy's eager, tense face stammered and glared back at you."[62] Transmissibility is paramount in their translation aesthetic, which aims at fluency, vehemence, and an embodied orality that debunks the Free State's erotophobic discourse of purity.[63] "Wild horses could not have kept Yeats from helping with [the translations]," O'Connor recalls, "and sometimes, having supplied some felicitous line of his own, he promptly stole it back for one of his original poems." The opening stanza of "The Curse of Cromwell" contains two such retrievals, the *ubi sunt* from the anonymous "Cill Chais" ("Kilcash") and the closing line of "Cabhair Ní Ghairfead" ("No Help I'll Call"), a satiric valedictory poem by Aogán Ó'Rathaille, the author of "Gile na Gile." "Kilcash" moves from decrying the ecological trauma of plantation—"What shall we do for timber?/The last of the woods is down"—to lamenting the destruction of the Gaelic social order: "And the great earls where are they?/The earls, the lady, the people,/ Beaten into the clay." In "Cabhair Ní Ghairfead" (1729) the destitute and dying Ó'Rathaille disdains to call for the patronage that would not be forthcoming anyway and instead declares sole allegiance to his matrilineal ancestral patrons, the MacCarthy clan, supplanted by the Brownes over a century before. By incorporating an *ubi sunt* intertext from "Kilcash" into Ó'Rathaille's closing lines, O'Connor/Yeats weaves his isolated protest into the common plaint and accents the theme of death grinding personality into anonymity: "I shall go after the heroes, ay, into the clay—/My fathers followed theirs before Christ was crucified."[64]

The tension between expropriation and affiliation is acute in the drive to translate Ó'Rathaille's valedictory lines. If one interprets Ó'Rathaille's valediction as a definitive refusal to collaborate with the new English dispensation and to address himself exclusively to the Gaelic patrons who predeceased his birth, the translation of his *non-serviam* into English is a highly questionable intervention. O'Connor's (or perhaps O'Connor/Yeats's) retitling of "No Help I'll Call" (the literal translation of "Cabhair Ní Ghairfead") as "Last Lines" overdetermines as terminus the last poem written by a poet who saw himself as the last in line of a bardic caste. The title links Ó'Rathaille with the emblematic figure of "the last bard" in a way that can be seen to treat the Gaelic source as part of a concluded (rather than an ongoing) tradition, a politically charged move when a central goal of the Gaelic Revival is to reverse the Anglocentric stereotyping of it as anachronistic.[65] Yeats aspired to the culminative status of being "the last," but the appropriation of Ó'Rathaille's words into his own final summation also involves a resonant affiliative gesture on Yeats's part, namely the reprise of a satiric declaration of atavistic allegiance to a literary milieu that the colonizer had destroyed before his lifetime. Yeats made Ó'Rathaille's last line his own: the *ubi sunt* of "Kilcash" features in his epitaph poem, "Under Ben Bulben," and the last poem he wrote, "The Black Tower," is a militant statement of unswerving loyalty to the ancestral dead. With an eye on the future, the last line is circulated as a bottom line through song: "That we in coming days may be/Still the indomitable Irishry" ("Under Ben Bulben").

Yeats writes to Dorothy Wellesley that "The Curse of Cromwell," which "echo[es] old Gaelic ballads which friends translated to me," was composed during a storm of creativity following the deep despondency that beset him when the controversial (and false) news broke that the Roger Casement diaries were forgeries. The scandal so stirred his "old Fenian conscience" that he was confined to bed before emerging, "more man of genius, more gay, more miserable. I write poem after poem, all intended for music, all very simple—as a modern Indian poet has said 'no longer the singer but the song.' "[66] "I have recovered a power of moving the common man I had in my youth[;] [t]he poems I can write now will go into the general memory," Yeats adds jubilantly, confident of realizing the old ambition of producing lyrics like Hyde's which would be sung by the people "without their knowing whose words they sang." The traumatic affront to his

Fenian conscience, which at first debilitated and then released him into song ("the poems I *can* write now"), precipitated a similar creative breakthrough to that of 1929, when the "audacious speech" of the licentious Crazy Jane (based on "a local satirist" from Gort) brought access to the "all impersonal . . . emotion" of "song."[67]

Crazy Jane has an atavistic power of rebound and insurrectionary energy which was crucial to the cultivation of Yeats's "ultimate style," Richard Ellmann's apt term for the impression of abandon which is partly colloquial artifice and partly real nonchalance in the late work. The "all impersonal . . . emotion" of song provides essential propulsion for what Theodor Adorno, writing about Beethoven's late style, calls "the irascible gesture with which [the power of subjectivity] takes leave of the works themselves," when "the conventions are no longer penetrated and mastered by subjectivity, but simply left to stand" ("no longer the singer, but the song").[68] The return-to-song emotion engages the formulaic and gregarious features of song which the young Yeats had felt he had to struggle against, namely the mellifluousness that threatens to overwhelm the lyric's intellectual content and the "facile charm" of folksong which he faults in his early work and in the boilerplate patriotism of Young Ireland verse.[69] The aristocratic "style" he prided himself on contributing to Revivalist collaborations was partly a defense against the inchoate "Jacobin rage" that he inherited from his mother and the "roystering humour" of "dialect,"[70] Yeats admits, but in later years he harnessed feminized "fanaticism" and ethnicized cursing power as a source of creative empowerment. This is the raw repudiatory energy of the "denouncing and remembering" mad old slum woman who remembers to curse *before* she recollects her grievance and the refrains of patriotic balladry which bind past, present, and future generations of "the Irishry," in Ireland and abroad, into one resounding plaintive chorus: "The Irish race—our scattered 20 millions—is held together by songs."[71] As Crazy Jane declaims the wisdom of Diotima, her irrepressible vituperation is less a "Celtic" relic of independence from "our workaday Western world" than the incantatory groundswell of savage indignation subtending the alternate sense of Irishry, a peoplehood based on a collective memory of persecution.

Crazy Jane's slum invective has insurrectionary brio, and it connects with the magical efficacy attributed to cursing rituals within the Gaelic tradition which has been made an object of urbane English satire since the early modern period.[72] Yeats was fascinated by the bards' manipulation of public fear of satire to maintain their high prestige, as the frequent mentions of his Gaelic precursors' curse poems (*aoir*, satires) and treatment of the poet Seanchan's hunger strike cursing ritual in the 1903 play *The King's Threshold* attest. He was also intrigued by the hierarchical inversion in cursing ritual whereby the weak have greater magical powers of redress than the strong, which is why Seanchan's cursing power increases as his strength ebbs and the widow's curse is especially feared.[73] Yeats changed the ending of The King's Threshold in 1920 to commemorate Terence MacSwiney's death by hunger strike, and in a lecture on "Modern Ireland" for U.S. audiences in the early 1930s he explores Irish "fanaticism" by pondering, on the one hand, how deliberate self-sacrifice had become "a chief instrument in our public life" since 1916 and, on the other, how Joyce's "unique self-absorption [in] . . . all that was sordid and casual in the life of Dublin" was the pinnacle of "a movement of imagination that was a direct expression of national self-contempt that followed the death of Parnell."[74]

The "Modern Ireland" lecture, which was the occasion on which Yeats met Marianne Moore,[75] is also significant because it reconfigures the literary renaissance around Ulysses—"from the local hate [Joyce] passed on to all that had remained unspoken in the European mind for generations" (263)—in ways that accord with Hugh MacDiarmid's ecstatic reception of Ulysses in 1922. In the lecture Yeats recalls having once asked Synge whether he wrote out of love or hatred of Ireland, and Synge had replied "that is a question I have never been able to answer," and he likewise detects a Swiftian misanthropic fury in how the young Joyce had bristled with "almost ungovernable rage" against passersby in Dublin streets (263). For Yeats and MacDiarmid alike, the "masculinity" of Joyce's and Synge's harsh disillusionment and saeva indignatio appeased their gender anxiety about aligning themselves with the victimized subject position.[76] Even as his "old Fenian conscience" identifies viscerally with the ambivalent rage informing the satiric genius of Swift, Synge, and Joyce, the gutter speech of the feminized outcast, and popular rebellious song, such angry hostility remains somehow alien to Yeats. To the aging poet with naught but "lust and rage / . . . to spur me into song" (VP 591), identification with the atavistic "local hate" that quickens the Irishry has elements of self-conscious artifice, philosophical and ironic detachment from the upcoming generation's ire, and canny appreciation for the aptness of a satiric swan song to the career arc of the phantasmagoric Yeats-in-the-oeuvre.

The title of "The Curse of Cromwell" is ambiguous, for it could denominate a historical ballad, a psychological portrait of the dislocating impact of colonialism, or a magical utterance intended as a retributive curse. The revenant speaker of the poem reports on the devastation wreaked by Cromwell to "you," an inferred audience that can be imagined as the underworld dead greeting the dead, another post-Cromwellian bard, or a contemporary audience hearing how it was:

You ask what I have found and far and wide I go,

Nothing but Cromwell's house and Cromwell's murderous crew,

The lovers and the dancers are beaten into the clay,

And the tall men and the swordsmen and the horsemen where are they?

And there is an old beggar wandering in his pride,

His fathers served their fathers before Christ was crucified.

> O what of that, O what of that,
>
> What is there left to say?

The ironic pressure placed on the revenant's narrative by the dramatic monologue form is intensified, even parodied, by the refrain's mockery of all effort at
interpretation and communication: "*O what of that, O what of that, / What is there
left to say?*" Both the refrain and the revenant are metapoetic analogies for the
"afterlife" of translation and for the unforeseen transports to the past provoked by
"haunting" tunes and unexpected encounters with reminders of former times.

Even though Yeats had once argued all evening with O'Connor about the latter's
proposed translation "Has made me a beggar before you, Valentine Brown" ("'No
beggars! No beggars!' he roared," presumably because he thought Ó'Rathaille
would never abase himself in this way), he switches Ó'Rathaille's parting words of
proud atavistic fealty to the third person and applies it to "an old beggar wandering
in his pride."[77] "Wandering in his pride" has near-antithetical connotations: it
could signify delusions of grandeur and hence position "No Help I'll Call" close to
the social powerlessness of the "denouncing and remembering" slum woman's
repudiation of what is not on offer, or it could signify the "uncompromising
literary pride" of the outcast-poet refusing to collaborate with the oppressor.[78] It
soon becomes apparent that the revenant shares the beggar's ethos: "What can
they know that we know that know the time to die?" (13). His contempt for
"money's rant" masks anxiety about the delusion that the swordsmen and ladies
"can pay a poet for a verse . . ./That I am still their servant though all are
underground" (ll. 20–21). His material conditions and requirements for a literary
life are entirely at cross-purposes, and by serving the dead patrons he laments
being unable to serve he "proves that things both can and cannot be" (l. 18). The
dialectic of self-canceling knowledge is represented with a simile of being consumed analogous to the "eater and eaten" trope: "But there's another knowledge
that my heart destroys/As the fox in the old fable destroyed the Spartan boy's"
(ll. 16–17).

The indeterminacy of the revenant's Orphic gaze is first sounded in "Nothing
but Cromwell's house and Cromwell's murderous crew." The annihilative bitter-

ness of the statement, which is accented by the Irish negative-exemptive locution, communicates to one of his own that no further elaboration is necessary once the fatal name is invoked. To an outsider, however, the revenant's transfixed attention to nothing other than Cromwell may seem symptomatic of the mesmeric grip of catastrophe upon historical consciousness. Such an observer might see in the revenant Benjamin's "angel of history": "where we perceive a chain of events, he sees one single catastrophe . . . [but a storm of progress] irresistibly propels him into the future to which his back is turned, while the pile of debris before him grows skyward."[79] The opposed interpretations of "nothing but Cromwell," like those of "wandering in his pride," depend on whether one situates the normative *we* "inside" or "outside" the revenant's disaffection. This judgment is influenced in turn by the generic factor of where the lyric is placed on the high/low spectrum between literary satire, the witty refinement of aggression into a display of verbal mastery which disavows personal malice, and colloquial cursing, an artless outburst of undisguised malediction which is coded as cultural impoverishment. The satire/curse spectrum is of course thoroughly marked by "the Pale," which elevates the cultured satirist of the English core over everyone else (including the superstitious Irish, whose satire maintains a connection with annihilative magic), but the insider/outsider crux also governs judgments about whether or not Yeats succeeds in "transcending" his "old Fenian conscience" and the biases of his colonial acculturation.

The scenario of the final stanza, in which the revenant comes upon a ruined house where he had formerly received patronage, honor, and hospitality, is suffused through Swiftian allusion with Yeats's personal sense of loss at the passing of Anglo-Irish privilege.[80] Sorrow at the deforestation of Kilcash mingles with regret at the destruction of Anglo-Irish Ancestral Houses and wooded estates (especially Coole Park).[81] The Jacobite poet's dream of a precolonial Utopia regained where the supremely isolated bard enjoys the conviviality of former times is shadowed by the Anglo-Irish nightmare of a ruined Big House, which anticipates the lit-up house in *Purgatory* which offers no release from "dreaming back" an originary colonial mésalliance. "I never knew the dream so deep," Yeats writes of *Purgatory* (1938), and his 1934 séance play about Jonathan Swift, *The Words upon the Window-Pane* (which speculates about whether Swift avoided having children out of dread of transmitting congenital madness or horror at imminent demagoguery), likewise explores the theme of degeneracy. Although the figure of the post-Cromwellian bard seems to rue colonialism, the palimpsestic image of a ruined great "house" also seems to lament the leveling of the colonial elite:

I came upon a great house in the middle of the night
Its open lighted doorway and its windows all alight,
And all my friends were there and made me welcome too;
But I woke in an old ruin that the winds howled through;
And when I pay attention I must out and walk
Among the dogs and horses that understand my talk.
                    O what of that, O what of that,
                    What is there left to say?

Awakening to the ruin surrounding the *aisling*, the revenant resolves not to follow the earls into the clay but to jettison human society, like Gulliver after his return from the land of the Houyhnhnms, for the companionship of animals. The double allusion to Swift's *Gulliver's Travels* (1726) and Ó'Rathaille's "Cabhair Ní Ghairfead" (1729), each composed out of the other's earshot under conditions of extreme cultural polarization, negotiates the chasm between eighteenth-century Ascendancy and Gaelic Ireland whose legacy is played out in the "hidden Ireland" debate. The copresence of Ó'Rathaille and Swift at the lyric's close makes Ó'Rathaille seem less remote and Swift less solitary to Yeats as he combines the "ghostly voices" of Ó'Rathaille's hatred of Gaelic ethnocide and Swift's hatred of colonial misrule in order to enlarge his "local hate" and to merge his antipathy to modern degeneracy with theirs.

"Swift haunts me; he is always just around the next corner," Yeats writes in the preface to *The Words upon the Window-Pane*, adding that the satiric vehemence of public oratory in Ireland often makes him wonder if Swift spoke "with just such an intonation."[82] Such "intonation" lies in the ears of the audience as much as in the utterance of the speaker, and thus the revenant's turning away from the inferred audience-within-the-poem toward those "that understand my talk" underscores the dearth of an audience to "catch" his exact intonation by resorting to the language of mute gesture. From the perspective of the putative last bard the satiric turning away acknowledges that last words are rendered idioglossic by the absence of any *we* who can understand them without translation. The Swiftian turn toward converse with beasts takes up Yeats's comparison of Swift's and Vico's philosophies of the end of civilization with the ends of their respective lives in *The Words upon the Window-Pane*'s preface, and by so doing, universalizes the post-Cromwellian bard's dilemma with Vico's concept of the second barbarism of reflection: "no matter how great the throng and press of their bodies, [humans] live like wild beasts in a solitude of spirit and will, scarcely any two being able to agree since each follows his own pleasure or caprice" (para. 1106). Parting words that cannot resound in the ears of a missing audience, which remain suspended like an unappeased ghostly voice, are counterpointed with the indignant song emotion of the Irishry. Vico's influence on the markedly different careers of Yeats, Joyce, and Beckett suggests a deep need to find a philosophical framework for the historical contingency of language—the recognition that all language "will be dead in time, just like our own poor dear Gaelic," as Mrs. Rooney puts it in Beckett's *All That Fall*[83]—and for negotiating de-Anglicization polemics.

Yeats's decision to displace the aftermath of the Williamite wars (1691) back to that of Cromwell's campaign of terror (1649–50) has a double effect: it simultaneously taps into the chorus of malediction associated with the arch-villain of Irish history and intensifies the ironic pressure on the revenant's point of view by situating the event as one in a pile-up of similar catastrophes. "The Curse of Cromwell on you!" (Scrios Cromuell ort!/May Cromwell destroy you!), which Patrick Power describes as the best known historical curse in Ireland, shows how Cromwell features as a satanic bogey man in Irish folk memory.[84] Through repeated imprecation "Cromwell" became a suprahistorical figure, tied to his historical deeds but exceeding them to the extent that his name became synonymous with destruction and a byword for vengeance. The temporal transposition of the post-Williamite poet back to "nothing but Cromwell" situates the lyric against an incantatory undertow that is not unlike the magical effect achieved by the retrotranslation of "Aengus" into the druidic tapestry behind all Irish history. Yet even as the contextual shift would seem to overdetermine the lyric as a refrain of the name that is a curse, that horizon of expectation is countered by Cromwell's archetypal status in Yeats's philosophy of history.

Cromwell doubles for Yeats as an incarnation of colonial persecution and a "Great Demagogue" who exemplifies how the desire to "enslave and be enslaved" creates cycles of tyranny and epitomizes the leveling of social privilege, state coercion, and rule by "the mob." No one understood the state repression proposed by Spenser's *View*, Yeats writes, "till the Great Demagogue had come and turned the old house of the noble into 'the house of the Poor, the lonely house, the accursed house of Cromwell,'" because Cromwell, "another Cairbre Cat-Head" (a legendary usurper-king who revolted against ancient Irish nobility), "found his own head in Spenser's book, for Spenser, a king of the old race, carried a mirror which showed kings yet to come though but kings of the mob" (*EI* 376). He confides to Wellesley that the lyric, which is "about Oliver Cromwell who was the Lennin [*sic*] of his day . . . is very poignant because it was my own state watching romance & nobility disappear." Cromwell's abstract role in the gyring class dialectic subtending history (class trumps nationality in the genealogy connecting

Cairbre Cat-Head and Lenin) makes the lyric more detached as a philosophical poem at the same time as the Cromwellite setting makes it more partisan as a colloquial Irish song.

The first use of the refrain, abutting Ó'Rathaille's last line, dispels the overwhelming sense of dèja vu which can collapse the escalating debris of colonial violence into the name of Cromwell. Instead of voicing the reflex curse, the refrain nonchalantly dismisses the rehearsal of past grievances and immemorial fealties and reconstitutes the last line as a point of departure. The *so what?* gesture, very much in line with the "what matter!" riff of Yeats's late poetry, establishes a new expectation of contrapuntal deflation which is confounded by subsequent repetitions. The final refrain chants that there is indeed nothing left to say, so that the ensuing silence becomes a form of protest not unlike the self-gagging of Ó'Rathaille's rhetorical "No Help I'll Call." The refrain enacts the backward/onward hesitations of the Orphic gaze and at the same time cuts loose its narrative ties to preceding and succeeding stanzas to become *fol-de-rol* filler, "no longer the singer, but the song." Yeats opens book 3 of *A Vision* by decrying the cliché that all human life must pass and recalling, by contrast, a beautiful young girl who, thinking "herself alone, stood barefooted between sea and sand [and] sang with lifted head of the civilizations that there had come and gone, ending every verse with the cry: 'O Lord, let something remain'" (220). The reiterative drive of the refrain sings a "let something remain" tune even as the words query their use value.

Yeats was enormously gratified to learn that a gathering of Royal Irish academicians spontaneously sang "Cromwell" late one evening. Because the lyric can be sung, it evokes an aura of intimacy between the bardic Yeats persona and the coterie audiences that represent quasi-organic "world[s] that sing and listen" within the mass-mediated "world that reads and writes." The importance of these legitimating coterie audiences to the construction of "Yeats" can be observed in how Yeats orchestrated the dissemination of "Cromwell" through the following diverse channels: a limited Cuala broadside (no. 8, in August 1937) with a commissioned illustration of "a rambling peasant poet" by Maurice MacGonigal (i.e., a collector's item under the guise of a popular street ballad); a commissioned musical accompaniment by Edmund Dulac for broadcast on the BBC; a performance at a Royal Irish Academy banquet at which Fenian Dr. Patrick McCartan presented Yeats with an honorarium from an American testimonial committee and eulogized him as "a Fenian in practice"; the correspondence with Wellesley commiserating about the proto-Leninist; "A General Introduction"; and *New Poems* (1938).[85] Although the lyric has not been a readers' favorite, perhaps because of its compaction and unresolved ambiguities, it was (maybe for the same reason) a personal favorite of Yeats's, who remarks that " 'The Municipal Gallery Revisited' is perhaps the best poem I have written for some years, unless 'The Curse of Cromwell' is."[86]

Yeats's quotation of "The Curse of Cromwell" in "A General Introduction" (omitted from the *Essays and Introductions* version) is of particular interest because, though it is the only Yeatsian verse used to exemplify his poetics, he cites it for the purpose of self-censure. The opening stanza is quoted to illustrate how "the 'Irishry' have preserved their ancient 'deposit' through wars [of extermination]." It makes an appropriate exemplum, given that the lyric was composed out of the convergence between the Gaelic literary "deposit" and the Casement scandal triggering the collective memory "deposit" that manifests itself as a corrosive reflex hostility. "No people hate as we do in whom that past is always alive," Yeats declares, amplifying the latter sense of *deposit* before introducing the verse with a disclaimer: "there are moments when hatred poisons my life and I accuse myself of effeminacy because I have not given it adequate expression[;] it is not enough to have put it in the mouth of a rambling peasant poet." The dissatisfaction is at odds with an earlier assertion in the essay that "I can put my own thought . . . into the mouth of rambling poets . . . and the deeper my thought the more credible, the more peasant-like, are ballad singer and rambling poet," and with the decisive influence on Yeats's poetics of the formative discovery that "[Young Ireland poets] were not separated individual men; they spoke or tried to speak out of a people to a people; behind them stretched the generations" (516, 510–11). It also shows how the "irascible gesture" of recapitulating and letting go the arsenal of Yeatsian motifs does not break free from the language, gender, and class hierarchies in which he embeds Irish "satiric genius." Whether Yeats dislikes how ventriloquism through a peasant mouthpiece disavows the hatred as a personal passion or if he finds the mask of the aggrieved Gaelic poet emasculating, the problem behind the "effeminacy" censure would seem to lie in a perceived impassable divide (or Pale) between the rambling poet persona and the Yeats persona. After applying the "eater and eaten" simile to the predicament of being unable to get "outside" either the English language through which "everything [he] loves has come" or insatiable atavistic hatred, he concludes: "This is Irish hatred and solitude, the hatred of human life that made Swift write *Gulliver* and the epitaph upon his tomb, that can still make us wag between extremes and doubt our sanity."

Although Swift supported Gaelic linguicide, opining that "their language . . . might easily be abolished, and become a dead one in half an age, with little expence, and less trouble,"[87] he sided implacably with "*we* [Irishry] in whom that past [of persecution] is always alive." The detached "solitude" from the Irishry which gave Swift analytic purchase on his subject matter paradoxically seems to have aggravated rather than defused his ire, and Yeats represents him as even more consumed and possessed by the memory of persecution than the Irishry on whose behalf he inveighs. Swift's fraught partisanship illustrates how contact with the dominated "other" culture can nurture indignation at English dominance even among those who are strongly English-identified, so that the counter-memory of antipathy to colonialism vies with the colonizer's presumptive right to dominate. Yeats laces Swiftian *saeva indignatio* and O'Rathaille's "concentrated passion" into his own power to admonish from the grave as he resolves to "intensify [his] hatred" in the "Whither?" peroration in order to draw closer the "counter-Renaissance" to the antipathetic "modern heterogeneity" observable from O'Connell Bridge and in the works of "the young English poets [who] reject dream and personal emotion" and whose "verse kills the folk ghost" (GI 526).

According to Yeats's Vichean "first principle," the poet makes "the common and its befitting language," and in the making the poet-qua-phantasmagoric Poet is formed to produce the Yeats figure that "has been reborn as an idea, something intended, complete" across the body of the poetry as an intelligible microcosm of his linguistic milieu. The lovelorn dreamer, towering senator, and denouncing and remembering Jeremiah who constitutes the phantasmagoric Yeats corresponds on a concrete plane with the verifiable lived life of W. B. Yeats. On a subliminal, abstract plane it adumbrates the beginning, middle, and end of a Vichean cycle of a culture and of the life of the Poet which is "more type than man, more passion than type" (GI 511, 509). The characteristic use of rhythm, intonation, and diction and the figurative and prosodic bent that composes the textual entity we denominate "Yeatsian" moves perceptibly from the enchanting romance in the early work through the vigorous discursiveness of the middle period to the disenchantment of the anarchic curse. As he wrought his style in the contact zone between English and Gaelic, written and oral, and elitist and popular literary traditions, Yeats collaborated closely with several influential translators. Even as he maintained a resolute caste difference from Gaelic, he left his imprint on the early Revivalists' infusion of the demotic with "ancient idealism" and, a generation later, on post-Independence writers' iconoclastic use of translation to satirize state officialdom and censorship. The national language became the antithetical lodestone of his literary vernacular as he strove to reconstruct the fabulous origins of the Irish nation, to cultivate a Homeric "folk" imagination, to harness the vituperative edge of the Irishry's plaint, and to become a representative national bard by engaging in colloquy with the Irish public. The evolution of his style can be tracked in relation to the changing symbolic status of Gaelic in the national imaginary brought about by the de-Anglicization movement and its aftermath. The impression of "something intended, complete" in the sweep of the Yeatsian oeuvre derives in no small part from how the manifold retranslations of the matter of Ireland into the "Collected Yeats" recapitulate the history of Gaelic from the early mythological cycles to its decline in the eighteenth and nineteenth centuries. The "haunted English" of Yeats's literary vernacular is animated by "the ghostly voice" of the subjugated national language whose revivification coincided with his career.

Hugh MacDiarmid and Marianne Moore's identities as "Celtic" poets were profoundly influenced by Yeats, the collective achievement of Irish modernists, and the far-reaching political impact of Irish cultural nationalism. Like several other commentators, Marianne Moore was impressed by Yeats's extraordinary prospective grasp of the cohering arc of the "Collected Yeats": "He has been from the first a chooser and a hoarder remaking and reshaping without fatigue even the memories he had taken from his hoard and made into poems[;] [y]et always willing to wait until his imagination is ready."[88] Her identification of Yeats as a fellow "chooser and hoarder" and the famous characterization of her own poetics as a "hybrid method of composition" highlights the salient common feature of the respective haunted Englishes of the three poets, the manner in which they fashion a literary vernacular out of the "intentional hybridization" of their colonial mother tongue.[89] "Talk to me of originality and I will turn on you in rage," Yeats thunders in "A General Introduction" (GI 522), and MacDiarmid and Moore, part successors and part peers to the senior poet, likewise eschew notions of originality for a poetics that recombines, refashions, and realigns the cultural archives, or "hoards," they find around them. Whereas for Yeats the eater-and-eaten process involves chewing the cud of personal and folk memory into an oeuvre that "seem[s] traditional," MacDiarmid and Moore embrace the particularism, topicality, and incorrigible plurality of the "modern heterogeneity" that so appalls him.

CHAPTER THREE

Hugh MacDiarmid's Poetics of Caricature

In 1977 a BBC interviewer asked Hugh MacDiarmid, then the grand old man of Scottish letters, what difference it would have made had he been born ten miles farther south and hence an Englishman. Growing up in Langholm had imbued him with "a border spirit where differences are accentuated by proximity," Mac-Diarmid replied, "the frontier feeling" that made him a fervent Scottish national-ist and an unremitting vanguardist.[1] The "frontier feeling" is evident in Mac-Diarmid's nationalism, which is defiantly bellicose toward the powerful English neighbor, and in his eagerness to experiment, to push the boundaries of con-sciousness, and to innovate restlessly, ceaselessly. When he describes his life in his autobiography, *Lucky Poet: A Self-Study in Literature and Political Ideas* (1972), "as an adventure, or series of adventures, in the exploration of the mystery of Scotland's self-suppression," he is as dogmatic about the diagnosis of thwarted national potential as he is willing to vary the series of forays made to comprehend the pathology (381).

One of the marvels of literary modernism's annus mirabilis, 1922, was the genesis of "Hugh MacDiarmid" out of an encounter between Christopher Mur-ray Grieve (1892–1978), a minor Scottish poet in English, and a Scottish ety-mological dictionary. Grieve had turned to the dictionary in order to lampoon what he saw as the mindless sentimentality of the "Kailyard" verse found in the "poetry corner" of the provincial newspapers. G. Gregory Smith's *Scottish Litera-ture: Character and Influence* (1919), a work that exerted considerable influence on Grieve's poetics, satirizes Kailyard poets as poor imitators of Robert Burns, "poeti-cules who waddle in good duck fashion through *Jamieson's* [*Etymological Diction-*

ary of the Scottish Language, 1808], snapping up fat expressive words with nice little bits of green idiom for flavoring" (138–39). In the course of caricaturing a literary praxis he despised, however, Grieve discovered a nascent literary vernacular in the play of "differences accentuated by proximity" between the Scots headwords and their English glosses. The process whereby the modernist makar Hugh MacDiarmid "was reborn as an idea, something intended, complete" as a result of Christopher Murray Grieve ingesting the national vocabulary from *A* to *Z* sketches a comically accelerated version of the laborious Vichean quest for "the common and its befitting language" encapsulated by Yeats's "eater-and-eaten" trope. He had cannibalized the Scots dictionary-dredging procedure in a spirit of parody, only to be bitten by the bug and to undergo what he would later characterize as "a religious conversion."[2] He swiftly patented his new voice with a "de-Anglicizing," ultra-Scottish, authorial signature: "an immediate realization of th[e] ultimate reach of the implications of my experiment made me adopt, when I began writing Scots poetry, the Gaelic pseudonym of Hugh MacDiarmid" (*LP* 6). "Synthetic Scots," the stuff out of which "MacDiarmid" is forged, is composed in an ambiguous zone of inter- and intra-lingual translation between Scots and English, under the remote influence of Scotland's third language, Gaelic. Grieve/ MacDiarmid had expected to write parodic verse but was surprised by "poetry." The conversion experience of unearthing a plastic literary medium from an antiquarian tome of Scotticisms, and the literary accomplishment of the MacDiarmid persona's first lyric, "The Watergaw," convinced the poet that the vernacular could be renovated as an international literary language.

The story of the making of MacDiarmid tends toward caricature, but this may be apt for a poet whose poetics develop out of a memory, on conscious and unconscious levels, of the genre of caricature. The conscious and unconscious "memory" of the genre pertains to two distinct but related forms of caricature, a hackneyed notion of Scottish "national character" which shapes Scotland's image at home and abroad and the exaggerated othering of a Scottish way of speaking which sets the vernacular apart as a residual "dialect," a hodgepodge of "Scotticisms." The formation of the stereotypic Scot and the profiling of Scots as "dialect" can be tracked to the anomalous formation of Scottish civil society within the British state after the Act of Union (1707), which made the Scottish people almost, but not quite, a European nation and almost, but not quite, an equal partner in empire.

The title of MacDiarmid's classic, *A Drunk Man Looks at the Thistle* (1926), conjures an immediate image of the stereotypic Scot: one readily clothes the drunk man in tartan regalia and assumes that he drinks whiskey, has strongly accented, idiomatic speech patterns, and is named "MacSomebody." The rustic thistle evokes a panoramic Highland setting whose romantic aura is augmented by the distant echo of bagpipe music. The drone of the bagpipes indirectly cites a diehard clannishness and vestigial messianic Jacobitism; one might even surmise that the drunk man is a nationalist. The international legibility of the stereotypic Scot is shown by the near-reflex ease with which associated ethnic signifiers (*tartan, bagpipes,* and *clannish*) supplement the "drunk" and "thistle" cues to complete a fixed yet phantasmatic image in line with a well-known preexistent schema. At one stage in his nocturnal Odyssey the "fou" (drunk) speaker of *A Drunk Man* likens the magnetic sway of stereotype to a "siren sang" whose insistent refrain persecutes him:

> But what's the voice
> That sings in me noo?
> —A'e hauf o' me tellin'
> The tither it's fou!
>
> It's the voice o' the Sooth
> That's held owre lang
> My Viking North
> Wi' its siren sang. . . .

Fier comme un Ecossais.   (2296–2305)[3]

The words of the formulaic refrain remain the same, but the manifold historic and geopolitical resonances they have accreted through repetition serve to explicate the forces of ambivalence which hold the stereotype in place and perpetuate its global currency.[4] "Fier comme un Ecossais" (Proud as a Scotsman) is the voice of Europe singing the contrast between the aloof hard drinkers of the "the North" and the sensual wine drinkers of "the South"; the voice of "the Anglo" upbraiding "the Scot"; and, as will later become apparent, the voice of a divided self disavowing the uncanny "tither hauf" of "the canny Scot."

The obsessive replay of the refrain suggests that the speaker's self-image is branded by a genre he experiences as name-calling. The incantatory voice bears a residue of slanging rituals, connecting *Fier comme un Ecossais* with the popular blazon, a speech genre that Mikhail Bakhtin defines as epithets of praise or more usually denigration for "the best" attribute of a nationality, city, or group which merge praise-abuse in an indissoluble unity.[5] The congealing of such popular expressions of neighborly hostility into commonplaces furnished the basis for Diderot and D'Alembert's *Encyclopédie* entry under *caractère des nations:* "National

characters are a certain habitual predisposition of the soul, which is more preva-
lent in one nation than in others . . . it is a sort of proverb to say: airy as a
Frenchman, jealous as an Italian, serious as a Spaniard, wicked as an Englishman, proud as a Scot, drunk as a German, lazy as an Irishman, deceitful as a
Greek."[6] David Hume's essay "Of National Characters" (1748) discusses the cool
North/warm South bipolarity, but "the proud Scot" is neither given a separate
mention nor implicitly subsumed under the "English" ("the least national character") category of his typology.[7] The elision of his own national type from the
international lineup may have been more than authorial tact on the part of Hume,
whose self-Anglicizing makeover was so ardent that it was said he would confess
not his sins but his Scotticisms on his deathbed.

   During the nineteenth century, under the influence of J. H. Herder and of
comparative philology, many nation-states articulated an idealized "national character" through literature. The common European pattern was distorted in Scotland, Tom Nairn argues in *The Break-Up of Britain* (1977), because material self-
interest encouraged the bourgeoisie and intelligentsia to neutralize or suppress
protonationalist separatism, leading to the émigré/Kailyard split in Scottish intellectual life.[8] An émigré intelligentsia migrated, literally and/or psychologically, to
a London-centered transnational republic of letters, and, according to Nairn, the
Kailyarders developed a "stunted, caricatural . . . cultural sub-nationalism" of
tartanry, which, "uncultivated by 'national' experience in the usual sense, [became]
curiously fixed or fossilized . . . to the point of forming a huge, virtually self-
contained universe of kitsch" (163). Scotland's imageme, the ambivalent and
unfalsifiable polarity within which a given national character is held to move,[9] is a
compromise formation, a symptom of a contradictory desire to enjoy the comforts
of empire without relinquishing those of nationality. The stereotype is flagrantly
over the top, for the fabricated nature of tartanry betokens a contrived refashioning
of authenticity. The telltale features of the national imageme have a disavowed
provenance in *Gàidhealtachd* culture that hark back to the complex influence of
"Ossianic" translations on the Enlightenment reconfiguration of the Pale/Fringe.

   The influence on Scotland's self-image of its ambiguous status as something
more than a province and less than a nation-state can be seen in how *Jamieson's
Etymological Dictionary of the Scottish Language* profiles Scots "as somehow less
than a language but more than a dialect" (*halbsprache*).[10] Roy Harris writes that
monolingual dictionaries met the need to codify national vernaculars as self-
sufficient *langues*, independently of Latin, in a proto-Saussurean procedure that
deploys words to define other words in the same language systematically in such a
way that no word is left undefined. National lexicons are symbols of linguistic

autonomy to other nations and function domestically to regulate and "fix" the variable spoken vernacular in line with the scriptist codes of alphabetical ordering, standardized orthography and pronunciation guides, and the use of literary citations. Harris contends that such "endemic scriptism," manifested by the commonsense notion that "there is no such word" unless it can be found in a dictionary, radically altered linguistic psychology. The "existence" of words no longer depends upon their being current but on their being "admitted" to the self-enclosed system by the unchallengeable impersonality of the lexicographer (130–33). The monolingual English dictionary after Dr. Johnson delineates a Pale between the English "of the most elegant speakers who deviate least from the written words" and the "fugitive cant" of Creole Englishes, dialect, and slang.

In 1781, when Rev. John Witherspoon coined *Americanism* as "exactly similar in its formation and signification to the word Scotticism,"[11] American English and Scots were deemed equally provincial, but their subsequent fortunes are anticipated and reinforced by the contrastive lexicographical approaches adopted in *Jamieson's* and Noah Webster's *American Dictionary of the English Language* (1828). Webster combines American lexis, orthography, and key redefinitions ("in this country the distinction between *constitution* and *law* requires a different definition," the preface declares) with a general reference function and confidently predicts that an ever-expanding catalogue of U.S. literary citations will enhance the declared ascendancy of U.S. English. The title of *Jamieson's* asserts that Scots is a *language,* but by confining itself to a peculiarly Scots vocabulary and mediating the "local" Scots idiom through the explanatory apparatus of "universal" standard English, it codifies the vernacular as ancillary. In contrast to the default mode of impersonal, up-to-date, informational English, the Scots headwords are profiled as colorful, quaint, arcane, vanishing "fossil-poetry," and as substandard or deviant idioms. The documented etymologies linking Scots with other languages independently of English (though Jamieson repeatedly downplays ties with Gaelic)[12] and the sheer heft of literary citations in the multi-volume opus, however, legitimize the "existence" of Scots as "something more than a dialect." Scotland's relative privilege vis-à-vis the undocumented condition of most Creole Englishes can be surmised from Tom Paulin's impassioned plea for a Hiberno-English dictionary to redress "the enormous cultural impoverishment [of] a living, but fragmented speech, untold numbers of *homeless* words, and an uncertain or *derelict* prose [style]."[13] Webster assumes his work is the seed of future U.S. lexicography, but Jamieson's bid "to rescue the language of the country from oblivion by compiling a Dictionary of it" treats Scots as a residual language whose future obsolescence merits compensatory preservation in an archive (preface, vi).

By adapting the Johnsonian "elegant speaker" precept to advance a U.S. hegemony of plain spelling (which was inculcated domestically through the homogenizing influence of *Webster's Spelling-Book* on American styles of enunciation), Webster helped to reconfigure the Pale in the United States along distinctively American lines. Jamieson's use of English orthography to script Scottish habits of pronunciation has the contrary effect of reinforcing the hegemony of the English Pale because it profiles Scots as sounding unlike the idiom of "the most elegant speakers" by placing undue emphasis on phonological traits that ring strangely to English or Anglicized ears. The centrality of scriptism and print technology to the profiling of Scots as aberrant can be illustrated by way of reference to the figurative derivation of the term *stereotype* from a typographic technique "consisting in transforming the pages constituted of mobile type into a unique slate of cast iron" which was used to publish almost all books between 1850 and 1900.[14] Stereotyping freezes an endless potential for the disassembly and reassembly of print signifiers into a fixed and reusable mould. Webster treats standard English as a contingent mode of extracting constants from variables and reshuffles them into a reusable American standard, but Jamieson codifies Scots in terms of deviation from an inflexible and absolute standard and, by so doing, seals the image of the vernacular as anomalous, anachronistic, and falling short of received norms.

The Pale/Fringe diglossia that makes English the "high" vernacular of civic life and Scots the "low" vernacular of family and provincial life creates the unequal clout of Scots and English speakers in everyday social interactions. In such encounters the "differences accentuated by proximity" between the mutually intelligible vernaculars are routinely exaggerated into a high-profile caricatural image of deviant Scots versus a low-profile image of the Pale's received norms. Memories of the Pale/Fringe linguicism that stratifies the two vernaculars into contrastive genres—a neutral English *language* and deviant Scots *dialect* consisting primarily of *Scotticisms*—activate the tendentious othering of phonological and idiomatic differentiae which causes Scots speech to resound like a distorted parody of itself. The reconditioning of Scotland's linguistic habitus was popularly regarded as "improvement," but because the proscription of Scots from the hub of civic life and the inhibition of Scottish styles of articulation and spontaneity of speech required repressing the social body, it often *felt* coercive. In this linguistic milieu the symbolic status of the "Scotticism," an utterance that *sounds* distinctly and distinctively Scottish to one's own or others' ears, becomes fraught with ambivalence. Associated with loss of public face and innermost expressivity, Scotticisms are the object of overt condescension and covert pride. Like Irish bulls, Scotticisms come into existence as a genre when the auditor tags them as such, but unlike bulls, whose solecisms supposedly go unnoticed by their speakers, the auditor of the Scotticism is often also the speaker of it. Scotticisms exemplify Mikhail Bakhtin's theory that "speech genres are the drive belts from the history of society to the history of language" because they disclose the ambivalent slippage between Anglo mask and unreconstructed Scottish ethnicity which delineates the contours of the Pale/Fringe in Scotland.[15]

The ambivalent status of the Scotticism accounts for the apparently contradictory stance taken by Grieve before his conversion in the epistolary "guerrilla warfare" he waged in the *Aberdeen Free Press* in December 1921 against the Doric revival proposed by the recently established Vernacular Circle of the London Burns Club (*Letters* 69). Grieve opines that a vernacular revival would "cloak mental paucity with a trivial and ridiculously over-valued pawkiness!—and bolster up [the peasant's] instinctive suspicion of cleverness and culture" which keeps Scotland in "an apparently permanent literary infancy," dwarfed by "the swaddling clothes of the Doric." It would elevate the collective wallowing in the national imageme that takes place at annual Burns Suppers into a populist orthodoxy that would stifle all serious intellectual, literary, and artistic endeavor. Lest anyone mistake his opposition for cultural cringe or intellectual snobbery, Grieve stresses that he desires the preservation of the Doric and "love[s] it as jealously [as anybody]" and that "[he] was brought up in a braid Scots atmosphere [and his] accent could be cut with a knife" (754). Almost in the same breath, Grieve portrays vaunting the vernacular as a hokey impersonation of stock Scottish "character" and cites his Scots accent and speaking style as proof of personal authenticity.

Responding to the Revivalist argument that Anglicizing makeovers were "mere caste mimicry," Grieve asks if there is anything to choose between going "Anglo" and going "Scot" "as far as mob-psychology goes, other than the peculiar virtue die-hards may attach to minority manifestations?" (*Letters* 753). The rhetorical question arranges the repertoire of available articulatory styles in Scotland between "talking like a book" in the etiolated style of the Pale and "talking like a character from a book" in the colorful (because ethnicized) hyperbole of the national imageme. Convinced that the latter route was a "cul-de-sac" that would render a susceptible public "practically idea-proof," Grieve took up the cudgels against the specter of "a Doric boom just now" by parodying the stock-in-trade of the Kailyard poeticule (756, 755).

The first published poem in Scots by "Hugh M'Diarmid," "The Watergaw," appeared with an appended glossary in October 1922 in the third issue of the *Scottish Chapbook*. A month earlier he had presented and commented on the lyric in a series on "Scottish Books and Bookmen" in which it was attributed to an anonymous "friend."[16] The prevarication reveals Grieve's ambivalence about being publicly identified with Doric revivalism and his assumption that some mediating introduction is necessary to bring the reader to the text:

Ae weet forenicht i' the yow-trummle
I saw yon antrin thing,
A watergaw wi' its chitterin' licht
Ayont the on-ding;
An' I thocht o' the last wild look ye gied
Afore ye deed!

There was nae reek i' the laverock's hoose
That nicht—and nane i' mine;
But I thocht o' that foolish licht
Ever sin' syne;
An I think that mebbe at last I ken
What your look meant then.[17]

Reading is slowed by the recondite vocabulary, some of which would be opaque even to Scottish readers. A hesitant first reading allows readers to adjust to the inflections of emphasis created by Scots orthography and "transitives" (William James's composite term for grammatical elements such as conjunctions and prepositions which order syntactic relations) and to seek contextual clues to the meanings of abstruse diction (James's "substantives"). This hesitancy prompts a phonic reading strategy, so that even a reader entirely unused to spoken Scots becomes sufficiently acclimated to guess that "ye gied" and "ye deed" mean "you gave" and "you died" and to understand that the arcane imagery evokes memories of "the last wild look ye gied/Afore ye deed!" The "wild" last look suggests a sudden access of energy or insight and heightens the mystery of the estranging vocabulary. The glossary allows one to reread the lyric translingually, and the play between substantives (the "hard words" in Scots and their explications in English) recapitulates the lexicographic wordplay out of which the lyric was composed. The *antrin*, or rare sight, of a *watergaw*, an indistinct or gap-toothed rainbow, is glimpsed through the *on-ding*, an onset of heavy rain, during *the yow-trummle*, a cold spell after the July sheepshearing, when ewes tremble.[18] The unpretentious sound and meterological precision of *watergaw* revitalizes an emblematic cliché in English. *Yow-trummle* evokes a graphic image of shorn sheep shivering in the rain which induces an empathetic feeling of nakedness, and at the same time, because it remains grounded in the mundane seasonal-work routines of the sheep farmer, it conveys a sense of ordinariness edged with metaphysical resonance.

The "novel" diction inaugurates a translational play between *rainbow/watergaw* and *autumn/yow-trummle* which draws attention to lacunae in English. Before his conversion Grieve might have perceived such translingual interaction in terms of the ancillary language supplementing the dominant one along the lines of Kailyard poets spicing up English with fresh local idioms. In the course of subsequent reflection upon what distinguishes "Synthetic Scots" from "dialect," however, he appears to have arrived at an incipient sense of the "novelistic" and polyphonic word as it is theorized by Bakhtin when he remarks in February 1922 on "a moral resemblance" between "the prodigious, uncontrollable, [outpouring that is] utterly at variance with conventional morality" in Joyce's *Ulysses* and the "*vis comica* that has not yet been liberated [but is] bound by deseutude and misappreciation in the recesses of the Doric" between the covers of a dictionary (*TR* 129). Synthetic Scots, then, is neither the stylization of Scots from the normative perspective of English that produces "dialect verse" nor in any straightforward sense a macaronic blend of the two vernaculars but, rather, a Bakhtinian "double-voiced," "double accented," and "double-languaged" hybridization.[19] Each vernacular refracts the foreignness of the other from the outside and at the same time subjects their interpenetration (an outcome of the "organic" hybridization that occurs between vernaculars) to the ironic pressure of "intentional" hybridization. The dialogism of Synthetic Scots pertains not only to the cultural difference from the fleecy sheep of English pastoral flagged by *yow-trummle* but also to how the hierarchical struggle between an accent-free, context-free, and explicit usage of vehicular English and an accented, context-bound, and implicit usage of vernacular Scots is waged within and through the poetic utterance itself.

The contrast between the rotund sound and austere sense of *yow-trummle*, which encapsulates the semantic burden of *shorn*, also engages the history of auditory discrimination against Scots-speakers that shapes the reception of "double-accented" Synthetic Scots. The rusticism contains two telltale phonological Scotticisms, the failure to diphthongize the "pure labial sounds /ju/ and /ʌu/" in *yow* (ewe) and the "consonantal cluster simplification" of the suppressed *b* in *trummle* (tremble) which contributes to an overall impression of "fewer harsh combinations of consonants" in Scots.[20] The former "Scotticism" is one among several related manifestations of Scotland and Northumbria's divergence from Southern English after the Great Vowel Shift, which lengthened such vowel sounds as those in *ae*, *nae*, and *nane* (one, no and none); *gie* (give); *hoose* (house) and *puir auld*

Scotland. "The Watergaw" gives prominence to the voiceless velar fricative /x/ (as in *loch*) in *licht, nicht,* and *thocht,* which, together with the rolled alveolar /r/, is a shibboleth of Scottishness.[21] When combined with another instance of consonant effacement, the substitution of a glottal stop in *wi'* (with; *wi'oot,* without) and *i* (in), the assonantal /x/ phoneme keys the sonic texture of the lyric to the short *i* sound that is anchored in the *licht* of the third line in both (*abcbdd*) stanzas.

The typographic scripting of Scots pronunciation is obtrusive, but its phon-aesthesic texture creates a barely audible hum of background down-home talk that draws the reader into the "braid Scots atmosphere" that had surrounded Grieve as a child. The attunement to the tonal modulations of Scots speech is reinforced by participation in the deictic frame of reference established by the speaker. Scots retains a "three term deictic system, in which *this* refers to objects close to the speaker, *that* to objects further away, and *thon, yon* to objects even further away, or 'over there.' "[22] "Yon" watergaw is beheld from a relational dis-tance that is travestied by "this" or "that" watergaw. *Yon* points to *ayont* in the euphonious "yow . . . yon . . . ayont" murmur and in the noncoercive assertion of thereness in "yon antrin *thing*" (over there).[23] The expressiveness of "yon antrin thing" illustrates William James's point in "The Streams of Thought" that perva-sive overreliance on substantives (epitomized by the error "of supposing that where there is *no* name no entity can exist") and concomitant inability "to say a feeling of *and,* a feeling of *if,* a feeling of *but,* and a feeling of *by,* quite as readily as we say a feeling of *blue* or a feeling of *cold*" reduces transitives to functional use alone and deprives our thinking of those shadings of relation which inhere "in an adverbial phrase, syntactic form, or inflection of voice."[24] Getting the feel of the speaker's "ayont" and "ever sin' syne" orients the reader in relation to the water-gaw's gawky "foolish licht" in the wintry pall of impending July rain. The experi-ence of not knowing "which to prefer/the beauty of inflections/or the beauty of innuendoes" helps to induce the synaesthesic shudder that "kens" the look of "yon watergaw i' the yow-trummle."[25] An intuitive apprehension of the internal character of Scots is caught from the nuances of "the vague" as much as from the grammar of substantives, in those subliminal dimensions of language use—rhythm, rhyme, meter, tone, inflection, figurative mode, way of situating oneself as a speaker—which are purposively shaped by poetry. The binding effect of the lyric's aural texture, which creates an inchoate yet cohesive impression of an underlying prosodic unity, gels the reader's sense of what Bakhtin in *The Dialogic Imagination* calls "the specific linguistic habitus" of a language. Because the habitus of one's own language or idiom can only be objectified in the light of another one, Bakhtin writes that what stands out for the creating literary consciousness is that side of an idiom *"that pertains to its world view . . . [and makes it]* ultimately untranslateable . . . *the style of the language as a totality* (62).

The process of getting a feel for the habitus of the vernacular as a whole is disrupted by the contrary alienating effect of the orthography, which sets the lyric apart as dialect verse. George Lang writes that a "sense of contingency pervades the reading of creoles, since none has as yet achieved, nor in the short or medium run is likely to attain, a stable enough written form to escape occasional *hetero-graphic* effects, the sensation that a parallel phantom text haunts the original, if only by way of the alternative spellings" (109). At least three phantom orthographies ghost "The Watergaw": the "correct" mode of standard English; competing regional variants, such as the northern pronunciation of *ane* as *een;* and the absence of a standard national orthography for Scots. The pull of standard English is so strong that it is no exaggeration to say that the first of these phantom orthographies leaves a ghostly trail of correctional red ink on the page, circling dropped fricatives with apostrophes and underscoring deviations from Received Pronunciation with nonstandard spellings. A reader of "The Watergaw" who mentally corrects the orthography and feels a sense of oppression while so doing experiences a reactivated generic memory of "dialect" and "Scotticism" in the ambivalent tug between the habitus of the Pale and the desire to appreciate "the style [of Scots] in its totality" without regard to the Pale. The physicality of the memory is important, not least because the conscious suppression of the schooled reflex illuminates the difference between the general meaning of *linguistic habitus* (the physical makeup and demeanor of a language as a translator might perceive it) and Pierre Bourdieu's restricted definition of *habitus* as the set of dispositions inculcated by overt and covert social conditioning which forms the basis of my definition of the *Pale.* By attempting to convey the habitus of Scots as it might be without the gravitational pull of the Pale through the scriptist codes of the Pale, "The Watergaw" represents how the habitus of the Pale both does and does not contain the habitus of Scots. The strongest pull against containment comes from the need to convey the distinctive sound of Scots, since it seems counterfactual when writing Scots to maintain the illusory "accent-free" effect of the Pale. The transliteration of a Scottish articulatory style into a modified English orthography reinscribes the containment, however, by transposing the intimate conviviality of the spoken vernacular into a specimen of reported idiomatic "dialect."

The speaker of "The Watergaw" narrates how an evocative object, "yon water-gaw i' the yow-trummle," stirs up an unresolved preoccupation (the meaning of the absent addressee's dying look), which he mulls over and in some sense re-solves by means of the imagistic cluster that brought it to consciousness. A later poem, "Kinship," confirms the disavowed autobiographical basis of the lyric.[26] His father had looked intensely at a photograph of his two sons shortly before he died, then-sixteen-year-old Grieve was told, and years later the burden of this speculative parting look could be worked through by way of "yon watergaw." One might surmise that the attenuated covenantal overtones of *rainbow* in *watergaw* afforded Grieve emotional distance from his father's devout Presbyterianism while connecting them by way of their home vernacular, but this is to overrationalize a necessarily obscure subconscious process. The experience convinced MacDiarmid that an imagistic verbal cluster or a "certain Slant of light" (to cite a corroborative lyric on the theme, Emily Dickinson's poem 258) could induce the self-altering bodily cognition that leaves "no scar / But internal difference, / where the Meanings, are—."

The insight informs MacDiarmid's argument in "Braid Scots and the Sense of Smell" (1923) that "the amazing difference in effect upon us when exactly the same thing is said in two different dialects . . . is a question not of logical but of vital values." Unlike the "moral censorship" of English, "amoral" braid Scots can tap into the synaesthesic fusion that occurs on an unconscious level when visual and auditory percepts "become, in ways which there is no terminology to describe, olfactory too," and hence it does not matter if "Braid Scots [is] only a dialect of English" because "we [can] produce physical-spiritual effects by employing Braid Scots which we cannot encompass through standard English."[27] In "Music—Braid Scots Suggestions" (1923) MacDiarmid writes that the words *Crune, Deedle, Lilt,* and *Gell,* indicate "a Scottish scale of sound-values and physico-psychical effects completely at variance with those of England" which can be reactivated through experiment with "the essence of deedling" (*RT* 88–89). For MacDiarmid braid Scots is more "vital" and intensively synthetic at a prelinguistic level than the dominant English of his everyday life because it cathects with the "unthought known" of the receptive unconscious to elaborate the "psychic genera" around which aesthetic form nucleates.[28] The appellation *synthetic* refers not only to how Synthetic Scots is an artificially "made" vernacular, a combinatorial synthesis of disparate regional and historic strata of Scots culled from primarily print sources rather than a naturalistic representation of a vernacular as it is purportedly spoken.[29] It also refers to the plasticity of a poiesis that allows the poet to elude the subjugation of the Pale by facilitating the synthesis of "vital" expressive gestalts.

When Grieve mimicked Kailyard praxis, he presumably proceeded by loading his parodic verse with those traits that are distinctly and distinctively Scottish and which make Scots stand out in marked contrast to standard English.[30] The tendentious motive was apparently superseded when the improvisatory compositional procedure of caricature, "to doodle and watch what happens," began to form the poetry that confounded his mainstream prejudices about the limited literary range of Scots dialect. E. H. Gombrich writes that graphic caricaturists start from the generic norm and systematically vary the configuration of cues by loading (Ital. *caricatura,* act of loading) component parts and using their personal instinctive reactions to the expressive gestalts that result as a basis for further experiment.[31] Although he underwent an attitudinal sea change, the subsequent development of MacDiarmid's poetics shows that he preserved the caricaturist's procedure, "to doodle and deedle and observe what happens." His freeform method of verbal doodling and deedling connected him with the Mallarméan touchstone that poetry is "not an idea gradually shaping itself in words, but deriving entirely from words" and enabled him to treat the entire range of Scots and English vocabulary as open to endless reordering and continuous variation instead of automatically subordinate to the dictates of the Pale (*LP* xxiii). Caricature no longer serves solely as a measure of how the odds are loaded against dialect but has "de-Anglicizing" potential for loosening and outwitting the procrustean grip of standard English.

MacDiarmid did not refer to his synthetic poiesis as caricatural except implicitly, such as when he describes Synthetic Scots as "aggrandized Scots" or stresses the anti-decorous bias of art: "literature is the written expression of revolt against accepted things."[32] In his de-Anglicizing polemic "A Theory of Scots Letters" (1923), MacDiarmid draws on G. Gregory Smith's concept of "Caledonian Antisyzygies" to theorize the "disinterested" potential of a freeform caricatural poiesis.[33] Smith coined *Caledonian antisyzygy* to designate the commingling of two contrary moods in Scottish literature, a meticulous observation and "zest for handling a multitude of details" which sometimes borders on "a maudlin affection for the commonplace" and a "whimsical delight" in the fantastic, "the airier pleasure to be found in the confusion of the senses [and] in the fun of things thrown topsy-turvy" (4, 5, 19). Smith introduces the neologism with playful archness, commenting in a parenthetical aside that either Sir Thomas Browne or Sir Thomas Urquhart (the translator of *Gargantua and Pantagruel*) might have so named the trait,[34] but it is evident that disjunctive-conjunctions, "almost a zig-zag of contradictions," encapsulate the "character" of Scottish literature for him (4). Caledonian antisyzygies show how "the Scot, in that medieval fashion which takes all things as granted, is at his ease in both 'rooms of life,' and turns to fun, and even profanity, with no misgivings" (35). Smith regrets that much literary evidence of the Scottish "delight in the grotesque and uncanny" has been lost through the "decorous" bias of canon formation, and he detects a generic kinship between an aesthetics that appreciates "the absolute propriety of a gargoyle's grinning at the elbow of a kneeling saint" and the uncanny doubles of Robert Louis Stevenson (23, 35).

Caledonian antisyzygies are a riposte to the Victorian dichotomy of Celtic whimsy and Anglo-Saxon despotism-of-fact, and Smith takes issue with Arnold's ethnological assumption that any trait that is at variance with England's self-image "may, must, and does come from an outside source; given a spiritual lightness and vivacity in the dull, heavy, practical genius of Teutonic England, it must have come from the Celts" (29). "We have grown suspicious" of ethnic stereotyping that "separate[s] the contrasts in character [by placing] the obverse of a coin in one bag and the reverse in another," Smith remarks, and he posits instead a dualistic notion of identity, drawn from Scottish literature, in which "the real and fantastic . . . invade [one another] without warning" like the "polar twins" of Robert Louis Stevenson's *Dr. Jekyll and Mr. Hyde* (29, 33, 20). Like Bakhtin, Smith intuits a similarity between the discrowning doubles of the medieval grotesque and the anguished doppelgänger narratives of the Romantic grotesque. He connects a "constitutional liking for contrasts," "contrariety," and enjoyment of "things thrown topsy-turvy" to the Scottish "fine sense of the value of provocation" and "the sheer exhilaration of conflict" manifest in "the old fun of *flyting*" (19–20, 33). An antisyzygical attitude is antagonistic and dialogical in a Bakhtinian sense; it favors the witty rejoinder and cheerful insult over pious flattery. Smith, like Grieve before his conversion, discerns no antisyzygical potential, however, in the literary antiquarianism and dictionary-dredging of the Kailyard "poeticules." It took the galvanic influence of the 1922 publication of *The Waste Land* and *Ulysses* to open Grieve's eyes to the "moral resemblance" between these groundbreaking classics and the untapped "*vis comica*" of Synthetic Scots contained in Jamieson's. The avant-garde texts filled him with confidence that the antisyzygical potential of Synthetic Scots "would be no less prodigious, uncontrollable, and utterly at variance with conventional morality than was Joyce's tremendous outpouring" (*TR* 129).

Through the lens of a Joycean *vis comica* the antisyzygical play among "differences accentuated by proximity" in the lexicon—the abrupt shifts of register between the "poetic" Scots entries and their "prosaic" English glosses; the arbitrary contiguities imposed by alphabetical order; the disjunctive anachronism of diachronic series of changing connotations; and the artificial synchrony created by containing the vocabulary within a single opus—becomes a vast resource for polyphonic deedling and doodling. The dizzying zigzag of clashing registers liberates Scots from the "enemy" who cries, "Hands off our fine old Scottish tongue" and promotes "a mere renewed vogue of the letter" while remaining blind to the fact that " 'the letter killeth but the spirit giveth life' " (*TR* 128, 133). The revivifying *spirit* of a true revival would, by contrast, hold nothing sacrosanct except the cultivation of an antisyzygical consciousness "in accord with the newest tendencies of human thought" (128, 133).

"A Theory of Scots Letters" refers to contemporary developments in the Irish Gaelic Revival, and MacDiarmid basically concurs with Hyde's "De-Anglicizing" thesis that the anomalous habit of slavishly imitating English custom while staying hostile to the English, and denigrating the [Scots] vernacular while espousing nationalist aspirations, has resulted in "colossal cringing" and widespread lack of initiative, though his polemics draw on a much wider repertoire of intellectual support (including Freud, Marx, and Nietzsche) than Hyde's. In 1924 MacDiarmid relates "the decay of the Doric" to "a 'specific aboulia' [a Freudian term for a pathological inability to make or act on decisions] caused by the suppression imposed by the rigours of Puritanism and accentuated by Anglicisation."[35] An uncompromising socialist and Marxist intellectual, his political commentary and autobiographical disclosures repeatedly highlight class antagonism as a motive for de-Anglicization: "Class antagonism has been strong in me from the start[;] when I was a boy to speak English was to 'speak fine' i.e. to ape the gentry, and the very thought of anything of the sort was intolerable" (*LP* 17). (In Ireland, by contrast, the animating influence of class antagonism on the De-Anglicization movement was consistently euphemized and downplayed.) A violent antipathy to bourgeois gentility lies behind the unfavorable comparison MacDiarmid draws between a popular poet such as Burns, whose ready assimilation into the drawing room secured his decline "from genius to 'gauger,' " and an unpopular one such as Baudelaire, who deliberately made himself into "a bogey to horrify the bourgeois."[36]

The antagonism to gentility has a misogynist element for the poet who opines in "MacDiarmid's" first prose writing in Scots, a quasi-review of Rebecca West's novel *The Judge,* that the "verra last thing Scottish literature needs is *lady-fying*" because "it'll tak a man tae write aboot Edinburgh" or, better yet, "an almark [a beast that breaks down fences] like Joyce."[37] The chauvinism is in tune with Joyce's remark that *The Waste Land* "ends the idea of poetry for ladies."[38] Along with asserting the male prerogative to dominate literary production, the display of machismo bristles against the refinement of poetry into effete marginality on the one hand and the tethering of the "mither tongue" to the hearth on the other. The tangle of gendered assumptions fuels the drive to make it BIG ("I'm all for GIANT-ISM in the arts," he declares [*TR* xvi]) by becoming an *almark,* or bogey, who defies orthodoxy and bourgeois complacency. As a political corollary to the antisyzygical revolt against accepted things, he elaborates a "Russo-Scottish parallelism" around the example of Fyodor Dostoevski, whom he hails (following Spengler) as the first delineation of "a 'Faustian' or modern type" (TR 137, 135). The "Dostoevskian debris of ideas—an inexhaustible quarry of subtle and significant sound" in Scots makes it "the only language in Western Europe instinct with those uncanny spiritual and pathological perceptions alike which constitute the uniqueness of Dostoevski's work, and word after word of Doric establishes a blood bond at once infinitely more thrilling and vital and less explicable than those deliberately sought after by writers such as D. H. Lawrence in the medium of English" (TR 131).

MacDiarmid grafts the Spenglerian-Nietzschean Faustian/Appollonian binary onto the Celtic/Teutonic one and reinstates coin-splitting stereotyping by separating the "the true Scot, rapid in his transitions of thought, taking all things as granted, turning to fun and even to profanity with no misgivings, at his ease in both rooms of life," from "the false Scot—the douce travesty, the methodical, level-headed, self-conscious creature of the popular tradition" (TR 135–36). The "canny Scot," whose sobriety, stern conscience, and thrift make him the linchpin of empire, kirk, and industry, is transformed into the Scottish counterpart of the Irish "false-national" scapegoat, the "West Briton." The "future depends upon the freeing and development of that opposite tendency in our consciousness which runs counter to . . . the canny Scot tradition," and hence "the slogan of a Scottish literary revival must be the Nietzschean 'Become what you are'" (TR 136–37). The de-Anglicizing nature of MacDiarmid's poetics of caricature is twofold: it is an expressionist mode of combinatorial doodling and deedling which releases him from the reified biases of Scots/English diglossia; and a poetics of indignation which bridles against the complex sociolinguistic and psychocultural realities that profile Scots as anachronistic, subordinate, and marginal. The conjoined disjunctive tendencies toward disinterested expressionism and counterhegemonic assault on the Pale each hold the other in check, so that his caricatural poetics serves simultaneously as a means of not reacting to and of reacting against the Anglocentrism of Scottish letters.

The catalytic effect of the publication of *Ulysses* and *The Waste Land* on the genesis of "MacDiarmid" owes much to how these works were celebrated as classics because they flouted generic conventions. From the outset MacDiarmid was determined to shatter the generic expectations that consign poetry, and especially vernacular poetry, to the margins by giving epic treatment to the hitherto "unfulfilled" uncanny Scot tradition. His breakthrough occurred when the composer F. G. Scott suggested that he "write a poem about a drunk man looking at the thistle," and MacDiarmid realized that as a "symbol of the miseries and grandeurs of the human fate in general" as well as one of Scottish nationality, it was the "[perfect] theme for a very long poem and a complicated poem" because "it was capable of all sorts of applications and extensions."[39] His confidence that the topos was endlessly complicated and capable of infinite variation is likely to baffle the reader who would be turned off by the prospect of a 2,684-line poem that contains no action except that of a drunk man looking at the national emblem. Such a topic conjures up a cartoon image that seems all too susceptible to the "two-beat" reception process that dogs the reception of graphic caricature and imagist verse, namely surprise at an unexpected equivalence followed by reintegrating laughter as it is put in its provisional place.[40]

MacDiarmid seized upon the topic's potential for upsetting stable categories of "normal" and "bizarre," however, by developing the antisyzygical point of view of the drunken beholder. An "Author's Note" to the 1926 edition picks up on Smith's observation that drunkenness can serve writers as a tongue-in-cheek device for justifying the sudden dislocations of Caledonian antisyzygies (23). "Drunkenness has a logic of its own," MacDiarmid writes, and then he counsels the teetotaler "to be chary . . . of such inadvertent reflections of their own sober minds" which they may catch in the "distorting mirror" of these pages (*ADM* 196). The speaker of *A Drunk Man* overtly dices with reader expectation. "I amna fou' sae muckle as tired—deid dune," he declares in the opening line (1), establishing his bona fides by denying that the adulterated whiskey ("the stuffie's no' the real Mackay" [9]) has made him drunk. He adds parenthetically that a drunken stream of consciousness gratifies stereotypical images of Scotland and the canny Scot's image of his reprobate brethren, "To prove my soul is Scots I maun begin/Wi' what's still deemed Scots and the folk expect" (21–22), which he can then "whummle" (overturn [25]) by overwhelming readers with the intoxicating "logic" of drunkenness.[41]

Scott's suggested topic also appealed to MacDiarmid's long-standing fascination with the formative influence of visual images on narratives of national identity, for as early as 1916, when stationed amid "the curious polyglottery" of army life at Salonika, he was "scribbling" on the following topics: "I have my *The Scottish Vortex* (as per system exemplified in *Blast*), *Caricature in Scotland—and lost opportunities, A Copy of Burns I want* (suggestions to illustrators on a personal visualization of the national pictures evoked in the poems), *Scottish Colour— Thought* etc." (*Letters* 9). Ezra Pound's Vorticist solution to the problem of developing the imagist aperçu into the "intensive art" of a long poem assumed fresh significance for the project of anatomizing the emblematic thistle. "The image [i.e., thistle] is not an idea," Pound writes, "it is a radiant node or cluster; it is what

I can, and must perforce, call a VORTEX, from which, and through which, and into which, ideas are constantly rushing."[42] Scott also helped to arrange the draft version of *A Drunk Man* into a sequence in accordance with musicological principles, and MacDiarmid acknowledges the collaboration by dedicating "this galli-maufry [hodgepodge]" ("flytin' and sclatrie" in the dedicatory verse) to Scott.[43] MacDiarmid also styled *A Drunk Man* a gallimaufry in advance press notices for the want of a better generic label for the ambitious work he felt would fail unless it took "its place as a masterpiece—*sui generis*—one of the biggest things in the range of Scottish literature" (*Letters* 89).

Peter McCarey contends that MacDiarmid draws on the Menippean tradition, very much as Bakhtin argues Dostoevski does, by fashioning the unclassifiable genre out of the "Dostoevskian debris of ideas" he found awaiting polyphonic treatment in Synthetic Scots.[44] *A Drunk Man* hails an apostrophized Dostoevski as the avatar of a new epoch, "This Christ o' the neist thoosand years" (1800), when the "canny Scot" shall give way to the uncanny one. Menippean satire, a genre of ultimate questions which mixes fantasy, slum naturalism, moral-psychological experimentation, and mysticism with inserted genres such as the diatribe and soliloquy, takes the topicality of the immediate and unfinalizable present as its starting point.[45] Dostoevski "sought the sort of hero whose life would be concentrated on the pure function of gaining consciousness of himself and the world" because such a hero fuses the artistic dominant of becoming self-conscious with the characterological dominant of the represented person.[46] The task of gaining consciousness of himself necessarily absorbs an intellectual and/or drunk who "dinna ken as muckle's whaur I am/Or hoo I've come to sprawl here 'neth the mune" (95–96).[47] The Dostoevskian hero's discourse as "he looks at himself, as it were, in all the mirrors of other people's consciousnesses," creates the *"interior infinite"* of "an individual carnival, marked by a vivid sense of isolation" and fearful and watchful secretiveness that has a residual generic kinship with the praise-abuse decrownings and fearless regenerative laughter of the carnival square.[48]

The thistle, skewed by moonlight and intoxication, is the "distorting mirror" that refracts back to the drunk man how he and his nation are perceived by others: "My ain soul looks me in the face, as it twere,/And mair than my ain soul—my nation's soul" (335–36).[49] The speaker calls attention to his drunken, or "loaded," state as he zeroes in and magnifies one aspect of the thistle and then veers off in another direction as a new perception initiates a different associative tack. "There's nocht sae sober as a man blin' drunk," the speaker confides (277), baiting the reader with *A Drunk Man*'s constitutive antisyzygy about whether the fixity on the thistle attests to an unsteady grip on reality or to an intensive analytic sobriety. Although but a "bairn at thee I peer," the drunk man declares that, like Dostoevski, he is a microcosm of his nation in all its contrariety, "For a' that's Scottish is in me,/As a' things Russian were in thee," and resolves "To pit in a concrete abstraction/My country's contrair qualities" (2014–18).[50] "Speaking somewhat paradoxically," Bakhtin writes in *Problems of Dostoevsky's Poetics*, "one could say that it was not Dostoevski's subjective memory, but the objective memory of the very genre in which he worked, that preserved the peculiar features of the ancient menippea" (121). In a similar vein I contend that the thistle VORTEX, which provides a stereoscopic means for looking at national identity in the very aspect of its looked-at-ness, preserves an "objective memory" of the Menippean subgenres of caricature and popular blazons.[51] The thistle is an abstract signifier of Scottish nationality, but these abstractions are woven into the concrete physiognomy of the plant "from which, and through which, and into which, ideas are constantly rushing." An extended blazon to the emblematic icon of nationality, *A Drunk Man* ponders "the mystery of Scotland's self-suppression" by subjecting the puzzling entelechy of the flora to minute scrutiny.

The thistle's catalytic effect on MacDiarmid's comic genius owes much to his childhood experience of a living carnival, the annual Common Riding. Celebrated to this day in Langholm, the Common Riding evolved from an ancient custom of riding round the boundaries of the burgh's common lands. In the ritual procession children bearing heather brooms join standard bearers behind a leader who carries aloft a flagpole bearing a specially cultivated eight-foot-high thistle. The thistle standard makes a resplendent spectacle in a MacDiarmid story based on the event: "Tied to the tap o' a flag pole it made a bonny sicht, wallopin' a' owre the life, an a hunner roses dancin' in't, a ferlie o' purple and green" (*TR* 349).[52] The "concretely sensuous language of carnival" epitomized by the presiding thistle evokes memories of "a free and familiar contact among people" which the young Grieve had otherwise seldom enjoyed.[53] An unalloyed joy is palpable in the verses recounting the Common Riding, which weave an accompanying traditional children's chant into the ballad measure that supplies the cantus firmus of *A Drunk Man:*

Drums in the walligate, pipes in the air,
Come and hear the cryin' o' the Fair.

A' as it used to be, when I was a loon
On Common-Ridin' Day in the Muckle Toon.

The bearer twirls the Bannock-and-Saut-Herrin',
The Croon o' Roses through the lift is farin',

The aucht-fit thistle wallops on hie;
In heather besoms a' the hills gang by.   (455–62)[54]

Swept up in the "jolly relativity" of the communal chorus, the drunk man happily recollects his wife, Jean, "as she was on her wedding day" and is then seamlessly transported into the heroic position of thistle carrier, as the narrative segues to one of the sequence's few full-blown paeans to the thistle (476):

Nerves in stounds o' delight,
Muscles in pride o' power,
Bluid as wi' roses dight
Life's toppin' pinnacles owre,
The thistle yet'll unite
Man and the Infinite!   (477–82)[55]

The overwhelmingly positive connotations of the thistle's "language of carnival" is counterpointed by the pejoration of the thistle in biblical allegory. The thistle is figured in Genesis as the blighted fruit of expulsion from Eden: "cursed is the ground for thy sake; in sorrow shalt thou eat of it all the days of thy life; thorns also and thistles shall it bring forth to thee" (3:17–19). The Scottish-Renaissance objective announced in the manifesto issue of the *Scottish Chapbook* in August 1922, "to meddle wi' the Thistle and pick the figs," incongruously gestures toward the futility of the task by alluding to Matthew 7:16: "Ye shall know them by their fruits. Do men gather grapes of thorns, or figs of thistles?" Biblical allegory receives extensive metaphorical play in the sequence in which the thistle signifies sinfulness and shriveled potential as well as the pathos (and bathos) of wrongful scapegoating. The thistle's reprobate status has a decidedly Calvinist tincture in *A Drunk Man:*

O stranglin rictus, sterile spasm,
Thou stricture in the groins o' licht
Thou ootrie gangrel frae the wilds
O' chaos fenced frae Eden yet.   (1294–95)[56]

Manichaean allegory facilitates the proliferation of oppositional pairs along a damnation/salvation axis—wilderness/civilization; sterile/fertile; evil/good; grotesque/beautiful—which helps to "fix" the construction of the thistle as "other."[57] The wide currency of the commonplace that the thistle has a reprobate "character" illustrates the peculiarly bogus yet unfalsifiable nature of stereotypes noted by imagologists such as Joep Leerssen.

The thistle's status as the "devil's vegetable" in European folk consciousness led to its adaptation into the genre of popular blazons, those popular expressions of praise-abuse for neighbors' most pronounced "best" trait among which the Scotticism is classified. In "The Foreigner as Devil, Thistle, and Gadfly" Felix Oinas tracks a pattern of name-calling which demonizes a despised and/or threatening neighbor by association with the hapless plant. Oinas writes that Finnish folk names for thistles mean "Swede" and "Russian," and the Russian folk name for them means "Tartar." By anthropomorphizing the thistle with the name of an unwanted or malign alien and projecting their racial physiognomy onto the weed, a Russian peasant can simultaneously vent his antagonism by figuratively uprooting "Tartars" from the land and access a surcharge of zeal for an irksome task. The thistle blazon humanizes the weed in order to demonize the human in a concrete proto-caricatural form that highlights the intimate link between name-calling and ascribing a disfigured human face to the ostracized party in order to profile them as beyond the pale. There is no evidence that MacDiarmid was consciously aware of the thistle blazon described by Oinas, but *A Drunk Man*, which at one point likens the thistle's "nervous shivering" to that of "a horse's skin aneth a cleg [gadfly]" (1437–38), draws on an "objective memory" of the xenophobic folk custom.

Signifying as it does a stubborn rootedness and a foreign trespass that invites extirpation, the thistle seems an anomalous choice of national emblem because it betrays an ambivalent or precarious sense of entitlement to domicile. The thistle became current as the Scottish emblem around the time the rose was adopted by the Tudors and first appeared on silver coins in 1470. William Dunbar's 1503 epithalamium for the marriage of James IV to Margaret Tudor, later entitled "The Thrissill and the Rois" by Allan Ramsay, celebrates a complementarity between the warlike yet protective thistle and the beautiful rose which became a staple of Anglo-Scottish diplomacy. In her appraisal of Dunbar's innovative literary use of the insignia, Priscilla Bawcutt notes that Lorraine also adopted the thistle as a defiant emblem after René II's successful struggle to preserve the small duchy's independence from Burgundy.[58] The thistle's message of deterrence has obvious emblematic appeal for ethnic groups who see themselves as withstanding a political takeover against the odds.

The Latin motto emblazoned on the Scottish emblem, "Nemo me impune lacessit" reinforces the visual "hands off" message with a verbal warning. The two markedly different registers of the translated motto in English ("No one assails me unharmed") and in Scots ("Wha daur meddle wi' me") encapsulates the divergent paths of Dunbar's "Inglishe" into English and Scots. The English motto, like the Latin one, issues a universal caution to potential aggressors by conveying the threat of retaliation through the measured tones of understated menace. The all-purpose concision of the Latin and English mottoes is highly reproducible, suited to imprinting on coins and dissemination as a national slogan within international diplomatic channels. The motto in Scots, by contrast, is cast in the form of a rejoinder to an enemy within earshot who is at once overbearing and conspicuously anonymous. The fragment from an ongoing altercation has the stentorian tones of an already injured "me" whose rage is edged with paranoia. The oscillation between declarative, interrogative, and exclamatory speech acts makes the "wha daur" rejoinder impossible to punctuate. Aggrieved without establishing either the grounds or source of grievance, the loud rejoinder is too "charged" to circulate within the stable decorum of print media and diplomatic protocol. The English and Scots mottoes are mutually intelligible and semantically contiguous, but the social configurations of their expressive cues are incompatible and disjunctive. If one envisions each motto on identical thistle-emblazoned coins and compares their profile, the contrastive "faces" of the two idioms become apparent. The equilibrium of the official motto in English has a neutralizing, normative effect that makes the thistle seem as commonplace as any other emblematic flora, whereas the bellicose motto in Scots sets "the devil's vegetable" huffing and bristling before our eyes. If the Scots rejoinder seems to skid and waver without the traction of a stable syntax, its errancy has an open-ended plasticity about it which makes the Latinate English motto seem flat and devitalized by comparison.

The vitalist dance of the contrary pulls of regulatory constants and destabilizing variations forms the core of *A Drunk Man*'s poetics of caricature. The thistle VORTEX as beheld by the drunk man becomes a kind of mediating third term, an iconicity that allows us to apprehend the almost semaphoric language of the carnivalesque thistle working variations upon the scriptist thistle of the coin insignia. "The munelicht that owre clear defines/the thistle's shrill cantankerous lines" highlights the contrast in the silhouette between spiny leaves and fleshy capitulum which in turn gives prominence to the antithesis between pointed spite and puffy pretension on which caricature depends (1903–4). As caricaturist Edward Koren remarks, caricature "is thought of as 'barbed,' it 'skewers human frailties and foibles,' it 'punctures pretensions,' it 'pricks and deflates pomposity,' it 'explodes fatuousness' " and the dynamics of comic deflation are enacted on a plastic level as the thistle swells and recoils into its habitual shrunken shape.[59]

The "shrill cantankerous lines" of the thistle VORTEX arouse the parodic travesty-ing and antisyzygical consciousness that brings MacDiarmid "Back to Dunbar!" and the heyday of Middle Scots (1455–1555) and connects him with the thistle blazon of the folk tradition.

MacDiarmid's labeling of *A Drunk Man* as "my flytin' and sclatrie" announces that his blazon to the alliance between the "grugous thistle" and "o'er sonsy rose" is a palinode to "The Thrissill and the Rois" by way of Dunbar's "The Flyting of Dunbar and Kennedy."[60] Dunbar's work was composed when blazons, then de-fined as "continuous praise or constant abuse of the object to be blazoned," were an ambivalent genre that "could render praise ironical and flatter that which was not usually to be flattered."[61] Bakhtin writes in *Problems of Dostoevsky's Poetics,* that "a free and ambiguous praise-abuse," as alien to official genres as it is characteris-tic of folk culture, underwent "rhetorical degeneracy" toward the end of the sixteenth century, when literary blazons attenuated to eulogy (under the growing influence of antique forms of praise) and genres of abusive language kept an insulting edge without an attendant positive regenerative pole until eventually they became categorically "unprintable" (166, 427). Meanwhile, as Bakhtin ex-plains in *The Dialogic Imagination,* the parodying images of dialects which belong to every peoples' most ancient store of language images began to receive more profound artistic formulations and to penetrate major literature (80).

In "The Flyting of Dunbar and Kennedie" (c. 1500) Dunbar feels sufficiently secure in his "Inglis" makar superiority at the court of James IV (the last monarch who knew Gaelic) to taunt bilingual Highlander poet Walter Kennedy with a scatological pun on Erse (from *Erische,* Irish) which became a staple slur: "Ane Lawland ers wald mak a bettir noyis" (l. 56).[62] The virtuoso punning on the purloined term shows how Dunbar's mastery of the "high" genre of *flyting* (styl-ized invective and raillery) draws on the "low" genres of *sclatrie* (obscenities, billingsgate, and popular blazons) by debasing his antagonist's mother tongue into a resounding fart-expletive. The burlesque echoes and mooning gesture are essential to the sophisticated wit of the mud-slinging retort that, in the *Gall-dachd's* view, the *Gàidhealtachd* shows a wrong-way-round-and-upside-down-and-inside-out (*erselins*) face to the world when speaking and enunciates weakly. The rude gesture of blending a contemptuous allusion to the other's linguistic heri-tage with making raspberries extends back to Greeks mouthing *bar-bar-os* at non-Greeks and beyond. An Orkney expression to signify making an Irish bull, "gaun erselins wi'd," shows the witty slander's effectiveness in promoting an image of Anglicized Gaels as congenital speakers of barbarisms.[63] Much in the man-ner that the thistle blazon humanizes the weed in order to demonize the human,

Dunbar's use of the lowercase *ers* as a generic term for speech elevates the neighboring language to the economy of the same in order to debase it more roundly with the travestying boast that Inglis outshines Gaelic in ers-eloquence. Interestingly, the substitution of *ers* for *Ers* mimics in reverse the semantic shift in Gaelic from [lowercase] *beurla*, "speech," to [uppercase] *Beurla*, "English."[64] The *beurla/parole* synonymy illustrates Bakhtin's thesis in *The Dialogic Imagination* that one can only objectivize one's own linguistic habitus and worldview in the light of another's language, an ability to see the literary word "with a sideways glance" which Dunbar's *ers/parole* hyperbole exploits to the fullest (61–62).

Memories of past struggles between languages and dialects are "retained not only as congealed traces in languages but also in literary and stylistic figuration," Bakhtin argues in *The Dialogic Imagination*, "preeminently in the parodying and travestying verbal forms" (66). Memories of Pale/Fringe linguicism also animate cross-cultural altercations and stoke the aggressive impulse to demean or retaliate which fuels popular blazons. The simmering hostility is at play in the apostrophic blazon "Grugous thistle, to my een" and the attendant "quarrel wi' th' owre sonsy rose" (2347, 2372). Although the Gaelic derivations of *grugous* (*grùgach*, scowling) and *sonsy* (*sonas*, prosperity) add satiric weight to MacDiarmid's use of them, he may have been unaware of their Gaelic etymons.[65] The habit of using a pejorative epithet for affectionate praise is rife in vernacular usage, and the thistle's "grugous" aspect is shadowed by the latent possibility of incursion by its antithesis when a smile overtakes a scowl, and vice versa. The frequent recourse to the diminutive *ie*, as the Gaelic *ín* (anglicized as *een*), for terms of endearment and/or derision in the vernacular is a striking instance of the Janus-faced ambivalence of blazons when deployed orally which is largely elided when they are transposed into print. The fine line between belittlement and exaltation in vernacular blazons inflects the tone of *A Drunk Man* with edginess, and it delineates the antisyzygical architectonics of the drunk man's intellectual odyssey.

Grugous has an antisyzygical gruesome/gorgeous ring to Anglophone ears, a semantic working-together-at-cross-purposes that sets in motion the ramifying "zig-zag of contradictions" of the intoxicating "logic" of drunkenness. The "loaded" speaker's swings between grandiosity and self-abasement are mimicked by the thistle's careenings in scale between mythic grandeur and puny insignificance, a collapsing of subject/object differentiation which disorients the reader's internal sense of proportion and harmony. E. H. Gombrich argues that the tendency of caricature to distortion and exaggeration exploits the role of muscular empathy in the cognition of equivalence by playing upon the radical disparity between our inner sense of dimension and harmony and our visual perception of proportion.[66] The transmogrification of scale works on the level of doodling, as the zooming up close to and back away from the thistle keeps the reader focused on visualizing the ever-shifting contours of the semaphoric thistle VORTEX. The variations upon scale also operate on the plane of deedling, for MacDiarmid maintained that the Caledonian antisyzygy "goes far deeper than language" and is best understood analogously to atonal music, to the "fantastic experimental clowning" of " 'the father of atonality,' " Erik Satie, whose mother was Scottish (*TR* 144–45), and to the twelve-tone "serial" technique of composition developed by Arnold Schönberg. (*A Drunk Man* alludes to Schönberg in l. 424.) Avant-garde musicology, mediated through F. G. Scott, informs MacDiarmid's developing interest in using *piobaireachd* (bagpipe music) as a basis for unsettling the inexorable sway of the Pale's home key.

Antisyzygy is a prosodic term, and MacDiarmid's antisyzygical deedling resembles Gilles Deleuze's concept of an "art of inclusive disjunctions" which "follow[s] a rolling gait" that "makes the language as such stutter: an affective and intensive language, and no longer an affectation of the one who speaks" (*Essays*, 110, 107). Great writers "carve out a nonpreexistent foreign language *within* [their] own language," Deleuze writes, "they make the language take flight, they send it racing along a witch's line, ceaselessly placing it in a state of disequilibrium, making it bifurcate and vary in each of its terms, following an incessant modulation . . . much as in music, where the minor mode refers to dynamic combinations in perpetual disequilibrium" (110, 109). Although Deleuze and Felix Guattari sharply distinguish their concept of "minor" literature from literary creolization, they note that it has the conjoined tendencies of "impoverishment" and "overload" with which "the so-called minor languages" are routinely faulted, namely the shedding of syntactical and lexical forms that allow one to sidestep a constant instead of tacking it head on and a taste for paraphrasis and proliferation of shifting effects which bear witness to the unlocalized presence of an indirect discourse at the heart of every statement.[67] In the guise of a "stuttering" drunken stream of consciousness MacDiarmid incorporates the twin tendencies of caricature toward elision and overload into the structural rhythms of the sequence as a whole in order to activate the antisyzygical doodling and deedling that places dominant scales and hierarchies in "perpetual disequilibrium." Caricature plays with and against "a mutable context of expectation" in ways that can either temporarily dislodge and then rapidly reinstate the normalcy of the relational model or that can disclose its arbitrary conventionality and enable one to sidestep it.[68]

An earnest botanical dissection of an abstract emblem of nationality is no more bizarre, from the "perpetual disequilibrium" of an antisyzygical point of view, than the whimsy of allowing the profile of the thistle to determine the trajectory of philosophical inquiry. The long vigil with the thistle has the intense earnestness of the soul-searching doppelgänger and the outlandish comedy of what Bakhtin describes as "the half-real, half-play-acted" decrownings of carnival (*Problems*, 123). Notwithstanding the residual generic kinship between the medieval and Romantic grotesque, the registers of their disjunctive worldviews are almost entirely at odds. The post-Enlightenment spectating hero is unable to laugh at his own absurdity as he confronts his spectral double, while the participants in the jolly relativity of carnival decline to take the inversions of customary hierarchies seriously. Nonetheless, they belong to an uncanny-comic continuum that is preserved in the colloquialism "Funny-ha-ha or funny-peculiar?" and in the semantic transformation of the French *drôle* which Ernst Kris invokes to illustrate a general rule of the comic, "that what was feared yesterday is fated to appear funny today" (213). Kris cites how gargoyles aroused terror in the thirteenth century and amusement in the fifteenth to support the thesis that a once feared or dreaded sinister shape lurks behind all comic figures. Kris's rule contains an implicit narrative of modernity progressively surmounting "medieval" phobias which can be juxtaposed with Smith's contention that an "antisyzygical" ability to intuit "the absolute propriety of a gargoyle's grinning at the elbow of a kneeling saint" fosters the nimble-wittedness necessary to envision life as " 'varied with a clean contrair spirit' " (35, 4).[69] The different emphases of Kris's and Smith's interpretations of the gargoyle illustrate how our sense of the comic and the uncanny depends upon mutable contexts of expectations. *A Drunk Man's* dicings with expectation and modes of working variations upon customary scales promotes the antisyzygical outlook that what is judged incongruous or jarringly unfunny by the mainstream today may be considered *heimlich*, or comic, in other epochs or cultural contexts.

The antisyzygical segues between uncanny and comic registers are reinforced on a linguistic level by two key strata in *A Drunk Man's* Synthetic Scots: an "enigmatic" idiom, based on the estrangement (*ostranie*) of the Romantic grotesque, which restores uncanny complexity to a disparaged vernacular; and a "rogue" idiom, derived from the popular grotesque of late-medieval folk genres, which affronts bourgeois gentility. The "ambiguous praise-abuse" of the national/ alien thistle becomes a means of blazoning the comic-uncanny virtuosity of Scots. The drunk man explores the mysterious entelechy of "the language that but sparely flooers/And maistly gangs to weed" (1219–20) by pondering the intermingling of the base and the beautiful which "A Theory of Scots Letters" identifies as a special province of Scottish genius (*TR* 131).

The craft that hit upon the reishlin' stalk,
Wi'ts gausty leafs and a' its datchie jags,
And spired it syne in seely flooers to brak
Like sudden lauchter owre its fousome rags
Jouks me, sardonic lover, in the routh
O' contrairies that jostle in this dumfoondrin' growth. $(1107-12)^{70}$

The assumption that the thistle's purpose lies in disclosing its "routh o' contrar-ies" to the beholder betrays an inability "to imagine the 'other' as anything but a [cryptic] message pertaining to the state of his own soul."[71] The solipsistic self-regard is confounded by the contrastive lack of affectation in the beheld object: "For who o's ha'e the thistle's poo'er/To see we're worthless and believe 't?"[72] (1413–14). The thistle's freedom from pretension delivers momentary in-sight into the absolute fallenness of humanity, and the speaker envisions the thistle spilling over into the philosophical laughter of the Baudelairean "absolute comic." Baudelaire defines the "true subject" of caricature as "the introduction of this indefinable element of beauty in works intended to represent his [moral and physical] ugliness to man; [a]nd what is no less mysterious is that this lamentable spectacle excites in him an undying and incorrigible mirth."[73]

The returning gaze of the thistle VORTEX mocks and confounds the drunk man's sense of personal embodiment to such an extent that he questions whether he can distinguish between them:

Is it the munelicht or a leprosy
That spreids aboot me; and a thistle
Or my ain skeleton through wha's bare banes
A fiendish wund's begood to whistle? $(369-72)^{74}$

The resounding reply is immediate diabolical laughter in which he, the thistle, and the devil become a composite "my face" that splits to reveal everything humankind keeps under wraps:

The devil's lauchter has a *hwyl* like this.
My face has flown open like a lid
—And gibberin' on the hillside there
Is a' humanity sae lang has hid! . . .   (373–76)

The infernal *hwyl* is glossed by MacDiarmid as *ululation,* connoting a rever-berating pure sound that spans the gamut of triumph, grief, despair, degrada-tion, defiance, revenge, and mockery. The italicized *hwyl* provokes a muscular response to the unpronounceable Welsh loanword, a facial contortion that might in turn evoke a visualization of a grimace like that of a signature Expressionist painting, Edvard Munch's *Scream* (1895). The choice of a Welsh shibboleth (the absence of vowels is foreign to English, Scots, and Gaelic orthography) sets the barbarous *hwyl* apart as though it were too hot to handle and offloads it onto a neighboring language without relinquishing a remote Celtic kinship with it. The "profound, primitive, and axiomatic" laughter of the Baudelairean "absolute comic" in this scene is a Babelized gibbering that sunders the connections between speaker and addressee (157), signifying sound and print signifier. Along with bringing a ramifying carnivalistic aesthetic into play (much as Peter McCarey argues the Dostoevskian loanword *nadryv* [tragical crack, l. 870] does), the shibboleth highlights the issues of translation and reception with which A *Drunk Man* is centrally engaged.

A *Drunk Man* opens with the speaker inveighing against the Burns cult, a diatribe that reactivates international readers' latent familiarity with Scots and introduces the stereotype he intends to "whummle." He then recalls a vision of "a silken leddy" which he had had in the pub earlier that evening by reciting an inserted verse translation (italicized and footnoted as "from the Russian of Alexander Blok"). The interpolation creates an illusion of direct interlingual contact between Russian and Scots which can withstand and coexist with readers' correct surmise that the drunk man speaks on MacDiarmid's behalf when he confesses that "I ken nae Russian and you [Dostoevski] ken nae Scots" (l. 2224). MacDiarmid's retranslation into Scots of Babette Deutsch and Avrahm Yarmolinsky's cotranslation of Blok's "Neznakomka" (The Unknown Woman) and "Predchuvstvuya tebya" (I have foreknown you) belongs to that burgeoning subcategory of translations whose ambiguous provenance is flagged by such equivocal prepositional markers as "after *x*" or "based on *y*" in a tacit pact to leave open to conjecture whether the text is a direct interlingual translation from the stated source or an intralingual retranslation of intermediary translations. MacDiarmid's retranslation, aimed through his image of the Russian source culture and an oppositional image of the intermediary English target language, substitutes whiskey for wine, inserts a parenthetical aside about the drunk man's Penelope-like spouse, and assigns a returning gaze to the blazoned silken leddy on the basis of two muted references to the "eyes" of the Blok hero's doppelgänger and of the azure sea. Aside from these semantic modifications and the Scots diction, he stays close to the Deutsch and Yarmolinsky translation, a stanza of which I quote here, by way of contrast with the MacDiarmid version that directly follows it:

But every evening, strange, immutable,
(Is it a dream no waking proves?)
As to a rendezvous inscrutable
A silken lady darkly moves.

But ilka evenin' fey and fremt
(Is it a dream nae wauk'nin' proves?)
As to a trystin'-place undreamt,
A silken leddy darkly moves.   (193–96)

The natural assurance in conveying an enigmatic register is indebted to the rich lexis pertaining to the uncanny in Scots. The "English" words *uncanny, canny, eerie,* and *fey* (fated) are actually Scots loanwords, and Scots also has many other less familiar words, including *fremt* (estranged), *oorie* (weird), *wanchancy* (unfortunate), and *drumlie* (troubled). The success of "fey and fremt/ . . . undreamt" over "strange, immutable/ . . . inscrutable" is reinforced by how the colloquialized aureate diction, trystin'-place and *silken leddy*, seems a plausibly unaffected idiom for a speaker with ready access to a trove of romantic ballads. The aura of ease with romance and enigma creates mixed familiarizing and defamiliarizing effects that have the paradoxical result of making MacDiarmid's version seem more "true" than the intermediary source, which is relegated by contrast to "crib" status. Russian critic D. S. Mirsky's claim that MacDiarmid "produced 'the only real *re-creations* of Russian poetry' in any form of English" seems counterintuitive *(ADM* viii; my emph.), since one would not expect a retranslated translation by someone who does not know Russian to be true to the original. MacDiarmid's success may be due to how retranslation into Scots can minorize the intermediary text with specific subcommunity registers that are otherwise lost in translating a polyphonic literary idiom into a dominant vehicular language. The truth effect depends on how the play between English crib and Scots retranslation objectifies those sides of Scots and English which pertain, in Bakhtin's formulation in *The Dialogic Imagination,* to its "specific linguistic habitus . . . which makes its worldview ultimately untranslateable, the style of the language in the totality" (62). Along with objectifying a vein of uncanniness in Scots, MacDiarmid's retranslation brings about a triangulated confrontation between the English and Scots versions before an imagined "internationalist" bar of Communist Russian opinion. The popular reception of such retranslations into vernacular Englishes as "the real Mackay" in preference to the purportedly transparent standard (the "crib" pejoration) is a measure of the ideological appeal of a de-Anglicizing aesthetic.

The recollection/translation of the exalted muse segues into a manic fun-house mirror quest for "my bonnie lass" (the vanished *Neznakomka*) during which the speaker, "feel[ing] like Dr. Jekyll/Tak'n' guid tent o' Mr. Hyde," observes from the thistle's "shaggy mien" that "I'm sair-hic-needin' a shave" (223, 231–32, 234–35). The near-slapstick burlesque is shadowed by a mounting paranoia that culminates with the questing speaker withering under the contemptuous gaze of the muse quarry:

> Or dost thou mak' a thistle o' me, wumman? But for thee
> I were as happy as the munelicht, withoot care,
> But thocht o' thee—o' thy contempt and ire—
> Turns hauf the warld into the youky thistle there,
>
> Feedin' on the munelicht and transformin' it
> To this wanrestfu' growth that winna let me be.
> The munelicht is the freedom that I'd ha'e
> But for this cursed Conscience thou hast set in me.   (253–60)

The latter-day Eve endows him with "the knowledge o' Guid and Ill,/Fear, shame, pity, like a will and wilyart growth . . . that twists Life into a certain shape" and fills the speaker with a crippling sense of moral and sexual inadequacy. The hamming-up of the doppelgänger narrative climaxes with the comic unmasking of classic farce as the discrowning mésalliances of carnival are brought into play by a "wumman's" sardonic look: "Till his puir warped performance is/To a' that micht ha' been, a thistle to the mune" (271–72). The deflation of male ego merges with the shrunken thistle to represent a Rabelaisian "body in the act of becoming," with special emphasis on the processes of digestion, elimination, and reproduction which, according to Bakhtin, are "performed on the confines of the body and the outer world, or on the confines of the old and new body" (*Rabelais*, 317). Thistledown becomes "a cloody blash o' sperm": "The wasted seam that dries like stairch/And pooders aff, that micht ha' been/A warld o' men and syne o' Gods" (1250, 1260–62).[75] The grotesque corporeality calls for a vulgar diction that relishes vibrant expressions of "scunner" (disgust) and draws on the rich lexis for bodily functions found in uncensored vernaculars and slang (such as "rumple-fyke [itch-in-the-anus] in Heaven's doup [backside]" [1333]). This "rogue" idiom aims to shock, titillate, and intrigue and by so doing to bring back down to earth the sacred writ of bourgeois decorum. The Nietzschean precept to "become what you are" finds expression through the earnest phallomorphism that riffs through *A Drunk Man*, "The thistle rises and forever will" (2231), and its irreverent comic underbelly, a detumescent sequel.

MacDiarmid further carnivalizes the man-thistle body-in-the-act-of-becoming with an inspired hermaphroditic touch when he names the thistle florets "roses" and thereby unsettles the antinomies between male and female, the grotesque and the beautiful, and Scotland and England. The conceit of "a rose loupin' out" of the thistle's "scrunts of blooms" structures the ballad of the crucified rose about the General Strike of May 1926 (1119–1218). The news of the union leaders' humiliating settlement broke when MacDiarmid (an active labor organizer in his capacity as the only Socialist town councilor in Montrose) was addressing a mass meeting of railwaymen, and "most of them burst into tears—and I am not ashamed to say I did too . . . it was one of the most moving experiences I ever had . . . weeping like children . . . because we knew we had had it."[76] Very much in the spirit of menippea, "the journalistic genre of antiquity" according to Bakhtin (*Problems*),[77] MacDiarmid wrote that he was incorporating the ballad ("which I think will rank as one of the most passionate *cris-de-coeur* in contemporary literature") into the then advanced work-in-progress, though there is no overt reference in the allegorical ballad to the contemporary events that inspired it:

> A rose loupt oot and grew, until
> It was ten times the size
> O' ony rose the thistle afore
> Had heistit to the skies.
>
> . . . .
>
> And still it grew until it seemed
> The haill braid earth had turned
> A reid reid rose that in the lift
> Like a ball o' fire burned.
>
> . . . .
>
> Syne the rose shrivelled suddenly
> As a balloon is burst;
> The thistle was a ghaistly stick,
> As gin it had been curst.
>
> . . . .
>
> And still the idiot nails itsel'
> To its ain crucifix
> While here a rose and there a rose
> Jaups oot abune the pricks.   (1155–58, 1163–66, 1171–74, 1203–6)[78]

The utopian aspiration, camaraderie, and gathering momentum of mass political action is conveyed by the semaphoric language of the carnival square as a new body politic almost emerges out of the old only to be destroyed anew by reactionary forces. The fact that a thistle "heisted to the skies" is invoked to celebrate a near-triumph by *British* labor activists rather than by *Scottish* nationalists may seem paradoxical, but it is less an index of the historical contingencies of 1926 or of socialism trumping nationalism for MacDiarmid than of how *A Drunk Man's* caricatural poetics is more in tune with mass protest by the proletariat than with constitutional nationalism. The ballad measure and the symbolic freight of the carnivalesque thistle enables MacDiarmid to plumb a generic memory of the popular blazon that infuses the cri de coeur with a profound sense of human solidarity and regenerative idealism. The exuberance of the ballad is a measure of the near-perfect match of poet and topos immediately intuited by MacDiarmid when Scott suggested to him that he write a poem about a drunk man looking at the thistle and which he subsequently gave as a reason why he did not reproduce anything comparable to the sui generis masterpiece.

When Christopher Murray Grieve adopted the Anglicized Gaelic pseudonym Hugh MacDiarmid, he patented himself as a national bard by affiliating with a Scottish clan (*Mac* is Gaelic for "son of"). Like the Scotticism, an utterance that sounds distinctly and distinctively Scottish, a "MacSomebody" signature is a hallmark of ultra-Scottishness as well as a signature of other-than-Englishness. The apparently illogical step of marking the discovery of Synthetic Scots by jettisoning a Lowland Scots name for an Anglo-Gaelic pseudonym was explained by MacDiarmid as a symbolic declaration of "the ultimate reach of the implications of my experiment."[79] Unlike the Irish Revivalist practice of re-Gaelicizing a family name that has been bowdlerized by Anglicization, the Scottish practice of renaming oneself "MacSomebody" replaces a given family name with an overtly Scottish pseudonym that projects the unstable genuine/caricatural registers of Scottish national character. The de-Anglicization of Irish names is a comparatively straightforward act of retranslation, whereas the Scottish practice eschews direct descent in order to align with the Highland Romance animating the nationalist subculture of tartanry. MacDiarmid's name change is an act of hyperbole, a flamboyant avowal of a core nationality that is located over there, on yon horizon. The "charge" of the charged declaration of nationality inheres in the unavowed identification with *Gàidhealtachd* culture toward which the hyperbolic gesture tacitly points, without ever quite acknowledging its Gaelic provenance. Such indirect mentions of what MacDiarmid terms "the Gaelic idea" are a constitutive part of

Scottish nationalist rhetoric. The Gaelic idea invoked to endorse "MacDiarmid" as a representative national bard is the theme of MacDiarmid's next major work, *To Circumjack Cencrastus* (1930).

Although one might surmise from MacDiarmid's pseudonym choice that he "ultimately" aspires to write in Gaelic, he declares in "The Caledonian Antisyzygy and the Gaelic Idea" (1931–32) that "from the point of view of the Gaelic idea, knowledge of, or indeed the existence of, Gaelic is immaterial" and then adds insult to the injurious expropriation by opining that "almost all the Gaelic speakers have been hopelessly false or unequal to their trust."[80] MacDiarmid represents the abstracted "Gaelic idea" as a complementary "dynamic myth" to Dostoevski's "Russian idea," a "Scotia Irredenta" that he equates, on the one hand, with an exclusivist racial homogeneity among Gaels (citing Wyndham Lewis on *Blutsgefühl*) which somehow enables them to reconnect with the "Ur-motives" behind the damaging neoclassicism of the Renaissance and, on the other, with a latent antisyzygical spirit freed from *"any cut-and-dried scheme* [and allowed to] *find its own forms* no matter how unrelated to anything in our past history [it] may be" (67, 70, 73). The paradoxical goal of de-Anglicization for MacDiarmid is to regain an Ur-character and to eschew all preconceptions of national character. In "English Ascendancy in British Literature" (1931), published in the *Criterion*, MacDiarmid proposes tempering the "formlessness" of Scots with the "excessive formalism" of Gaelic in order to create the "national art" that, citing Daniel Corkery's *Hidden Ireland*, is posited as the antithesis of the "second hand" classicism of the Renaissance.[81]

MacDiarmid's Gaelic idea enacts what George Lang identifies as a recurrent feature of Creole literatures, a "trope of deep speech" which conveys the sense that their authentic registers are at the furthest remove from the high cultures with which they are in contact.[82] The poet-speaker of *Cencrastus* seeks such a "coontervailin' force" to bridge the spiritual gulf isolating him from his countrymen.[83] Considering his distance from the stars "faur away," he muses:

Yet no' sae faur as 'gainst my will I am
Frae nearly a'body else in Scotland here.
But a less distance than I'll drive betwixt
    England and Scotland yet
(Wrang-heidit? Mm. *But heidit! That's the thing.*)   (206)[84]

The Gaelic idea exaggerates and augments the "heiditness" needed to polarize Scotland from England and provides a phantasmagoric image of the bardic community that the poet-speaker craves. A *wrang-heidit* feature of this polarization is that it suppresses the genetic relationship between the cognate dialects of English and Scots (MacDiarmid elsewhere aptly characterizes Scots as "not a dialect, but a sister language to English" [*TR* 147]) and inserts an image of a Celtic English with a Gaelic basilect (Anglicized Gaelic, as it were) in its stead.[85] The move is akin to Lang's description of Atlantic-Creole writers' endeavors "to retrieve and resurrect the missing core of their Creoles, to found their texts on a shared sense of a phantom center" (142), except that the missing core is clothed in Highland regalia borrowed from the neighboring speech community. A Gaelic-derived core nationality is legitimately key, however, to MacDiarmid's bid to make *Synthetic* Scots a *national* literary vernacular.[86] In contrast, for example, with Sorley MacLean and Basil Bunting's literary responses to the respective linguistic milieux of the *Gàidhealtachd* and Northumbria, MacDiarmid's Synthetic Scots is less an effort to fashion a literary vehicle from a low-status vernacular than it is a plastic medium for "explor[ing] the mystery of Scotland's self-suppression." The vernacular's "national" significance is not so much a question of attributing special eminence to Scots over and above English and Gaelic, therefore, as it is a matter of locating the traces of Scotland's anomalous national development in the Scotticism and the national imageme and synthesizing that history through autopoiesis. Ironically, this emphasis obliges MacDiarmid to stay focused on what keeps the Anglo-centrism of Scottish letters in place, and when he writes in 1926 of his new work-in-progress that "where the *Drunk Man* is in one sense a reaction from the 'Kailyard,' *Cencrastus* transcends that altogether" (*Letters* 91), one senses that the quest for transcendence is itself a reaction against the reactive nature of his de-Anglicizing poetics.

In his fullest gloss of *To Circumjack Cencrastus* MacDiarmid writes that the "Homage to Consciousness" is concerned "to glorify the Gaelic element in our heritage (which I believe underlies our Scottish life and history in much the same way that consciousness underlies and informs the whole world of man)" (*Letters* 128–29). The title words are from *Jamieson's*: *to circumjack* means "to encompass" in an explicative sense and *cencrastus* is a coiling snake, associated by MacDiarmid with a beloved Langholm haunt, an ascending woodland path known as the curly snake.[87] He glosses *Cencrastus* as a Scottish-Gaelic *uroboros* whose movements underlie the pattern of history (an extension of the Spenglerian-Yeatsian Great Wheel that concludes *A Drunk Man*) and as a Gnostic demiurge, influenced by Russian philosopher Vladimir Solovyov, which develops the Sophianic muse borrowed from Alexander Blok. The search for quintessence as the poet-speaker attempts to lay hold of the curly snake, which is as elusive in *Cencrastus* as the thistle is omnipresent in *A Drunk Man*, unfolds in two obscurely overlapping spheres. It is enacted along an abstract metaphysical plane as the poet-speaker, knowing he cannot grasp the logos (*uroboros*), persists in attempting to do so. At the same time, he conducts an equally nebulous quest for a phantom *omphalos* that might connect him with an ancestral past hidden in the recesses of the Jacobite-Gaelic tradition.

W. N. Herbert characterizes *To Circumjack Cencrastus*, which incorporates extensive translated Irish- and Scottish-Gaelic poetry and several macaronic fragments of Gaelic verse, as a "distended *aisling*" (74). Aside from a fleeting encounter in boyhood, MacDiarmid had had minimal contact with Gaelic culture,[88] and he drew his material from two books that strive to put Free-State Ireland in touch with its Gaelic past, Daniel Corkery's *Hidden Ireland* (1925) and Aodh de Blácam's *Gaelic Literature Surveyed* (1929). MacDiarmid's *Scotia Irredenta* concept is indebted to *The Hidden Ireland*, a work of subaltern literary criticism which implicitly relates the 1916 insurrectionists' "dream" to the *aislingí* (dream vision poems) and satires of pauperized eighteenth-century Munster poets. The broad survey by Ulster critic de Blácam includes Scottish-Gaelic poetry, and this, together with the Jacobite politics of the *aisling*, stoked MacDiarmid's enthusiasm for a "Gaeldom"-based counteroffensive against the hegemony of the Pale.

By the late 1920s the *aisling*'s clandestine call to arms by the *spéirbhean* was an open secret. The genre had apotheosized into a typological proof of a Jacobite "delusion" vindicated by time and sunk into the bathos of a propagandistic and pietistic mantra. The "excessive" genre aroused deep ambivalence among Scottish intellectuals, whose embarrassment about the Jacobite kitsch that Tom Nairn calls the "cultural subnationalism" of tartanry had to contend with the demonstrable success of that sentimental subculture in fomenting revolution in Ireland. I argued in the first chapter that because the *aisling* transcodes erotic, aesthetic, and political spheres, the genre facilitates literary transference by enmeshing personal fantasy with the collective fantasy of a redemptive Jacobite comeback. In the course of writing the long (over three thousand lines) and uneven work, MacDiarmid was beset by a marital crisis that culminated with his wife leaving him for another man in 1930. In 1935, by then remarried to Valda Trevlyn and living in spartan seclusion on the Shetland island of Whalsay with their son, he had a nervous breakdown diagnosed as "a summation of numerous subconscious 'insults' arising from domestic difficulties a few years previously."[89] The confluence between MacDiarmid's "poetic life" and the culturally overdetermined genre suggests an alternative definition for "distended *aisling*" to Herbert's. Herbert characterizes the genre as one "in which the visionary moment is the subject of examination in itself and can no longer be trusted as a convention" (74), but this implies an authorial analytic distance that is often noticeably lacking in *Cencrastus*. I would like to revise Herbert's definition to argue, instead, that *Cencrastus* explores and *acts out* the "dream-work" that is thematized by the *aisling*. The poem presents a mottled picture of the next major transition in MacDiarmid's career, the turn toward epic encyclopedism in "Synthetic English" (a vernacular loaded with scientific terminology) which dominated the remainder of his work, though he continued to compose new verse in Synthetic Scots.[90]

To inaugurate his narrative, the speaker of *Cencrastus* establishes the collusive pact between marketer and consumer which invests the unreal "real Scotland" with some semblance of actuality by leading a French visitor "to the islands/ Where the wells are undefiled/And folk sing as their fathers sang/Before Christ was a child" (*CP* 208). (The dependence upon a French tourist to encounter the domestic other is oddly reminiscent of Matthew Arnold's "daughter of Gomer" device.) Their literary tour is brought up short by a mirage of a Jacobite pantheon, "Phoenix-flight frae the ashes upbeatin'—/Raifteire, Ó'Rathaille, Ó'Súilleabháin/ Feiriter, Haicéid, and Céitinn," which emerges from the great Beyond: "Syne fifty miles owre the mist-ocean/Wha but Alasdair MacMhaighstir stude?" (*CP* 210–11). The poet's Jacobite precursors, "pricked oot in the blue and gowd" of the sunlit sea, appear in the iridescent guise of a *spéirbhean* who resembles Aphrodite and the Virgin Mary "as frae the Ark at Ararat/The warld was then to me." The blurring of boundaries between the phantasmagoric bard and the *spéirbhean* he immortalizes in verse creates an impression of chimerical fusion "as though in him the *eidolon* of the nation spoke" (to cite de Blácam's praise for Ó'Rathaille [310]). The *eidolon* (the elusive cencrastus) is approached by way of retranslating James Clarence Mangan's translation of Aogán Ó'Rathaille's *Gile na Gile* (reprinted in *The Hidden Ireland*).

Despite Mangan's "slow-paced, dull-voiced attempt to reproduce [*Gile na Gile's*] rhythm and melody" and "[Mozartian] compact of brilliancy, spontaneity and poise," Corkery writes, "it is this translation that must serve" because, for reasons discussed in the first chapter, the ornately wrought lyric defies translation. Mac-Diarmid wisely does not attempt to recreate the intricacy of the original but, instead, highlights two features of *Gile na Gile*/Brightness of Brightness's radiance, her crystalline eyes and the golden ringlets that sweep dew from the grass. The aisling's baroque hermeticism, which was nurtured by Ireland's removedness from the heart of Jacobite activism in contrast to the militancy of Scottish-Gaelic Jacobite verse, is brought home to the "lanely glen" in the casual dress of a popular ballad:

Aodhagán Ó'Rathaile sang this sang
That I maun sing again;
For I've met the Brightness o' Brightness
Like him in a lanely glen,
And seen the hair that's plaited
Like the generations o' men.

'Wha'e'er she is, I daurna look,
Eidolon o' a fallen race,
Wi' lifted e'en, as fain I wad,
Upon her noonday face
—Tholin' my ancestors' assize
For centuries in a minute's space!

And yet as tho' she didna see
The hopeless boor I was
She's taen me to her white breists there,
Her bricht hair owre us fa's.
She canna blame me gin I fail
To speir my fortune's cause.   (CP 224)[91]

MacDiarmid's familiar ease with the "brightness of brightness" epithet and candor about her bedazzling appearance and voluptuous white breasts has a directness that respects one of the original's most striking qualities, the way in which the tension between formal abstraction and intense sensuality generates an overall impression of incandescence.

It is highly unlikely that MacDiarmid could have been aware of the major semantic change introduced by Mangan in the climactic scene in which the poet-speaker inserts himself into the role of the avenging prince, because Corkery never mentions it in the course of a lengthy discussion of the translations' inadequacies. My surmise is that Corkery never adverts to the license of substituting "a bridegroom such as I" for the Stuart prince because he was so accustomed to identifying with the role of chivalrous avenger—like those nationalists who attended *Cathleen Ni Houlihan* as "a sort of sacrament"—that the alteration went unnoticed by him. The very simplicity of the *aisling*-plot which causes the genre to teeter on the maudlin also makes *Gile na Gile* into an evocative transferential object for the recently cuckolded poet. The identification with Mangan's poet-speaker is apparent in MacDiarmid's innovative treatment of the *spéirbhean*'s hair, a conventional mane of golden curls in the original. The personal erotic charge in the image of the unloosed plaits enveloping the embrace of speaker and *spéir-bhean* is borne out by its recurrence in "Of My First Love" (*CP* 1046), in which the "golden tumult" of the beloved's cascading hair is likened to Eas-Coul-aulin, a waterfall whose Gaelic etymon means "tresses of hair." Perhaps in tribute to Ó'Rathaille's aural filigree (the focus of Corkery's commentary) and interlacement in Celtic design, MacDiarmid represents her hair in a phrase that would garner tremendous symbolic resonance for him, "plaited like the generations of men." The hair blazon, at once sensuous and abstracted, develops a note of chill inhuman splendor in Ó'Rathaille's treatment of *Gile na Gile*'s radiance by responding to how the steely control of the original accents the cataclysmic shock of the enforced witness of her violation.

In his encounter with *Gile na Gile* the speaker anticipates that the good fortune that "she didna see . . . the hopeless boor I was" will vanish once she *hears* him speak and then *sees* him for the boor that he is: "when I ope my mooth / In horror yet she'll flee." "O wad at least my yokel words / Some Gaelic strain had kept," he laments, bemoaning the fact that scarcely a vestige of "MacMhaighstir's fire," which "stirred, alas, but couldna kyth [emerge, appear]," survives in the "Burns clay" of his Scots diction (CP 225–26). Although his speech lacks the requisite Gaelic timbre, it would be even more offensive to her were it more Anglicized: "And gin I aped the gentry's tongue / 'Ud flee wi' greater speed" (226). *Gile na gile*, an emissary from the imagined "pure" Celtic core, tarries with those whose brogue, syntax, and idiomatic speech identify them as members of the extended clan on condition that they do not strive to pass as Anglicized subjects in the rival realm of the Pale. The auditory cues that keep Anglo-Celts on the lower rungs of the Pale are signifiers of authenticity to the fugitive national *eidolon*, the personification of the other-than-English component of Anglo-Celtic subjectivity which *Cencrastus* attempts to circumjack. The speaker imagines *Gile na Gile* / Cencrastus as inevitably deserting him, and the expected abandonment fuels his ire against his lot: "Curse on my dooble life and dooble tongue, / —Guid Scots wi' English a' hamstrung" (236).

The speaker's denunciation of his "yokel words" imitates seventeenth-century Gaelic poets' practice of citing the transition from classical to popular verse as an index of the bardic elite's fall into penury: "At every Cross in Scotland I pause, / Crying (in Scots) like O'Heffernan / *Ceist cia chinneochadh dán?* [Who would desire a poem?]" (*CP* 213). By so doing, MacDiarmid taps into a vein of misanthropic elitism in Gaelic verse (which is not emphasized by Corkery or de Blácam) and adds a keener register to the churlish denunciations of an unworthy audience ("the dreich mob" [*CP* 183]) by setting them against the groundswell of Dáibhí Ó'Bruadair's anguished cry, "*Is mairg nach fuil 'na dhubhthuata*" (Woe to him who isn't a black boor). The gesture of alluding to an idealized bardic past to critique present degeneracy is key to the rhetorical appeal of the "Gaelic idea" and of the "national" bard. The Gaelic idea trades on the halycon international image of an Ossianic community in which the bard wields enormous cultural authority; it identifies with the bards' despair and anguish in the face of cultural desolation; it wields the strategic counter-image of indomitable resistance for withstanding the incursions of English Ascendancy; and it appeases remorse for Lowlanders' long-standing discrimination against Gaels by claiming consanguinity. This rich and contradictory symbolic capital underwrites the national bardic signature "MacDiarmid." By making the Jacobite revenant part of his bardic persona, Mac-Diarmid reinforces his role as a "bogey" by mobilizing shock troops of phantom Highlanders behind the Borderer's "heiditness."

The Jacobite revenant is portrayed as one who has been cruelly isolated from the group that determines his personal identity and hence functions as a synecdoche for the shared sense of a phantom core nationality in the Scottish cultural unconscious. The vicarious status of the revenant is emphasized in *Cencrastus*, in which he features as one among a dynasty of phantasms that shimmer in the mist of the Atlantic Ocean. Although MacDiarmid enlists Ó'Rathaille as an exemplar several years before Yeats uses Ó'Rathaille to position himself as "the last bard," MacDiarmid places Yeats in the phantasmagoric Jacobite pantheon and invokes him to ratify his disdain for the popular poet:

> I blink . . .
>
> .   .   .   .   .
>
> At Yeats, my kingly cousin, and mind hoo
> He prophesied that Eire 'ud hae nae Burns
> (Tho' it has tried to mair than aince) but haud
> Its genius heich and lanely.   (*CP* 185)[92]

MacDiarmid embraces the Yeatsian idea that the national poet is the more representative for being atypical because he mirrors an antithetical image of itself to the nation. The "heich and lanely" genius of "Gaeldom" as it is refracted through MacDiarmid's image of Yeats has the dual registers of a superior caste (the hereditary privileges of the bards during the classical period, which Yeats merges with what he saw as the innate leadership of the Anglo-Irish "Ascendancy") and of a persecuted "lanely" outcast. The identification of "Yeats," and by exten-

sion his "kingly cousin," "MacDiarmid," with "Raifteire," "Ó'Rathaille," "Ó'Súilleabháin," and the Gaelic tradition as a whole invests them with enormous authority as bardic keepers of national memory. The living Yeats is supplanted by his
literary remains, the revenant Yeats. The larger-than-life figure of the national
bard who returns, peremptory yet full of pathos, to remind the nation of the as-
yet-unfulfilled "destiny" they hold in trust from their ancestors, is profoundly
spectral, a kind of phantom limb that calls attention to what is missing.

The "Collected Yeats" and the "Collected MacDiarmid" call attention to their
respective national traditions, but they also occlude much from representation.
The many other stories hidden by the "story of Scotland" (and Ireland) can be
illustrated by way of MacDiarmid's blazon for *Gile na Gile*, "plaited like the generations of men," which, along with "the terrible crystal," became a master metaphor for his poetics (*CP* 223, 876).[93] "Plaited like the generations of men" depicts
the stresses of what "to circumjack" the hypostatized *Scotia Irredenta* entails for
MacDiarmid, his effort to pin down and define, and yet to leave open, "our
national genius which is capable of countless manifestations at absolute variance
with each other, yet confined within the 'limited infinity' of the adjective 'Scottish.' "[94] The reactionary politics of the *Blutsgefühl* section of "The Caledonian
Antisyzygy and the Gaelic Idea" can be seen at play in how MacDiarmid reworks
the verse of Ó'Rathaille—an intensely genealogical poet who, as de Blácam put it,
"loved to sing of the *Cárrth 'fhuil*, the Carthy blood" (310)—by plaiting the loose
ends of a heterogeneous history into a monolithic Gaelic idea and *Blutsgefühl*
patrimony. The vast symbolic capital invested in the Gaelic idea and in the venerated womb-of-the-nation is inversely proportionate to the subordinate status of
Gaelophones and women in Scotland and Ireland.

As editor of the *Dial*, Moore was kept up to date with how the gendered
symbolic status of the revered-yet-abjected Gaelic Idea was informing contemporary debates about the status of Irish in Free-State Ireland. One wonders what she
made of John Eglinton's ruminations on the troubling effects of the "indefeasible" claims of Irish on the nation in one of the *Dial*'s occasional series of "Irish
Letters" (July 1928):

> I have a private impression that the newly constituted Free State Government is
> seriously embarrassed by [the Irish-language] problem. I hardly think the language
> is now much loved really for its present self: in itself it is rather a cross-grained
> ignorant old survivor, addicted to cursing and crooning snatches of ancient song in a
> voice which makes one creepy. There are indeed many who love it for what it was;
> and when, like Edmund Spenser in his day, we cause the passionate love-poems

written in Irish even one hundred years ago "to be translated unto us" we cannot but feel towards this old language as we might when gazing upon the withered age of some village crone, renouned in former days for her matchless beauty and romantic history. (144)

Elsewhere, Moore notes laconically that in Yeats's work "woman is pitied and pitiless—a concept which one will always resist."[95] Her "Irish" poems seek modes of resistance which can both represent, and protest, the silencing of women and the colonized. MacDiarmid's and Moore's respective styles seem close to gendered parodies of one another: her reticent candor, understated concision, and deliberate omissions versus his garrulous "guerrilla warfare," hyperbole, and epic overreach. Yet Moore, too, is faulted for whimsical encyclopedism (i.e., for being too antisyzygical) and like MacDiarmid, she uses a "hybrid method of composition" to explore and contest the politics of reception which shape Pale/Fringe cross-cultural contact.

CHAPTER FOUR

An Irish Incognita

The Idiosyncrasy of Marianne Moore

Marianne Moore isn't read as an "Irish" or a "Celtic" poet. Readers may be taken aback by the complexity of her verse "in plain American which cats and dogs can read!" but are unlikely to doubt its American provenance.[1] Although she seems an unlikely poet with which to explore the gendered discourse of Celticism and the long history of colonization in Ireland, Moore's poetry engages these subjects in ways that suggest an abiding identification with her ethnic homeland. Indeed, it is precisely the combination of deep attachment and her physical and temporal distance from the gender politics of the Pale/Fringe in "the greenest place I've never seen" that makes Moore such an intriguing and compelling figure for this study.

Moore's Irish poems mix the derogatory commonplaces the poet-speaker "h[as] heard men say" about Ireland into declarations of Irishness which simultaneously represent the dynamics of colonial and gender discrimination and camouflage personal disclosure. "Sojourn in the Whale" (1917) examines how the Victorian stereotype of "the essentially feminine" Celt is experienced by those on the fringe. Apostrophizing Ireland, the poet-speaker observes how the colony, which "ha[s] heard men say:/There is a feminine temperament in direct contrast to ours," resists domination. The gender politics of the colonial encounter are investigated through a bricolage of ethnographies about Ireland in "Spenser's Ireland," a poem that culminates with a resounding, if ambivalent, declaration of Irishness: "I am troubled, I'm dissatisfied, I'm Irish." "Spenser's Ireland" explores the contact zone between cited and spontaneous speech acts in which cultural identity is formed through a clandestine citational practice Moore borrows from Maria Edgeworth (1768–1849). Both poems weave reductive observations about Ireland into a poetics of subterfuge and camouflage and place a distinctively Moore-ish spin on "the spell of feminine idiosyncrasy" which Arnold assigns to Celts.

Moore's memorable wit and editorship of the *Dial* placed her at the hub of American modernism at the same time as her private life as a celibate who lived with her mentor-mother until she was sixty put her at odds with its mores. Against the backdrop of "mongrel Manhattan," where prescribed gender, race, class, and sexuality scripts were energetically revised on the street, in the new media, and in print, she appeared extravagantly proper. Although she hazards the prejudice and condescension that her poetry seeks to redress by so doing, Moore assumes the posture of a flamboyantly "spinsterish anti-poetess" and espouses the aesthetic and moral value of the "idiosyncrasy" she sees as the essence of her poetic identity.[2]

Moore's precept that "a poet does not *speak* language but *mediates* it" develops the Emersonian idea that "by necessity, by proclivity, and by delight . . . all minds quote" and that we find our language and culture "readymade: we but quote them."[3] Moore's hallmark "hybrid method of composition," which borrows from an eclectic range of high and middlebrow sources that remain marked as derivative and other because they are quoted, has received extensive critical commentary.[4] Artists achieve a laudable singularity for Moore because they are "idiosyncratic" in the precise etymological sense of *idio* (one's own, distinctive) + *synkrasia* (mix); that is, their take on their material lends it distinction. In "Humility, Concentration, and Gusto" Moore writes that "humility, indeed, is armor, for it realizes it is impossible to be original, in the sense of doing something that has never been thought of before" (*CPr* 421). Although the humble armor has a reclusive dimension, hiding the self-effacing poet behind an assemblage of words that she doesn't quite own, it also combats and refashions Romantic concepts of originality and lyric subjectivity by transgressing and placing in the foreground the boundaries between the self-enclosed lyric and its cultural matrix. "Concentration" encompasses rhythm ("the rhythm is the person, and the sentence but a radiograph of personality"); the "lion's leap" of a syntax arranged in accordance with the anacoluthic and elliptical cadences of conversation; and the punctilio of precise diction, intonation, and timing (*CPr* 396). Artists develop "gusto" by trusting their personal taste and predilections, which for Moore often means being "prepossessed" by the "impassioned explicitness" and "infectious" compressed ambiguity of those peers who obey her moral injunction to go "right on doing what idiosyncrasy tells [them] to do; to see the vision and not deny it; to care and admit that we do" (422–23, 426).

Moore's own combinatorial verve, lambent irony, and brio of delivery imbues her material with gusto, which in turn can impart to readers the singular "spin" that has been wrought on her material. Gusto is ambiguously a property of the verse and a quality discerned in it by the reader, who is expected to catch and savor the implicit messages flowing through Moore's writerly inscription of a dazzling conversational style. The loose-knit conversational hum reassures the reader that it isn't necessary to catch *every* nuance, while the bracing "fragrance of iodine" spurs one to intuit "implicit" ironies ("If tributes cannot/be implicit,/give me diatribes and the fragrance of iodine" [*CP* 151]). Although she can be a devastating ironist, Moore disarms as frequently through appreciative enthusiasm. In "Idiosyncrasy and Technique" she expresses regret that in an age of "too much sarcasm" any "touch of unfeigned gusto" is deflated by "our smart press" (*CPr* 511). Deeply attuned to how reception determines what and how things get said, Moore is fully committed to trusting personal predilections, even at the risk of obscurity. "Voltaire objected to those who said in enigmas what others had said naturally, and we agree," she opines, and then adds a characteristic retroactive qualifier, "yet we must have the courage of our peculiarities" (*CPr* 398). The commitment to idiosyncrasy means that Moore's poems can occasion the kind of reception difficulties they comment upon, as she acknowledges in a 1960 interview with Donald Hall: "the most difficult thing for me is to be satisfactorily lucid, yet have enough implication in it to suit myself."[5] The carapace of quotation that can make her verse appear opaque "seems under compulsion to set down an unbearable accuracy," and this tension between private meaningfulness and public engagement infuses her poetics (CPr 398). A contemporary, Randall Jarrell, captures the effect: "But the most extreme precision leads inevitably to quotation; and quotation is armor and ambiguity and irony all at once—turtles are great quoters. Miss Moore leaves the stones she picks up carefully uncut, but places them in an unimaginably complicated and difficult setting, to sparkle under the Northern Lights of her continual irony."[6]

In 1919, his curiosity piqued by "Black Earth," a poem that ponders how "The I of each is to/the I of each,/a kind of fretful speech" from the perspective of "This elephant skin/which I inhabit . . . Black/but beautiful," Ezra Pound wrote, offering publication assistance to the poet he had hailed the previous year as an exemplar of "logopoeia or poetry that is akin to nothing but language, which is a dance of intelligence among words and ideas."[7] "Does your stuff 'appear' in America?" Pound queries before signing off a letter that is very taken up with how the poet herself appears, asking "how much youngness there is to go into the work" and "are you a jet black Ethiopian Othello-hued, or was that line in one of your *Egoist* poems but part of your general elaboration and allegory, and designed to differentiate your color from that of the surrounding menagery?"[8] With characteristic forbearance Moore's response protests the relative dullness of her background, portrays herself as the granddaughter and sister of a Presbyterian clergyman, and declares: "I am Irish by descent, possibly Scotch also, but purely Celtic . . . and contrary to your impression am altogether blond and have red hair."[9] Although Moore's self-representation as a daughter of the manse advertises her Scotch-Irishness, the declaration that *"I am Irish* by descent, *possibly* Scotch also, but *purely Celtic"* suppresses the colonialist and sectarian overtones of Scotch-Irishness to identify with the colonized Irish and to lay claim to the considerable cachet of a Celtic background in Anglo-American literary circles at the time.

Marianne Craig Moore's matrilineal roots can be traced back to Craigs on the 1610 list of Scottish undertakers, participants in the Stuart plantation of Ulster, who resettled in the colony of the Penns in 1719 (they were denied entry at Boston) with four other "Dissenter" families who were unwilling to conform to the Articles of Perth; and to Moore's Warner great-grandparents, who left Ireland in the 1815–21 diaspora. Although the Irish domicile in the Scottish-Irish-American chain migration is of comparatively short duration, their isolation there from English colonists and native Irish (and from Boston Brahmins and "famine Irish" in the United States) consolidated their group identity and clannishness. The family history by Mrs. Moore's cousin Mary Craig Shoemaker, *Five Typical Scotch-Irish Families of the Cumberland Valley,* tracks an unwaveringly high level of intermarriage among the five families over six generations.[10]

It is significant that the Scotch-Irish and Irish Catholics, who both regard their emigration from Ireland as compelled by oppression, are more Irish-identified as a group than Anglo-Irish immigrants. Ireland figures as the place whence they were wrongfully evicted.[11] The sense of grievance nurtures the adversarial identity, (the Presbyterian "Dissenter" identity tag is especially revealing in this respect), which prompts the Moores to categorize their impatience, perseverance against adversity, and clannishness as "Irish" traits. The mix of racial entitlement and grievance fostered by the Anglo-Celt's junior-partner role in British imperialism is pithily captured by Shoemaker when she observes that the Ulster plantation freed northern England from border insurgents while providing Ulster with industrious settlers (7). Thus, the Celtic Fringe became an imperial vanguard, and Anglo-Celts developed an ambivalent self-image of Anglo-identified industry and Celt-identified insurgency. Anglo-Celts' adversarial identity suppresses their complicity with colonialism, and their ambiguous postcolonial status in settler colonies continues to generate controversy. In a U.S. context *Irish* signifies "white" and "not-WASP," a racial identity that Moore's letter features as at once mainstream (the privilege, and ordinariness, of "altogether blond") yet ultimately resistant to assimilation (because "purely Celtic" represents indefeasible otherness).

In what must have seemed to Pound as an unnecessarily detailed chronology of the family's relocations, beginning with her grandfather's manse and culminating with the tacit wish that she and her mother might yet join her brother Warner in his, Moore obliquely conveys the supreme importance to her of the devout and intensely close-knit family that formed the first audience for her poetry.[12] "My mother lost him early" is Moore's only reticent comment on the father she never met and knew little about.[13] When Moore corresponded with Pound, she and her mother were recovering from the impact of her brother Warner's marriage in 1918, a trauma presaged in 1915 when Mrs. Moore objected to his courtship of a woman who was "not of [her] 'race.'" On that occasion Warner ("Badger") wrote to assure his mother ("Mole") that he was of her "race" (he also accents *race* with quotation marks) and that "we shall move as 3 in 1" to "Badger Hollow" (his future manse), adding, "we are not of a race to flinch" at the self-denial involved.[14] *Race* presumably refers to their Scotch-Irishness, inextricable from Presbyterianism for Mrs. Moore and Warner, but it also treats the family as a racialized enclave whose private idiom Warner admiringly detects in Moore's writing "in our own special 'language' but so marvellously handled that the 'aliens' could & can understand them & enjoy them" (RML 5:23:19). The corollary extravagant nicknaming in family correspondence anticipates the many animal personae of the poems and over a decade's work on translating *The Fables of La Fontaine* (1954) and evinces what Ernest Renan identifies as the "invincible attraction to fables [which] must have discredited the Celtic race in the eyes of nationalities that believed themselves to be more serious" (*Poésie*, 57). The use of animal personae in the family argot shows how "own special 'language'" works as a kind of communal "thick skin" insulating their circle from the outside world and intimates how a "near-obsession with the idea of the belligerence of being" underlies their playful camaraderie.[15] The family argot is a particular instance of what may well be a common practice among diasporic families, the tendency to categorize family foibles and customs as Irish and, perhaps, to follow the atavistic narrative logic of family lore and assign a blanket "Irish" label to the mysterious gaps opened up by the unknown texture and undisclosed secrets of their forebears' lives. Under these conditions "the story" of the family and the "story of Ireland" are each held to represent the other metonymically.

Moore's acquaintance with her ethnic homeland was exclusively textual (she first visited Ireland in 1964 in her late seventies), a "memory" composed out of extensive reading, family lore, visual images, artifacts, and hearsay. Her reviews and reading notebooks reveal a thorough knowledge of Irish literature and other writings about Ireland. The depth of Moore's admiration for Maria Edgeworth (1767–1849) can be deduced from her adaptation of *The Absentee* (1812), a novel that Edgeworth had first attempted as a play, into Moore's only play, *The Absentee* (1962), which has never been produced. She praises Yeats's *Ideas of Good and Evil,* which includes the "Celtic" essay, as "worth their weight in gold," and her annotations underscore the influence on both poets of Blake's visionary poetics.[16] Written in bold red superscript over other penciled marginalia on Yeats's opinion that Blake's intensity of vision made him "a too literal realist of imagination" (Yeats is commenting on the Blakean principle that "ideas cannot be given but in their minutely appropriate words") is Moore's revisionary phrase "literalists of the imagination." The phrase is famously incorporated into the alternate long version of "Poetry," a manifesto that declares that we shall not have poetry until "literalists of the imagination" present "imaginary gardens with real toads in them" (*CP* 267). Moore published odes to Yeats, Shaw, and George Moore and a regular "Irish Letter" when she edited the *Dial* and was exceptionally well informed about Irish history, literature, and politics.

In the preface to *On the Study of Celtic Literature* (1867) Matthew Arnold recalls reading *Times* editorials about the 1865–66 lectures as "arrant nonsense" and "a foolish interference with the natural progress of civilization" and thinking to himself, "*Behold England's difficulty in governing Ireland!*" The ad hominem attack characterized Arnold as "a sentimentalist who talks nonsense about the children of Taliesin and Ossian, and whose dainty taste requires something more flimsy than the strong sense and sturdy morality of his fellow Englishmen" (*SCL* xiii). The censure indicates the near-reflex association of the "inferior" race and/or subjugated people with the "weaker" sex, a cultural commonplace that was consolidated in Ernest Renan's influential assertion that Celts are "an essentially feminine race" but which has a much wider provenance than it. The spectacle of a scion of English culture identifying with Celts provokes a stern reprimand that to "go Celtic" is "to go soft and effeminate" and to risk losing credibility in a public sphere in which the "sturdy morality" of the progressive, political, and worldly Englishman rules over everyone else—women, children, Celts, lower classes, and lesser races—by virtue of innate superiority. The Celt serves as a foil of effeminacy to the "sturdy morality" of the Englishman and bolsters "that imperturbable faith in its untransformed self which at any rate ma[kes] it imposing" (*SCL* xviii).

As a mark of biological difference and necessary interdependence, gender is a malleable construct for simultaneously naturalizing a binary opposition between Anglo/Celtic spheres while also rehabilitating the subordinate role as a complementary one, the junior partner of British imperialism. Marjorie Howes writes that the "Celt's femininity stood . . . for a combination of racial difference and racial affinity" which structures the "imperial romance" that Arnold promotes with his "insistence that the English should be capable of 'attaching' the Irish" (20–21). This imperial romance has exerted enormous influence on regulating and narrating Anglo-Celtic cross-cultural relations. Criticism of the gendered racial stereotype has focused on deconstructing gender roles, either by examining compensatory hyper-masculine revisions of Celticism (as they are variously exemplified by the revivalist cult of Cuchulain, Yeats's struggle to master "the sweet insinuating feminine voice" of the *sidhe,* and MacDiarmid's warfare against "Doric infantilism" and "ladyfying") or by analyzing how patriarchal uses of the (Renanean) "ideal of woman" or the Jacobite *spéirbhean* as a custodian of national honor occludes and reinforces the oppression of women.[17] My focus, however, is on how the Anglo-Celtic imperial romance masks and reifies the structural inequalities of Pale/Fringe cross-cultural contact.

Moore's Irish poems bring her poetics of idiosyncrasy to bear on the "charmante pudeur" concept at the heart of Ernest Renan's influential representation of Celts as "a domestic race," a "people so eminently dowered with feminine tact" that they have graciously retired to the remote fastnesses of Europe, where their "indomitable hope, that tenacity in the affirmation of a [Breton/Celtic] future," makes "an invincible resistance to its enemies" (16, 24, 6). By portraying Celts as contractile, Renan at once manages to gratify a colonialist fantasy of consensual dispossession through an image of Bretons' gallant withdrawal to the fringe and to assuage native pride by depicting an "indomitable" and "invincible" people. Bretons are assigned the feminized role of moderating the harsh ethos of commercial and public life with their aesthetic, moral, and spiritual values, but they also constitute pockets of radical dissent from dominant mores. Renan approaches the Celtic Fringe with the double-consciousness of a worldly ethnographer perturbed by natives' aloof taciturnity and an insider who takes a certain pride in "that powerful individuality, that hatred of the foreigner" and (albeit "stifling") "spirit of family" which isolates his home culture. Crossing the Pale separating Breton Brittany from French France "seems like entering on the subterranean strata of another world . . . [resembling being led by Dante counterclockwise] from one circle of his Inferno to another." The Dantean allusion is in keeping with Renan's portrayal of the Celtic Fringe as a primary source of early modern European literature, but the disorienting experience of entering the antipodal zone and following the withershins directionality of riddance magic suggests to the traveler that he has somehow transgressed a sacred space. *Charmante pudeur* has an edge of repudiation that conveys a subliminal "back-off" message.

Arnold mutinies against Renan's portrayal of the shamefast, contractile Celt because he experiences the shameless, sponging Irish as an intrusive nuisance. Moreover, Renan's taciturn Celts are altogether too Teutonic for Arnold's taste and could not deliver "the expansive, eager Celtic nature" and "the Titanism of the Celt, his passionate, turbulent, indomitable reaction against the despotism of fact" needed to counteract the humdrum philistinism (*die gemeinheit*) of the Anglo-Saxon (131, 85). He sidesteps the issue of whether "chivalry and romance and the glorification of a feminine ideal spring" from a Celtic source, conceding only "that there is a Celtic air about the extravagance of chivalry." "No doubt the sensibility of the Celtic nature, its nervous exaltation, have something feminine in them," he assents, "and the Celt is thus peculiarly disposed to feel the spell of feminine idiosyncrasy; he has an affinity to it; he is not far from its secret"; he "half-divines" it (90–91). A tutelary female mediates "the secret of natural beauty and natural magic" to the impressionable male Celt and beyond him to the observing Anglo ethnographer, who is enthralled by the extravagance (as opposed to the decorum) of chivalric romance. *Charmante pudeur* has seductive appeal for Arnold, "and very often, for the gay defiant reaction against fact of the lively Celtic nature one has more than sympathy; one feels, in spite of good sense disapproving, magnetized and exhilarated by it" (91–92).

Moore's poetics of idiosyncrasy calls attention to a structural homology between *the Pale* and *pudeur* manifest in the casual use of the colloquialism "beyond the pale." In *Histoire de la pudeur* (1986) Jean Claude Bologne defines *pudeur* as "the socially agreed upon border between what one conceals and what one reveals to others, a border which always exists but whose placement is largely arbitrary and continually shifting."[18] Renan and Arnold's dissenting interpretations of Pale/Fringe relations demonstrate Bologne's point about the arbitrary placement of *pudeur*. The Pale-*pudeur* separating Anglo and Celt is not a bilaterally agreed-upon border between equal partners but is determined by the interests and point of view of the dominant Anglo partner. This Anglocentrism empowers the Anglo observer and subordinates the Celt to the feminized position of to-be-looked-at-ness. The one-way traffic from Gaelic source to English target culture that dominates translation practice also structures Celticist ethnography in English. The Celtic source is expected to yield what the Anglocentric ethnographer collects and interprets. The positional superiority of the Anglo interpreter over the Celtic

source is strengthened by disavowing the discriminatory structure of their relations, but the denial falters when confronted with an opaque, unyielding, and
enigmatic source. The unyielding source is veiled with the femininity of one who
withholds favors or guards esoteric knowledge, and the enigmatic source shifts
the burden of translation back onto the ethnographer, who must decipher whence
and in what idiom she speaks. The uncanny authority of "the spell of feminine
idiosyncrasy" belongs to the "feminine" sphere of the local, the particular, the
magical, and the beautiful, as opposed to the "masculine" sphere of worldly
universality.

The Pale can be said to constitute itself in relation to an outside, the excluded
Fringe that lies beyond the pale, but it is also the case, Moore shows, that the Fringe
confronts the Pale with a display of reticence, "omissions [that] are not accidents,"
and opaque cultural practices that mark "the outside" as a withheld limit, a
guarded domain of unknowable reserves.[19] The elliptical style of "Sojourn in the
Whale" comments upon the need for subterfuge under repressive conditions and
calls attention to how enigmatic reserve can convey the depths of feeling, eloquence, and power that are thus held back: "Not decorum, but restraint," as Moore
puts it in another poem (CP 76). In "Spenser's Ireland" she adapts Edgeworth's
deployment of Spenser's citation of Herodotus on the Irish-Scythian mantle as a
means to represent the remote land "which, like Herodotus,/I have not seen
except in pictures," in terms of its elusiveness (CP 78). "The Greeks liked smooth-
ness, distrusted what was back/of what could not be clearly seen," Moore writes of
the chroniclers of antiquity (CP 75), and this warranted distrust, also manifested in
Spenser's proposals to ban the mantles that afford the Irish protective obscurity,
informs her representation of Pale/Fringe cross-cultural exchange.

In my discussion of Renan and Arnold's quarrel over Celts' "shamefastness" in
the first chapter, I argue that the "poetic life" of the Breton native and Anglo
conqueror and their respective positions on opposite sides of the Pale/Fringe color
their purportedly disinterested ethnographies. The "fixed feelings" of contempt
and shame which keep Pale/Fringe diglossia in place are also fluid and ambivalent, with Renan sublimating the shame of conquest into indomitable pride and
Arnold's confidence in the Anglo-Saxon ability to conquer foundering on "hauntings" of Celtic doom. Because "Celt" is a notional construct, an artificial pan-
ethnic tag that the Irish, Scottish, Welsh or Scotch-Irish can avow or disavow at
will, it is very amenable to psychological transference. Hence, the received script
can be freely adapted by Renan to offer homage to his close-knit family and by
Arnold to qualify his father's Teutonic bias. The role occupied by family as an
intermediary zone between the individual and inherited discourses of race is of

particular interest in relation to Moore, whose unusually close family bears a remarkable resemblance to Renan's.[20] Renan's image of the Breton fastness resonates with Moore's depiction of the mollusk shell as sanctuary and poem in her ode to contractility, "To a Snail," and her paean to maternal solicitude, "The Paper Nautilus." "If 'compression is the first grace of style,'/you have it," the snail is told: "Contractility is a virtue/as modesty is a virtue," for what we value "in the curious phenomenon of your occipital horn" is what we value in style, "the principle that is hid." Restraining and constrained mothering in "The Paper Nautilus" is associated with productive hindrance, a theme revisited with the "hindered characters" of "Spenser's Ireland":

> her glass ram's horn-cradled freight
>   is hid but is not crushed;
>   as Hercules, bitten
>   by a crab loyal to the hydra,
> was hindered to succeed,
>   the intensively
>   watched eggs coming from
> the shell free it when they are freed.

Moore shares with Renan (and arguably with Edgeworth) a sense that their beleaguered minority cultures are an extension of their precarious and resilient homesteads. Renan's family was a crucial first audience for *Poésie,* and Maria Edgeworth's extensive collaboration with her father and relative isolation in a Big House meant that she too addressed a familial audience before engaging a public one.[21]

The "delicacy" and "reserve" that consign Celts to the hearth in Renan's schema are regarded by Moore as essential *civic* virtues. She views modesty as a necessary tempering of behavior to allow individuals to meet and come to terms with one another and is supremely aware of how social decorum is rigged to impose an unequal burden of deference on women and the lower orders of society.[22] Nor, for that matter, does she agree that the aesthetic influence of tact culminates with medieval romance, for she finds a rhetoric of reticence at the forefront of American modernism in the "reticent candor" of Wallace Stevens and T. S. Eliot and the "perspicuous opacity" of Gertrude Stein.[23]

In December 1915, at the time of the averted crisis over Warner's courtship, Moore made a decisive visit to Manhattan, where she was introduced to the Stieglitz circle by Alfred Kreymbourg (who published her poetry in *Others*) and which she recounts as her "big time in the whale" and "my passage to the Red Sea" in ecstatic letters to Warner. Her "sojourn in the whale" was a vocational Rubicon, as the Jonah allegory suggests, and after the Easter Rising in Ireland the following year Moore conflated the two watershed events in the poem "Sojourn in the Whale" (1917).[24] Yeats's "Easter 1916" inscribes the poet in the national pantheon—"I write it out in a verse"—and the poem is frequently cited as an authoritative testimony of the event and the poet's indirect contribution to it. As the title of the poem preceding "Sojourn" declares in a different context, "He Wrote the History Book," and Moore's inscription of her poetic career into Irish history meanwhile goes unremarked, by contrast. She is not considered to have had any involvement in the event she represents as an abstract gendered altercation between Ireland and the oppressor. The allusion in "Sojourn['s]" title to her correspondence with Warner is the only clue that the confirmation of her vocation as a poet is a theme, and the date of publication and extended apostrophe to "you, Ireland" are the sole indicators of its engagement with the 1916 insurrection. The reticence hardly gainsays, however, the boldness of conflating her own destiny as a poet with Ireland's destiny. This quality of reclusive assertiveness can be seen at play in the effacement of the speaker's "I" from the poem, which must be inferred from the fiction of conversational reciprocity established by her apostrophic address to "you, Ireland." The retiring omniscient speaker nevertheless speaks out assertively on Ireland's behalf by orchestrating a confrontation in which she ventriloquizes the pejorative commonplaces Ireland has "heard men say" and lends her ethnic homeland a perfect putdown for the oppressor.

"Sojourn" is a parable of resurgence which conveys its message through the ironic juxtaposition of the two quotations that constitute the verbal showdown and through the rhythmic undertow of water in motion. The emphasis on the ocean that connects and separates Ireland and the speaker reinforces the reiterative timelessness of apostrophe by grounding the I-thou reciprocity in the ebb and flow of the sea. The "Ireland" addressee is a dystopic Atlantis of indeterminate gender since Jonah's role is occupied by a Rumpelstiltskin-like spinster, but s/he "has heard men" refer to her as "she." Hidden by its opaque devourer, Ireland is enveloped in layers of legend and interpretation. The chronicler of its privations approaches through a convoluted fairytale topography:

> Trying to open locked doors with a sword, threading
>   the points of needles, planting shade trees
>   upside down; swallowed by the opaqueness of one whom the seas

love better than they love you, Ireland—

you have lived and lived on every kind of shortage.
    You have been compelled by hags to spin
    gold thread from straw and have heard men say:
"There is a feminine temperament in direct contrast to ours,

which makes her do these things. Circumscribed by a
    heritage of blindness and native
    incompetence, she will become wise and will be forced to give in.
Compelled by experience, she will turn back;

water seeks its own level":
    and you have smiled. "Water in motion is far
    from level." You have seen it, when obstacles happened to bar
the path, rise automatically.

The de-individuated personae, imprisonment theme and imagery, and the atemporality of lyric apostrophe all contribute to the impression of a self-enclosed poem remote from the historical personal and Irish national events that occasioned it and create a feeling of claustrophobia which prepares for the sensation of release at the close.

The worldliness of the lyric, and the particular spin Moore places on discourse about Ireland, is made plain by examining her reading diaries to see how she deploys her borrowed sources. Identifiable background sources include excerpts from newspaper articles defending Ireland against calumny,[25] studies of wave rhythm cadences in Isaiah and Synge's *Aran Islands,* and verse featuring a lovelorn speaker weaving her shroud by Irish poet Ethna Carbery. For the words dryly attributed to "men" she amplifies a recorded unattributed fragment, "without disparagement to women there is a feminine temperament which is in direct . . ."[26] She drops the giveaway "without disparagement to women" and preserves the blah, blah, blah effect by expanding the ellipsis to a bombastic pronouncement that finds its level by enjambing three stanzas. By quoting a misogynist commonplace whose immediate source is obviously nugatory, Moore represents the binary stereotype as specific, but not limited, to Ireland.

The only annotated source, "water in motion is far from level," is the shortest sentence in the poem and the anchor of its rhythmic design. Culled from *Literary Digest,* it is a mundane explanation for the general reader of a principle of physics: "It is perfectly true that 'water seeks its level' but this aphorism holds true only for still water. Water in motion is far from level. The elevation of the center of a stream during a flood is generally the result of the roughness of its bed." Moore's gift for inflecting borrowed phrases with her own rhythm and tone—that is, her own spin or idiosyncrasy—can be observed in how she catches a nascent rhythmic and ironic inflection in the simple sentence that may have been missed by the author of it. Taking his cue from Moore's statement that her verse is "governed by the pull of the sentence," Jerrald Ranta makes a persuasive case that she structures her sentences to reproduce the motion of waves in the series of sea poems which begins with "Sojourn."[27] The effect is achieved in "Sojourn" by a progressive shortening of the six sentences to the terse penultimate sentence, a pivotal trough that is followed by the gathering force and implied continuing swell of the long closing sentence. The subtle euphony of " 'Water in motion is far/from level,' " scores the crescendo of resurgence against the overbearing weight of what "men say." In the setting provided by Moore, the laconic statement cuts through the misogyny with leveling irony. The deflating rejoinder debunks the fallacious logic used to bolster men's masculine, innately insightful and competent, and solid selves as the antithesis of Ireland's feminine, congenitally blind and incompetent, and fluid identity. Rejoinders necessarily take up the antagonist's terms, and so Moore deploys a law of physics to overturn men's law of antipodal "feminine" temperament. The upward lift of the melodious line and the cutting edge of the leveling irony converge in a delicate pulsation of rhythm and intonation which imparts the invigorating gusto of irony to the borrowed phrase. The sentence is the moral of the poem, but the efficacy of that moral inheres less in its semantic content than in the "radiograph of personality" invested in the phrase by the upbeat satire.

Idiosyncrasy is a style of delivery, a way of sending a message so that it catches on, even against the odds. The message acquires a doubleness when it is relayed through the ironic juxtaposition of quotations because one receives both the ironic commentary of the sender and the objectified quotations that may be construed differently by the reader. The abstractedness of quotation in the men/colonized Ireland exchange has a strong "as-if" effect that makes the rejoinder more freely available to other oppressed groups and less embedded in the particularities of the Irish insurrection. The very artifice of juxtaposition begs the question of whether the staged exchange is in fact a dialogue, and this in turn raises the fictive status of the apostrophe dialogue that unfolds as if "you, Ireland" might in turn address the speaker. At the same time as one exults vicariously in the witty rejoinder, the as-if echo rebounds to suggest that neither "you, Ireland" nor "men" are listening to what is said by the speaker or the oppressed Irish. The perceptual split opens the gap between what gets said and what gets heard to make tangible the lopsidedness of the Pale between colonizer and colonized, the *pudeur* between the sexes, and the transatlantic separation of the diasporic speaker from her ethnic homeland. The sense of impasse has the paradoxical effect of conveying a sense of the Pale much as the men of the leveling imperium envisage it—an impermeable cordon sanitaire that keeps a lid on the subjugated other—but from the wrong side of the divide. On the wrong side of the Pale/*pudeur* one is forced "to spin" and "to give in" and is given many occasions to bridle at what "men say."

Helen Vendler's observation that Moore's wit shows the aggression of the silent well-brought-up girl who thinks up mute rejoinders during boring parlor room conversations is pertinent for appreciating why the shamefast lady and the underclass are both so practiced at crafting unspeakable rejoinders.[28] The art of the mute rejoinder is one of pointing and gesture, and it is signaled by punctuation in "Sojourn." The placement of the colon and the period in the sentence preceding the rejoinder—" 'she will turn back;/water seeks its own level': and you have smiled"—is important because the smile inflects "water seeks its own level" with a contrary intonation even *before* the rejoinder is uttered. The colon marks the Pale/*pudeur*: what "men say" is rebutted by the smile of "you [who] have seen it" otherwise, creating the ripple effects that can coalesce to "rise automatically." The power of the disempowered to not hear what men say in the way men intend them to hear it keeps shifting the contours of the Pale/*pudeur* and loosens its regulatory force by exposing its arbitrariness. The smile is a sign of "charming shamefastness," a semiotic gesture that obliquely highlights how *charmante pudeur* can be used as a ruse to uphold patriarchal order and colonial hegemony. Through this device Moore transforms reticence into an expository rhetoric that becomes a form of social critique. She deploys "you have smiled" to include readers who share the insurrectionary joy of a well-turned, well-timed, and well-deserved rejoinder, and thus the rhetoric of the "shamefast" smile works as a disarming armor that spreads and gathers and joins readers in an inclusive "you have smiled" insurgency against the inanities and injustices of men. The Pale/*pudeur* demarcates a history of shameful shaming, which, if one has the humility to yield to its insurrectionary counter-currents, can be turned in another direction.

All minds quote during the soliloquizing that accompanies the course of everyday life, according to Yeats, and Moore's rejoinder makes a genteel counterpoint to the "denouncing and remembering" slum woman speech that animates Yeats's reveries. Moore's retaliatory fantasies situate the speaker as Ireland's advocate, a self-insertion in the role of rescuer which resembles the poet-speaker's role in the

Jacobite *aisling*. The agency shown by "you, Ireland" seems diminished by contrast with that of the eloquent speaker, creating a fatalistic image of the insurrectionists rising "automatically" in what Moore and Yeats independently represent as a passive drama. Moore's allusion to the reluctant Jonah who tries to evade
his appointed destiny complicates the aura of passivity by bringing both Moore's
Presbyterian faith and her humor into play. Ignominiously spewed into fulfillment of his role, Jonah is one of the great seriocomic figures of biblical "literalism of the imagination." The Jonah allusion may express a wish to be catapulted
out of the inhibition induced by hearing "men say" one is incapable of self-
determination. Whatever the tenor of Jonah's private significance for Moore, the
allusion to Jonah to register the vocational Rubicon, and the enlargement of that
allusion to incorporate the 1916 Rising into a foundational myth for the construction of "Moore," suggests a profound affiliation to Ireland. As an activist for
the then-unrealized goal of nationwide women's suffrage in the United States,
Moore's gendered treatment of the "rise automatically" law broadens the Irish
event to encompass the anticipated enfranchisement of other groups.

Moore's work lives on the contagion of "touché!" Reading this connoisseur of
the well-turned rejoinder affords the pleasure of encountering phrases, which,
had we only thought of them, we would like to have coined ourselves. The lapidary
quality of Moore's work, which is so replete with memorable turns of phrase that it
is as if her words are always already quoted, makes the Irish bull an especially
congenial speech genre for her. Irish bulls are solecisms that are circulated as
laughable failures at verbal passing by the semi-Anglicized Irish. Although the
intended meaning of these utterances is clear and straightforward, they are so
infelicitously expressed as to be manifestly absurd and self-contradictory.[29] Bulls
are an aural genre, like Scotticisms, because they come into existence when the
verbal "blunder" is tagged as such by the auditor. Unlike the Scotticism, however,
the Irish bull is seized upon as an eminently *quotable* blunder to be kept until an
opportune moment for citing it arises. They provide an occasion for insiders of the
Pale to form a bond of pleasurable superiority at the disparity between their verbal
mastery and the blunderer's ineptitude, in accordance with the triangular dynamic of tendentious jokes. The coding of the speech genre as a bull is not a result
of hearing the explicit meaning and missing the implicit meaning but of adopting
a superior communicative stance that disdains to attend to the implicit meaning
and instead ridicules the speaker's incomplete mastery of the Pale's explicit style
of speaking. Bulls are cited, not said, if I may use a bull to define the speech
genre.[30] The citation of a bull uproots the utterance from the implicit conversa-

tional style of an oral context, in which it makes sense, and translates it into an explicit scriptist code that accentuates its ungrammaticality and rights (writes) it. They are usually cited for the injurious purpose of putting down the Irish and have been instrumental in widening the diglossic divide between those who speak and those who think up mute rejoinders.

Maria and Richard Lovell Edgeworths' *Essay on Irish Bulls* (1802) cites bulls not to mock the Irish but to reform the complacent reflex of their English and Anglicized readers, "wherever we hear [the brogue], we expect the blunder," by showing the figurative wit and bilingual double-consciousness of these idiosyncrasies of Irish speech (142).[31] My chapter title, "An Irish Incognita," refers to how Moore is not "read" as Irish and also alludes to a parable entitled "The Irish Incognito" in the Edgeworths' essay, which features a highly Anglicized Irishman who loses a wager that he can pass as English because he keeps betraying himself with bulls. His telltale slips include the enthusiastic commendation of a painting as "absolutely more like than the original" (212). The title of "The Irish Incognito" is intended as a contradiction-in-terms (i.e., a bull) by the Edgeworths, I believe, because they hope that Irish natives will continue to betray themselves through the irrepressible exuberance of their nonstandard speech. The Edgeworths' indignation that the Irish should be denied the social clout to persuade others to attend carefully to what they mean to say is mixed with proleptic nostalgia about the likely future demise of distinctively Irish ways of skewing English. Their wish to reform the conditions that entrench Anglo-Irish diglossia while yet desiring that Irish culture might somehow "stay the same" is a key for understanding both the ideological sway of "de-Anglicization" and the mix of grievance and nostalgia which shapes Irish-Americans' sentiment toward their ethnic culture. Ambivalence about the desirability of "total assimilation" is a driving force of the de-Anglicization movement and an unsettling preoccupation in a multiethnic United States bent on an *e pluribus unum* makeover.

The Edgeworths' antiquarian enterprise of amassing and preserving "collectible" Irish bulls is a congenial one for a poet who once described her verse as "a collection of flies in amber."[32] Although the curatorial metaphor suggests the mummification rather than the revivification of Irish culture, Moore's salvage of specimens of idiosyncrasy and sedimented history attests to a faith in their infectious gusto, a gusto that she believes can help to foster "the courage of our peculiarities" in individuals and societies. By treating the bull as a didactic tool, Moore effectively resignifies it as a kind of "bloother," a verbal blunder circulated among the Irish themselves for self-instruction and entertainment. Whereas the (implicitly monolingual) auditor of the bull detects an inadmissible mode of thought disrupting the proper one, the (implicitly bilingual) auditor of a *bloother* detects a collision between two incompatible linguistic consciousnesses which is simultaneously funny and enlightening, since it allows one to momentarily occupy a third space for perceiving the play between the two. In speaking/citing Irish bulls in "Spenser's Ireland," Moore attempts to tease out the history and dynamics of the anti-Irish discrimination encapsulated by the bull while yet preserving the contagious iterability of the genre. Her multidimensional citational practice seeks to create a poem that has the gusto and pithy éclat of a bull and yet packs in enough "implication" to gratify the troubled and dissatisfied poet-speaker and to provide an encrypted genealogy of subaltern Irish historiography.

"Spenser's Ireland" juxtaposes two magisterial "views" of Ireland, Edmund Spenser's *View of the Present State of Ireland* (c. 1596) and Irish expatriate Donn Byrne's photo-essay in the *National Geographic Magazine* (1927), with oral storytelling "fictions" by novelist Maria Edgeworth (*Castle Rackrent* [1800] and *The Absentee* [1812]) and translated Gaelic lore (from the late fifteenth century to the present) Moore heard from Irish writer, folklorist, and raconteur Padraic Colum.[33] Draft marginalia indicate that Giraldus Cambrensis's twelfth-century tract, *Topographia Hibernia,* was also a source, as is Herodotus, and the poem is an ambitious critical genealogy of ethnographies about Ireland and of the politics of the ethnographic encounter. It is a poem of great verve which sweeps from an arresting treatment of Ireland as a distant ethnographic object—"Spenser's Ireland/has not altered/a place as kind as it is green/the greenest place I've never seen"—to a resounding, if ambivalent, declaration of Irishness: "I am troubled, I'm dissatisfied, I'm Irish." The opening and closing sentences provide an autobiographical frame that makes any ultimate separation of speaker and poet difficult because they are the only ones in the poem without sources annotated in the notes (*CP* 280). Ireland *is* "the greenest place I've never seen" for Moore, and draft marginalia, in which she doodles with a hyphenated "I'm Ire-ish" (a play on the Elizabethan pun "land of Ire" and Shakespeare's "What ish my nation?") to accent the *I wish/Ire-ish* rhyme, indicate that she *is* troubled, dissatisfied, and Irish.[34] The closing sentence responds with mixed skepticism and disappointment to photo-essayist Byrne's claim that the extravagant reciprocity of Irish speech habits discloses Irish hospitality: "I wish/I could believe it:/I am troubled, I'm dissatisfied, I'm Irish." Moore's ambiguous mode of showing and hiding her Irish affiliation is signaled by the possessive case in the title, "Spenser's Ireland," which serves to draw attention to the colonialist attempt to define and disseminate its own view of Ireland at the same time as it oddly distances Moore from ownership of her poem.

Moore says that her poems start when "a felicitous phrase springs to mind," and it is evident from draft marginalia—"marvelous to say"—that she felt that the provocative opening statement formed a syntactic and rhythmic sentence that provided a nucleus for the isosyllabic stanzas.[35]

> Spenser's Ireland
>
> has not altered;—
>> a place as kind as it is green
>> the greenest place I've never seen.

The sentence defies credence, since Ireland couldn't *not* have altered since the late sixteenth century, and Spenser and Ireland were unquestionably not kind to one another. The speaker's opening admission that Ireland "is the greenest place I've never seen" undermines her credibility as an Irish ethnographer and makes her seem less authoritative than her precursors who lived in Ireland. At the same time, the admission paradoxically authenticates her as an Irish autobiographer by uttering an Irish bull (one cannot logically assert that an unseen place is the greenest). She is an outsider, but Irish culture is inside her, secreted within idiosyncratic usages of English.

One instinctively hears "the greenest place I've *never* seen" as a slip of the tongue and assumes that the speaker has said the contrary of what she means to say, the greenest place I've *ever* seen. The permanence of the printed poem re-channels the impulse to impute an error toward reading the solecism as an intentional catachresis, a rapid double take that betrays much about the almost automatic way print supersedes the spoken word to become the definitive version. The friction produced by the ambiguous *never/ever* slippage lends the utterance punch, however, which suggests in turn that the catachresis is preferable to its insipid correct counterpart. The hyperbole and elision responsible for the solecistic "greenest thing [I've heard about but] never seen" intensifies the antithesis between privation (*never seen*) and desire (*greenest*) which culminates with the closing "I wish"/"Ire-ish" rhyme. *Greenest* is charged with the systemic pejoration of the Irish in Irish bulls as "green" in the compounded sense of credulous and uncultured and Irish. The ingenue's praise for the greenest place rebounds to mark her as the greenest, the most Irish and the greatest dupe.

The Irish-American ingenue is the greenest because, to cite the second bull in "Spenser's Ireland," "Hindered characters / seldom have mothers / in Irish stories, but they all have grandmothers" (ll. 21–23). This motherless-but-grandmothered bull (which Moore covertly places to link family lore with translated Gaelic lore she heard from Padraic Colum about Spenser's antagonist, Earl Gerald) is a figure for the return of the repressed. Bulls are received as unconscious slips or bunglings in which a Gaelic substrate disrupts the imposing coherence of Arnold's "vast, visible Teutonic superstructure." They are rich in ulteriority and have the double-voiced parasitism of one mode of mental functioning disturbing another. "Hindered characters/seldom have mothers/in Irish stories, but they all have grandmothers" has a syntax of exemptive afterthought (a frequent source of contradiction in Irish bulls) which mimics its atavistic message by eliding the intermediate link with an ulterior antecedent. Instead of deriving Irishness from residency ("the same people in the same place," as Leopold Bloom puts it), the diasporic speaker redefines it with the borrowed Colum aphorism as the same hindrance in different places. Irish hindrance is transmitted through genes (grandmothers), quotations (stories), and the social web of interlocution which determines who is green. The "return of the repressed" figure encapsulated by the bull is also suggested by the typographic appearance of the quotational poem, which draws attention to the encroachments of prior texts on present writing, of an atavistic "deep speech" on the reigning symbolic order, and of juxtaposed competing narratives.

David Kadlec argues that Moore's post-Darwinian pragmatist understanding of "the instability of generational transmission" has ethical and metapoetic repercussions, informing both her opposition to essentialist eugenics and restrictive immigration policies and her contingent procedure when composing isosyllabic verse: "I never plan stanzas[;] Words cluster like chromosomes, determining the procedure."[36] Moore's borrowed axiom of matrilineal hindrance plays with and against the patrilineal Emersonian precept that "everyman is a quotation from all his ancestors" and its contemporary restatement as an immigrant "principle of third-generation interest, 'what the son wishes to forget the grandson wishes to remember.' "[37] As these patriarchal aphorisms indicate, one's ancestors are not equally accessible to quotation, and hence, much citation practice is selective in the exclusionary sense. Because citation is selective in the sense of open to personal preference, however, it is possible to reconstitute "patrimonies." Moreover, because citation is selective in the evolutionary sense of open to happenstance, one may be surprised by unexpected outcomes as "[quotations] cluster like chromosomes, determining the procedure."

The citational strategy of "Spenser's Ireland" displays the ambivalent affiliations involved in autoethnography, self-writing that is mediated through one's scripted "ethno," or cultural, identity.[38] One does not get to select one's grandmothers or mainstream notions of what it means to be female, Irish, American, Irish-American, or Celtic, but one can selectively cite this heritage to affiliate with, and disaffiliate from, them. The selectivity of autoethnography raises interpretive challenges for readers, who must determine the extent to which the speaker owns, disavows, ironizes, and/or resignifies the quoted ethno, or group, identity. Cultural identity is formed in a public (and textual) arena. Because it is shaped by how individuals and groups are recognized, or "read," by others, it is located in the ambivalent slippage between spontaneous and cited speech acts marked by Moore's deployment of Irish bulls.

In "Mr. Colum's telling of the story of Earl Gerald, gusto as objectified made the unbelievable doings of an enchanter excitingly circumstantial," Moore remarks by way of explaining why she had to quote Colum's parenthetical aside about Irish storytelling (the "hindered characters" axiom) verbatim in order to preserve its "gusto": "The words have to come in just that order or they aren't pithy" (*CPr* 426). Colum's storytelling *style* and *locutionary mode* for expressing the parenthetical aside are crucial, and their pith would be lost through paraphrase or translation into standard English. One might say (as Edgeworth says of narrator "honest Thady Quirk" in *Castle Rackrent*) that the aside is "untranslateable," but from a Moore perspective it is more accurate to say that the parenthetical bull and her verbatim citation of it admirably achieves what she defines as "the first requisite of a translation . . . that it should not sound like a translation" but should convey a "simulacrum of spontaneity" (*CPr* 434).

Bulls are often translational catachreses, formed when the desire to express an Irish idiom in English generates a solecism that is apparent to the English-speaking auditor but not to the speaker of Irish-English whose thought is influenced by Gaelic syntax.[39] Many bulls are anacolutha (syntactically incoherent phrases whose semantic drift is nonetheless intelligible), which arise out of the incompatibility between an English grammar based on subordination and an inflected Gaelic language whose syntax can be freely reordered for emphasis (e.g., "I haven't taken a drop tonight but one drink") and euphonious redundancy (e.g., "this house will stand as long as the world does, and longer"). Such anacoluthic license is a feature of the implicit conversational style of vernacular usage, which eschews the sequential and explicit logic of a print-standardized communicative style to dart ahead, shift emphasis, make positive assertions through antiphrasis, exaggerate, abruptly change tack, and leave gapped or dangling phrases to be completed by interlocutors who can grasp what the speaker means to impart. "Those who are quick and enthusiastic . . . are apt to make elisions in speaking, which they trust the capacities of their audience will supply," the Edgeworths note, offering as an example: "the best way of boiling potatoes is in cold water."[40] Many of Moore's "sentences" have anacoluthic tails: "looking/upon a creature's error with the/feelings of a mother—a/woman or a cat" (*CP* 9), and an anacoluthic economy also governs the play of allusions across stanzas.

Another pronounced idiosyncrasy of Moore's, the tendency to make positive assertions through antiphrasis, is a significant cause of Irish bulls. Self-negating bulls can be traced to the paraphrastic affirmations and denials that may be attributed in part to the absence in Irish of words for *yes* and *no* and the distinctive Irish use of *but (ach)*. The contorted syntax of "we cannot say we are not enchanted with disenchantment in *The Plough and the Stars*" (*CPr* 197), as though Moore labors under extraordinary censorship when she is invoking *The Dial*'s royal *we* to make a positive assertion, attests to a deeply ingrained adversarial style. It seems a stretch to relate this grammar of "hindrance" to remote Gaelic contact, but the profusion of negative compounds in "Spenser's Ireland"—"dissatisfied," "discommodity," "invisible," "disappeared," "disuse," "unlearning obduracy," "'I'll never give in,'" "native genius for disunion"—makes it clear that Moore associates her ethnic homeland with a rhetoric of Dissent.[41] "Instinctively, we employ antithesis as an aid to precision," to create the "lion's leap . . . of impact and exactitude" found in conversation with "diction that is virile because galvanized against inertia," Moore writes in "Feeling and Precision" (*CPr* 396–97). The "greenest place I've never seen" yokes together with antithetical precision solution and need (*greenest place / never seen*) into a slogan that would make a catchy advertisement for Irish tourism (or for boosting *National Geographic* sales). Bulls' straightforward implicit meanings, enhanced by at-oddness with their explicit sense, lend them the "contagion" that "can hold people's attention," which Moore associates with "the shimmer of the unsaid," "terseness and the simultaneous double meaning of puns," and "rhythm, the pattern of the pauses in a piece of verse" found in the lively beat of nuanced conversation (*CPr* 435, 433).

Moore obliquely cues the reader into how the very quirkiness that provokes cultural condescension may also camouflage ulterior agendas with an obtrusive reference to Irish mantles in the last sentence of the opening stanza, which she annotates by citing Maria Edgeworth citing Spenser in *Castle Rackrent* (1800):

> They're natural,—
>   the coat, like Venus'
> mantle lined with stars,
> buttoned close at the neck,—the sleeves new from disuse.   (9–12)

Moore reads *Castle Rackrent* as an extended bull. The novel stages an ethnographic encounter in which the apparently guileless oral narrative of "an illiterate old steward," Thady Quirk, is recorded by an amanuensis editor who prefaces, footnotes, and concludes it (3). Quirk's claim that the shabby "great coat" he wears as a sleeveless mantle belies the fact that he is the father of a gentleman (a son he professes to disown for usurping the Rackrent family whom he loyally serves) is contravened by a parallel ulterior script inaugurated by the "editor" citing Spenser on the seditious Irish mantle (7). Spenser wants to ban the wearing of the traditional Irish garb because mantles frustrate surveillance and facilitate covert subversive activity: "the commodity doth not countervail the discommodity . . . for [the mantle] is a fit house for an outlaw, a meet bed for a rebel, and an apt cloak for a thief" (qtd. in Edgeworth, *Castle Rackrent*, 8). Spenser also recommends excluding Irish jurors from the judicial system so that they cannot "picke some quirke or devise some subtill evasion" to acquit Irish defendants (*View* 31), and thus the underground counter-narrative demarcated by the mantle suggests that the unlettered Thady's stream of anecdotes, told in an "idiom incapable of translation . . . into plain English," is duplicitous subterfuge.

Quirk's deferential tale could be a sly "Irish answer," the extravagant feigned obsequiousness that the Edgeworths argue is also shown to their colonial masters by intermediaries in India and the West Indies (*Bulls* 179). The editor's footnote places Thady's narrative within quotation marks, mantling every word with the ironic possibility that Thady may—but also may not—mean the opposite of what he says. In the scene of the encounter when the ethnographer "writes" the native source, the quirks and idiosyncratic idiom that guarantee "the authenticity of [Thady's] story" also make it impossible to "read" whether or not Thady's "partiality to *the* [Rackrent] *family* in which he was bred and born" is feigned or genuine (3–4). The scrim-like image conjured by the cited "mantle" sets the main text apart from the parallel editorial paratext of notes in a way that makes it easier to visualize the covert counter-narrative. In the duplex economy established by the mantle footnote, "Quirk" exemplifies the Irish bull "None but himself can be his parallel" (*Bulls* 177). The citation of the mantle does not ironically invert Thady's intentions but renders them profoundly indeterminate.

"None but himself can be his parallel" radically upsets the stabilities of antecedence and, by so doing, sets in train a logic of inclusive disjunctions and "the zig-zag of contradictions" which G. Gregory Smith terms "Caledonian antisyzygies."[42] Many bulls feature the self-reflexive topics of identity and literacy in ways that are at odds with customary modes of perception. A bull greeting such as "When first I saw you I thought it was you, but now I see it is your brother" abashes personal egotism (*Bulls* 166). "I should have written a better letter, only I had not time to take a copy of it before I wrote it," another generic staple, calls attention to the role of scriptism in delineating the Pale (and the mantle) which separates the English Original from the lesser copy, its Anglicized inferiors (*Bulls* 164). "Quirk" offers an instructive contrast with "The Irish Incognito," Phelim

O'Mooney, in this respect. To pass as English, O'Mooney has to jettison his giveaway name for a pseudonym. To honor the "curious coincidence, that the name of that species of blunder, which is so peculiar to the Irish, should be, to a letter, the same as the distinguishing appellation of the English nation," he chooses Sir John Bull (9). Rather than lose the wager, Sir John Bull "stands mute" on his forgery of Phelim O'Mooney's signature and goes to jail,[43] until the comic resolution sets all to rights "and Phelim O'Mooney never relapsed into Sir John Bull" (224). The Irish Incognito's practical bull of using his own signature rebounds back upon the fake pedigree of "the distinguishing appellation of the English nation" to suggest that the English Original is itself a counterfeit, an empty signifier masking a social ailment that imperils would-be Englishmen with "relapses." Whereas the scriptist apparatus of legal signatures and writs surrounding "Sir John Bull" unravels in comic farce, the idiosyncratic style of narrating ephemeral gossip practiced by "Quirk" has remarkable staying power. Unlike the arbitrary and imitable "standard," the vernacular *quirk* is peerless (no parallel but itself) and this non-fungible value can hold its own against the permanence of print. "Quirks" have de-Anglicizing potential because they "keep" a residue of inassimilable difference and because they set the standard at antisyzygical odds with itself.

As Moore's dangling allusion to Edgeworth's narrative sleight of hand suggests, the "greenest" ingenue-speaker is a direct descendant of Quirk, and Moore's "hybrid method of composing" her Irish mantle, like Edgeworth's, is profoundly double-voiced and ambivalent. Moore's mantle can be read transversally, as a curatorial montage of Irish memorabilia, anecdotes, and idiosyncrasies, spliced and quilted to the arbitrary template of isosyllabic stanzas. The overt display of a bricolage of citations is supplemented by the covert citation of "Earl Gerald" to show how the "discommodity" (citing Edgeworth's footnote on Spenser on the mantle) of vernacular quirkiness enables the Irish to evade surveillance: "Discommodity makes/them invisible; they've dis-/appeared" (ll. 61–63). The poet-speaker exhibits items that appeal to her taste, showing a predilection for meticulously crafted, simple objects such as angling-flies and an eye for unusual sumptuary customs. "When large dainty/fingers tremblingly divide the wings/of the fly for mid-July," she says admiringly, "their pride,/like the enchanter's/is in care, not madness" (38–40, 43–45).

Fashion is a prominent motif, and the poem "quotes" *National Geographic* photographs, featuring prepubescent boys dressed in red petticoats in order to repel the fairies, a damask weaver, a grandmother knitting in front of a "purple-coral" fuchsia tree, and an assortment of megalithic twisted gold "torcs" and "lunulae":[44]

Concurring hands divide

flax for damask
    that when bleached by Irish weather
    has the silvered chamois-leather
water-tightness of a
skin. Twisted torcs and gold new-moon-shaped
        lunulae aren't jewelry
like the purple-coral fuchsia-tree's. Eire—   (45–52)

The proud care lavished on these feminized weaving and twisting techniques (*métissage*) demonstrates "the great amount of poetry in unconscious/fastidiousness" which Moore extols in "Critics and Connoisseurs," and their pleasing idiosyncrasy is exhibited with "unfeigned gusto" by their curator. (Like Sir John Bull, Moore does not "practice the art of 'not to admire,' so as to give a justly high opinion of his [or her] taste" [*Bulls* 203]). The citation of *National Geographic* photographs in a poem that demonstrates the importance of reading in ethnic makeovers is significant because it attests to the influence of mass-mediated images of the "Emerald Isle" in magazines, advertisements, and movies on how Irish-Americans could cite, and be seen to cite, their Irish ethnicity.

In Moore's poem "Venus' mantle" archly glosses the fashionably *démodé* garb in which the altogether blond and redheaded poet "appears" (recalling Pound's query "Does your stuff appear in America?"). Richard Avedon's famous portrait of Moore wearing a mantle and tricorn and bearing a bouquet of flowering quince captures the mixed messages of her sartorial masquerade as a "spinsterish antipoetess": the woman who in the late 1940s "walked into a milliner's shop and asked to be fitted as Washington crossing the Delaware" is at once a founding father and a benign witch of American letters.[45] Moore displays her signature mantle in a spirit of camp: she postures boldly (Fr. *se camper*) and stands out (Ital. *campeggiare*) in the mantle she also hides behind. Alive to the continuity between the Spenserian rebel's use of the mantle as a nightly camp and the Greenwich Villager's campy use of a mantle to withstand social control, she weaves an Irish-Scythian warp into the ultra-American woof of her Washingtonian garb.

"Venus'/mantle lined with stars," quotes Edgeworth, citing Spenser's ostentatiously "fair" use of classical allusion in the dialogue format of Spenser's *View*: Eudoxus cites the Greek precedent of Venus' mantle to qualify Irenius' assertion that the sumptuary custom, along with the customs of nomadic pasturage, keening, and war cries, proves that the Irish descend from the Scythian barbarians (*View* 66, 77). Moore's multileveled citation of Edgeworth/Spenser/Herodotus suggests that Spenser's display of bipartisan even-handedness in "venus mantle lyned with starrs" not only masks the exclusionary use of "classical quotation [as] the literary *parole* of literary men all over the world" but also represses a dread of the baleful "feminine" and "native" influences it holds at bay.[46] The resplendent "Venus" is shadowed by an image of Irish "monashuts" (vagrant women, from *mná siubhail*) whose mantles provide cover for "lewde exercyse, [and] when she hath fylled her vessell, under yt shee can hyde both her burthen and her blame" and swaddle bastards (69). Irish women's "sucke" exposes settler families to the "three most dangerous Irish infeccions, fostering and marriage with the Irish" and, above all, "the evill custome of the language" because "the speache beinge Irish, the harte must needes bee Irishe" (88–89). Earl Gerald, a figure of Irish "literalism of the imagination" who marvelously enacts Spenser's neurosis about the ineradicable influence of Irish "sucke," is cited in a circuitous and multidimensional manner by Moore to unmask the "Venus' mantle" cover-up and similar cover-ups by the gentlemen's club of "fair" citation.

The complexity of Moore's citational method can be elaborated by examining her use of *angling-flies:*

> When large dainty
> fingers tremblingly divide the wings
>   of the fly for mid-July
> with a needle and wrap it with peacock-tail,
> or tie wool and
>   buzzard's wing, their pride,
> like the enchanter's
> is in care, not madness.   (38–45)

Moore annotates Edgeworth's novel *The Absentee* (1812) as the source, and on turning to the novel one finds that she alludes to the pivotal scene in which the hero, Colambre, forswears absenteeism (116–20). Colambre and some newly quartered English militia visit patriotic antiquarian Count O'Halloran, and Colambre distinguishes himself to his host by catching an allusion to Herodotus' account of the Scythians' cryptic gift of a mouse, a frog, a bird, and five arrows as a warning to the invading Persians. O'Halloran gives the English militia the angling-flies they admire (with the Swiftian barb that they are of Irish manufacture), and Colambre, by then dissociated from the militia, receives the funerary urn that eventually proves his beloved's honorable birth. By allegorizing the host's parting gift of angling-flies as a cryptic Scythian rejoinder that assimilates Colambre and excludes the militia in the same gesture, Moore renders the politics of *The Absentee* more radically anticolonial than the conciliatory text would seem to warrant.

Learning how to read Ireland by catching the inflections "between the lines" is key to the Hibernicization of "the absentee," Colambre, and reading likewise plays a crucial role in "purely Celtic" and hyphenated-American makeovers.[47] The encryption of the Scythian rejoinder assimilates Edgeworth into a clandestine Amazonian-Scythian sorority with Moore, a gesture she repeats in her play *The Absentee* (1962).[48] In the same move as she puts the most radical spin on Edgeworth's allusions to the Irish-Scythian mantle, Moore mantles their radicalism by representing the cryptic bait as beautifully wrought angling-flies to be appreciated qua angling-flies in the poem. By so doing, she salvages the Scythian mantle "as a strategy which imposes a way of life," a way of nomad warfare, camouflage, and aporia which is so devised, according to Herodotus, "that none who attacks them can escape and none can catch them if they desire not to be found."[49] Latter-day Scythian nomads use citational strategies that allow them to be found by others on a similar wavelength and to stay hidden from hostile outsiders.

Moore's multidimensional citational practice in "Spenser's Ireland" engages specific subcommunities, including those attuned to a campy performance of "purely Celtic" ethnicity and those cued into Moore's Irish allusions. "Camp is a mode of seduction, with a witty meaning for cognoscenti and another, more impersonal, one for outsiders," Susan Sontag writes. Those who can find, with the speaker, "a private zany experience of the thing" in "the fly in mid-July" are likely to intuit how the exquisite pride and care invested in the quirky Irish manufacture of angling-flies is "like the enchanter's" (l. 44).[50] For the cognoscenti of purely Celtic American camp, the angling-flies are neither fish bait nor a cryptic allusion to something else, though they may also be those things, but a flamboyant act of citation which signifies an affiliation to a marginal or subcultural group that shares their ironic relation to the mainstream. "Camp sees everything in quotation marks," Sontag writes, "it is not a lamp, but a 'lamp' "; not a mantle but a "mantle"; not Earl Gerald, but "Earl Gerald" (56).

Camp renders theatrical and hyperbolic the Emersonian precept that we find "our country, customs, laws, our ambitions, and our notions of fit and fair . . . readymade; we but quote them" (200). Such aficionados can read the catalogue of idiosyncrasies that "bespeak relentlessness" and culminate with "Earl Gerald": "Then/they are to me/like enchanted Earl Gerald" as a synchronic montage and get a panoramic overview of what Ireland "is like" for the speaker (ll. 56–58). Unlike many of their American counterparts, Irish cognoscenti "know" that Quirk speaks out of both sides of his mouth at once and that Earl Gerald is none other than Gearóid Iarla (1338–98), a fourteenth-century Anglo-Norman colonist who became "more Irish than the Irish" and is therefore one of the "degenerate" Old English haunting Spenser's *View*. To cite *Earl Gerald* is to cite six centuries of colonial oppression, and thus many Irish readers are predisposed to detect a covert anticolonial narrative between the lines of the quirky mantle and to engage in a diachronic, politicized reading "for the plot."

The citational appeals to these two distinct, if potentially overlapping, audiences highlight the different ways in which Moore's Irish-Scythian mantle is structured like a bull. Bulls, idiosyncrasies, and quirks have intrinsic value for Moore as "fossil poetry" and as an exemplary style of interpreting the world from an odd vantage. At the same time, and paradoxically, bulls only come into existence when they are cited as such and thus are void of intrinsic worth. When the Irish Incognito commends the Romney portrait as "absolutely more like than the original," he makes a metapoetic observation about bulls which also applies to camp taste: both are predicated on the assumption that the ironic citation of the utterance or thing "is absolutely more like than the original." The playful imposition of "one's own spin" (idiosyncrasy) on an utterance or a thing is at the opposite end of the spectrum to the concept of idiosyncrasy as a resistant cache of indefeasible otherness, and yet both aspects have a role in creating "nomadic" coteries among those excluded from the gentlemen's club. Blatant bulls are cited as laughable failures at verbal passing, but milder bulls (like the two in "Spenser's Ireland") can operate as a passing code, "a freemason sign by which we Hibernians know each other" (*Bulls* 217–18). Just as camp taste inverts the dominant art of "not to prefer" to form a cult that excludes, for once, those who are otherwise dominant, vernacular quirks can be made into a clandestine code to strengthen a marginalized group.

Moore's selective citations in "Spenser's Ireland" hinder the reader by muddying the literary excavation trail that connects "Earl Gerald" with Spenser and with Moore family lore about their Irish heritage. She thereby reproduces the contrastive transmission histories of the dominant written and subordinate oral texts so that the reader can come to perceive the mantle (Pale/*pudeur*) dividing Anglo and Gaelic Ireland and the "hindrance" connecting the diasporic and resident Irish. The strategy also facilitates a crossover of reading styles among camp cognoscenti (who perceive bulls as ahistorical antisyzygies) and Irish readers (for whom the bull is charged with memories of linguistic imperialism and social ostracism). If she can reproduce the "gusto as objectified" which she admires in Colum's "telling of the story of Earl Gerald" and Edgeworth's quirky narrator, readers can be "hindered to succeed" by hobbling the tendencies to read "Spenser's Ireland" either as purely Celtic textual pastiche or as Manichaean allegory (*CP* 121).

When Spenser "caused diverse [Gaelic poems] to bee translated unto [him]" (97–98), it is possible that the following fourteenth-century verse was recited to him:

> *Binn a mbriathra, gasta a nglór,*
> *aicme rerab mór mo bháidh;*
> *a gcáineadh is mairg nár loc:*
> *mairg adeir olc rís na mnáibh.*

> Sweet their voices, true their tact,
> Their kind wins my allegiance;
> Scorn on them I will not brook:
> Woe to those who malign women!

The "sweete witt and good invencion," "good grace and Comlyness," and chivalric sentiment of the verse would surely have appealed to the courtly English poet (*View* 98), but the pleasure would evaporate once he heard the poet's name: *Gearóid Iarla*/Earl Gerald, the third earl of Desmond, one of the "brave and worthy" Norman Butlers and Geraldines who "grewe insolente and bente . . . as degenerate . . . as the wilde Irishe, yea and some of them have quite shaken of theire Englishe names, and putt on Irishe, that they might bee altogeather Irishe" (83–84). The third Earl Gerald (1338–98) pulled off the remarkable feat of serving as justiciar (the king's representative) of Ireland when Gaelic was outlawed by the 1366 Statutes of Kilkenny and yet was an accomplished Gaelic poet, credited with introducing *amour courtois* into Gaelic poetry.[51]

According to legend, Gerald was the son of Maurice, the first earl of Desmond, and the Munster sovereignty goddess, Áine, a "tradition" that the Geraldines evidently encouraged because a poem by the family bard, Gofraidh Fionn O'Dálaigh, names him "the son of Áine's knight" (*a mheic marcaigh fionnÁine*) when Gerald was a child.[52] The sovereignty goddess legendarily chooses and mates with the rightful king. In a coded representation of rape, tradition holds that Gerald's father only succeeded in mating with Áine because he had first seized her mantle. Gerald's grandson, Thomas, the eighth earl, ruled Munster like a Gaelic king, and Spenser blames the Norman-Irish alliance on the "huge wronge" of his execution in 1468 (85). By the time the fourteenth earl, also named Gerald, was released from prison in London in 1573, the lore had mythologized him into a messianic hero, a role he acknowledged upon his arrival at Lough Gur by the ritual (and illegal) divestment of English dress and donning of the Irish mantle. The fourteenth Earl Gerald was the symbolic quarry of the 1580–82 campaign of terror which Spenser helped Lord Grey execute in Munster, and his defeat cleared the way for the plantation of Munster, in which Spenser was granted an estate at Kilcolman.

Earl Gerald, the composite figure of the oral tradition, encompasses everything Spenser's View seeks to avert: the Gaelicization of English settlers, the poor English governance shown by the eighth earl's wrongful execution, and the fourteenth earl's continuing popular legitimacy after the Munster planters had destroyed him and usurped his lands. Above all, Elizabethans wanted the Irish to forget Earl Gerald and his ilk (an "Act of Oblivion" was passed in 1585 providing for the surcease of suits concerning anything occurring before 1583). Under these circumstances the survival and resurfacing of Earl Gerald cheek by jowl with Spenser in Moore's poem some 350 years later is as fascinating a tale as the one encrypted in the lore itself.

Dáithí Ó'hÓgáin dates the dissemination of Geraldine lore to the traumatic aftermath of the eighth earl's death, when the oral tradition merged the folk motif of an enchanted hero who awaits an opportune moment to deliver his people from bondage with shape-shifting lore about the third earl, Gearóid Iarla, who was famed as a magician. In the fifteenth and sixteenth centuries the typological lore had the political prestige of "history" and foundational myth, as demonstrated by the first earl's planting of the legend of Gerald's birth and the fourteenth earl's citation of the myth by donning the outlawed mantle. After the 1585 Act of Oblivion the myth gradually receded into the fugitive and feminized genres of clandestine coded allusions and rumor.

Moore heard it in the twentieth century as a children's story, albeit one that alludes to Geraldine typology by mentioning in an aside that the Earl resurfaced "just before Earl Gerald's descendent, Lord Edward Fitzgerald, was making the people ready for an uprising" (in the 1790s).[53] The plastic lore adapted to circumstances to feature local heroes such as Donall O'Donoghue of Killarney and to reflect changing historical circumstances, from the contest for dynastic supremacy in medieval Ireland to the survival of Gaelic culture in early modern Ireland to the struggle to regain the land in the eighteenth and nineteenth centuries. The constant elements in the lore are revealing: the naming of a native or assimilated Irish chief, the embedding of that name in a known locale, and an emphasis on the illegitimacy of the reigning political order. Earl Gerald's disappearance under the fairy mounds of Kildare (in Colum's variant) or his inundation under Lough Gur, a lake overlooked by Knockainey, Áine's "hill" or breast (in the Munster variant), shows the importance of naturalizing leadership by wedding it to the landscape (as the first earl set out to do). This trope of locality-based sovereignty, which is also a staple of the *aisling*, was crucial in delegitimizing London-based sovereignty in popular consciousness. The legitimacy of English rule is further displaced by the same question posed to or by the earl on his rare sightings: "An é an t-am fós é?" (Is it the time yet?). The assurance that the untimeliness of the present moment would change at some juncture in the future is central to the lore's messianic promise.

The oral transmission of the lore to Moore mattered a great deal to her because Colum's storytelling performance "made the unbelievable doings of an enchanter excitingly circumstantial" (*CPr* 426). True to the vagaries of the oral tradition, this leaves open to conjecture how the "lecture" (her unforthcoming annotation is "from a lecture by Padraic Colum" [*CP* 280]) and conversations with Colum could have supplemented or differed from the version of the lore which Colum published as "The Wizard Earl" in *The Big Tree of Bunlahy: Stories of My Countryside* (1933).[54] In *The Big Tree* Colum's adult narrator recalls for Irish and American children the stories he heard as a boy from various villagers who used to congregate under the eponymous tree. The wealth of unobtrusive contextual detail provided by the connecting frame narratives allows the individual tales to unfold as their storytellers might plausibly have told them. Because it was Midsummer's Eve, the villagers ask "Martin the Weaver to tell them a tale that only he had aright," and he begins: "To gather Fern-seed and get any good out of it, you must gather it on Midsummer's Eve just as the sun is going down, neither a minute before nor a minute after" (102, 103). Fern-seed collection must be unwatched by mortal eyes, but "the country people" hid to watch the earl and broke the enchantment. Because iron taboos magic, he wasn't carrying his sword and had to repel them by changing himself into a stag, and meanwhile the opportune moment had passed. His young bride hears about the incident and longs "to know [him] in all [his] shapes" (108). She prevails upon him to perform his shape-shifting, assuring him that she won't "be made afraid of the change" and thereby cause him to disappear (109). He changes into a stag, a cat-of-the-mountain, and a miniature of himself which is then seized by a monkey, whereupon his wife breaks the taboo against showing surprise by screaming. He disappears into the Fairy-Mounds, where he is the leader of "the heroes who are to help in the deliverance of the land," and rides around the Curragh with his horsemen every

Midsummer's Eve. When his stallion's silver shoes have worn away, the time will have come.

In "Spenser's Ireland" Moore ironically juxtaposes Geraldine lore, a military rescue fantasy that anticipates a return to locality-based sovereignty, with Spenser's apologia for an intensified campaign of terror to secure Elizabeth's sovereignty. She hybridizes two texts—one, in Gaelic and Irish-English, circulated orally to shape the political unconscious and foster resistance; the other, in English, disseminated through print to influence official policy—which were not in dialogue though profoundly implicated in one another. Spenser simultaneously dominates the poem and is located outside it, in the paratext. The title, "Spenser's Ireland," is the first line of the first (twelve-line) stanza, but this line is dropped from the eleven-line isosyllabic stanza frame for the following five stanzas, making it into a kind of phantom line in the quantitative prosodic economy. The note on "Venus'/mantle lined with stars" cites Edgeworth's citation of Spenser's proposal to outlaw mantles (*CP* 280). "Earl Gerald" is cited in a carefully arranged series of symmetrical parentheses. The opening and closing autoethnographical sentences enclose (1–4, 65–67), respectively, Donn Byrne's discussion of Gaelic-derived vernacularisms and interactive styles in the *National Geographic* (5–8, 63–65); the citation of Edgeworth's mantle footnote (9–12, 61–63); and Geraldine lore (13–20, 57–61). Earl Gerald is secreted in the innermost layer, inside the mantle, in the onion-like arrangement. The weak lead in the notes, "from a lecture by Padraic Colum" (*CP* 280), refers only to line 58, in which he is named ("enchanted Earl Gerald"), and there is nothing to indicate that there is any connection between the shape-shifting enchanter and the quest to gather fern-seed (ll. 13–20). She withholds Earl Gerald's significance as Spenser's antagonist from her Anglo-American audience. She further attenuates the residual presence of the messianic oral history in Colum's story by restricting herself to the zoo-morphic trickster figure of a children's tall tale. In short, Spenser's *View* and Geraldine lore coexist in the poem but potentially without mutual engagement. Moore brings the charged, antagonistic texts together for readers and remains reticent about it.

After cataloguing Irish crafts and fauna, the speaker of "Spenser's Ireland" apostrophizes "Eire" (resuming the conversation with "you, Ireland" while marking the 1937 constitutional name change) in the final stanza and asks whether they

—bespeak relentlessness? Then

they are to me
    like enchanted Earl Gerald who

changed himself into a stag, to

a great green-eyed cat of

the mountain. Discommodity makes

    them invisible; they've dis-

appeared.

The lilting portrayal of the enchanted earl is brought up short by the obtrusive "discommodity" that has caused them to "dis-/appear." *Discommodity* summons the mantle footnote in Edgeworth on how, for Spenser, "the commodity of the mantle [versatility] doth not countervail the discommodity [camouflage for rebels]" (8). The allusion registers how English convenience determines what got recorded as visible history and topography and what was proscribed as obscure myth. The shape-shifting earl appears in the ephemeral guise of fairy tale. Because the feminized genre is orally transmitted from mother to child, it eludes regulation and imperils the state with the "most dangerous infeccion": Irish "sucke." Earl Gerald returns, fleetingly, and then slips beyond the mantle or through the typographical black hole of *dis-/appeared.*

The return of the repressed Earl Gerald in "Spenser's Ireland" shows how "literalism of the imagination" in Geraldine lore not only encodes Irish desire for a messianic reversal of fortune but also succeeds in graphically parodying Spenser's feared implosion of the colonial enterprise, "in which the domestic triumphs over the state, female over male, and Irish over English."[55] The coupling of the two texts creates the kind of hybridity which Homi Bhabha defines as one "that reverses the effects of colonialist disavowal, so that other 'denied' knowledges enter upon the dominant discourse and estrange the basis of its authority" (114). Moore diverts the likelihood of this counter-knowledge taking politico-historical epistemological form by hiding "the facts" and using the magical ethos of legend to decenter realism. She seeks to estrange the empirical ground of ethnography by re-creating the antisyzygical worldview of the proverbial Irish bull "Of course I don't believe in fairies, but they're there."

The fern-seed passage of the second stanza, which is cast as a skeptical and wistful question to which the Colum bull replies, suggests that Ireland needs a magical remedy for "obduracy":

If in Ireland

    they play the harp backward at need,

    and gather at midday the seed

of the fern, eluding

their "giants all covered with iron," might

there be fern seed for unlearning obduracy and for reinstating
the enchantment?

The esotericism of these lines, unmoored from Geraldine lore, is mystifying. No source is given for "giants all covered in iron" (nor does the phrase arise in the published version of "The Wizard Earl"), though the concept that iron taboos magic comes across. In the convivial milieu of Colum's tale it would be easy to substitute *grown-ups, the authorities, village gossips,* or even *colonizer* for *giants,* but in the poem they are an abstraction that creates a subliminal sense of a hostile force of surveillance. The emphasis on eluding surveillance recalls the constitutive role of magic in ethnography to suggest that native opacity is perceived by the observer as a kind of mana, which is impenetrable, unpredictable, and potentially antagonistic. Such mana represents native power apparently to disappear and then make a surprising comeback. The "if/might there be" grammar casts the untimely motif of Geraldine lore as a problem that requires redress. Puzzlement about why magic needs reinstatement in this taboo-riven land of ironclad giants prompts a retracing of the convolutions of "unlearn-/ing obduracy" and the quest for antidotal fern-seed. Harpists play the harp backwards to undo musical enchantment,[56] and the rereading follows the withershins directionality of riddance magic, drawing the reader (who might otherwise remain at a nonplussed distance) into the speaker's esoteric quest.

The reply to the speaker's question (the Colum axiom) raises more ambiguities: are the hindering grandmothers the source of the obduracy or of the restorative enchantment? The phrase "Secret sly hint" is written beside the axiom in draft, indicating that the concealment of the link between Geraldine lore and the speaker's family lore is intentional. Much as legendary grandmothers elide mothers, remote clan lore may mask more immediate family narratives, and generalized cultural explanations such as "it was Irish" afford safe distance from inadmissible knowledge.

Hindered characters
seldom have mothers
in Irish stories, but they all have grandmothers.

It was Irish;
a match not a marriage was made
when my great great grandmother'd said
with native genius for

disunion, "Although your suitor be
        perfection, one objection
    is enough; he is not
    Irish." Outwitting
            the fairies, befriending the furies,   (21–32)

It is Irish to close ranks against the not-Irish and to favor the reproduction of sameness ("a match") over a marriage. The taboo on exogamy does not nurture solidarity but, instead, a "native genius for disunion." Irish matriarchs are held responsible for the militant clannishness, and we know from Mary Craig Shoemaker's genealogies and the controversies over Warner's courtships that marriage outside the "race" was taboo for the Craig-Moores. Although Moore's citation of Edgeworth celebrates the cryptic genius of the Amazonians' repulsion of invaders, "Outwitting/the fairies, befriending the furies" adopts a critical stance toward women's role as ethnic border guards. The phrase, like "Venus' mantle," conflates a classical Greek allusion with a clandestine Irish sumptuary custom.

"Outwitting the fairies" refers to a *National Geographic* photograph that displays how Irish mothers protect their sons from fairy abductors by dressing them in red petticoats: "Along the Connemara coast," reads the accompanying text, "boys were dressed in red flannel skirts up to the age of twelve . . . in order to deceive the fairies who are supposed . . . to run away with male children if they have the opportunity, but who will not touch little girls" (314). The covert criticism of the endogamy taboo is made by citing an unannotated photographic image of a "backward" custom, which, frozen in the glossy modernity of *National Geographic*'s pages, seems altogether alien to a U.S. readership. In Ireland "the touch" of the *sidhe* provides a vehicle for articulating taboo subjects such as maternal incest and miscegenation dread. In the United States the ethnographic frame of an archaic survival of fairy belief defuses the specter of excessive mother-love raised by the vivid image of the boys' mothers' cross-dressing stratagems. The masquerade of worthless femininity by the sons illustrates the cost exacted upon daughters by vigilant maternal protectiveness. As Moore's draft version riffs, "so kind to everyone else/to itself so inhumanely bind" (RML 1:4:21). Spenser's beleaguered garrison outlook was transmitted by great-great-grandmothers to the United States, where it survives in "Irish" and "Scotch-Irish" enclaves as well as in U.S. nativist ideology.

The hidden allusion to the Wizard Earl in the fern-seed passage, and the significance of the relationship established by the shared Geraldine provenance of the second and final stanzas, becomes clearer in the light of the great-great-grandmother anecdote and the ensuing reflections about "supreme belief" which connect the two stanzas:

> whoever again
> and again says, "I'll never give in," never sees

> that you're not free
>> until you've been made captive
>> by supreme belief,—credulity
> you say? When large dainty
> fingers tremblingly . . . [make the angling-flies and other quirky artifacts that]
>
> .   .   .   .
>
>   —bespeak relentlessness? Then
>
> they are to me
>> like enchanted Earl Gerald who
>> changed himself into a stag.   (Ll. 33–39, 57–59)

Earl Gerald's powers of metamorphosis are enviably unconstrained except by the permissive maternal taboo that Colum delightfully renders as "if anyone who loved [him] was made afraid of the change, [he'd] have to disappear [into the Fairy-Mounds]" (109). Gerald is "made captive/by supreme belief" in the shape-shifting arts of provisional identity and nomadic camouflage and is dubious about his bride's assurances that she will honor the taboo against registering surprise at his metamorphoses. The odds against the shape-shifter's family accepting a radical metamorphosis without surprise are about as remote as the likelihood of a human becoming a stag. Áine's taboo protects Gerald against those whose solicitude or censure may inhibit his freedom to assume "the courage of [his] peculiarities."

Moore, like Herodotus, is interested in the supervening shape assumed by past events after "they have *fought their way*, past credence, into the country of myth," whence it is amenable to return.[57] The mantled quotation of Earl Gerald shows how occluded history returns under an occult guise that Moore associates with gusto. The exciting circumstantiality she admires in Colum's storytelling style is achieved by the "compressed ambiguity" with which she encrypts Geraldine lore that has "impassioned explicitness" when explicated in relation to the texts it hybridizes (*CPr* 422–23). The concentrated idiosyncrasy is made contagious by the deferred release of the correspondences of allusion, which emulates the syntax of scrupulous hyperbole in Colum's optimally deferred "but they all have grandmothers" bull. Earl Gerald's "magic" inheres in the "gusto-as-objectified" by his extraordinary persistence in popular memory and his remarkable capacity to resurface across generations and cultures as a quotation. His traversals back and forth "beyond the Pale" or across "the mantle" recapitulate how the justiciar-cum-Gaelic poet was figured in the lore as the offspring of military rapine and native magic; how his adoptive literate Gaelic culture was forced into underground oral channels and then underwent a change of vernacular and a diaspora; and how it can now be salvaged as a "purely Celtic" totem.

When asked in a survey whether she regarded herself as part of the "American tradition" or as a poet simply, dissociated from nationality, Moore replied "yes, as implied above, an American chameleon on an American leaf" (*CPr* 675). Maria Edgeworth, who preceded Moore by a century, and Gearóid Iarla, who lived four hundred years before that, are improbable precursors for a modernist American poet. Their citation in "Spenser's Ireland" shows why their contributions, enmeshed as they are in the particularities of Irish colonial history, offer the American chameleon resources that no U.S. writer could replicate. By so doing, they highlight how the "most American" poet (like his or her "more-Irish-than-the-Irish" settler-Irish counterpart) is most American when traversing the borders between cultures in which the writing of cultures takes place.

Notes

INTRODUCTION

1. See Frederick Loewe, *My Fair Lady: A Musical Play in Two Acts*, adaptation and lyrics by Alan Jay Lerner (New York: Coward-McCann, 1956), 27–29. On the multiple remakes of Shaw's "shameless potboiler," see Keith Garebian, *The Making of My Fair Lady* (Toronto: ECW Press, 1993), esp. 12.

2. Shaw writes to Ellen Terry on September 8, 1897, that he wants to write a play starring Stella Campbell as "an east end dona in an apron and three orange and red ostrich feathers." See *Collected Letters of George Bernard Shaw*, ed. Daniel Laurence, 4 vols. (London: Max Reinhardt, 1965): 1:803.

3. See Yeats, *The Collected Plays of W. B. Yeats* (London: Macmillan, 1982), 56.

4. "Celtic" is a branch of Indo-European languages, including the Goidelic group of Irish- and Scottish-Gaelic and Manx and the Brythonic group of Welsh, (French) Breton, and Cornish. Manx and Cornish are no longer spoken, though an effort to revive Manx is afoot. On the discourse of Celticism, see Joep Leerssen's introductory essay in Terence Brown, ed., *Celticism* (Amsterdam: Rodopi, 1996).

5. On the racialism of Celticist discourse, see L. P. Curtis, *Anglo-Saxons and Celts: A Study of Anti-Irish Prejudice in Victorian England* (Bridgeport, Conn.: Conference on British Studies at the University of Bridgeport, 1968); Seamus Deane, *Celtic Revivals: Essays in Modern Irish Literature, 1880–1980* (London: Faber and Faber, 1985); David Cairns and Shaun Richards, *Writing Ireland: Colonialism, Nationalism, and Culture* (Manchester: Manchester University Press, 1988); Malcolm Chapman, *The Celts: The Construction of a Myth* (London: Macmillan, 1992); Robert Young, *Colonial Desire: Hybridity in Theory, Culture, and Race* (New York: Routledge, 1995); Marjorie Howes, *Yeats's Nations: Gender, Class, and Irishness* (Cambridge: Cambridge University Press, 1996); Joep Leerssen, *Remembrance and Imagination: Patterns in the Historical and Literary Representation of Ireland in the Nineteenth Century* (Notre Dame, Ind.: University of Notre Dame Press, 1997).

6. See Robert Phillopson, *Linguistic Imperialism* (Oxford: Oxford University Press, 1992), 50–57, 104–7. On "killer" imperial languages, see Daniel Nettle and Suzanne Romaine, *Vanishing Voices: The Extinction of the World's Languages* (New York: Oxford University Press, 2000). Several advocates of linguistic diversity favor the ecological metaphor.

7. Confirming Spenser's adage, R. D. Grillo observes in *Dominant Languages: Language and Hierarchy in Britain and France* (Cambridge: Cambridge University Press, 1989), that a

considerable range of evidence from diverse times and places indicates that "an integral feature of the system of linguistic stratification in Europe is an ideology of contempt: subordinate languages are despised languages" (173–74).

8. See Louis-Jean Calvet, *Linguistique et colonialisme: un petit traité de glottophagie* (Paris: Payot, 1974); and discussion in Phillopson, *Linguistic Imperialism*, 98–107.

9. My concept of "the Celtic Fringe" is in broad agreement with that of Joep Leerssen and Murray Pittock; I am indebted to their scholarship. On the Celtic fringe, see Murray Pittock, *Celtic Identity and the British Image* (Manchester: Manchester University Press, 1999), 1–7. My work differs from theirs in its focus on linguistic imperialism and on the Pale/Fringe as a contact zone for remaking cultural identity through "de-Anglicization."

10. I use *Gaeltacht* to encompass Irish-Gaeltacht and Scottish-Ghàidhealtachd enclaves.

11. See Mary Louise Pratt, *Imperial Eyes: Travel Writing and Transculturation* (New York: Routledge, 1992), 6–7.

12. In the 1905 Carnegie Hall speech Hyde says: "Now it has been objected to me that that word, which I coined long ago for want of a better, de-Anglicization, contained in it something harsh, something virulent, something rebellious; and that it was calculated to alienate the good will of many people who would, otherwise, be our supporters; and, as that may possibly be so, and especially in a cosmopolitan city like New York [he wishes to assure his audience that he honors and respects everything that is good in the English race and its culture]." See *Language, Lore, and Lyrics: Essays and Lectures*, ed. Breandán O'Conaire (Dublin: Irish Academic Press, 1986), 179–80.

13. See *Tractatus* 5.62: "The world is *my* world: this is manifest in the fact that the limits of *language* (of that which I alone understand) mean the limits of *my* world." *Tractatus Logico-Philosophicus*, trans. D. F. Pears and B. F. McGuinness (London: Routledge and Kegan Paul, 1961).

14. See Geoffrey Galt Harpham, *Language Alone: The Critical Fetish of Modernity* (New York: Routledge, 2002), esp. 5.

15. The omission of Welsh Wales means that *Haunted English* relinquishes any claim to making a comprehensive argument about the Celtic Fringe as a whole. As the third term in my subtitle suggests, this study radiates out from Hyde's de-Anglicizing manifesto to Spenser's *View*, Jacobitism, and Celticism to track a key factor in the formation of the Celtic Fringe, the disavowed linguicism that structures Anglo/Celtic relations, and to explore several Celtic modernists' response to it.

16. This book treats Anglicization as an acculturation process that subordinates the interests of the colonized and the lower classes to those of the Anglo elite. There are many different histories of Anglicization, but in the British Isles, the United States, Africa, and most former commonwealth countries, linguistic diversity has been proscribed as inimical to Anglo hegemony. The term *English-only* is intended to highlight the de-legitimation of competing vernaculars which has been a marked feature of the ascendancy of English as a world language and to resonate with twenty-first-century politics of global English by alluding to contemporary "English-only" ideology in the United States. On the English-only movement in the United States, see James Crawford, *At War with Diversity: US Language Policy in an Age of Anxiety* (Clevedon, UK: Multilingual Matters, 2000).

CHAPTER 1. BEYOND THE PALE

1. See Edmund Spenser, *A View of the Present State of Ireland*, ed. W. L. Renwick (London: Eric Partridge, 1934), 197, 121.

2. See Homi Bhabha, *The Location of Culture* (New York: Routledge, 1994), 89.

3. See Bassnett's introduction to *Post-Colonial Translation: Theory and Practice*, ed. Susan Bassnett and Harish Trivedi (London: Routledge, 1999), 2, 4.

4. See Maria Tymoczko, *Translation in a Postcolonial Context: Early Irish Literature in English Translation* (Manchester, UK: St. Jerome, 1999), 17.

5. See Tony Crowley, *The Politics of Language in Ireland, 1366–1922: A Sourcebook* (London: Routledge, 2000), 12–17.

6. The relationship between linguistic imperialism and cultural imperialism is complex and controversial. Some would argue that a culture can survive relatively unscathed by a change of vernacular; others would contend that an Anglicized Gaelic culture is no longer "Gaelic" in any meaningful sense. Instead of trying to resolve the chicken-and-egg conundrum, my goal is to emphasize the specificity of linguistic imperialism, both as an element of cultural imperialism and as a cultural phenomenon in its own right. For Spenser the goal of extirpating the Gaelic language (linguicide) is inextricable from the task of extinguishing the culture (ethnocide).

7. I treat Spenser's *View* as a blueprint for Anglicizing Ireland and the overseas colony, though of course the actual Anglicization of Ireland diverged in several ways from his draconian prescriptions. Historian Nicholas Canny explores Spenser's considerable influence on colonial policy and ideology, most recently in *Making Ireland British, 1580–1650* (Oxford: Oxford University Press, 2001). There is a growing literature on Spenser and Ireland, including Andrew Hadfield, *Edmund Spenser's Irish Experience: Wilde Fruit and Salvage Soyl* (Oxford: Clarendon, 1997); Willy Maley, *Salvaging Spenser: Colonialism, Culture, and Identity* (New York: St. Martin's, 1997), which includes treatment of Irish/Scottish/English relations; and Richard McCabe, *Spenser's Monstrous Regiment: Elizabethan Ireland and the Poetics of Difference* (Oxford: Oxford University Press, 2002), which examines Gaelic and English sources. Spenser's dual status as a major English poet and colonialist ideologue is especially germane to *Haunted English* because *The Faerie Queene* and *A View* exemplify the Benjaminian thesis that "there is no document of civilization which is not at the same time a document of barbarism." See Walter Benjamin, *Illuminations*, ed. Hannah Arendt, trans. Harry Zohn (New York: Schocken, 1969), 256.

8. In a best-seller in the 1880s J. R. Seeley opines that "we seem, as it were, to have conquered and peopled half the world in a fit of absence of mind." See *The Expansion of England*, ed. John Gross (Chicago: University of Chicago Press, 1971), 12.

9. In his caustic critique of the "barbarism" of the colonial enterprise in *Discours sur colonialisme* (1955), Aimé Césaire observes that colonization has not really placed civilizations in contact because "between colonization and civilization there is an infinite distance" (11). He cites apologist of empire French-Celt Ernest Renan to the effect that the goal of colonization is to widen inequalities and make them into a law by reducing the overseas

colony to "a country of serfs" (15). Thomas Macaulay's 1835 "Minute on Indian Education" famously defines the role of Anglicization in creating a class of intermediaries: "to form a class of persons, who may be interpreters between us and the millions whom we govern; a class of persons, Indian in blood and colour, but English in taste, in opinions, in morals, and in intellect." See reprint in Bill Ashcroft, Gareth Griffiths, and Helen Tifflin, eds., *The Post-Colonial Studies Reader* (New York: Routledge, 1995), 428–30.

10. See Maggie Kilgour's essay "The Function of Cannibalism at the Present Time," in *Cannibalism and the Colonial World*, ed. Francis Barker, Peter Hulme, and Margaret Iversen (Cambridge: Cambridge University Press, 1998), 280.

11. Although preceded by an "ogham" alphabet, Gaelic written literature developed after Latin grammar was introduced along with Christianity in the fifth century, and this monastic literary tradition in Latin and Gaelic flourished over the next six hundred years alongside the more ancient oral tradition of the *filí* (poets). A hereditary caste of bards flourished from the end of the twelfth to the sixteenth centuries. Gaelic was spoken throughout most of the area covered by modern Scotland (along with some Anglo-Saxon in the southeast and Old Norse in Shetland, Orkney, and Caithness) until the eleventh-century reign of the Gaelic-speaking Malcolm Canmore and his English queen, Saint Margaret, when Gaelic began to recede to the Highlands and "Inglis" replaced it in the Lowlands. For the history of Gaelic in Scotland and Ireland, I've consulted Roger Blaney, *Presbyterians and the Irish Language* (Belfast: Ulster Historical Foundation and the Ultach Trust, 1996); Malcolm Chapman, *The Gaelic Vision in Scottish Culture* (London: Croom Helm, 1978); Nancy Dorian, *Language Death: The Life Cycle of a Scottish Gaelic Dialect* (Philadelphia: University of Pennsylvania Press, 1981); Victor Edward Durkacz, *The Decline of Celtic Languages: A Study of Linguistic and Cultural Conflict in Scotland, Wales and Ireland from the Reformation to the Twentieth Century* (Edinburgh: John Donald Publishers, 1983); William Gillies, ed., *Gaelic and Scotland/Alba agus a 'Gha'idhlig* (Edinburgh: Edinburgh University Press, 1989); David Greene, *The Irish Language* (Dublin: Three Candles, 1966); Michael Hechter, *Internal Colonialism: The Celtic Fringe in British National Development, 1536–1966* (Berkeley: University of California Press, 1975); Reg Hindley, *The Death of the Irish Language: A Qualified Obituary* (London: Routledge, 1990); Donald MacAulay, *The Celtic Languages* (Cambridge: Cambridge University Press, 1992); Aodán Mac Póilín, ed., *The Irish Language in Northern Ireland* (Belfast: Ultach Trust, 1997); Brian Ó'Cuív, ed., *A View of the Irish Language* (Dublin: Stationery Office, 1969); and Charles Withers, *Gaelic in Scotland, 1698–1981: The Geographical History of a Language* (Edinburgh: John Donald, 1984). For an introductory overview relevant to the dominant concerns of *Haunted English*, see Maureen Wall, "The Decline of the Irish Language," in Ó'Cuív, *View of the Irish Language;* and Nancy Dorian, *Language Death*, 10–41.

12. See Durkacz, *Decline of Celtic Literature.*

13. See Durkacz, *Decline of Celtic Literature*, 17. See also R. D. Grillo, *Dominant Languages: Language and Hierarchy in Britain and France* (Cambridge: Cambridge University Press, 1989). In Wales, by contrast, the publication of a Welsh Bible "ensured the continuity of the literary tradition in Wales" (qtd. in Grillo, *Dominant Languages*, 98).

14. See David Murison, *The Guid Scots Tongue* (1977); Charles Jones, *The Edinburgh*

History of the Scots Language (1997); Derrick McClure, *Language, Poetry, and Nationhood: Scots as a Poetic Language from 1878 to the Present* (East Linton: Tuckwell Press, 2000). For a pithy and insightful analysis of the ambiguous status of Scots, see Tom MacArthur, "Scots and Southron," *The English Languages* (Cambridge: Cambridge University Press, 1998), 138–59.

15. On diglossia, a sociolinguistic concept developed by Charles Ferguson (1959) and Joshua Fishman (1967), see Louis-Jean Calvet, *Language Wars and Linguistic Politics*, trans. Michel Petheram (Oxford: Oxford University Press, 1998), 26–40; and Grillo, *Dominant Languages*, 78–83.

16. Competence in the credentialed speech functions as "linguistic capital" in the "linguistic market" that potentially earns the speaker a "profit of distinction" on each occasion of social exchange. See Bourdieu, *Language and Symbolic Power*, esp. 55.

17. Many Scots flocked to Irish actor Thomas Sheridan's lectures on elocution in 1754, published as *A Course of Lectures on Elocution* in 1796 and republished in an "American Linguistics, 1700–1900" series in 1991 because of its U.S. influence (Delmar, N.Y.: Scholars' Facsimiles and Reprints, 1991), 33. Sheridan's lecture-course identifies mannerisms and phonological features that are deemed "provincial or vicious . . . [and] have some degree of disgrace annexed to them" (47). He anatomizes the proper use of voice (articulation, pronunciation, accent, tone, tempo, and pitch), countenance, and gesture, which, when fully integrated into one's bodily habitus, would convey the high-prestige signature of fully Anglicized Britishness.

18. See Bourdieu on competence/recognition gap (*Language*, 62).

19. On the "obsession" with accent, see Linda Mugglestone, *Talking Proper: The Rise of Accent as Social Symbol* (Oxford: Clarendon, 1995), esp. 6; and Grillo, *Dominant Languages*, esp. 151. The cultural preoccupation is linked to how the sociolect of the ruling caste, the "Public School English" of the aristocracy's elite institutions, maintains a conspicuous lofty disdain for the punctilious English of the bourgeois monitors of the Pale. Cultural anxiety about accent and articulatory style generated heated controversy during the modernist period about how to inculcate "RP" ("Received Pronunciation" aka Public School English) through the schools and media.

20. *Brogue* may derive from *barróg teangain* (a wrestle-hold on the tongue, a speech impediment), in which case the purloined word acknowledges the strain of adapting one's linguistic habitus to another tongue, or it may derive from *bróg* (shoe, orig. rawhide shoe), and thus convey contempt for maladroit speech along with the expectation (summed up by Jonathan Swift as whenever we hear the brogue we expect the blunder) that the Anglicized Gael speaks only to put his or her foot in their mouth. On English contempt towards the brogue, see Swift, "On Barbarous Denominations in Ireland" (1740) in Tony Crowley, ed., *The Politics of Language in Ireland, 1366–1922: A Sourcebook* (London: Routledge, 2000), 114. "Brogue" is associated particularly with the Irish, and to a lesser extent, Highlanders, though the OED also cites Scott (1828): "the Doctor . . . has done much for the Lowland Scottish brogue."

21. See "Standardness" in MacArthur (1998): 102–59; and "Standards" in Raymond Williams, *Keywords: A Vocabulary of Culture and Society* (New York: Oxford University Press, 1985), 296–99. On standard English, see also Tony Crowley, *The Politics of Discourse:*

The Standard Language Question in British Cultural Debates (Basingstoke, UK: Macmillan, 1989); and Richard Bailey, *Images of English: A Cultural History of the Language* (Ann Arbor: University of Michigan Press, 1991).

22. Harris, *Language Makers.*

23. Johnson, 2:1, qtd. in Mugglestone, 208; see Mugglestone (1995): 208–57, on literature and "the literate speaker." On "the orthography of the uneducated," see also Raymond Williams, *The Long Revolution* (New York: Columbia University Press, 1961), 222.

24. Qtd. in Charles Jones, *A Language Suppressed: The Pronunciation of the Scots Language in the 18th Century* (Edinburgh: John Donald, 1995), 4.

25. See Duncan's and other essays in *The Scottish Invention of English Literature*, qtd. in 37, 41.

26. The 1996 Republic of Ireland census returns 1,430,205 Irish speakers (2,049,443 non Irish-speakers); the 1991 census returns 65,000 people with knowledge of Gaelic in Scotland and 142,00 in Northern Ireland. Because few people have learnt Gaelic as a second language in Scotland, and the Scottish Gaeltacht is concentrated in the Western Isles (where 79 percent of the population can speak Gaelic according to 1981 census returns), Gaelic is the first language of most of the documented 65,000 speakers. In the Republic of Ireland by contrast, there is a high level of partial bilingualism because Irish is taught in the schools. Irish is the predominant vernacular of only a small proportion of documented Irish speakers, however, perhaps about 60,000. Various surveys (e.g., McGreil and Winston [1989], ITÉ [1993] indicate that roughly 10 percent of the population declare themselves fluent in Irish, 40 percent have partial fluency, and 50 percent know little or no Irish.

27. The provocative title of Éamon Ó'Cíosáin's *Buried Alive* makes the point. See *Buried Alive: A Reply to Reg Hindley's* The Death of the Irish Language (Dublin: Dáil Uí Chadhain, 1991).

28. On the politics of *Aiseirigh's* preface, see Robert Welch, *A History of Verse Translation from the Irish, 1789–1897* (1988), 19–24. A vibrant corpus of verse was also produced by Duncan Bàn Mac an tSaoir (1724–c. 1818), Iain MacCodruim (c. 1710–96), Rob Donn MacAoidh (c. 1715–78), and Dùghall Bochanan (1716–68), among others. See Derick S. Thomson, ed. *Gaelic Poetry in the Eighteenth Century: A Bilingual Anthology* (1993) and John L. Campbell, *Orain Ghàidhealach mu Bhliadhna Theàrlaigh: Highland Songs of the Forty-Five* (1984). During the seventeenth century the Gaelic literati translated European literature into Gaelic, but in the eighteenth-century one-way translation from the Gaelic "source" to the English "target"-culture became the rule in Scotland and Ireland. In *Translating Ireland* (1996), Michael Cronin identifies Gaelic-poet Hugh MacCurtin's (Aodh Buí MacCruitín) preface to *A Brief Discourse in Vindication of the Antiquity of Ireland* (1717) as a watershed in English/Gaelic translation-activity: the author declares that "though he felt himself 'not sufficient to write correctly in the English language,' he would have to do so in order to vindicate his compatriots" (92).

29. The translation is Malcolm Chapman's (59–60), except I've substituted "Lowland churls" for *"Gallbhodaich"* (meaning Lowland peasant/carle/churl) in the light of MacInnes's discussion of Gaelic terminology for Scots and English speakers, "The Gaelic

NOTES TO PAGES 13-17   195

Perception of the Lowlands," in *Gaelic and Scotland: Alba agus a' Ghàidhlig,* ed. William Gillies (Edinburgh: Edinburgh University Press, 1989), 94.

30. In 1780 the Scottish lexicographer and grammarian William Shaw, a friend of Dr. Johnson and opponent of Macpherson, called Gaelic "the language of Japhet, spoken before the Deluge, and probably the speech of Paradise." Before later developments in Indo-European philology the idea had wide currency outside the Gaeltacht. See Joep Leerssen, *Mere Irish and Fíor-Ghael* (1986), 361.

31. It is significant that Irish antiquarian Charles O'Conor's 1766 refutation of the Scottish Ossian was concerned less with a proprietary reclamation of the "vulgar" lore than with the way the emphasis on oral tradition threatened to displace the thesis of O'Conor's 1753 *Dissertations on the Antient History* of Ireland that pre-Christian Ireland had an aristocratic, literate culture, and not a barbarous one. See Clare O'Halloran, *Ossian* 76-77.

32. See Fabian, *Time and the Other: How Anthropology Makes Its Object* (New York: Columbia University Press, 1983), 31. See also Robert Crawford, *Devolving English Literature* (Oxford: Clarendon, 1992), 20, on Adam Smith's contribution to the nascent discipline of anthropology in 1750-51.

33. See Fiona Stafford *The Sublime Savage* (1988) 77-84, qtd. on 78.

34. See Ann Dooley and Harry Roe's translation of *Acallam na Senórach/Tales of the Elders of Ireland* (New York: Oxford University Press, 1999); and Bo Almqvist et al., eds., *The Heroic Process: Form, Function, and Fantasy in Folk Epic* (Dublin: Glendale Press, 1985). See also James MacKillop, *Fionn MacCumhaill: Celtic Myth in English Literature* (Syracuse, N.Y.: Syracuse University Press, 1986), on English literary adaptations of the Gaelic heroic figure, from John Barbour's allusion to "Fyngall" in Scots to *Finnegans Wake.*

35. See Macpherson, "A Dissertation concerning the Antiquity, &c. of the Poems of Ossian, the son of Fingal," in Gaskill, ed., *The Poems of Ossian and Related Works* (Edinburgh: Edinburgh University Press, 1996), 52. On the "literal" translation, see Derick S. Thomson, *The Gaelic Sources of Macpherson's Ossian* (Edinburgh: Published for the University of Aberdeen by Oliver and Boyd, 1952), 42. On the forgery question, see Howard Gaskill's editorial introduction to *Ossian Revisited* (Edinburgh: Edinburgh University Press, 1991), 1-17; and on the pre-Romantic Ossian, see Gaskill and Fiona Stafford's introduction to *From Gaelic to Romantic: Ossianic Translations* (Atlanta: Rodopi, 1998), esp. xii.

36. See Talal Asad, "The Concept of Cultural Translation in British Social Anthropology," in *Writing Culture: The Poetics and Politics of Ethnography,* ed. James Clifford and G. E. Marcus (Berkeley: University of California Press, 1986), 160.

37. See Paul DeGategno's essay "'The Source of Daily and Exalted Pleasure': Jefferson Reads the Poems of Ossian," in Gaskill, *Poems of Ossian,* 94.

38. See Peter Womack, *Improvement and Romance,* esp. 169.

39. See Uwe Böker, citing Alexander Gillies (1933), in "The Marketing of Macpherson: The International Book Trade and the First Phase of German Ossian Reception," in Gaskill, *Poems of Ossian,* 84, 87.

40. See Schwab, "Cultural Texts and Endopsychic Scripts," *SubStance* 30, nos. 1-2 (2001): 171-73; and "Words and Moods: The Transference of Literary Knowledge," *SubStance* 26, no. 3 (1997): 107, 111.

41. On transformational "evocative objects," see Christopher Bollas, *Being a Character*, 33–46.

42. See Schwab, introduction to *Imaginary Ethnographies*, 3, quoted with permission of the author from an unpublished manuscript; Schwab borrows *transcoding* from Fredric Jameson.

43. See Foster, *Irish Story*, 8, citing Michel de Certeau.

44. Brendán O'Buachalla estimates that "Gile na Gile" was composed in response to the dashed hopes of "the fifteen" Jacobite rising (550); Seán Ó'Tuama suggests 1707–9 as a likely date of composition (1978, 154). For a magisterial study of the *aisling* genre, and Ó'Rathaille's contribution to it, see O'Buachalla, *Aisling Ghéar*. For *Aisling Ghéar's* donnée in English, see O'Buachalla, "Irish Jacobite Poetry," *Irish Review* 12:40–49. On Ó'Rathaille, see also Seán Ó'Tuama, *Filí Faoi Sceimhle*, 87–124, an abridged English version of which appears in *Repossessions*, 101–18. See also MacDiarmid's sources: Daniel Corkery, *The Hidden Ireland: A Study of Gaelic Munster in the Eighteenth Century* (Dublin: M. H. Gill and Son, 1925) 155–83; and Aodh De Blácam, *Gaelic Literature Surveyed* (Dublin: Talbot Press, 1929), 309–14.

45. See Mary Louise Pratt, "Linguistic Utopias," *The Linguistics of Writing: Arguments between Language and Literature*, 46–66 (New York: Methuen, 1987).

46. See O'Buachalla, *Aisling Ghéar*, 296, 345–46, 652–54.

47. See Corkery, *Hidden Ireland*, 175–77; and James Clarence Mangan, *The Poets and Poetry of Munster* (Dublin: James Duffy, 1850), 23–25. See also translations by Patrick Dinneen and Tadhg O'Donoghue of Ó'Rathaille, *Dánta Aodhagáin Uí Rathaille* (London: Irish Texts Society, 1911), 18–21; Seán Ó'Tuama and Thomas Kinsella, *An Duanaire: Poems of the Dispossessed, 1600–1900* (Dublin: Dolmen Press, 1981), 150–51; and Frank O'Connor, *Kings, Lords and Commons* (1959; rpt., Dublin: Gill and Macmillan, 1991), 104–5. Despite misgivings, O'Connor provides an unsatisfactory translation of "Gile na Gile" "to complete the picture of O'Rahilly's poetry"; the opening quatrain reads:

> Brightness of brightness lonely met me where I wandered,
>> Crystal of crystal only by her eyes were splendid,
>> Sweetness of sweetness lightly in her speech she squandered,
>> Rose-red and lily-glow brightly in her cheeks contended.

48. See Ó'Rathaille, *Dánta Aodhagáin Uí Rathaille*, ed. Dinneen and O'Donoghue, xxxviii–lii, for a lucid metrical exposition. Because their diacritics are not reproducible, I supply their gloss instead: *i* as in the Irish *rith*, English *sin; u* as in Irish *cor*, English *cur; ee* as in Irish *bí*, English *free;* and *ua* as in Irish *fuar*, English *truant* (except shorter).

49. *Ní* features on the playbill but is not mentioned onstage. The headnote was written by John O'Daly, Mangan's editor.

50. In the oral tradition, humans visited by the *sidhe* (fairies) are said to be "touched."

51. Quoting P. S. O'Hegarty. Stephen Gwynn writes "I went home asking myself if such plays should be produced unless one was prepared for people to go out to shoot and be shot." See Conor Cruise O'Brien, "Passion and Cunning: the Politics of Yeats," in *In Excited Reverie: A Centenary Tribute to William Butler Yeats, 1865–1939*, ed. A. Norman Jeffares and K.G.W. Cross (New York: Macmillan, 1965), 221.

52. "Working to free Ireland from foreign rule" was added to the organization's objec-

tives. In "The Coming Revolution" (1913) Pearse declares that whenever Hyde produces his dove of peace at a Gaelic-League meeting, he "tantalize[s] him by saying that the Gaelic League has brought into Ireland 'not peace, but a sword,'" and declaims that "the Gaelic League, as the Gaelic League, is a spent force, and I am glad of it . . . it was a prophet . . . but not the Messiah . . . the vital work to be done in the new Ireland will be done . . . by men and movements that have sprung from the Gaelic League or have received from the Gaelic League a new baptism and a new life of grace . . . and will tend toward the common objective: the Irish revolution" (qtd. in Tom Garvin, *Nationalist Revolutionaries in Ireland, 1858–1928* [Oxford: Clarendon, 1987], esp. 99; and F.S.L. Lyons, *Ireland since the Famine* [London: Weidenfeld and Nicolson, 1971], 334–39). Hyde retired to scholarship, but after the Irish Free State was reconstituted as the Republic of Eire, he became its first President (a largely ceremonial position) in 1938. Marianne Moore writes "we are encouraged by Douglas Hyde's election" in an otherwise gloomy international scene (*SL* 392).

53. See Arnold, *The Study of Celtic Literature* (1867), 2nd ed. (London: Kennikat, 1970), xiv–xv; hereafter cited as *SCL*.

54. Arnold writes to his mother on May 8, 1959: "I could not help but think of you in Brittany, with Cranics and Trevenecs all about me, and the peasantry with their expressive, rather mournful faces, long noses, and dark eyes, reminding me of dear Tom and uncle Trevenen." In 1864 he writes of the vacation in Wales: "The poetry of the Celtic race and its names of places quite overpowers me, and it will be long before Tom forgets the line, 'Hear from thy grave, great Taliesin, hear!'—from Gray's 'Bard,' of which I gave him the benefit some hundred times a day on our excursions." Later he visited the Highlands: "I have a great penchant for the Celtic races, with their melancholy and unprogressiveness." See notes to R. H. Super, ed., *Complete Prose*, 3:490–92.

55. On Arnold's oedipal rejection of Thomas Arnold's "Teutomania," see Robert Young, *Colonial Desire*, 68.

56. On Arnold's interest in Irish issues, and especially on the influence of Fenian activism on the "Celtic" essay, see Owen Dudley Edward, "Matthew Arnold's Fight for Ireland," in *Matthew Arnold: Between Two Worlds*, ed. Robert Giddings (London: Vision, 1986), 148–201. Fenians John O'Leary (Yeats's mentor) and Thomas Luby Clarke (later one of the executed 1916 leaders) were sentenced to twenty years' hard labor a week before Arnold delivered his first lecture.

57. On the chronotope, see *Remembrance and Imagination*, 188–95. Leerssen does not address the language issue as I do here. I quote from an earlier version of Leerssen's argument, "Outward Bound: The Locale and Ontology of Cultural Stereotypes in the Case of Celtic Exoticism," in *Proceedings of the Twelfth Congress of the International Comparative Literature Association*, ed. Bauer et al. (Munich: Iudicum, 1990), 4:214.

58. *La Poésie des races celtiques* was first published in *Revue des Deux Mondes*, February 1, 1854. Yeats uses the 1896 translation by William Hutchinson (which, in circular fashion, met the market demand for things Celtic fanned by Yeats) for his "Celtic Element" essay. I use a reprint of Hutchinson's edition, *The Poetry of the Celtic Races and Other Studies* by Ernest Renan (Port Washington, N.Y.: Kennikat, 1970), 1–2.

59. See René M. Galand, *L'Âme celtique de Renan* (New Haven, Conn.: Yale University Press, 1959): esp. 10, on Renan's Breton background. Galand cites Renan's letter of August

17, 1885: "Je passe l'été près de Perros, au milieu d'un hameau de très pauvres gens . . . Des que je leur ai parlé breton, ils m'ont tenu absolument pour un des leurs." On March 9, 1954, Renan writes to his mother: "I have recently sent you separately a proof of an article that I placed in the *Revue des Deux Mondes*. I thought it would give you pleasure because it is about Brittany and the Bretons. I have spoken, as you see, with love and patriotism. While writing it I thought of our walks together, and of all our memories" (Je vous ai envoyé les jours derniers un tirage a part d'un article que j'ai inséré dans la *Revue des Deux Mondes*. J'ai pensé qu'il vous ferait plaisir, parce qu'il y est question de la Bretagne et des Bretons dont j'ai parlé, comme vous voyez, avec amour et patriotisme. Je pensais en l'écrivant, à nos promenades d'autrefois, à tous nos souvenirs). See *Lettres familières, 1851−71* (Paris: Flammarion, 1947), 37.

60. See John V. Kelleher, "Arnold and the Celtic Revival," *Perspectives of Criticism* (Cambridge, Mass.: Harvard University Press, 1950), 209. The R. H. Super edition (1962) corrects the error.

61. Renan maintains that "[the French language] will say quite diverse things, but always liberal things . . . it will never be a reactionary language either . . . Fanaticism is impossible in French . . . A Musulman who knows French will never be a dangerous Musulman . . . the preservation and propagation of the French language are important for the general order of civilization." Qtd. in Tzvetan Todorov, *On Human Diversity: Nationalism, Racism, and Exoticism in French Thought* (Cambridge, Mass.: Cambridge University Press, 1993), 145−46. Renan was a major contributor to Orientalist ideology, a discourse of Otherness that parallels Celticism in many ways. On Renan's orientalism, see Edward Said, *Orientalism*, esp. 130−48.

62. Arnold borrows the phrase from Henri Martin's *Histoire de France;* see discussion, Frederic E. Faverty, *Matthew Arnold: The Ethnologist* (Evanston, Ill.: Northwestern University Press, 1951), 134−35.

63. The *Pilot* published fourteen articles by Yeats headed "The Celt in London" between August 1889 and November 1892. See *Letters to the New Island*, ed. George Bornstein and Hugh Witemeyer (New York: Macmillan, 1989), xvi.

64. See Leerssen, *Remembrance and Imagination*, esp. 67; and on Yeats, esp. 191.

65. See Geoffrey Hartman, *Saving the Text: Literature, Derrida, Philosophy* (Baltimore: Johns Hopkins University Press, 1981), 141; cited by Schwab.

66. *Language, Lore, and Lyrics: Essays and Lectures*, ed. Breandán O'Conaire (Dublin: Irish Academic Press, 1986), 157; hereafter cited as *LLL*.

67. See W. B. Yeats, "A General Introduction," in *Essays and Introductions* (New York: Macmillan, 1961), 509. Since "A General Introduction" is a touchstone text, I cite it parenthetically as GI with the page numbers of the *Essays and Introductions* version. I also draw on the version edited by Edward Callan, which I cite specifically as "Callan ed."

68. The term *oral tradition* or *folklore* is more commonly used in Ireland than *orature* (a word that seeks to eliminate the scriptist bias of *literature* from the term for orally composed and transmitted narratives). I use *orature* as an umbrella term for orally transmitted legends, tales, songs, and lore, and as a subcategory of *folklore*, which I use in a very broad sense. There is extensive Irish scholarship on folklore, and my ideas on folklore are indebted to Nuala Ní Dhomhnaill, Angela Bourke, Diarmuid Ó'Giolláin, Daithi Ó'hÓgáin,

and other scholars published in the journal *Bealoideas*. See also Mary Helen Thuente, *W. B. Yeats and Irish Folklore* (Totowa, N.J.: Barnes and Noble, 1981); and the useful annotated anthology *W. B. Yeats: Writings on Irish Folklore, Legend and Myth*, ed. Robert Welch (London: Penguin, 1993).

69. On *volksseele* and common sense, see Isaiah Berlin, *Vico and Herder: Two Studies in the History of Ideas* (New York: Vintage, 1976), 61; and Giambattista Vico, *The New Science of Giambattisto Vico* (1744 ed.), trans. Thomas Goddard Bergin and Max Harold Fisch (Ithaca, N.Y.: Cornell University Press, 1948), para. 142.

70. See note and appended ballad in Hyde, *Leabhar Sgeulaigheachta*, 231-38.

71. See introduction by Dominic Daly to *Abhráin atá leagtha ar an Reachtúire/Songs Ascribed to Raftery*, vii.

72. Gaelic catechisms and twenty editions of *Pious Miscellany* published between 1802 and 1840 were produced in this form. See Niall Ó'Cíosáin, "Printed Popular Literature in Irish," in *The Origins of Popular Literacy in Ireland: Language Change and Educational Development, 1700-1920* (Dublin: Department of Modern History, Trinity College; Department of Modern History, University College, 1990), 48-49.

73. See *Fairy and Folk Tales of the Irish Peasantry*, 8; hereafter cited as *FFT*. In 1895 Bridget Cleary was burned to death as a suspected changeling by her family (the fairy associations of "new milk" played a role in the tragedy). For an excellent study of the psychological and artistic subtlety of the residual belief system as it collides with the modernity supplanting it, see Angela Bourke's study of the incident and the public controversy about it, *The Burning of Bridget Cleary: A True Story* (Pimlico, 1999), esp. 142-43, on Yeats's "The Stolen Bride" (1893), retitled "The Host of the Air."

74. See Joseph Hone, *W. B. Yeats, 1865-1939* (London: Macmillan, 1943), 114. The play enjoyed a long run on a double bill in London with Shaw's *Arms and the Man*. The program note anticipates Brian Friel's dramaturgical device in *Translations* (1980), but the illusion of Gaelic speech does not work in Yeats's play.

75. Yeats was a confirmed English monoglot. Donald Pearce recalls George Yeats's response to his question about why Yeats had such a hard time with foreign languages: " 'Probably it was more a matter of personality than of language skills' she said. 'W. B. liked to be decisive and impressive when he spoke. He couldn't bear stumbling about in a language as a beginner. And that, I would think, would make it impossible for him to get started in a foreign language—don't you agree?—even to speak commonplaces' " (490). See "Hours with the Domestic Sibyll: Remembering George Yeats," *Southern Review* 29, no. 3 (1992): 485-502. Yeats briefly studied Irish at Coole, but didn't persist with it. He writes to Lily Yeats on July 11, 1898—"I had almost forgotten, by the by, that I have begun Irish and am getting on fairly well with it." Despite his difficulty with languages, the feeble effort is surprising when the symbolic stakes were so high. He held aloof from Irish by envisioning it as a primordially "other" tongue that he had not "been born to": "One could still, if one had the genius, and had been born to Irish, write for these people plays and poems like those of Greece." See *Essays and Introductions*, 213; hereafter cited as *EI*. The psychological distance is apparently bound up with his image of his Anglo-Irish identity, though his Anglo-Irish peers, Synge and Hyde, were fluent and well-read in the language, and Gregory attained considerable proficiency. Likewise, though he hadn't "been born to Irish," Yeats's

brother, the artist Jack Yeats, studied it. On Yeats's vestigial knowledge of Irish, see James MacKillop, "'Beurla on It': Yeats, Joyce, and the Irish Language," *Eire-Ireland* (Spring 1980): 138–48; and Brendan O'Hehir, "Kickshaws and Wheelchairs: Yeats and the Irish Language," *Yeats: An Annual of Critical and Textual Studies* 1 (1983).

76. See *Collected Letters*, 1:303.

77. Hyde singles out the Anglicization of *Táiltín*, an ancient site of national gatherings, as "Telltown"; by not telling the "place-of-assembly" connotation, the homonymic substitute "make[s] sure that no national memories should stick to it" (*LLL* 166). On how the seventeenth-century remapping of Munster usurped natives' "cognitive ownership" of their land, see Mary Hamer, "Putting Ireland on the Map," *Textual Practice* 3, no. 2 (1989): 184–201.

78. The 1851 census was the first one with language data and records 1.5 million Irish speakers (23 percent); the 1892 census records a drop to 15 percent. The scholarly consensus is that these figures are an underestimate, but they are in any case overshadowed by the likely number of Irish speakers—estimates range from a third to one half—in the pre-famine population of 8.5 million. By the century's close the population had almost halved as a result of over a million lives lost to famine and the remainder to the mass emigration that continued unabated throughout the period. See Cormac Ó'Gráda, *Black '47 and Beyond* 216, 84–121. I find Seán De Fréine's controversial thesis that the desire to create symbolic distance from the famine trauma intensified "the mass flight from the Irish language" persuasive, but the impact of the famine on language attitudes remains inadequately researched. See de Fréine in *The English Language in Ireland,* ed. Diarmaid O'Muirithe (Cork: Mercier, 1977), 83.

79. See *LLL* 78, 80; and preface to *Beside the Fire* (1890): xliv. Although the Danish, Dutch, Finnish, Flemish, Norwegian, and Swedish language communities were smaller than the Irish-Gaelic community at the time of the famine, their economies thrived unhindered by the preservation of their minority languages. See J. J. Lee, *Ireland, 1912–1985* (Cambridge: Cambridge University Press, 1989), 662–77. Ireland's embrace of English-only Anglicization was shaped by a singular combination of push-pull factors, but the visceral rejection of bilingualism that Hyde calls "suicidal mania" has relevance for understanding the psychodynamics of language shift and reversing language-shift elsewhere (*LLL* 181).

80. Hyde delivered the address as a stump-speech many times; a footnote in the inaugural version is reworked for rhetorical effect in the 1905 version.

81. *LLL* 154–55; my emph.; my paraphrase of Hyde's catalogue retains its sense.

82. See Cheng, *Melancholy of Race,* 7.

83. Here I adapt Etienne Balibar's observation that "it is not race which is a biological or psychological human 'memory,' but it is racism which represents one of the most insistent forms of the historical memory of modern societies" (45). Balibar argues that "racism is not an 'expression' of nationalism, but . . . *a supplement internal to nationalism,* always in excess of it, but always indispensable to its constitution and yet"—the qualification is crucial—"always still insufficient to achieve its project." See "Racism and Nationalism," in *Race, Nation, Class: Ambiguous Identities,* ed. Balibar and Immanuel Wallerstein (New York: Verso, [1995], 54).

84. On the "false-national" scapegoat, see Balibar, "Racism and Nationalism," 60. On Arnold's appropriation of Heine's use of *Philistine* as "enemy," see Stephen Prickett, "Matthew Arnold and Ernest Renan," *Franco-British Studies* 16 (1993): 1–12.

85. As John Hutchinson and Joep Leerssen argue, the bifurcation of Anglo/Celtic cultural spheres—small-scale versus mass; heroic versus utilitarian; visionary versus political; poetic versus prosaic—correspond with the traditional *community*/anonymous *society* antithesis popularized by Ferdinand Tonnies's sociological treatise, *Gemeinschaft und Gesellschaft* (1887). See Leerssen, *Remembrance and Imagination: Patterns in the Historical and Literary Representation of Ireland in the Nineteenth Century,* Field Day Monograph (Notre Dame, Ind.: University of Notre Dame Press, 1997), 164; and Hutchinson, *The Dynamics of Cultural Nationalism: The Gaelic Revival and the Creation of the Irish Nation State* (Boston: Allen and Unwin, 1987), 133.

86. Louis-Jean Calvet defines the *tendencies* toward "vernacular" usage (the language of a particular class or group of people) and "vehicular" (language of wider communication) relationally (*Language Wars,* 55–66). Any utterance can aim toward the maximal explicit intelligibility of a lingua franca *(langue véhiculaire)* or toward the implicit intimacy of vernacular usage *(langue grégaire).* Language marks "where we differ [from excluded others] and where we belong [with included others]" (56). Calvet's concept of a vernacular as a *"langue grégaire"* resonates with how Hyde envisions the use of spoken Irish in a dominant Anglophone context.

87. On Arnold's erasure of class interests through the "tribal nicknames" of barbarian, philistine, and populace, see Chris Baldick, *The Social Mission of English Criticism* (Oxford: Clarendon, 1983), 36. See Garvin, *Nationalist Revolutionaries,* on "status resentment" and class antagonism among de-Anglicizers (86, 90).

88. On the primitivism of the Revivalist construction of the peasant, see Philip O'Leary; Gregory Castle; Marjorie Howes; and Deborah Fleming, *"A Man Who Does Not Exist": The Irish Peasant in the Work of W. B. Yeats and J. M. Synge* (Ann Arbor: University of Michigan Press, 1995).

89. See Breandán MacAodha, in *The Gaelic League Idea,* ed. Seán Ó Tuama (Dublin: Mercier Press, 1972), 21. On the social composition of Gaelic League membership (returned émigrés are a significant cohort), and rise in membership after 1899, see Martin J. Waters, "Peasants and Emigrants," in *Views of the Irish Peasantry, 1800–1916,* ed. D. Casey and R. Rhodes (Hamden: Archon, 1977). Waters's argument that the Boer War was the crucial catalyst in popularizing cultural nationalism supports my thesis about the significance of anti-imperial sentiment to the movement.

90. See *LLL* 21. The drastic efficacy of the tally stick can be judged from Garret Fitzgerald's analysis by age cohort and district of the declining numbers of Irish speakers—in the barony of Kilmallock, County Limerick, to take one dramatic instance, the number of Irish-speaking children fell from 100 percent in 1811 to 3 percent in 1861. See Fitzgerald, *Proceedings of the Royal Irish Academy* 84, C, 3:133. A similar surveillance system, where children pass around a button to identify those who lapse into Gikuyu and other African languages in Kenya, is described by Ngũgĩ wa Thiong'o in *Decolonising the Mind: The Politics of Language in African Literature* (London: Heinemann, 1986), 11.

91. Hyde provides an apt figure for the personal vigilance practiced by ardent revivalists

when he confides the year before the "De-Anglicizing" manifesto that he had placed himself "under *geasa* (prohibitions) as they said in the old Irish . . . never to utter an English word except when I would not be understood in Irish" (trans., *LLL* 49).

92. See Baldick, *Social Mission*, 23, quoting Arnold on the preparatory function of criticism.

93. When questioned about the prospects of the Language Movement in a San Francisco *Leader* interview in 1906, for example, Hyde parries that he distrusts taking stock of the future and prophesying because, with "immense inertia" to combat, "if we had done so at any time during the past ten years, what could we have foreseen but failure?" (*LLL* 196).

94. R. V. Comerford, *The Fenians in Context: Irish Politics and Society, 1848–82* (Dublin: Wolfhound, 1995), 30.

95. All citations from the letter can be found in *Uncollected Prose*, 2 vols., 1:255–56; hereafter cited as *UP1* and *UP2*.

96. See W. B. Yeats, *The Variorum Edition of the Poems of W. B. Yeats*, ed. Peter Allt and Russell K. Alspach, 3rd ed. (New York: Macmillan, 1966), 778; hereafter cited as *VP*.

97. See *Vision*, 261; hereafter cited as *V.*

98. On the autodidacticism of the (Gramscian) organic intellectual, see Said, *Orientalism*, 25; and *Beginnings*, esp. 349.

99. Hyde was impatient with how Yeats held forth at social gatherings about literature, mythology, and aesthetics. His diary for January 29, 1887, reads, "Yeats was there; I was bored to death with his blather." See Dominic Daly, *The Young Douglas Hyde: The Dawn of the Irish Revolution and Renaissance, 1874–1893*, foreword by Erskine Childers (Totowa, N.J.: Rowman and Littlefield, 1974), 90; and Janet and Gareth Dunleavy, *Douglas Hyde: A Maker of Modern Ireland* (Berkeley: University of California Press, 1991), 131–33.

100. See W. B. Yeats, *Mythologies* (New York: Macmillan, 1959), 336; hereafter cited as *Myth*.

101. See W. B. Yeats, *Explorations*, ed. Mrs. W. B. Yeats (New York: Macmillan, 1962), 400; hereafter cited as *Ex*.

102. See "J. M. Synge and the Ireland of His Time," *EI* 314. The posthumous homage to "a pure artist" who "sought for the race . . . in the depths of the mind" treats Synge as an exemplar of the "first principle" of Yeats's poetics. Yeats treats "poet" in the restricted sense of maker-of-verse in "A General Introduction" and viewed the "Collected Yeats" as a fable of the self-making poet, but the Synge essay—which focuses on his ethnographical journals, *The Aran Islands*, as well as his plays—suggests that he occasionally has the broader category of literature in mind.

103. Vico writes that the discovery that the peoples of remote antiquity thought in poetic images and fables is the axiomatic "master key" of *The New Science* and "cost [him] the persistent research of almost all [his] literary life, because with our civilized natures we cannot at all imagine and can understand only by great toil the poetic natures of these first men." See *The New Science of Giambattista Vico*, trans. Thomas G. Bergin and Max H. Fisch, 22, para. 34; and Benedetto Croce, *The Philosophy of Giambattista Vico*, 45–46. My ideas on Vico are indebted to the work of Edward Said.

104. See Callan ed., 62–63 and 104–7, on the inclusion of the "Curse of Cromwell" in "A General Introduction." See also GI 518–19.

105. See Yeats/Gonne letters, 449.

106. Yeats may have heard the simile from the Shri Purohit Swami or Mohini Chatter-jee. W. H. O'Donnell's annotations in the Cornell edition of Yeats marks the wild beast simile as "unidentified," and I have been unable to track any direct source for it. A. K. Ramanujan glosses the lines "caterpillar on a leaf, eating,/being eaten" in his poem "Ele-ments of Composition" with his own translation of the Taittiriya Upanishad, "What eats is eaten,/and what's eaten, eats/in turn." See *Norton Anthology of Modern and Contemporary Poetry*, 3rd ed., 2 vols., ed. Jahan Ramazani, Richard Ellmann, and Robert O'Clair (New York: Norton, 2003), 2:441.

107. See *UP1* 267–74. See also "Hopes and Fears for Irish Literature," published in 1892 before Hyde's de-Anglicizing lecture. Yeats cites the cultural difference he observes between London's Decadents, for whom "literature has ceased to be a handmaid of human-ity" and become "an end in itself," and Irish writers, who share his belief that "all great art and literature [depend] upon conviction and heroic life" as evidence that England is at the sunset of a lyric age and Ireland at the dawn of an epic age (*UP1* 248).

108. The term *autopoiesis,* which I use because it encapsulates so exactly the Vichean-Yeatsian "first principle," was coined by Humberto Maturana and Francisco Varela in the 1970s to designate the circular self-referring organization of "self-producing" systems. See John Mingers, *Self-Producing Systems: Implications and Applications of Autopoiesis* (New York: Plenum, 1995).

109. See Niklas Luhmann, "The Work of Art and the Self-Reproduction of Art," *Essays on Self-Reference* (New York: Columbia University Press, 1990), 191–214.

110. A felicitous illustration of the different modes of cognition occurs when John Mingers signs off his expository study of "autopoiesis" as follows: "I will close this book with a quotation from a poem by W. B. Yeats, 'Among Schoolchildren,' which evokes in me the feeling of autopoiesis: '*O body swayed to music, O brightening glance,/ How can we know the dancer from the dance?*'" The couplet embodies Mingers's "feel" for his subject; the lines explain little, and yet they say it all.

CHAPTER 2. "EATER AND EATEN"

1. "The Message of the Folklorist," *UP1* 284.

2. See Halbwachs, *On Collective Memory,* esp. 182–83.

3. *UP2* 56; and Pierre Nora, *Realms of Memory: Rethinking the French Past* (*Les Lieux de mémoire,* trans. Arthur Goldhammer) (New York: Columbia University Press, 1996).

4. Yeats thus sums up his "private philosophy" in a letter written shortly before his death to Ethel Mannin about *The Death of Cuchulain* adding, "there must be no sign of [this philosophy]; all must be like an old faery tale." See Allan Wade, ed., *The Letters of W. B. Yeats* (New York: Macmillan, 1955), 917–18; hereafter cited as *Letters* in the text.

5. My concept of the "Yeats"-in-the-oeuvre is indebted to James Olney and the partici-pants in the National Endowment for the Humanities seminar on "Yeats and Autobiogra-phy" held at St. Angela's College, Sligo, in 1993. For the distinction between the "autobiogra-phy"-of-the-Poet which may be gleaned from the oeuvre and the conventional notion of the poet's autobiography, see Olney, "Where Is the Real T. S. Eliot? or, The Life of the Poet."

6. See W. B. Yeats, *The Variorum Edition of the Poems of W. B. Yeats*, ed. Peter Allt and Russell K. Alspach, 3rd ed. (New York: Macmillan, 1966), 800; hereafter abbreviated as *VP*. See also note to *Collected Letters*, 2:663–69 for an account of the order and Virginia Moore, 78–79 on the "Aengus" ritual.

7. *Collected Letters*, 2:99.

8. See W. B. Yeats, *Autobiographies* (Dublin: Gill and Macmillan, 1955), 377–78; hereafter cited as *Au*. Noting [apropos of his 1890s "seership"] how he associated the ghostly "white jester [AE saw] about the corridors at Coole" with Aengus, Yeats writes of this "time of great personal strain and sorrow" that "I was tortured by sexual desire and disappointed love; [o]ften as I walked in the woods at Coole it would have been a relief to have screamed aloud" (*Memoirs*, ed. Denis Donoghue [New York: Macmillan, 1972], 125; hereafter cited as *M*).

9. See "Tradition and the Individual Talent," *Selected Prose of T. S. Eliot*, ed Frank Kermode (New York: Farrar, Strauss, and Giroux, 1975), 11.

10. Yeats famously associates apple blossoms with his first meeting with Maud Gonne (*M* 40). Deirdre Toomey writes that Yeats knew from Sigerson's *Bards of the Gael and Gall* that it was "a favourite figure of recent [i.e., Jacobite] Irish bards to describe a maiden as a blossom of the Apple-tree." "Bards of the Gael and Gall: An Uncollected Review by Yeats in *The Illustrated London News*," *Yeats Annual*, no. 5, ed. Warwick Gould (London: Palgrave, 1987), 203–12. Allen Grossman cites the alchemical reading of Deuteronomy 33:13–16 in the form Yeats knew it from Westcott's *Hermetic Arcanum* (181).

11. See Helen Vendler, "Technique in the Earlier Poems of Yeats," 17–18.

12. See Jean Laplanche and J. B. Pontalis "Fantasy and the Origins of Sexuality," 26; they reject the reality illusion opposition to argue that fantasy needs to be understood as "the stage-setting of desire."

13. See Butler, "Force of Fantasy," 110.

14. See Wade, *Letters*, 324; *Myth*, 115.

15. See *Field Day*, 1:3–7, 18–19, on *Aislinge Óenguso*. Caer, the beloved, an uncoupled solitary swan with thrice fifty accompanying maidens/swans may be recalled in the "nine-and-fifty swans" in "The Wild Swans at Coole," and John Rhys's *Legends on the Origin and Growth of Religion as Illustrated by Celtic Heathendom* suggests the connection with the Leda myth (173). Edward Muller's translation of the British Museum Egerton MS 1782 (47) in *Revue Celtique* 3 (1876–82): 342–50, is the source for Rhys, for Lady Gregory's tale in *Cuchulain of Muirthemne* (118–22), and for what was probably Yeats's source, Henri D'Arbois de Jubainville's *Le Cycle mythologique irlandais et la mythologie celtique*, 282–89, along with Rhys. Gonne may have read the de Jubainville text with Yeats; he bills it in 1895 as "so important that no right knowledge of Irish legend is possible without it" (*UP1* 387). AE (George Russell) shares Yeats's fascination with Aengus, the "Celtic Eros," who features in several of his poems, including "Carrowmore," "The Winds of Angus," and "Transformations." AE writes Yeats in 1903 about plans to publish a cosmogony, perhaps a shared "Celtic Mystical Order" project. His "Celtic cosmogenesis" features Manannan, the divine imagination, whence springs the Sacred Hazel, the symbol of life ramifying everywhere, from which the Many, Angus the Young, seeks through myriad forms of illusion for the infinite being it has left. See *The Candle of Vision* (London: Macmillan, 1918), 153–61.

16. See James Pethica's essay in *Yeats Annual*, no. 15 (2002) on the Gregory/Hyde/Yeats collaborations at the turn of the century.

17. See Douglas Hyde, *Abhráin Grádh Chúige Connacht: Love Songs of Connacht* (Dublin: Gill and Son, 1893), 75–76.

18. In *Autobiographies* Yeats recalls his first meeting with Hyde, who "filled [him] with surprise, partly because he had pushed a snuffbox toward me, and partly because there was something about his vague serious eyes, as in his high cheek-bones, that suggested a different civilization, a different race[;] I had set him down as a peasant, and wondered what brought him to college, and to a Protestant college . . . Years afterwards I was to stand at his side and listen to the Galway mowers singing his Gaelic words without knowing whose words they sang . . . He was to create a great popular movement, far more important in its practical results than any movement I could have made, no matter what my luck" (216–18).

19. See George Moore's amusing account of this experiment in *Hail and Farewell*, 246–55.

20. See Philip O'Leary's *The Prose Literature of the Gaelic Revival, 1881–1921: Ideology and Innovation*, esp. 9–16, 45–49.

21. See "Modern Ireland: An Address to American Audiences, 1932–3," ed. Curtis Bradford, *Massachusetts Review* 5, no. 2 (1964): 256–68.

22. In *Synge and the Irish Language* Declan Kiberd argues that much of Synge's idiom is a direct translation from Irish (204–9).

23. Qtd. in O'Leary, *Prose Literature*, 288; see his chapter on the uneasy alliance between the Gaelic Revival and the Irish Renaissance.

24. See Lady Augusta Gregory, *Poets and Dreamers: Studies and Translations* (1903; rpt., Oxford: Oxford University Press, 1974), 248–51; and W. B. Yeats, *Explorations*, ed. Mrs. W. B. Yeats (New York: Macmillan, 1962), 205, 206; hereafter cited as *Ex*. Note the asymmetry in verb tense in the final quotation.

25. *Collected Letters*, 583.

26. See "Phases of the Moon" and "Blood and the Moon" (*VP* 406, 420, 480–81).

27. See "To Be Carved on a Stone at Thoor Ballylee" and "Meditations in Time of Civil War" (*VP* 406, 420).

28. See "A Prayer for My Daughter" and "Coole Park, 1929" (*VP* 405, 489); the "swallows" refer to Hyde, Synge, and himself, making Gregory the hegemonic hub of the Revival.

29. See Smith, *Rhetoric of Renewal*, 163, 176.

30. In *The Oxford Book of Modern Verse* Yeats writes, "A Boy of seventeen, Walt Whitman in his pocket, had little interest in a querulous, sensitive scholar" (Gerard Manley Hopkins). Yeats knew and admired Whitman from the 1880s, and Whitman admired an article Yeats wrote on Samuel Ferguson in 1886. On Whitman and Yeats, see Terence Diggory, 18–30. For a dual-language text of "Seanchus na Sceiche"/"The Dispute with the Bush," see Douglas Hyde, *Abhráin atá Leagtha ar an Reachtúire: Songs Ascribed to Raftery Being the Fifth Chapter of the Songs of Connacht* (1903), coll., ed., and trans. Douglas Hyde, intro. Dominic Daly (New York: Barnes and Noble, 1973), 282–321.

31. See *New Science*, 323.

32. See Mary Hanley, *Thoor Ballylee: Home of W. B. Yeats*, ed. Liam Miller (Dublin: Dolmen Press, 1965), esp. 26.

33. See Benedetto Croce, *The Philosophy of Giambattista Vico*, 184, 190; and Vico, para. 313.

34. See Vico, para. 313–14; and Donald Verene, *Vico's Science of Imagination* (1981), 110.

35. See "The Second Coming": "the center cannot hold" (2).

36. See *Senate Speeches*, June 11, 1925, 99.

37. See Alasdair MacIntyre, "Poetry as Political Philosophy: Notes on Burke and Yeats."

38. On J. R. Seeley's opinion that "we seem, as it were, to have conquered and peopled half the world in a fit of absence of mind," see chap. 1 n. 8. See also Mary Louise Pratt's *Imperial Eyes* (1992).

39. See David Simpson, "Destiny Made Manifest: The Styles of Whitman's Poetry," in *Nation and Narration*, ed. Homi Bhabha (London: Routledge, 1990), 182, 191.

40. Ezra Pound's Canto 81 proclaims "(To break the pentameter, that was/the first heave)." In *History of the Voice: The Development of Nation Language in Anglophone Caribbean Poetry* Edward Kamau Brathwaite writes that "nation-language" seeks to renovate "syllabic intelligence" by breaking the pentameter because "the hurricane does not roar in pentameters" (10).

41. See Welch, *History of Verse Translation;* O'Donoghue, "Translator's Voice"; and Seán Lucy, "Metre and Movement in Anglo-Irish Verse," *Irish University Review* 8, no. 2 (1978).

42. The key passage in Vico's *New Science* (bk. 3: *Discovery of the New Homer*), from which Donald Verene draws his thesis about *fantasia*, reads: "in that human indigence [of common script not yet being invented], the peoples, who were almost all body and almost no reflection, must have been all vivid sensation in perceiving particulars, strong imagination in apprehending and enlarging them, sharp wit in referring them to their imaginative genera, and robust memory in retaining them. It is true that these faculties appertain to the mind but they have their roots in the body and draw their strength from it. Hence memory is the same as imagination, which for that reason is called *memoria* in Latin" (313). See also Croce on "Homer and Primitive Poetry," esp. 191.

43. Moore writes that there are moments "when the [Yeatsian] stanza is perhaps too neat [and] summary; the rhymed line, unduly firm—dispatched-and-dealt-with-and-buried-from-sight—lending a touch of disdain that seems to apply to the reader rather than the thing written of" (*CPr* 295).

44. See Barrington, *Ireland,* 39; and Torchiana, *W. B. Yeats and Georgian Ireland* (Washington, D.C.: Catholic University Press, 1966), 305–6.

45. See O'Connor, *Kings, Lords and Commons,* ix.

46. See Michael Yeats, "W. B. Yeats and Irish Folk Song," 164.

47. See P. L. Henry (1957), 200; and Markku Filppula (1999), 213–15, on the substratal influence of the Gaelic *ná/ach* (but) on the Irish-English tendency toward "initial negation followed by exemptive but/only."

48. See Gilles Deleuze, "He Stuttered" (1997), 113.

49. The "forgotten" text describes how that night, inside a daylight-brightened house at Slieve Echtge, Hanrahan found the sovereignty goddess Echtge and her attendant crones

who bore the four treasures of Danu, the cauldron, stone, spear, and sword (the treasures structured many Celtic Mystical Order rituals). Because he failed to ask who she was and what she was waiting for he was "touched" and wandered aimlessly, forgetting his beloved Mary Lavelle, until the next *Samhain*, by which time he had lost her (*Secret Rose*, 90–95).

50. See Deirdre Toomey, "Labyrinths: Yeats and Maud Gonne," in *Yeats Annual*, no. 9, ed. Toomey (London: Macmillan, 1992).

51. See Said, *Culture and Imperialism* (1995), 225–26, first published in *Nationalism, Colonialism, and Literature*, ed. Seamus Deane (Minneapolis: University of Minnesota Press, 1990).

52. See conclusion to *La Topographie légendaire des évangiles en Terre Sainte* (1941) in *On Collective Memory*, 193–225; and Patrick Hutton's account of Halbwachs's *La Topographie* in *History as an Art of Memory*, 73–90, esp. 82, 84. Ernest Renan's *Vie de Jésus* is a key source text for Halbwachs.

53. See Beckett, *A Samuel Beckett Reader*, ed. Richard Seaver (New York: Grove Press, 1976), 119.

54. Drumahair = *Droim dhá hEithiar*/the ridge of the two demons; Lissadell = *Lios-a'-Doill*/the fort of the blind man; Lugnagall = *Lug-na-gall*/Hollow of the Strangers; Scanavin = *Sceanmhan*/[a place of] fine shingle (near Collooney). See Jeffares, *Commentary* 34–36. See *Myth* 177–83, for the lore about Lugnagall; according to tradition, Cromwellians who sacked Sligo Abbey were led there by the *sidhe* to their deaths.

55. See Patrick Maume, *"Life That Is Exile": Daniel Corkery and the Search for Irish Ireland* (Belfast: Institute of Irish Studies, 1993), 96.

56. See letter to Olivia Shakespear, Oct. 9, 1922, in Wade, *Letters*, 690.

57. See "Compulsory Gaelic," *UP2* 439–49; qtd. on 441, 443, 446, 448.

58. See Maume, *"Life That Is Exile,"* 22, 122.

59. See O'Connor's autobiographical work *An Only Child*, 145.

60. See *Irish Tribune*, August 13, 1926, 23.

61. On the ideological sway of an Irish-Ireland "vision of national fragility" on Free-State cultural politics, see Terence Brown, *Ireland: A Social and Cultural History, 1922–79* (London: Fontana, 1981), 79.

62. See O'Connor, "Two Friends: Yeats and A.E.," *Yale Review* 29 (Sept. 1939): 72.

63. See my essay "Putting Words in a Rambling Peasant-Poet's Mouth: Frank O'Connor and W. B. Yeats's Translations 'from the Irish'" on the collaboration in *Yeats Annual*, no. 15 (2002), 190–218. See also Richard Ellmann (1964), 190–201; and, on the erotics of the ballad, Elizabeth Butler Cullingford (1996), 165–84.

64. "*Rachad 'na bhfasc le searc na laoch don chill,/na flatha fá raibh mo shean roimh éag do Chríost*" is translated by Patrick Dinneen and Tadhg O'Donoghue as "I will follow the beloved heroes to the churchyard,/the nobility my ancestors served before the death of Christ," and by Seán Ó'Tuama and Thomas Kinsella as "In the grave with this cherished chief I'll join those kings/my people served before the death of Christ" (167).

65. See Fiona Stafford's *The Last of the Race: The Growth of a Myth from Milton to Darwin*. Her thesis that the mid-eighteenth century "stress on the last of the race can be seen as an attempt (albeit unconscious) to free the age from its melancholic preoccupa-

tions, since the death of the last bard has a finality which is hard to reject" gives a therapeutic interpretation to the trope (94), though the cultural preoccupation may also be regarded less benignly as symptomatic of an annihilative urge to finish off the culture.

66. See *Letters on Poetry from W. B. Yeats to Dorothy Wellesley*, 123, hereafter cited as *LDW*.

67. Yeats writes to Olivia Shakespear on March 2, 1929, that "I am writing *Twelve poems for music* . . . not so much that they may be sung as that I may define their kind of emotion to myself. I want them to be all emotion and all impersonal" (Wade, *Letters*, 758); and on the "local satirist," see 785–86.

68. See Adorno (1993), 105.

69. See *Oxford Book of Modern Verse*, xiii.

70. See *EI* 335, on "roystering humour"; and entry for January 13, 1909, in *Memoirs*, 156–57, on how "style" enabled him to escape from the "Jacobin rage" he inherited from his mother.

71. See Wade, *Letters*, 895.

72. See F. N. Robinson (1911).

73. See Patrick Power, *The Book of Irish Curses*, on the widow's curse (73–78); Power speculates that the social taboo on cursing in the presence of women may be motivated by an atavistic fear of women's superior cursing power stemming from their comparative social powerlessness (93). A Gaelic curse translated by Gregory in 1903 in *Poets and Dreamers*, "The Curse of the Boers on England," reads:

> O Lord, let there fall
> Straight down on [Victoria's] head
> The curse of the peoples
> That have fallen with us
> The Lord does not listen
> To the curse of the strong.

74. See Yeats, "Modern Ireland," 263.

75. The poets met and exchanged compliments after Yeats's lecture at the Brooklyn Institute in December 1932. Her copious notes on the lecture are in the Rosenbach Museum Library 7:5:9.

76. The introduction to the *Oxford Book of Modern Verse* reinforces the "Modern Ireland" argument: "John Synge brought back masculinity to Irish verse with his harsh disillusionment" (xiii).

77. See *My Father's Son*, 118. O'Connor kept the "beggar" line, and Yeats substituted his preferred line in *OBMV*. "The Death of Yeats" was the working title of *My Father's Son*, a memoir of three surrogate father-figures, Corkery, AE, and Yeats.

78. In "Literature and Life: Egan O'Rahilly," *Irish Statesman*, Jan. 30, 1926, 653–55, O'Connor praises the "intolerable pathos" of Ó'Rathaille's "uncompromising literary pride" and claims that he comes closest of all Gaelic poets to "our idea of personal utterance"; Corkery celebrates how Ó'Rathaille "outLears Lear" in *The Hidden Ireland*, 179.

79. See *Illuminations*, 257–58.

80. See Daniel Hoffman, *Barbarous Knowledge: Myth in the Poetry of Yeats, Graves and Muir* (New York: Oxford University Press, 1967), 58.

81. Ó'Rathaille's nemesis, Valentine Browne, made twenty thousand pounds by felling eight hundred thousand trees (sixpence a tree) on his estate (Corkery, *Hidden Ireland*, 35). Between December 1922 and March 1923, 192 Big Houses were burned down; see Terence Brown (1981), 86.

82. See *Ex* 345.

83. See Samuel Beckett, *Complete Dramatic Works* (London: Faber and Faber, 1986), 194.

84. See Power, *Book of Irish Curses*, 25. In "Oliver Cromwell in Irish Oral Tradition" Seán Ó'Suilleabháin (1976) notes that half of the catalogued archives in the folklore archives at University College, Dublin (UCD), refer to Cromwell. For a recent treatment of the "Cromwell" theme, see Brendan Kennelly's book-length poetic sequence, *Cromwell* (1983).

85. See copy of the Broadsheet with the MacGonigal illustration in the Edward Callan edition of "A General Introduction," 20; Wade, *Letters*, 890–91 for correspondence with Dulac; John Unterecker, "Yeats and Patrick McCartan: A Fenian Friendship," *Dolmen Press Centenary Papers*, no. 10, ed. Liam Miller (Dublin: Dolmen Press, 1968), 406; *LDW* 119, 123; and, on his gratification at hearing that RIA members spontaneously sang "Cromwell" after he had left the gathering, *LDW* 144.

86. See Wade, *Letters*, 897.

87. See "On Barbarous Denominations in Ireland" (c. 1740), in Tony Crowley, *The Politics of Language in Ireland, 1366–1922: A Sourcebook* (London: Routledge, 2000), 114.

88. See 1916 reading diary on Yeats's *Reveries upon Childhood and Youth*, Rosenbach Museum Library 7:1:1. She adds, "I believe he was a boy, just as I believe my first bishop was nude once upon a time."

89. See Moore, *Complete Poems*, 262; and Bakhtin, *Dialogical Imagination*, 361.

CHAPTER 3. HUGH MACDIARMID'S POETICS OF CARICATURE

1. See "Valedictory," interview with Tom Vernon, in *The Thistle Rises*, ed. Alan Bold, 287; hereafter cited as *TR*.

2. See Kenneth Buthlay, "An Awkward Squad," in *Scotland and the Lowland Tongue*, ed. J. Derrick McClure (Aberdeen: Aberdeen University Press, 1983), 149.

3. I cite by line number from Kenneth Buthlay's excellent annotated edition (Scottish Academic Press, 1987), to which I am indebted; hereafter referred to as *ADM*. *Noo*, now; *A'e*, one; *o'*, of; *tither*, the other; *fou*, drunk; *owre lang*, over long; *wi'*, with; *fier comme un Ecossais*, proud as a Scot.

4. On the stereotype, see Joep Leerssen's imagological studies of the Celt (1986; 1997; and esp. the summative "A Rhetoric of National Character" [2000]); Homi Bhabha (1994), 66–84; and Mireille Rosello, *Declining the Stereotype: Ethnicity and Representation in French Cultures* (Hanover, N.H.: University Press of New England, 1998).

5. See Bakhtin, *The Dialogic Imagination*, ed. and trans. Caryl Emerson and Michael Holquist (Austin: University of Texas Press, 1981), 429.

6. Qtd. in Leerssen, "A Rhetoric of National Character: A Programmatic Survey," *Poetics Today* 21, no. 2 (2000): 273. Leerssen's point about the unfalsifiability and ambivalence of stereotypes is illustrated by how the refrain, perhaps because of the translational pun on

fier/fiery, is variously translated by Kenneth Buthlay as "touchy as a Scot" and by Mac-Diarmid as "free-spirited as a Scot."

7. See *The Philosophical Works of David Hume*, 4 vols. (Boston: Little, Brown, 1854), 3:244–58, esp. 253–56.

8. See Tom Nairn, *The Break-Up of Britain: Crisis and Neo-Nationalism* (London: New Left Books, 1977), 146; MacDiarmid received a copy shortly before his death and replied to Nairn commending "the only serious work on Scottish nationalism." See *Letters*, ed. Alan Bold, 889; hereafter cited as *Letters*.

9. See Leerssen, "Rhetoric," 279.

10. See Tom MacArthur (1998), 142.

11. See Witherspoon, "The Druid," no. 5 in *The Beginnings of American English*, ed. M. M. Matthews (Chicago: University of Chicago Press, 1931), 17.

12. William Ferguson cites Jamieson's failure to note the obvious Gaelic provenance of *glen* as indicative of his "disingenuous approach," in *The Identity of the Scottish Nation*, 260.

13. See Tom Paulin, *Ireland and the English Crisis* (Newcastle-upon-Tyne: Bloodaxe Books, 1984), 192; my emph.

14. The contemporary usage of *stereotype* to signify a mental image or idea that has become fixed through being widely held was promulgated in a 1922 book, as it happens, Walter Lippmann's *Public Opinion*. See Mireille Rosello (1998), 21–23.

15. See Bakhtin, *Speech Genres and Other Late Essays*, ed. Caryl Emerson and Michael Holquist; trans. Vern McGee (Austin: University of Texas Press, 1986), 65.

16. See *The Raucle Tongue*, 30–33; Grieve used Sir James Wilson's *Lowland Scotch as Spoken in the Lower Strathearn District of Perthshire* (1915) for his groundbreaking literary experiment.

17. See *Collected Poems* 17; hereafter cited as *CP*.

18. *Ae weet forenicht*, one wet early night (the time between twilight and the night proper); *i'*, in; *wi' its chitterin' licht*, with its shivering light; *ayont*, beyond; *thocht*, thought; *afore*, before; *there was nae reek i' the laverock's hoose*, (lit. there was no smoke in the lark's house), a Perthshire saying glossed by Grieve as "It was a dark and stormy night"; *sin syne*, since then; *mebbe*, maybe; *I ken*, I know.

19. See *The Dialogic Imagination* (1981), 360; on the distinction between "organic" and "intentional" "novelistic"/"dialogical" hybridization, see 358–61.

20. See Charles Jones, in *Edinburgh History of the Scots Language*, 309, 327.

21. See David Murison, *The Guid Scots Tongue* (Edinburgh: Blackwood, 1977) 25. For an overview of Scots phonology, see 24–37; and Jones, *Edinburgh History*, 267–334. On shibboleths of Scottish pronunciation, see Tom MacArthur, *The English Languages* (Cambridge: Cambridge University Press, 1998), 156.

22. See Joan Beal in Jones, *Edinburgh History*, 351.

23. My reading is indebted to Richard Poirier's Jamesian reading of Robert Frost's "idea of sound" in *Poetry and Pragmatism* (Cambridge, Mass.: Harvard University Press, 1992), 138–54; James calls for "the reinstatement of the vague."

24. See James, *The Writings of William James*, ed. John J. McDermott (Chicago: University of Chicago Press, 1977), 38.

25. I quote from Wallace Stevens's "Thirteen Ways of Looking at a Blackbird," which continues "the blackbird whistling/or just after."

26. Grieve resisted autobiographical interpretations of "The Watergaw," but it is significant that the dictionary-dredging conversion experience evoked memories of his father's tragic early death, not least because the breakthrough was marked by jettisoning his patronymic for the pseudonym that would define his career.

27. See *The Raucle Tongue*, 72–73, hereafter cited as *RT*.

28. Psychic "genera," the antinomy of "trauma" in Bollas's theory of a receptive unconscious, organize unconscious material in an open-ended, generative, and vital manner rather than in a repetitive way to foster the elaboration of the "unthought known" at the core of aesthetic experience. See Bollas, *Being a Character*, esp. 88.

29. David Murison, the editor of *C–Z* in the ten-volume *Scottish National Dictionary*, observes that MacDiarmid's conversation was almost entirely in English and "to questions about where he got this or that word he most frequently referred one to a book" (86). His Synthetic Scots "sticks cautiously to Jamieson" in practice and, notwithstanding the "Back to Dunbar!" manifesto and the oft-touted model of Landsmaal's construction from Old Norse, "there is surprisingly little Middle Scots in his work" (88, 95). Although his selection procedure was often programmatic (alliterative passages, and even whole lyrics, are composed out of proximate items in Jamieson), "his touch is remarkably sure" (96). See *The Age of MacDiarmid*, ed. P. H. Scott and A. C. Davis (Edinburgh: Mainstream, 1980), 93–99. See also W. N. Herbert, *To Circumjack MacDiarmid* (Oxford: Clarendon, 1992), 26–41.

30. Such "distinctly and distinctively" traits are what Joep Leerssen calls "the *effets de typique*" on which stereotyping is based ("Rhetoric," 283).

31. See "The Experiment of Caricature" (1960), 302; "to doodle and watch what happens" is Gombrich's phrase.

32. On "aggrandized" Scots, see *A Lap of Honour* (1965), 11; the latter phrase is Thomas Hardy's, and MacDiarmid invokes it in the 1923 "Theory of Scots Letters," (*TR* 129) the 1931–32 "The Caledonian Antisyzygy and the Gaelic Idea" (63) and in the 1977 "Valedictory" where he says it "sums up my whole position" (294).

33. See *TR* 133; MacDiarmid cites A. R. Orage, "The Criteria of Culture" as an authority for "disinterestedness" (126). T. S. Eliot reviewed Smith's *Scottish Literature: Character and Influence* (1919) under the revealing title, "Was There a Scottish Literature?"; see Robert Crawford (1992), 254.

34. David Reid describes "Urquhart's writing [as] a freak compound of all that Scottish prose after Knox is not" in *The History of Scottish Literature*, 4 vols., ed. Cairns Craig (Aberdeen: Aberdeen University Press, 1987–88), 1:195.

35. See Buthlay's annotation to MacDiarmid's use of *aboulia* in l. 319 (*ADM*, 29).

36. See "Burns and Baudelaire," *Raucle Tongue*, 71. MacDiarmid's ambivalence toward Burns is extremely complex; in terms of their respective "national" traditions, there are several resemblances between MacDiarmid's dispute with Burns and Yeats's with Thomas Davis.

37. See "Following Rebecca West in Edinburgh: A Monologue in the Vernacular," reprinted and introduced by Nancy Gish in *The Gender of Modernism*, ed. Bonnie Kime Scott (1990), 282, 281, 279. Grieve's reaction against "Doric infantilism" in December 1921 was

probably inflamed by what was for him the feminized topic of Bulloch's talk "Diminutives in the Doric" (e.g., *lassie* and *pinkie*).

38. See Richard Ellmann, *James Joyce* (New York: Oxford University Press, 1959), 510.

39. See Bold (1988), 181.

40. See Adam Gopnik, *Modern Art and Primitive Culture* (New York: Abrams, in association with the Museum of Modern Art, 1990), 133.

41. *Amna fou*, am not drunk; *sae*, so; *muckle*, much; *deid dune*, dead done, done in; *stuffie*, stuff; *no'*, not; the *real Mackay*, colloquialism of unknown origin (perhaps connected with the Reay Mackay clan of Sutherland) for "the real thing," "the genuine article" (G. Mackay and Co. distillers adopted the proverbial phrase as an advertising slogan in 1870); *maun*, must.

42. See Pound, *Gaudier-Brzeska*, 106–7. On Pound's influence, see MacDiarmid's essay "Ezra Pound" in *The Company I've Kept*, 170–83; and W. N. Herbert, "Pound and MacDiarmid," in *Sons of Ezra: British Poets and Ezra Pound*, ed. Michael Alexander and James McGonigal (Atlanta: Rodopi, 1995).

43. On the collaboration with Scott, the dedicatee of *A Drunk Man*, see *ADM* xvi–xxiii. Scott set over 70 of MacDiarmid's lyrics, including "The Watergaw," to music.

44. Qtd. in *TR* 131. See McCarey, *Hugh MacDiarmid and the Russians*, 17–27. For a Bakhtinian approach to MacDiarmid's work, see also Robert Crawford, *Identifying Poets: Self and Territory in Twentieth-Century Poetry* (Edinburgh: Edinburgh University Press, 1993).

45. On the generic elements of the menippea, see Bakhtin, *Problems of Dostoevsky's Poetics*, ed. and trans. Caryl Emerson (Minneapolis: University of Minnesota Press, 1984), 114–20; hereafter cited as *Problems*.

46. See *Problems*, 50. Although MacDiarmid arguably falls short of Dostoevski's "radically new . . . *integral* authorial position" with regard to the drunk man, he (like the German Expressionists) takes the "artistic dominant of self-consciousness" as a goal (see Bakhtin, *Problems*, 56–57, 54).

47. *Dinna ken*, don't know; *as muckle's*, as much as; *whaur*, where; *hoo*, how; *'neth*, beneath.

48. See Bakhtin, *Problems*, esp. 53, 156–57.

49. *Ain*, own; *twere*, it were; *mair*, more.

50. *Nocht*, naught; *sae*, so; *blin'*, blind; *bairn*, child; *a'*, all; *pit*, put.

51. Northrop Frye writes of the larger class of Menippean satire into which the subgenre of caricature falls that it "relies on the free play of intellectual fancy and the kind of humorous observation that produces caricature" (*Anatomy of Criticism: Four Essays* [Princeton: Princeton University Press, 1957], 310).

52. *Tap*, top; *bonny sicht*, beautiful sight; *hunner*, hundred; *ferlie*, marvel.

53. See Bakhtin, *Rabelais*, 123–24. In his autobiography MacDiarmid writes that the Grieves were "jeered at a little," making him "permanently incapable of 'going with the herd'" (*Lucky Poet*, 77). Nancy Gish writes that Valda Grieve recalled him as one of the loneliest people she ever met, one who shut himself off from others: "He just had this thing within himself. He was afraid of anything personal'" (*Hugh MacDiarmid: Man and Poet* [London: Macmillan, 1984], 8).

54. *Drums in the Walligate*, from a children's chant: "Ra-a-rae, the nicht afore the Fair! The drum's i' the Walligate, the pipes i' the air"; *the cryin' o' the Fair*, the proclamation of the

Fair; *loon*, boy; *the Muckle Toon*, the affectionate name by which Langholm is known, lit. the big town; *the Bannock-and-Saut-Herrin'*, a barley bannock and salted herring nailed to a wooden dish on a standard that signifies the duke of Buccleuch's rights in the mills and fisheries; *Croon o' Roses*, a floral crown on a standard; *lift*, sky; *wallops*, dances; *hie*, high; *heather besoms*, children were rewarded with new threepenny bits for carrying heather brooms in the procession.

55. *Stounds*, throbs; *bluid*, blood; *dight*, arrayed; *spauld*, shoulder; *wecht*, weight; *a' thing*, everything; *hauld*, hold.

56. *The groins o' licht*—see l. 1265, "As 'twere the hinderpairts o' God"; *ootrie*, foreign, outré; *gangrel*, vagrant; *frae*, from.

57. See Abdul JanMohamed (1983), esp. 4. The Manichaean cast of biblical allegory prompts Henry Champfleury to observe in 1865 that caricature and Christian doctrine work hand in glove: "What is the doctrine that, recalling man to his misery, showed him his humble nature, made him look down on grandeur, fortune and beauty, and incessantly cried out to him that his body formed of dust should return to dust? And what art stripped man of his vain ornaments, and delighted in magnifying and exaggerating his baseness, his vices, his passions? Caricature which, unbeknownst to it, served Christian doctrine" (trans. and qtd. in Michele Hannoosh, *Baudelaire and Caricature: From the Comic to an Art of Modernity* [University Park: Pennsylvania State University Press, 1992], 34).

58. See Bawcutt, *Dunbar the Makar*, 100–103.

59. See Judith Wechsler, "Speaking the Desperate Things: A Conversation with Edward Koren," *Art Journal* 43 (Winter 1983): 385.

60. Bawcutt writes that Dunbar's "art is the art of the caricaturist" (*Dunbar the Makar*, 239–40).

61. See Bakhtin, *Rabelais*, 427.

62. Lowland speech would make a better noise. See Priscilla Bawcutt, *William Dunbar: Selected Poems* (London: Longman, 1996), 266.

63. See *Scottish National Dictionary*.

64. See John MacInnes, "The Gaelic Perception of the Lowlands" (1989), 92.

65. *Jamieson's Dictionary of the Scottish Language* cites the Gaelic etymon for *sonsy* but not for *grugous*, but MacDiarmid may not have consulted the dictionary. *Grugous* is glossed as *grim* in *Jamieson's*; *grim, grisly* in *ADM*; and *ugly* in the *Complete Poems* glossary. One might ascertain the semantic and affective freight of *grugous* for MacDiarmid if one could tell whether he had hazarded upon (the hitherto-unknown?) word in *Jamieson's*, considered it slang like "youky," or recalled hearing an affectionate "what a grugous face!" or chiding "wipe that grugous look off your face!" in childhood. That such critical surmise proves elusive even for a bookish poet writing in a thoroughly documented vernacular attests to the "homelessness" of cultural memory in vernacular Englishes.

66. Gombrich notes how we feel the likeness between Philipon's notorious series of cartoons featuring King Louis Philippe as a *poire* (fathead) "only by knitting our brows and dropping our cheeks which corresponds to the feel of sluggish malice that belongs to the face from the first—all traces of false bonhomie have disappeared [from the final drawings of the series]" (1972): 39.

67. See Deleuze and Guattari, *A Thousand Plateaus* (1987): 102–4. Their concept of an unfinalizable "indirect discourse" is indebted to Bakhtin; see 523–24 nn. 5, 10. The corre-

spondence between antisyzygies, Bakhtin's concept of "hybridization," and Deleuze and Guattari's concept of "minorization" is suggested by MacDiarmid's comment in "English Ascendancy in British Literature" on "the vast amount of linguistic experimentation that has been going on in recent Russian literature, with the progressive de-Frenchification and de-Latinisation of the Russian tongue, the use of *skaz* (the reproduction of accentual peculiarities) and *zaumny* (cross-sense, as in Lewis Carroll)" (120). To illustrate his concept of disjunctive synthesis, Deleuze cites Lewis Carroll on portmanteau words: "If your thoughts incline ever so little towards 'fuming,' you will say 'fuming-furious'; if they turn, even by a hair's breadth, towards 'furious,' you will say 'furious-fuming'; but if you have that rarest of gifts, a perfectly balanced mind, you will say 'frumious.' " See *The Logic of Sense*, trans. Mark Lester (New York: Columbia University Press, 1980), 46.

68. Gombrich contends that the art of caricature demonstrates how portraiture "is not a faithful record of a visual experience but the faithful construction of a relational model," and relates the portraitist's mode of envisioning to the everyday profiling of others that accompanies social interaction ("we see the mask before we notice the face") and to draftsmen's techniques for drawing criminal suspects (*Art, Perception, and Reality* [Baltimore: Johns Hopkins Press, 1972], 89–90). Adam Gopnik contends that the apparent "economy" of graphic caricature depends not (as cognitive psychologists argue) on its intrinsic structure—"the artist overcharges his portrait so the viewer doesn't have to overcharge his mind"—but on its fixed place within the secure decorum of art and "on a mutable context of expectations" (*Modern Art and Popular Culture* [1990], 133).

69. Smith's gargoyle thesis is endorsed in *A Drunk Man*, ll. 426–28.

70. *Reishlin'*, rustling; *wi'ts*, with its; *gausty*, ghastly; *datchie*, hidden; *spired it*, made it soar; *syne*, then; *seely*, happy; *fousome*, disgusting; *jouks*, evades; *routh*, abundance.

71. Susan Manning attributes this tendency to Calvinism; see *The Puritan-Provincial Vision* (1990), 15.

72. *Who o's ha'e*, whom of us have, *poo'er*, power.

73. See "On the Essence of Laughter," *The Painter of Modern Life and Other Essays*, trans. and ed. Jonathan Mayne (1964), 147.

74. *Wha's*, whose; *banes*, bones; *wund's*, wind has; *begood*, begun.

75. *Cloody*, cloudy; *blash*, splash, downpour; *stairch*, starch; *pooders aff*, powders off; *micht*, might; *warld*, world, *syne*, thereafter.

76. See Alan Bold, *MacDiarmid: Christopher Murray Grieve: A Critical Biography* (London: John Murray, 1988), 184.

77. Bakhtin, *Dialogic Imagination*, 118.

78. *Loupt*, leapt; *oot*, out; *O ony*, of any; *afore*, before; *heisted*, hoisted; *haill*, whole; *braid*, broad; *reid*, red; *lift*, sky; *syne*, then; *gin*, if; *curst*, cursed; *ain*, own; *jaups*, splashes.

79. *Mac* lenites the patronymic, *MacDhiarmid* (pronounced *Mock Yearmuid*); Sorley MacLean Gaelicizes *Hugh MacDiarmid* as *Uisdean MacDhiarmid* and *Christopher Murray Grieve* as *Crìstean Moireach Mac a' Ghréidhir* (*Ris a Bhruthaich*, 258). The predestinative power of names is a motif of *Lucky Poet*, which opens, "My surname—the name *Grieve*—does not figure much in Scottish history" (1), notwithstanding the "MacDiarmid" cover autograph. MacDiarmid/Grieve claims that the root meaning of the name Grieve, "rough,"

fits his abrasive style (379–80) and his matrineal name, Murray, indicates his genetic predisposition to linguistics (3). He has a flyting with Roy Campbell over the latter's "libel" against his concealment of "a mean, lachrymose little patronymic" (7–8). MacDiarmid enjoyed doing alias reviews of his own work. The alias provided antisyzygical freedom to play devil's advocate against himself, for as he writes to Herbert Grierson, "MacDiarmid is by no means committed to Grieve's position" (*Letters* 309).

80. See *Selected Essays*, 68–69.

81. See *Selected Prose*, 74, 79.

82. See George Lang, *Entwisted Tongues: Comparative Creole Literatures* (Atlanta: Rodopi, 2000), 105–42.

83. See *Complete Poems*, 1:179–94; 205–6; citations are by page number.

84. *Faur*, far; *frae*, from; *a'body*, anybody; *wrang-heidit*, wrongheaded.

85. See C. I. Macafee and Colm O'Baoill, "Why Scots Is Not a Celtic English," in *The Celtic Englishes*, ed. Hildegard L. C. Tristram (Heidelberg: Universitätsverlag C. Winter, 1997), 245–86.

86. Synthetic Scots conforms in this sense to a "nuclear Creole" (Lang, *Entwisted Tongues*, 144); for an overview of the controversial term *Creole*, see 1–20. For useful comparative discussions of Scots as an English Creole, see Manfred Gorlach, "Jamaica and Scotland—Bilingual or Bidialectal?" in *Englishes* (1991): 69–89; and Tom McArthur, "English That Isn't English: Dialects and Creoles," 7–10. (MacArthur compares a passage from *The King James Bible* with both the *New Testament in Scots* [New York: Penguin, 1985], a landmark translation by William Lorimer; and the *Tok Pisin Nupela Testamen* [Canberra, 1969]).

87. The Curly Snake "has always haunted my imagination and has probably constituted itself as the ground-plan of my mind" (*TR* 153).

88. Boyhood vacations enabled Grieve "to learn a little Gaelic from the Ross-shire woman who was my uncle's second wife" (*LP* 5). As a result of the later collaboration with Sorley MacLean, MacDiarmid became far better informed about Gaelic culture, though he never became proficient in the language.

89. See Buthlay, "An Awkward Squad," 99; and, on the marriage breakup, see Bold, *MacDiarmid*, 255–68.

90. The poetry of the next decade (revised but not significantly expanded over the following thirty years) constitutes a small proportion of the mammoth epics planned but never completed by MacDiarmid. *Cornish Heroic Song for Valda Trevlyn* again takes up "the Gaelic Idea" that is pursued in *To Circumjack Cencrastus* in an epic form based on the quantitative measure of the *pibroch* (bagpipe music); the First and Second Hymns to Lenin are part of an unfinished five-volume autobiographical epic, *Clann Albain;* and "In Memoriam James Joyce" is part of a four-volume project, *Mature Art* (later called *A Vision of World Language*).

91. *Maun*, must; *lanely*, lonely; *wha'e'er*, whoever; *daurna*, dare not; *wi'*, with; *e'en*, eyes; *as fain I wad*, as I'd rather; *tholin'*, enduring; *taen*, taken; *owre*, over; *fa's*, falls; *gin*, if; *speir*, ask.

92. *Eire*, Ireland; *'ud*, would; *hae*, have; *nae*, no; *tho*, though; *aince*, once; *haud*, hold; *heich*, high; *lanely*, lonely.

93. In the final section of *In Memoriam James Joyce* (1955), entitled "Plaited like the Generations of Men," *braidbinding* is used to describe the task of the poet committed to a Solovyovian "interpenetration of all languages"; "the terrible crystal," from *Ezekiel* 1:xxii, connects with the image for *Gile na Gile*'s eyes.

94. "Caledonian Antisyzygies and the Gaelic Idea," *Selected Essays*, 68.

95. *Complete Prose of Marianne Moore*, 314.

CHAPTER 4. AN IRISH INCOGNITA

1. "England," *The Complete Poems of Marianne Moore* (New York: Macmillan, 1981), 46; hereafter cited as *CP*.

2. On the "spinsterish anti-poetess," see Sandra Gilbert, "Marianne Moore as Female Female Impersonator," in *Marianne Moore: The Art of a Modernist*, ed. Joseph Parisi (Ann Arbor, Mich.: UMI Research Press, 1990), 35. On contesting received identity scripts through passing and masquerade, see Ann Douglas, *Terrible Honesty: Mongrel Manhattan in the 1920s* (New York: Farrar, Strauss, and Giroux, 1995).

3. See *The Complete Prose of Marianne Moore* (New York: Viking, 1986), 379, my emph.; hereafter cited as *CPr*; and "Quotation and Originality," *Complete Works of Ralph Waldo Emerson*, 12 vols. (New York: AMS Press, 1968), 8:200, 178.

4. Her famous prefatory "A Note on the Notes" reads: "But since in anything I have written, there have been lines in which the chief interest is borrowed, and I have not yet been able to outgrow this hybrid method of composition, acknowledgements seem only honest" (*CP* 262). Almost all of Moore's critics have explored some aspect of her quotational poetics. In *Quotation and Modern American Poetry*, Elizabeth Gregory writes that while Moore's quotational poetics, like those of T. S. Eliot and William Carlos Williams, revalues the secondariness associated with their status as American modernists, it does so most markedly in terms of gender and analogously to hierarchies of all kinds (130). Lynn Keller (1991) argues that Moore plays off the nonhierarchical nature of intertextuality against a patrilineal model of influence in her masterpiece "Marriage." Cristanne Miller's *Questions of Authority* (1995) anatomizes how Moore combines intricate formalism, erudite allusion, and sententiousness with "culturally 'feminine' aspects of use" more commonly associated with inconsequential orality in "a feminist metapoetics of appreciative and non-hierarchical exchange." Miller identifies Moore's "culturally feminine aspects of language use" as "substitution of multivocality for an authoritative voice; inclusion of trivial, apparently irrelevant, information; excessive detail and excessive restraint; overemphasis on the mundane through marked quotations from the private sphere; and a didactic tone without accompanying transparent clarity" (191–92).

5. See "Interview with Marianne Moore by Donald Hall," in *Poets at Work*, ed. George Plimpton (New York: Penguin, 1989), 87.

6. See Charles Tomlinson, ed., *Marianne Moore: A Collection of Critical Essays* (Englewood Cliffs, N.J.: Prentice Hall, 1969), 120.

7. See Tomlinson, *Marianne Moore*, 46. "Black Earth" is not published in *Complete Poems*; see Robin Schulze, *Becoming Marianne Moore: The Early Poems, 1907–1924* (Berkeley: University of California Press, 2002), 45–47.

8. On the gender politics of the reprinted Moore/Pound correspondence, see Ronald Bush, "Ezra Pound," in *The Gender of Modernism,* ed. Bonnie Kime Scott (Bloomington: Indiana University Press, 1990), 353–66.

9. See *Selected Letters,* ed. Bonnie Costello et al. (New York: Penguin, 1997), 122; hereafter cited as *SL.*

10. Shoemaker's book (available at the Rosenbach Museum Library) was begun in the 1890s and published in 1922 (publisher not cited). Shoemaker's genealogical research participated in a surge of Scotch-Irish historiography after the Proceedings of Annual Scotch-Irish Congresses began to be published after 1889. George Chambers's *Tribute to the Principles, Virtues, Habits, and Public Usefulness of the Irish and Scotch Early Settlers of Pennsylvania* (1856) suggests the tenor of these works. Mrs. Moore published her late father's sermons in an encomiastic book at considerable expense in 1895. It is significant that Moore was aware of intersections between family and public history. Her grandmother, Jenny Craig, died of typhoid contracted from nursing Confederates at Gettysburg when Mrs. Moore was a year old, and two Craigs were scalped in 1754. Notes about the Warner family history are appended to Shoemaker's history of the Craigs. On his first visit to Ireland, Warner writes (June 23, 1927), "I visited Merrion Square twice and was much thrilled to think of [great-]grandfather Warner's early home being there," and his mother replies, "It is an exciting thought that today as I sit at the desk at 14 you are in Dublin! On the very streets that were walked by our great-great-grandparents. How *strongly* one yearns to see behind a closed door." (One wonders whether the yearning to see behind locked doors cites the 1917 poem "Sojourn in the Whale," or if the poem cites an oft-expressed wish of Mrs. Moore's.) Warner recounts "a life event" that moved him profoundly, when on a chance private visit to St. Patrick's Cathedral the organist played his favorite hymns for him as he stood at Dean Swift's tomb. Dean Swift is an especially poignant forefather for Warner, representing as he does his own and his beloved grandfather's vocation and his estranged father's fate. For the family correspondence, see Rosenbach Museum library archives (6:28:10); hereafter cited as RML. I am grateful to Evelyn Feldman of the Rosenbach Museum Library for her help with the Moore family history.

11. On the Irish diaspora to North America, see Kerby Miller, *Emigrants and Exiles* (1985). Donald Akenson, *The Irish Diaspora* (1994), a comparative study of Irish emigration worldwide, argues against Miller's exilic thesis (236–44) and the tendency to emphasize ideological motives for emigration over material ones. See also R. J. Dickson, *Ulster Emigration to Colonial America, 1718–1775* (1962); and E.R.R. Green, ed., *Essays in Scotch-Irish History* (1969) (Belfast: Ulster Historical Foundation, 1992). Different immigration histories and continuing colonial caste consciousness on both sides of the Atlantic have segregated Irish-Americans along sectarian lines. During the colonial period 60 percent of Irish immigrants were Presbyterian (Miller 137). Since the great diaspora of 1815–21, Irish immigrant demographics have reflected those of the homeland: 80 percent Catholic, 10 percent Presbyterian, and 10 percent Anglican. Protestant (Presbyterian and Anglican) dominance in Irish immigration to colonial America makes Protestants the majority among Irish-Americans, even though the absolute number of Catholic immigrants exceeds that of Protestants (Akenson, *Irish Diaspora,* 250, 221–23).

12. Moore's biographer Charles Molesworth writes, "Just as Mrs. Moore came to play

the role of first reader, collaborator, and strictest critic for Moore's poetry, Warner was often the distant, even transcendent audience for much of what she wrote" who characteristically praised her work in inspirational, religious term (*Marianne Moore*, 265).

13. He was institutionalized for a nervous breakdown before her birth. See Andrew Kappel (1994), 177.

14. Warner broke up with Mary White (whose "race" I haven't been able to ascertain) the following July and married Constance Eustis in 1918. On December 22, 1915, Mrs. Moore writes of Mary White, "Should she ever marry into my 'race,' God would help me to love her and count her as altogether mine; but such things God alone can accomplish . . . May God indeed make you 'worthy' of Mary; [but oh! God! I pray thee let her never have him—let her never come near to having him.] (That prayer must needs write itself down)," and adds a postscript to say that Marianne felt the letter would cause him displeasure. A letter from Warner Moore to Mary Warner Moore, from December 23, 1915, replies: "Badger (Warner) remembers that visit to Badger Hollow Mole (Mrs. Moore) made and how enthusiastic mole was over his house, noting how it could be enlarged or made smaller by the art of digging etc. and ever since Badger has known mole to be of his 'race' " (he also accents *race* with quotation marks). See RML 5:21:13. A letter from Warner Moore to Mary Warner Moore, July 9, 1916, confides that he has ended the relationship with Mary White, "and for once in my life I've put you in full charge of the ship . . . we shall move as 3 in 1," adding, "we are not of a race to flinch [at the sacrifice involved]" (RML 6:22:8).

15. For a persuasive account of the Moore family's ethos, see Andrew Kappel, "The World Is an Orphan's Home: Marianne Moore on God and Family" (1994), qtd. on 188.

16. See Molesworth, *Marianne Moore*, 111. Moore's marginalia on the "Celtic" essay isolate "idealism in love and hatred"; "reaction against the despotism of fact"; "unslakeable primitive melancholy"; and the "excess of the arts that must cry in the ears of our penury until the world has become a vision." I have been unable to verify whether she read Arnold or Renan's essays, from which Yeats quotes extensively, but she is evidently familiar with the broad contours of Celticist discourse.

17. On the gendering of Celticism, see especially Marjorie Howes's chapter " 'That Sweet Insinuating Voice,' " in *Yeats's Nations* (1996), which cites "Sojourn" as an epigraph, though Moore isn't included in her discussion. See also Murray Pittock's *Celtic Identity and the British Image* (61–93); David Cairns and Shaun Richards, *Writing Ireland* (42–57); and Declan Kiberd, *Inventing Ireland* (1996).

18. Qtd. in Ruth Yeazell, *Fictions of Modesty: Women and Courtship in the English Novel* (Chicago: University of Chicago Press, 1991), 240.

19. The epigraph for Moore's inaptly titled *Complete Poems*, "omissions are not accidents," is fitting for her work. Moore's mantled poetics—"a poet does not speak language but mediates it"—engages Gayatri Spivak's question, "Can the subaltern speak" (1988). Spivak's argument that "[Coetzee's Friday] is the arbitrary name of the withheld limit" applies to Moore's deployment of the three-tiered citation of "Venus' mantle lined with stars" (1999, 193).

20. Renan's father died when he was very young, and he was raised by his mother and beloved sister Henriette. Like Moore, leaving home to attend school induced a grave psychological crisis; by his own account, a life-threatening one and "the Breton part of me did

die" (*Recollections of My Youth*, 156). Renan wrote *Poésie* when living with Henriette in Paris before his marriage, when a difficult ménage-a-trois ensued. See Renan's *Ma Soeur Henriette* (1895); and H. W. Wardman's biography (1964), 60–68.

21. Neither Edgeworth nor Moore seem to have found their parents' monitoring of their writing exceptional. Edgeworth (1767–1849) moved to her father's estate at Edgeworthstown, Co. Longford from Oxfordshire when she was fifteen and lived there for the rest of her life. Editor George Watson notes that Castle Rackrent was the only work Edgeworth kept from her father, "her first independent novel, which she scribbled down fast and in secret—almost the only novel she ever wrote without her father's help, and her best" (x–xi). "Spenser's Ireland" was composed when Moore's mother was ailing, and may have held a similar clandestine significance for Moore.

22. I take this definition of modesty from Yeazell's *Fictions of Modesty*, ix.

23. See review essays by these titles, *CPr* 453–58 and 339–41. On Moore's "rhetoric of reticence," see Bonnie Costello (1981), 215–45.

24. See *SL* 107–12 for the third letter in the four-part sequence. See Linda Leavell (1995), 10–25, on the significance of the visit for her avant-garde aesthetics. Moore wowed Manhattan as much as it wowed her. Kreymbourg wrote of her in *Troubadour* as "an astonishing person with Titian hair, a brilliant complexion, and a mellifluous flow of polysyllables which held every man in awe" (qtd. in Leavell, 29).

25. The 1916 rising aroused considerable adverse media comment as an act of wartime treachery. Moore's reading diaries contain excerpts from articles defending Ireland, including Shane Leslie's rhetorical use of Walt Whitman's words as an Irish insurgent's in the *New York Tribune* (May 26, 1916) and Francis Hackett's article in the *New Republic* (August 19, 1916): "How would Americans feel if, because they loved their country and showed their love for it, they were hounded by armed police and traduced by officials and stigmatized by cads in a House of Lords as lawless, treacherous, untrustworthy, crafty and sordid?" (RML 7:1:6). Hackett's article continues, "In the face of such infamies . . . [Ireland] has aimed to endure. But endurance is not forever. There would be no manhood in Ireland if there could be no rebellion in Ireland: it is to the undying glory of Irishmen that in a state made so servile many still can choose death rather than such subjection" (62). Hackett, an expatriate Irish writer, was an acquaintance; Moore records meeting him after a dull author club meeting: "he was almost tearing his hair out with depression at having come" (RML 7:10:6).

26. See RML 7:1:2 and 6.

27. See "Marianne Moore's Sea and the Sentence," *Essays in Literature* 15, no. 2 (1988): 245–57. In the essay Jerrald Ranta also discusses "The Fish" (1921), "A Grave" (1921), and "Novices" (1923).

28. Helen Vendler, "Marianne Moore," in *Marianne Moore*, ed. Harold Bloom, *Modern Critical Views* series (New York: Chelsea House, 1987), 77.

29. On the reception of bulls from *Teagueland Jests* (1680) to recent times, see Brian Earls, "Bulls, Blunders and Bloothers: An Examination of the Irish Bull," *Béaloideas* (1988): 1–92.

30. Bakhtin's thesis that "speech genres are the drive belts from the history of society to the history of language" is key here, as it was in the MacDiarmid chapter (1986), 65.

31. The commonplace is an unmarked citation from Swift's "On Barbarous Denominations in Ireland" (c. 1740).

32. "Why the many quotation marks? . . . When a thing has been said so well that it could not be said better, why paraphrase it? Hence my writing is, if not a cabinet of fossils, a kind of collection of flies in amber" (*A Marianne Moore Reader* [New York: Viking Press, 1961], xv).

33. I use the following editions of these texts: Edmund Spenser, *A View of the Present State of Ireland*, ed. W. L. Renwick. (London: Eric Partridge, 1934); Donn Byrne, "The Rock Whence I Was Hewn," *National Geographic Magazine* 51, no. 3, 257–316; Maria Edgeworth, *Castle Rackrent*, ed. George Watson (New York: Oxford University Press, 1964); and *The Absentee*, ed. W. J. MacCormack and Kim Walker (New York: Oxford University Press, 1988). Moore also cites a local tour guide, Denis Sullivan's *Happy Memories of Glengarry* (ll. 53, 56).

34. See marginalia on "distrust," learning "how to be patient with impatience," and ambivalence, "There have been times that Ireland took my fancy . . . Ireland never took my fancy less than now." On the exogamy theme, she likens Ireland to a "[distrustful] hedgehog," and adds darkly: "I used to hear them say / Blood is thicker than water / It is but not in just the way in which they meant it" (RML 1:4:21).

35. See Hall interview, 85.

36. See David Kadlec, "Marianne Moore, Immigration, and Eugenics," *Modernism/Modernity* 1, no. 2 (1994): 21–49, qtd. on 22–23.

37. See epigraph to Emerson's "Quotation and Originality," *Complete Works* (1968), 8:175. On the principle of third-generation interest that subsequently became known as "Hansen's Law," expounded by Marcus Lee Hansen in 1938 and popularized by Oscar Handlin and Will Herberg in the 1950s, see Werner Sollors, *Beyond Ethnicity* (1986), 215–16.

38. As the combination of *ethnography* and *autobiography* in the portmanteau term implies, *autoethnography* adopts the language used to designate the self as other in order to represent the self. In *Autobiographical Voices* (1989) Françoise Lionnet theorizes the genre from Martinican poet Édouard Glissant's poetics of *métissage* (from *métis*, "hybrid"), the braiding of dominant written and occluded oral traditions to represent subaltern histories and multiple cultural affiliations (*Caribbean Discourse: Selected Essays*, trans. J. Michael Dash [Charlottesville: University of Virginia Press, 1989], 4). I am indebted to Lisa Botshon for our discussions of autoethnography.

39. A good example of translational catachresis arises from the Gaelic *marbhadh* (to kill but also to hurt or wound), which is responsible for many bulls about Irish who are "kilt and murdherred" but who survive to tell the tale. From an Anglocentric point of view, such bulls are crazy hyperbole; from a Gaelocentric point of view, they contain information about degree of injury because as *Castle Rackrent*'s editor notes, to be "kilt all over with rheumatism" is to be in a far worse state than to be merely "kilt with the cold." See footnote to the comic scene when "lady Rackrent was all kilt and smashed" (85): " 'She'll never ride no more on her jaunting car, (said Judy) for it has been the death of her sure enough.'—'And is she dead then?' says his honor.—'As good as dead, I hear,' " etc. Further citations of *Castle Rackrent* will be abbreviated *CR*.

40. See the Edgeworths' *Essay on Irish Bulls*, 164; hereafter cited as *Bulls*.

41. The tenacious insularity of Moore's Scotch-Irish milieu makes such conservatism a possibility, if a very remote one. The popular assumption that the Scotch-Irish were not Gaelic identified has been qualified by recent scholarship: see Roger Blaney, *Presbyterians and the Irish Language* (1996). Elizabeth Bishop speculates that Moore's "use of double or triple negatives, the lighter and wittier ironies" stemmed from Mrs. Moore "conversational style." See "Efforts of Affection," *Complete Prose* (New York: Farrar, Strauss, and Giroux, 1984), 129.

42. See chap. 3. The Edgeworths' argument that Irish bulls are precipitated by figurative extravagance and a crowding of ideas anticipates the tenor of Smith's argument in many respects. The Edgeworths portray the "phlegmatic" English reader as having a rather plodding and instrumentalist attitude toward language in contrast to (in Smith's terminology) the "antisyzygical" outlook of the Irish.

43. Irish idiocy in the public and judicial sphere is another staple of bulls, such as the "practical bull" of swearing to an et cetera or the "Irish orator who said, 'I am sorry to hear my honourable friend stand mute' " (181, 159).

44. See *National Geographic*, 264, 279, 372, 314.

45. On the Washington tricorn episode, see Costello, *Marianne Moore*, 248. On Avedon's portrait, see *Evidence, 1944–1994: Richard Avedon*, ed. Mary Shanahan (New York: Random House, 1994), 62–64.

46. Boswell citing Johnson, *The Life of Samuel Johnson, 1740–1795*, 4 vols., 3rd ed. (London: C. Dilly, 1799), 4:105.

47. Werner Sollors argues that reading played a key role in the ethnic conversion experiences of Americans as diverse as Jewish assimilationist Mary Antin and black nationalist Malcolm X (1986), 275.

48. See W. J. MacCormack and Kim Walker's introduction to Edgeworth's novel *The Absentee*, "an accessible fiction which is none the less rife with hermetic meanings" (xxxv), especially xix–xxi on the Scythian allusions. See Bruce Henderson, "Marianne Moore and *The Absentee*: The Poet as Playwright," in *Marianne Moore: Woman and Poet*, ed. Patricia Willis (Orono, Maine: National Poetry Foundation, 1990), 255–83, on the never-produced play. The most striking innovation in Henderson's view is the love declaration scene where they engage in verbal sparring about Irish thistles, Titania, and Bottom in *A Midsummer Night's Dream*, and the heroine Grace Nugent confesses that she is "quite suspicious of poetry and am still" (276–81). That Moore should associate Grace Nugent with Titania/Hippolyta, make her favorite flower a Scottish/Irish thistle, and have their love scene occur under the enchantment of Midsummer's Eve, is richly allusive to "Spenser's Ireland" and demonstrates the deep personal significance of her Edgeworthian allusions.

49. See François Hartog, *The Mirror of Herodotus* (Berkeley: University of California Press, 1988), 202; and Herodotus, *Histories*, 4.46.

50. See Susan Sontag, "Notes on Camp" (1964), reprinted and much contested in *Camp: Queer Aesthetics and the Performing Subject: A Reader*, ed. Fabio Cleto (Ann Arbor: University of Michigan Press, 1999), 57–58. See Cleto's introductory survey of controversial definitions of *camp*, especially the discussion of etymology, which discusses the mean-

ing of the Indo-European root of *kamp* (what is curved, flexible, articulated) and its connection with the Greek word *métis* (30).

51. See Thomas O'Rahilly, ed., *Dánta Grádha, an Anthology of Irish Love Poetry, 1350–1750* (1926), 4, for "Mairg adeir olc rís na mnáibh!" Gearóid Iarla's verse was preserved in the *Book of Fermoy* (mid-fifteenth century) and *Book of Dean of Lismore* (early sixteenth century). See also Robin Flower's introduction (in English) to *Dánta Grádha* (xi–xxxiv); Flower popularized the controversial idea that "Gerald the Rhymer" introduced *amour courtois* to Ireland. Gearóid MacNiocaill has edited Gearóid Iarla's verse in "Duanaire Ghearóid Iarla," *Studia Hibernica* 3 (1963): 7–59.

52. Conversation with Máire Mhac an tSaoi; see also Mhac an tSaoi, "Ar Thóir Ghearóid Iarla" (1990), 26. For Gofraidh Fionn O'Dálaigh's poem, see *Dioghlaim Dána*, ed. Lambert McKenna (Dublin: Oifig an tSoláthair, 1938), 205.

53. See Dáithí Ó'hÓgáin (1985) 142; and Colum, *Big Tree*, 112. Colum adds that Earl Gerald was asked, "Has the time come?" and he replied, "Not yet, not yet!" See also Ó'hÓgáin (1985), esp. chap. 3; and "An é an t-am fós é?" *Bealoideas* 42–44 (1974–76): 213–308. Ó'hÓgáin gathered fifty-one versions of the legend from sixteen counties in Ireland (Stith Thompson motif D1960.2).

54. As Patricia Willis suggests in "Notes to 'Spenser's Ireland' " (8), the undocumented lecture is probably based on a Kildare variant of the lore that he published in *The Big Tree of Bunlahy: Stories of My Countryside* (New York: Macmillan, 1933), 101–15, illustrated by Jack Yeats. (The only fragment set off in quotation marks, "giants all covered with iron," does not occur in the published tale.) Colum focuses on the Geraldines of Kildare, but Gearóid Iarla's fame as a poet and magician was such that Moore was probably made aware of the Munster connection. She may not have known Gearóid Iarla's poetry, since it wasn't widely disseminated, and she also may not have known the lore about his birth, though Colum's story features the maternal taboo. Ó'hÓgáin cites a variant of the enchanted earl riding around Lough Gur every seventh Midsummer's Eve but does not mention the fern-seed, which could be a syncretic addition of another folk belief by Colum.

55. See Ann Rosalind Jones and Peter Stallybrass, "Dismantling Irena: The Sexualizing of Ireland in Early Modern England," in *Nationalisms and Sexualities*, ed. Andrew Parker et al. (New York: Routledge, 1992), 164.

56. I am indebted to Renee Tursi and Treasa O'Driscoll for this information.

57. I quote Herodotus' translator, David Grene, citing Thucydides' criticism of Herodotus. Grene calls attention to how Thucydides' locution "fought their way" (*eknikan*) implies a willed transfiguration into myth and argues that Herodotus was more interested in the supervening shape of myth than in verifiable facts.

Select Bibliography

Adams, Hazard. *The Book of Yeats's Poems*. Tallahassee: Florida State University Press, 1990.

Adorno, Theodor. "Late Style in Beethoven." *Raritan* 13, no. 1 (Summer 1993): 102–7.

Akenson, Donald. *The Irish Diaspora: A Primer*. Belfast: Queen's University Institute, 1993.

Arnold, Matthew. *The Complete Prose of Matthew Arnold*. 11 vols. Ed. R. H. Super. Ann Arbor: University of Michigan Press, 1960–77.

———. *Letters of Matthew Arnold, 1848–1888*. 2 vols. Ed. George W. Russell. New York: Macmillan, 1895.

———. *The Study of Celtic Literature* (1867). London: Kennikat, 1970.

Bakhtin, Mikhail. *The Dialogic Imagination*. Ed. and trans. Caryl Emerson and Michael Holquist. Austin: University of Texas Press, 1981.

———. *Problems of Dostoevsky's Poetics*. Ed. and trans. Caryl Emerson. Minneapolis: University of Minnesota Press, 1984.

———. *Rabelais and His World*. Trans. Hélène Iswolsky. 1968. Rpt. Bloomington: Indiana University Press, 1984.

———. *Speech Genres and Other Late Essays*. Ed. Caryl Emerson and Michael Holquist. Trans. Vern McGee. Austin: University of Texas Press, 1986.

Baldick, Chris. *The Social Mission of English Criticism*. Oxford: Clarendon, 1983.

Balibar, Etienne, and Immanuel Wallerstein. *Race, Nation, Class: Ambiguous Identities*. New York: Verso, 1995.

Barker, Francis, Peter Hulme, and Margaret Iverson, eds. *Cannibalism and the Colonial World*. Cambridge: Cambridge University Press, 1998.

Barrington, Sir Jonah. *The Ireland of Sir Jonah Barrington: Selections from His Personal Sketches*. Ed. Hugh Staples. Seattle: University of Washington Press, 1967.

Baudelaire, Charles. *The Painter of Modern Life and Other Essays*. Ed. and trans. Jonathan Mayne. London: Phaidon, 1964.

Bawcutt, Priscilla. *Dunbar the Makar*. Oxford: Clarendon, 1992.

Benjamin, Walter. *Illuminations*. Ed. Hannah Arendt. Trans. Harry Zohn. New York: Schocken, 1969.

Benveniste, Émile. *Problems in General Linguistics*. Coral Gables, Fla.: University of Miami Press, 1971.

Berlin, Isaiah. *Vico and Herder: Two Studies in the History of Ideas*. New York: Vintage, 1976.

Bhabha, Homi K. *The Location of Culture*. New York: Routledge, 1994.

———, ed. *Nation and Narration*. London: Routledge, 1990.

Bold, Alan. *MacDiarmid: Christopher Murray Grieve: A Critical Biography*. London: John Murray, 1988.

———, ed. *The Thistle Rises*. London: Hamish Hamilton, 1984.

Bourdieu, Pierre. *Language and Symbolic Power*. Trans. Gino Raymond and Matthew Adamson. Cambridge, Mass.: Harvard University Press, 1991.

Bradford, Curtis. *Yeats at Work*. New York: Ecco Press, 1978.

Brown, Terence, ed. *Celticism*. Amsterdam: Rodopi, 1996.

———. *Ireland: A Social and Cultural History, 1922–79*. London: Fontana, 1981.

Buthlay, Kenneth. "An Awkward Squad: Some Scots Poets from Stevenson to Spence." In *Scotland and the Lowland Tongue*, ed. J. Derrick McClure. Aberdeen: Aberdeen University Press, 1983.

———. *Hugh MacDiarmid*. Edinburgh: Scottish Academic Press, 1982.

Byrne, Donn. "Ireland: The Rock Whence I Was Hewn." *National Geographic* 51:3 (March 1927): 257–316.

Cairns, David, and Shawn Richards. *Writing Ireland: Colonialism, Nationalism, and Culture*. Manchester: Manchester University Press, 1988.

Calvet, Louis-Jean. *Language Wars and Linguistic Politics*. Trans. Michel Petheram. Oxford: Oxford University Press, 1998.

Castle, Gregory. *Modernism and the Celtic Revival*. Cambridge: Cambridge University Press, 2001.

Campbell, John Lorne, ed. *Orain Ghàidhealach mu Bhliadhna Theàrlaich: Highland Songs of the Forty-five*. Edinburgh: Scottish Gaelic Texts, 1984.

Canny, Nicholas. *Making Ireland British, 1580–1650*. Oxford: Oxford University Press, 2001.

Carleton, William. *Traits and Stories of the Irish Peasantry*. Vol. 1. Philadelphia: E. L. Carey, 1834.

Carney, James. "Literature in Irish, 1169–1534." In *New History of Ireland II: Medieval Ireland, 1169–1534*, ed. Art Cosgrove et al., 688–707. Oxford: Clarendon.

Césaire, Aimé. *Discourse on Colonialism*. Trans. Joan Pinkham. New York: Monthly Review Press, 1972. Originally published as *Discours sur colonialisme* (1955).

Chapman, Malcolm. *The Celts: The Construction of a Myth*. London, Macmillan, 1992.

———. *The Gaelic Vision in Scottish Culture*. London: Croom Helm, 1978.

Cheng, Anne Anlin. *The Melancholy of Race*. Oxford: Oxford University Press, 2000.

Cleto, Fabio, ed. *Camp: Queer Aesthetics and the Performing Subject: A Reader*. Ann Arbor: University of Michigan Press, 1999.

Colley, Linda. *Britons Forging the Nation, 1707–1837*. New Haven, Conn.: Yale University Press, 1992.

Colum, Padraic. *The Big Tree of Bunlahy: Stories of My Countryside*. New York: Macmillan, 1933.

Comerford, R. V. *The Fenians in Context: Irish Politics and Society, 1848–82*. Dublin: Wolfhound, 1995.

Corkery, Daniel. *The Hidden Ireland: A Study of Gaelic Munster in the Eighteenth Century*. Dublin: M. H. Gill and Son, 1925.

Costello, Bonnie. *Marianne Moore: Imaginary Possessions.* Cambridge, Mass.: Harvard University Press, 1981.

Crawford, Robert. *Devolving English Literature.* Oxford: Clarendon, 1992.

———. *The Scottish Invention of English Literature.* Cambridge: Cambridge University Press, 1998.

Croce, Benedetto. *The Philosophy of Giambattista Vico.* Trans. R. G. Collingwood. New York: Russell and Russell, 1964.

Crowley, Tony. *The Politics of Discourse: The Standard Language Question in British Cultural Debates.* Basingstoke: Macmillan, 1989.

———. *The Politics of Language in Ireland, 1366–1922: A Sourcebook.* London: Routledge, 2000.

Cullingford, Elizabeth Butler. *Gender and History in Yeats's Love Poetry.* Cambridge: Cambridge University Press, 1993.

Daly, Mary, and David Dickson, eds. *The Origins of Popular Literacy in Ireland: Language Change and Educational Development, 1700–1920.* Dublin: Department of Modern History, Trinity College, 1990.

Deane, Seamus. *Celtic Revivals: Essays in Modern Literature, 1880–1980.* London: Faber and Faber, 1985.

———, ed. *The Field Day Anthology of Irish Writing.* 3 vols. Derry: Field Day Publications, 1991.

Deane, Sheila. *Bardic Style in the Poetry of Gerard Manley Hopkins, W. B. Yeats, and Dylan Thomas.* Ann Arbor, Mich.: UMI Research Press, 1989.

De Blácam, Aodh. *Gaelic Literature Surveyed.* Dublin: Talbot Press, 1929.

De Jubainville, H. D'Arbois. *Le Cycle mythologique irlandais et la mythologie celtique.* Paris: Ernest Thorin, 1884.

Delargy, J. H. "The Gaelic Storyteller." *Proceedings of the British Academy 31* (1945): 177–221.

Deleuze, Gilles. *Essays Critical and Clinical.* Trans. Daniel W. Smith and Michael A. Greco. London: Verso, 1998.

Deleuze, Gilles, and Felix Guattari. *A Thousand Plateaus: Capitalism and Schizophrenia.* Trans. Brian Massumi. Minneapolis: University of Minnesota Press, 1987.

Dickson, R. J. *Ulster Emigration to Colonial America, 1718–1775.* 2nd ed. Belfast: Ulster Historical Foundation, 1988.

Diggory, Terence. *Yeats and American Poetry: The Tradition of the Self.* Princeton, N.J.: Princeton University Press, 1983.

Doob, Penelope. *The Idea of the Labyrinth from Classical Antiquity through the Middle Ages.* Ithaca, N.Y.: Cornell University Press, 1990.

Dorian, Nancy. *Language Death: The Life Cycle of a Scottish Gaelic Dialect.* Philadelphia: University of Pennsylvania Press, 1981.

Douglas, Ann. *Terrible Honesty: Mongrel Manhattan in the 1920s.* New York: Farrar, Strauss and Giroux, 1995.

Dunne, T. J. "The Gaelic Response to Conquest and Colonisation: The Evidence of the Poetry." *Studia Hibernica.* 20 (1980):7–30.

Durkacz, Victor Edward. *The Decline of Celtic Languages: A Study of Linguistic and Cultural*

Conflict in Scotland, Wales and Ireland from the Reformation to the Twentieth Century. Edinburgh: John Donald Publishers, 1983.

Ellmann, Richard. *The Identity of Yeats.* Oxford: Oxford University Press, 1964.

Emerson, Ralph Waldo. "Quotation and Originality." *The Complete Works of Ralph Waldo Emerson.* 12 vols. New York: AMS Press, 1968. 8:175–204.

Earls, Brian. "Bulls, Blunders and Bloothers: An Examination of the Irish Bull." *Béaloideas* (1988): 1–92.

Edgeworth, Maria. *The Absentee.* Ed. W. J. MacCormack and Kim Walker. Oxford: Oxford University Press, 1988.

———. *Castle Rackrent* (1800). Ed. George Watson. Oxford: Oxford University Press, 1964.

Edgeworth, Maria, and Richard Lovell. *Essay on Irish Bulls.* 2nd ed. London: J. Johnson, 1803.

Ferguson, William. *The Identity of the Scottish Nation: An Historic Quest.* Edinburgh: Edinburgh University Press, 1998.

Filppula, Markku. *The Grammar of Irish-English: Language in Hibernian Style.* London: Routledge, 1999.

Flower, Robin. *The Irish Tradition* (1947). Dublin: Lilliput Press, 1994.

Foster, Roy. *The Irish Story: Telling Tales and Making It Up in Ireland.* London: Penguin, 2001.

Galand, René M. *L'Âme celtique de Renan.* New Haven, Conn.: Yale University Press, 1959.

Garvin, Tom. *Nationalists Revolutionaries in Ireland, 1858–1928.* Oxford: Clarendon, 1987.

Gaskill, Howard, ed. *Ossian Revisited.* Edinburgh: Edinburgh University Press, 1991.

Gaskill, Howard, and Fiona Stafford, eds. *From Gaelic to Romantic: Ossianic Translations.* Atlanta: Rodopi, 1998.

Gish, Nancy. *Hugh MacDiarmid: Man and Poet.* London: Macmillan, 1984.

Glen, Duncan. *Hugh MacDiarmid and the Scottish Renaissance.* Edinburgh: W. R. Chambers, 1964.

Glissant, Édouard. *Caribbean Discourse: Selected Essays.* Trans. J. Michael Dash. Charlottesville: University of Virginia Press, 1989.

Gombrich, E. H. *Art and Illusion.* Princeton, N.J.: Princeton University Press, 1960.

Gombrich, E. H., J. Hochberg, and M. Black, eds. *Art, Perception, and Reality.* Baltimore: Johns Hopkins Press, 1972.

Gopnik, Adam. "High and Low: Caricature, Primitivism and the Cubist Portrait." *Art Journal* 43 (Winter 1983): 317–16.

Görlach, Manfred. "Jamaica and Scotland—Bilingual or Bidialectal?" *Englishes: Studies in Varieties of English, 1984–88.* Philadelphia: J. Benjamins, 1991.

Gramsci, Antonio. *Selections from Cultural Writings.* Ed. David Forgacs and Geoffrey Nowell-Smith. Trans. William Boelhower. London: Lawrence and Wishart, 1985.

Greene, David. *The Irish Language.* Dublin: Three Candles, 1966.

Gregory, Augusta, Lady. *Cuchulain of Muirthemne: The Story of the Men of the Red Branch of Ulster.* Preface by W. B. Yeats. 5th ed. 1902. Rpt. Gerrards Cross, UK: Colin Smythe, 1970.

———. *Poets and Dreamers: Studies and Translations.* 1903. Rpt. Oxford: Oxford University Press, 1974.

Gregory, Elizabeth. *Quotation and Modern American Poetry: Imaginary Gardens with Real Toads.* Houston: Rice University Press, 1996.

Grillo, R. D. *Dominant Languages: Language and Hierarchy in Britain and France.* Cambridge: Cambridge University Press, 1989.

Grossman, Allen. *Poetic Knowledge in the Early Yeats.* Charlottesville: University of Virginia Press, 1969.

Halbwachs, Maurice. *The Collective Memory.* Trans. Francis and Vida Yazdi Ditter. New York: Harper and Row, 1980.

Hall, Donald. "Interview with Marianne Moore by Donald Hall." In *Poets at Work,* ed. George Plimpton. New York: Penguin, 1989.

Hardiman, James. *Irish Minstrelsy.* 2 vols. London: Joseph Robins, 1831.

Harpham, Geoffrey Galt. *Language Alone: The Critical Fetish of Modernity.* New York: Routledge, 2002.

Harris, Roy. *The Language Makers.* Ithaca, N.Y.: Cornell University Press, 1980.

Hartog, François. *The Mirror of Herodotus: The Representation of the Other in the Writing of History.* Trans. Janet Lloyd. Berkeley: University of California Press, 1988.

Hechter, Michael. *Internal Colonialism: The Celtic Fringe in British National Development, 1536–1966.* Berkeley: University of California Press, 1975.

Henderson, Bruce. "Marianne Moore and *The Absentee:* The Poet as Playwright." In *Marianne Moore: Woman and Poet,* ed. and intro. Patricia Willis, 255–83. Orono, Maine: National Poetry Foundation, 1990.

Henry, P. L. *An Anglo-Irish Dialect of North Roscommon.* Dublin: University College, 1957.

Herbert, W. N. *To Circumjack MacDiarmid.* Oxford: Clarendon, 1992.

Herodotus. *The History.* Ed. and trans. David Grene. Chicago: University of Chicago Press, 1987.

Hindley, Reg. *The Death of the Irish Language: A Qualified Obituary.* London: Routledge, 1990.

Howes, Marjorie. *Yeats's Nations: Gender, Class and Irishness.* Cambridge: Cambridge University Press, 1996.

Hutchinson, John. *The Dynamics of Cultural Nationalism: The Gaelic Revival and the Creation of the Irish Nation State.* Boston: Allen and Unwin, 1987.

Hyde, Douglas. *Abhráin atá Leagtha ar an Reachtúire: Songs Ascribed to Raftery Being the Fifth Chapter of the Songs of Connacht* (1903). Coll., ed., and trans. Douglas Hyde. Intro. Dominic Daly. New York: Barnes and Noble, 1973.

———. *Abhráin Grádh Chúige Connacht: Love Songs of Connacht.* Dublin: Gill and Son, 1893.

———, ed. and trans. *Beside the Fire: A Collection of Irish Gaelic Folk Stories.* London: David Nutt, 1910.

———, ed. *Leabhar Sgeulaigheachta.* Dublin: Gill and Son, 1889.

———. *Language, Lore, and Lyrics: Essays and Lectures.* Ed. Breandán O'Conaire. Dublin: Irish Academic Press, 1986.

Hymes, Dell. *Ethnography, Linguistics, Narrative Inequality: Toward an Understanding of Voice.* London: Taylor and Francis, 1996.

Jamieson, John. *An Etymological Dictionary of the Scottish Language.* 4 vols. Paisley: Alexander Gardner, 1879–82.

———. *Jamieson's Dictionary of the Scottish Language.* Paisley: A. Gardner, 1910.

JanMohamed, Abdul R. *Manichean Aesthetics: The Politics of Literature in Colonial Africa*. Amherst: University of Massachusetts Press, 1983.

Jones, Charles, ed. *The Edinburgh History of the Scots Language*. Edinburgh: Edinburgh University Press, 1997.

Kappel, Andrew. "The World Is an Orphan's Home: Marianne Moore on God and Family." In *Reform and Counterreform: Dialectics of the Word in Western Christianity since Luther*, ed. John C. Hawley, 173–91. Berlin: Mouton de Gruyter, 1994.

Keller, Lynn. "'For Inferior Who Is Free?': Liberating the Woman Writer in Marianne Moore's 'Marriage.'" In *Influence and Intertextuality in Literary History*, ed. Jay Clayton and Eric Rothstein, 219–44. Madison: University of Wisconsin Press, 1991.

Kennelly, Brendan. *Cromwell*. Dublin: Beaver Row, 1983.

Kiberd, Declan. *Inventing Ireland*. Cambridge, Mass.: Harvard University Press, 1996.

———. *Synge and the Irish Language*. Totowa, N.J.: Barnes and Noble, 1979.

Lang, George. *Entwisted Tongues: Comparative Creole Literatures*. Atlanta: Rodopi, 2000.

Laplanche, Jean, and Jean-Bertrande Pontalis. "Fantasy and the Origins of Sexuality." In *Formations of Fantasy*, ed. Victor Burgin, James Donald, and Cora Kaplan, 5–34. New York: Methuen, 1986.

Leavell, Linda. *Marianne Moore and the Visual Arts*. Baton Rouge: Louisiana State University Press, 1995.

Lecky, W.E.H. *A History of Ireland in the Eighteenth Century*. 5 vols. London: Longmans, 1912.

Leerssen, Joep. "Celticism." In *Celticism*, ed. Terence Brown, 1–20. Amsterdam: Rodopi, 1996.

———. *Irish and Fíor-Ghael: Studies in the Idea of Nationality, Its Development and Literary Expression prior to the Nineteenth Century*. 2nd ed. Field Day Monograph. Notre Dame, Ind.: University of Notre Dame Press, 1996.

———. *Remembrance and Imagination: Patterns in the Historical and Literary Representation of Ireland in the Nineteenth Century*. Field Day Monograph. Notre Dame, Ind.: University of Notre Dame Press, 1997.

———. "A Rhetoric of National Character: A Programmatic Survey." *Poetics Today* 21, no. 2 (2000): 267–92.

Lionnet, Françoise. *Autobiographical Voices: Race, Gender, Self-Portraiture*. Ithaca, N.Y.: Cornell University Press, 1989.

Lloyd, David. *Nationalism and Minor Literature: James Clarence Mangan and the Emergence of Irish Cultural Nationalism*. Berkeley: University of California Press, 1987.

Loewe, Frederick. *My Fair Lady: A Musical Play in Two Acts*. Adaptation and lyrics by Alan Jay Lerner. New York: Coward-McCann, 1956.

Lucy, Seán. "Metre and Movement in Anglo-Irish Verse." *Irish University Review* 8, no. 2 (1978): 151–77.

Luhmann, Niklas. *Essays on Self-Reference*. New York: Columbia University Press, 1990.

MacArthur, Tom. *The English Languages*. Cambridge: Cambridge University Press, 1998.

MacAulay, Donald. *The Celtic Languages*. Cambridge: Cambridge University Press, 1992.

Macauley, Thurston. *Donn Byrne: Bard of Armagh*. New York: Century, 1929.

McCabe, Richard A. *Spenser's Monstrous Regiment: Elizabethan Ireland and the Poetics of Difference*. Oxford: Oxford University Press, 2002.

McCarey, Peter. *Hugh MacDiarmid and the Russians*. Edinburgh: Scottish Academic Press, 1987.

McClintock, Anne. *Imperial Leather: Race, Gender and Sexuality in the Colonial Contest*. New York: Routledge, 1995.

McClure, J. Derrick. *Language, Poetry, and Nationhood: Scots as a Poetic Language from 1878 to the Present*. East Linton: Tuckwell Press, 2000.

———, ed. *Scotland and the Lowland Tongue: Studies in the Language and Literature of Scotland, in Honour of David D. Murison*. Foreword by A. J. Aitken. Aberdeen: Aberdeen University Press, 1983.

———. *Scots and Its Literature*. Amsterdam: John Benjamins, 1995.

MacDiarmid, Hugh. *The Company I've Kept*. London: Hutchinson, 1966.

———. *A Drunk Man Looks at the Thistle*. Ed. Kenneth Buthlay. Edinburgh: Scottish Academic Press, 1987.

———, ed. *The Golden Treasury of Scottish Poetry*. London: Macmillan, 1940.

———. *A Lap of Honour*. London: McGibbon and Kee, 1967.

———. *The Letters of Hugh MacDiarmid*. Ed. Alan Bold. London: Hamish Hamilton, 1984.

———. *Lucky Poet: A Self-Study in Literature and Political Ideas*. Berkeley: University of California Press, 1972.

———. *The Raucle Tongue: Hitherto Uncollected Prose*. Ed. Angus Calder et al. Manchester: Carcanet, 1998.

———. *Selected Essays of Hugh MacDiarmid*. Ed. Duncan Glen. London: Jonathan Cape, 1969.

MacDonagh, Thomas. *Literature in Ireland* (1916). London: Kennikat, 1970.

MacInnes, John. "The Gaelic Perception of the Lowlands." In *Gaelic and Scotland: Alba agus a' Ghàidhlig*, ed. William Gillies. Edinburgh: Edinburgh University Press, 1989.

MacIntyre, Alasdair. "Poetry as Political Philosophy: Notes on Burke and Yeats." In *On Modern Poetry*, ed. Verene Bell and Laurence Lerner, 145–57. Nashville: Vanderbilt University Press, 1988.

MacKillop, James. " 'Beurla on It': Yeats, Joyce, and the Irish Language." *Eire-Ireland* (Spring 1980): 138–48.

———. *Fionn MacCumhaill: Celtic Myth in English Literature*. Syracuse, N.Y.: Syracuse University Press, 1986.

MacLean, Sorley (Somhairle MacGill-Eain). "MacDiarmid, 1933–1944." In *The Age of MacDiarmid*, ed. P. H. Scott and A. C. Davis. Edinburgh: Mainstream, 1980.

———. *O Choille gu Bearradh from Wood to Ridge: Collected Poems in Gaelic and English*. Manchester: Carcanet, 1989.

———. *Ris a' Bhruthaich: Criticism and Prose Writings*. Ed. William Gillies. Stornoway, Isle of Lewis: Acair, 1985.

MacMhaighstir Alasdair, Alasdair. *Alasdair MacMhaighstir Alasdair: Selected Poems*. Ed. Derick Thomson. Edinburgh: Scottish Academic Press, 1996.

MacNeice, Louis. *Varieties of Parable*. Cambridge: Cambridge University Press, 1965.

Mac Niocaill, Gearóid. *Duanaire Ghearóid Iarla*. *Studia Hibernica* 3 (1963): 7–59.

Mac Póilín, Aodán, ed. *The Irish Language in Northern Ireland*. Belfast: Ultach Trust, 1997.

Maley, Willy. *Salvaging Spenser: Colonialism, Culture and Identity*. London: Macmillan, 1997.

Mangan, James Clarence. *The Poets and Poetry of Munster*. Ed. John O'Daly. Dublin: James Duffy, 1850.

Manning, Susan. *The Puritan-Provincial Vision: Scottish and American Literature in the Nineteenth Century*. Cambridge: Cambridge University Press, 1990.

Maume, Patrick. *"Life That Is Exile": Daniel Corkery and the Search for Irish Ireland*. Belfast: Institute of Irish Studies, 1993.

Mencken, H. L. *The American Language*. 4th ed. New York: Knopf, 1963.

Mhac an tSaoi, Máire. "Ar Thóir Ghearóid Iarla." *Oghma* 2 (1990): 20–34.

Miller, Cristanne. *Marianne Moore: Questions of Authority*. Cambridge: Cambridge University Press, 1995.

Miller, Kerby. *Emigrants and Exiles: Ireland and the Irish Exodus to North America*. Oxford: Oxford University Press, 1985.

Mireille, Rosello. *Declining the Stereotype: Ethnicity and Representation in French Cultures*. Hanover, N.H.: University Press of New England, 1998.

Molesworth, Charles. *Marianne Moore: A Literary Life*. New York: Atheneum, 1990.

Moore, George. *Hail and Farewell*. 2nd ed. Gerrards Cross, UK: Colin Smythe, 1985.

Moore, Marianne. *The Absentee*. New York: House of Books, 1962.

———. *Becoming Marianne Moore: The Early Poems, 1907–1924*. Ed. Robin G. Schulze. Berkeley: University of California Press, 2002.

———. *The Complete Poems of Marianne Moore*. New York: Macmillan, 1981.

———. *The Complete Prose of Marianne Moore*. New York: Viking, 1986.

———. *Selected Letters*. Ed. Bonnie Costello. New York: Penguin, 1997.

Mugglestone, Linda. *Talking Proper: The Rise of Accent as Social Symbol*. Oxford: Clarendon, 1995.

Muir, Edwin. *Scott and Scotland*. New York: Robert Spellar, 1938.

Muller, Edward. "Two Irish Tales." *Revue Celtique* 3 (1876–82): 342–60.

Murison, David. *The Guid Scots Tongue*. Edinburgh: Blackwood, 1977.

———. "The Language Problem in Hugh MacDiarmid's Work." In *The Age of MacDiarmid*, ed. P. H. Scott and A. C. Davis. Edinburgh: Mainstream, 1980.

Murphy, Maureen. "Lady Gregory and the Gaelic League." In *Lady Gregory, Fifty Years After*, ed. Ann Saddlemyer and Colin Smythe, 143–63. Gerrards Cross, UK: Colin Smythe, 1987.

Nairn, Tom. *The Break-Up of Britain: Crisis and Neo-Nationalism*. London: New Left Books, 1977.

Nettle, Daniel, and Suzanne Romaine. *Vanishing Voices: The Extinction of the World's Languages*. New York: Oxford University Press, 2000.

Ó'Buachalla, Breandán. *Aisling Ghéar: na Stíobhartaigh agus an tAos Léinn, 1603–1788*. Dublin: Clóchomhar Tta, 1996.

O'Callaghan, Margaret. "Language, Nationality and Cultural Identity in the Irish Free State, 1922–7: The *Irish Statesman* and the *Catholic Bulletin* Reappraised." *Irish Historical Studies* 24, no. 94 (Nov. 1984): 226–45.

O'Connor, Frank. *A Backward Look: A Short History of Irish Literature*. New York: Putnam, 1967.

———. *Kings, Lords and Commons*. 1959. Rpt. Dublin: Gill and Macmillan, 1991.

——. *My Father's Son*. Syracuse, N.Y.: Syracuse University Press, 1999.

——. *An Only Child*. New York: Knopf, 1961.

Ó'Cuív, Brian, ed. *A View of the Irish Language*. Dublin: Stationery Office, 1969.

O'Donoghue, Bernard. "The Translator's Voice: Irish Poetry before Yeats." *Princeton University Library Chronicle* 59, no. 3 (Spring 1998): 299–320.

Ó'Giolláin, Diarmuid. *Locating Irish Folklore: Tradition, Modernity, Identity*. Cork: Cork University Press, 2000.

O'Hehir, Brendan. "Kickshaws and Wheelchairs: Yeats and the Irish Language." *Yeats: An Annual of Critical and Textual Studies* 1 (1983): 92–103.

Ó'hÓgáin, Daithi. "*An é an t-am fós é?*" *Béaloideas* 42–44 (1974–76): 213–308.

——. *The Hero in Irish Folk History*. Dublin: Gill and Macmillan, 1985.

——. *Myth, Legend, and Romance: An Encyclopaedia of the Irish Folk Tradition*. New York: Prentice Hall, 1991.

Oinas, Felix. "The Foreigner as Devil, Thistle, and Gadfly." *Proverbium* (Helsinki) 15 (1970): 89–91.

O'Leary, Philip. *The Prose Literature of the Gaelic Revival, 1881–1921: Ideology and Innovation*. University Park: Pennsylvania State University Press, 1994.

Olney, James. "Where Is the Real T. S. Eliot? Or, The Life of the Poet." In *The Cambridge Companion to T. S. Eliot*, ed. A. David Moody, 1–13. Cambridge: Cambridge University Press, 1994.

Ó'Muirithe, Diarmid, ed. *The English Language in Ireland*. Cork: Mercier, 1977.

O'Rahilly, Thomas F., ed. *Dánta Grádha: An Anthology of Irish Love Poetry, 1350–1750*. Cork: Cork University Press, 1926.

Ó'Rathaille, Aodhagán. *Dánta Aodhagáin Uí Rathaille*. Ed. and trans. Patrick S. Dinneen and Tadhg O'Donoghue. London: Irish Texts Society, 1911.

Ó'Súilleabháin, Eoghan Rua. *Amhráin Eoghain Ruaidh Uí Shuilleabháin*. Ed. Pádraig ua Duinnín. Dublin: Connradh na Gaedhilge, 1902.

Ó'Tuama, Seán, ed. *The Gaelic League Idea*. Cork: Mercier, 1972.

——. *Repossessions: Selected Essays on the Irish Literary Heritage*. Cork: Cork University Press, 1995.

Ó'Tuama, Seán, and Thomas Kinsella, eds. *An Duanaire: Poems of the Dispossessed, 1600–1900*. Dublin: Dolmen Press, 1981.

Pethica, James. "Claiming Raftery's Curse: Yeats, Hyde, Lady Gregory and Writing of *The Marriage*." In *Yeats Annual*, no. 15, ed. Wayne K. Chapman and Warwick Gould, 3–35. London: Palgrave, 2002.

——. "Patronage and Creative Exchange: Yeats, Lady Gregory and the Economy of Indebtedness." In *Yeats Annual*, no. 9, ed. Deirdre Toomey, 60–94. London: Macmillan, 1992.

Phillopson, Robert. *Linguistic Imperialism*. Oxford: Oxford University Press, 1992.

Pittock, Murray. *Celtic Identity and the British Image*. Manchester: Manchester University Press, 1999.

——. *Poetry and Jacobite Politics in Eighteenth-Century Britain and Ireland*. Cambridge: Cambridge University Press, 1994.

Pound, Ezra. *Gaudier-Brzeska: A Memoir by Ezra Pound*. London: Laidlaw and Laidlaw, 1953.

Power, Patrick. *The Book of Irish Curses*. Cork: Mercier, 1974.

Pratt, Mary Louise. *Imperial Eyes: Travel Writing and Transculturation*. New York: Routledge, 1992.

——. "Linguistic Utopias." *The Linguistics of Writing: Arguments between Language and Literature*, ed. Derek Altridge et al., 46–66. New York: Methuen, 1987.

Ramazani, Jahan. *The Hybrid Muse: Postcolonial Poetry in English*. Chicago: University of Chicago Press, 2001.

Renan, Ernest. *Lettres familières, 1851–71*. Paris: Flammarion, 1947.

——. *La Poésie des races celtiques*. In *Oeuvres completès de Ernest Renan*, ed. Henriette Psichari, 2:252–301. Paris: Calmann-Lévy, 1947–61.

——. *The Poetry of the Celtic Races, and Other Studies by Ernest Renan*. Trans. William G. Hutchinson (1896). Port Washington, N.Y.: Kennikat, 1970.

——. *Recollections of My Youth*. Trans. C. B. Pitman. Boston: Houghton Mifflin, 1929.

Robinson, Fred Norris. *Satirists and Enchanters in Early Irish Literature*. Cambridge, Mass.: Harvard University, 1911.

Said, Edward. *Beginnings: Intention and Method*. New York: Columbia University Press, 1985.

——. *Culture and Imperialism*. New York: Knopf, 1993.

——. *Orientalism*. New York: Vintage, 1979.

Schwab, Gabriele. "Words and Moods: The Transference of Literary Knowledge." *SubStance* 26, no. 3 (1997): 107–27.

Scott, Bonnie Kime, ed. *The Gender of Modernism*. Bloomington: Indiana University Press, 1990.

Shoemaker, Mary Craig. *Five Typical Scotch-Irish Families of the Cumberland Valley*. N.p.p., 1922.

Smith, Gregory. *Scottish Literature: Character and Influence*. London: Macmillan, 1919.

Sollors, Werner. *Beyond Ethnicity: Consent and Descent in American Culture*. New York: Oxford University Press, 1986.

Spenser, Edmund. *A View of the Present State of Ireland*. Ed. W. L. Renwick. London: Eric Partridge, 1934.

Spivak, Gayatri Chakravorty. *A Critique of Postcolonial Reason: Toward a History of the Vanishing Present*. Cambridge, Mass.: Harvard University Press, 1999.

Stafford, Fiona J. *The Last of the Race: The Growth of a Myth from Milton to Darwin*. Oxford: Clarendon, 1994.

——. *The Sublime Savage: James Macpherson and the Poems of Ossian*. Edinburgh: Edinburgh University Press, 1988.

Taniguchi, Jiro. *A Grammatical Analysis of Artistic Representation of Irish English with a Brief Discussion of Sounds and Spelling*. Tokyo: Shinozaki Shorin, 1972.

Thomson, Derick S. *Gaelic Poetry in the Eighteenth Century: A Bilingual Anthology*. Aberdeen: Association for Scottish Literary Studies, 1993.

——. *The Gaelic Sources of Macpherson's Ossian*. Edinburgh: Published for the University of Aberdeen by Oliver and Boyd, 1952.

——. *An Introduction to Gaelic Poetry*. London: Gollancz, 1974.

Tomlinson, Charles, ed. *Marianne Moore: A Collection of Critical Essays*. Englewood Cliffs, N.J.: Prentice Hall, 1969.

Toomey, Deirdre. "Labyrinths: Yeats and Maud Gonne." In *Yeats Annual*, no. 9, ed. Deirdre Toomey, 95–132. London: Macmillan, 1992.

Torchiana, Donald. *W. B. Yeats and Georgian Ireland*. Washington, D.C.: Catholic University Press, 1966.

Vendler, Helen. "Marianne Moore." In *Marianne Moore*, ed. Harold Bloom, 73–88. Modern Critical Views series. New York: Chelsea House, 1987.

———. "Technique in the Earlier Poems of Yeats." *Yeats Annual*, no. 8, ed. Warwick Gould, 3–20. London: Macmillan, 1991.

Verene, Donald. *Vico's Science of Imagination*. Ithaca, N.Y.: Cornell University Press, 1981.

Vico, Giambattista. *The New Science of Giambattisto Vico* (1744 ed.). Trans. Thomas Goddard Bergin and Max Harold Fisch. Ithaca, N.Y.: Cornell University Press, 1948.

Walsh, Edward. *Irish Popular Songs*. 2nd ed. Dublin: Peter Roe, 1883.

———. *Reliques of Irish Jacobite Poetry*. 2nd ed. Dublin: John O'Daly, 1866.

Wardman, H. W. *Ernest Renan: A Critical Biography*. London: Athlone Press, 1964.

Watson, Roderick. *The Literature of Scotland*. London: Macmillan, 1984.

Whitman, Walt. *Leaves of Grass*. Brooklyn, N.Y., 1855.

Willis Patricia. "The Notes to 'Spenser's Ireland.'" *Marianne Moore Newsletter* 4, no. 2 (1980): 2–9.

Withers, Charles. *Gaelic in Scotland, 1698–1981: The Geographical History of a Language*. Edinburgh: John Donald, 1984.

Womack Peter. *Improvement and Romance: Constructing the Myth of the Highlands*. Houndmills, Basingstoke, Hampshire: Macmillan, 1989.

Yeats, John B. *Letters to His Son W. B. Yeats and Others, 1869–1922*. London: Faber and Faber, 1944.

Yeats, Michael. "W. B. Yeats and Irish Folk Song." *Southern Folklore Quarterly* 31, no. 2 (1966): 153–78.

Yeats, W. B. *Autobiographies*. Dublin: Gill and Macmillan, 1955.

———. *The Collected Letters of W. B. Yeats*. Vol. 1 (of projected 12+ vols.), ed. John Kelly. Oxford: Clarendon, 1986.

———. *The Collected Plays of W. B. Yeats*. London: Macmillan, 1982.

———. *Essays and Introductions*. New York: Macmillan, 1961.

———. *Explorations*. Ed. Mrs. W. B. Yeats. New York: Macmillan, 1962.

———, ed. *Fairy and Folk Tales of the Irish Peasantry* (1888). Foreword by Kathleen Raine. Gerrards Cross, UK: Colin Smythe, 1973.

———. *The Gonne-Yeats Letters, 1893–1938: Always Your Friend*. Ed. Anna MacBride White and A. Norman Jeffares. London: Hutchinson, 1992.

———. *The Letters of W. B. Yeats*. Ed. Allan Wade. New York: Macmillan, 1955.

———. *Letters on Poetry from W. B. Yeats to Dorothy Wellesley*. Oxford: Oxford University Press, 1964.

———. *Memoirs*. Ed. Denis Donoghue. New York: Macmillan, 1972.

———. "Modern Ireland: An Address to American Audiences, 1932–3." Ed. Curtis Bradford. *Massachusetts Review* 5, no. 2 (1964): 256–68.

———. *Mythologies*. New York: Macmillan, 1959.

———. *The Oxford Book of Modern Verse, 1892–1935*. Oxford: Clarendon, 1936.

———. *The Secret Rose, Stories by W. B. Yeats: A Variorum Edition*. Ed. P. L. Marcus, W. Gould, and M. J. Sidnell. Ithaca, N.Y.: Cornell University Press, 1981.

———. *The Senate Speeches*. Ed. Donald R. Pearce. London: Faber and Faber, 1961.

———. *Uncollected Prose, by W. B. Yeats*. 2 vols. Vol. 1 ed. John P. Frayne. Vol. 2 ed. John P. Frayne and Colton Johnson. New York: Columbia University Press, 1970.

———. *The Variorum Edition of the Poems of W. B. Yeats*. Ed. Peter Allt and Russell K. Alspach. 3rd ed. New York: Macmillan, 1966.

———. *A Vision* (1937). Dublin: Gill and Macmillan, 1937.

———. *W. B. Yeats: The Poems*. Ed. Daniel Albright. London: J. M. Dent, 1990.

Young, Robert J. C. *Colonial Desire: Hybridity in Theory, Culture, and Race*. New York: Routledge, 1995.

Index